MIDDLE AMERICA

MARY W. HELMS

Northwestern University

MIDDLE AMERICA

A Culture History

of

Heartland and Frontiers

PRENTICE-HALL, INC., Englewood Cliffs, New Jersey

Library of Congress Cataloging in Publication Data

Helms, Mary W.
  Middle America: a culture history of heartland and
frontiers.

  Bibliography: p.
  1. Mexico—History. 2. Central America—History.
3. Indians of Mexico—History. 4. Indians of Central
America—History. I. Title.
F1226.H43   917.2'03   74-18115
ISBN 0-13-582957-7

© *1975 by PRENTICE-HALL, INC.*
Englewood Cliffs, New Jersey

THE PRENTICE-HALL SERIES IN ANTHROPOLOGY
David M. Schneider, Series Editor

PRINTED IN THE UNITED STATES OF AMERICA

10 9 8 7 6 5 4 3 2 1

PRENTICE-HALL INTERNATIONAL, INC., London
PRENTICE-HALL OF AUSTRALIA, PTY. LTD., Sydney
PRENTICE-HALL OF CANADA, LTD., Toronto
PRENTICE-HALL OF INDIA PRIVATE LIMITED, New Delhi
PRENTICE-HALL OF JAPAN, INC., Tokyo

To J. W. V.

Contents

part two
THE VICEROYALTY OF NEW SPAIN

part three
THE CHALLENGE OF NATION-BUILDING

Preface

This volume is intended primarily for use as an introductory textbook or as general background reading for college courses dealing with peoples and cultures, past and present, of mainland Middle America. Its origins can be traced to lecture notes prepared for introductory courses on the culture history of Mexico and Central America. The book also owes its genesis to my interest in frontier areas of Middle America, which to date have not received as much historical or anthropological treatment as have the "heartland" regions of Mexico-Guatemala (Mesoamerica), but which are an integral part of the region as a whole and necessary components in the consideration of its cultural development. The primary goal of this text, then, is to present an outline of the culture history of Middle America which focuses not only on the high culture area of Mesoamerica but also includes northern Mexico and lower Central America. Hence the use of a general heartland-frontiers framework for presentation of material.

Within this broad orientation the book is divided into three major parts. Part 1 deals with the evolution of pre-Columbian civilization; Part 2 discusses the development of colonial culture patterns during the centuries under Spanish rule; Part 3 considers some of the problems and challenges of nation-building in our time. Because it is my intent to provide a basic background for readers making their first acquaintance with the land and its peoples, each part emphasizes the major course of cultural development and the basic structure of society as it is revealed by archaeological, ethnohistorical, and/or ethnographic materials. The picture is painted with a broad brush in order to provide both an overview of the course of Middle American culture history for those who wish a general knowledge of the area, and a preparatory framework for additional reading and investigation for those who wish to pursue the topic further. In so doing I have found it necessary to be selective in the materials presented. Consequently there are a number of topics and issues which, regrettably, either are not included in this overview or are not given the full attention which they merit. Nonetheless, an effort has been made to fashion a coherent and cohesive account of the development of basic economic, social, and political structures and organizations that is more or less complete within itself.

The text is amplified by references and notes, and a list of selected readings with brief annotations. These references and readings acknowledge most of my major sources; but I should like to acknowledge here my debt to the work of many more scholars. The references also provide the reader with a guide to additional materials. However, since it is anticipated that the readership will be primarily English-speakers, only English language publications have been listed.

I should also like to express my appreciation to those who aided and encouraged the preparation of this volume. My sincere thanks are due Donald Collier, Eva Hunt, Jeffrey Parsons, and G. Alexander Moore, Jr., who read portions of the manuscript in the course of preparation and offered invaluable comments, suggestions, and corrections. They are in no way accountable for the deficiencies of the finished work. I am also particularly grateful to Dr. Collier and to Michael D. Olien for their continued interest and constant encouragement. I was fortunate, too, to obtain the excellent typing skills of Shirley Walat, Ruth Andris, and Lenore Slenczka, and I thank them for their patience and diligence. To Ruben E. Reina, Thomas Hinton, Michael D. Olien, Alan B. Emmering, Thomas Charlton, and Michael L. Helms I am indebted for assistance with illustrations.

Finally, I wish to acknowledge the great debt I owe my husband, James W. VanStone, who read the manuscript, made available to me various materials from the Field Museum of Natural History, encouraged constantly, listened patiently. His continued enthusiasm was a major support, particularly during the periods of gloom that seem to be an inevitable part of the writing process. This volume is dedicated to him with affection and respect.

M. W. H.

Pronunciation Note

Indian words are spelled according to the Latin alphabet system used by Spanish missionaries of the sixteenth century. In general, phonetic values of vowels are very similar to those in Spanish.
Thus:

a is pronounced approximately as *ah*
e is pronounced approximately as the *e* in bet
i is pronounced as the *ee* in meet
o is pronounced as the *oa* in boat
u is pronounced as the *oo* in boot
y, as a semivowel, is pronounced as in yet

However, *u* before *a, e, i,* and *o* is pronounced as *w.*

Consonants are pronounced as in English with some important exceptions and modifications as follows:

tl, ts, and *tz* are pronounced as single sounds, as, for example, in the English ca*ts*
x is pronounced *sh* as in *sh*e
z is pronounced as *s*
qu is pronounced *k* before *e* and *i,* but as *kw* before *a*

Examples:

Quiche	kee-cheh
Uaxactun	wa-shac-toon
Chichén Itzá	chee-chén ee-tźa
Quetzalcoatl	ke-tzahl-koh-ahtl
Tenochtitlán	teh-noch-tee-tlaĥn
Teotihuacán	teh-oh-tee-wah-káhn
Tikal	tee-kahl

MIDDLE AMERICA

part one

THE EVOLUTION
OF
PRE-COLUMBIAN
CIVILIZATIONS

1

First Acquaintance

Introduction

When first encountered Middle America appears to be a confused jumble of mountains and valleys, jungles and deserts, and languages and customs—a kaleidoscope of bright and vibrant landscapes and peoples that confuses with strange sights and sounds and can be patterned into many relationships and perspectives.

This diversity has always characterized Mexico and Central America (including Panama), the region we are considering under the heading of Middle America. Even more, it has been a major factor determining the course of Middle America's culture history. The juxtaposition of cool highlands and warm lowlands; the extreme differences in rainfall; the varieties of microenvironments found in a single mountain valley as, to varying degrees and at varying altitudes, mountain slopes and valley floor receive the wind or are sheltered from it, face the sun or sit in shadow, and are drenched with rain or lie dry on the leeward side; the vast diversity of wild and cultivated plants, of useful and semiprecious stone, and of precious metals, woods, and other natural resources that this variegated landscape produces; all these are vital ingredients in the intricate complex of natural and cultural factors that made the temperate uplands of Mexico-Guatemala one of the primary centers of plant domestication in the world, gave impetus to the rise of early stratified societies, and supported the mighty state of Teotihuacán, the federated empire of the Mexica (Aztecs), the celebrated Maya centers, as well as lesser tribes and bands.

3

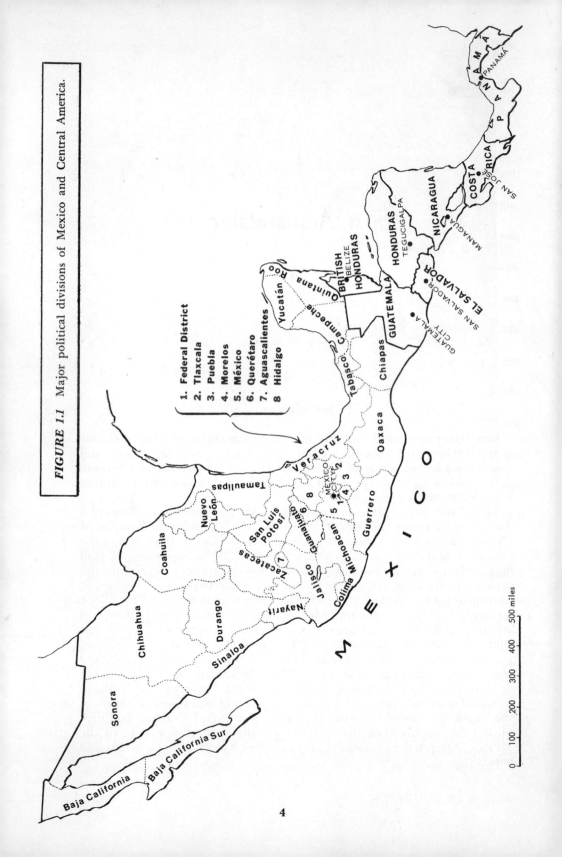

FIGURE 1.1 Major political divisions of Mexico and Central America.

4

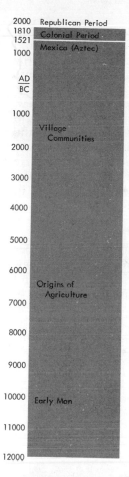

2000	Republican Period
1810	Colonial Period
1521	
1000	Mexica (Aztec)
AD/BC	
1000	
2000	Village Communities
3000	
4000	
5000	
6000	
7000	Origins of Agriculture
8000	
9000	
10000	Early Man
11000	
12000	

FIGURE 1.2 Temporal duration of Middle American culture periods—Pre-Columbian, Colonial, Republican.

Clouded mountain ranges, snow-capped volcanoes, torrential rivers, and fertile valleys also witnessed the daring explorations of Balboa and Cortés, Pedrarias and Alvarado, and a host of other self-assured conquistadors and barefoot friars seeking wealth, adventure, and souls to be saved for the greater glory of the monarchs of distant Spain. The humble populace of native villages met them too, as did the stately priests and rulers of bustling towns and gleaming cities. All fell before the power of the new lords of the land, all but a few rough tribes in distant deserts and isolated mountain fastnesses or humid lowlands. The fertile soil that for millennia had yielded maize, beans, squash, amaranth, and other native foods was planted now with new crops such as wheat, barley, sugar cane, and citrus fruits, while sheep, goats, horses, and cattle grazed where none had grazed before. Vast wealth was found beneath the landscape, too. Silver, in a seemingly endless stream, made fortunes for the lucky and fed the hopes of many more less fortunate.

The real wealth of the land, however, lay in its people, in the sons of

native forebears who now tilled the soil and built cathedrals for their
Spanish rulers and in the new race formed of Indian, Spaniard, and
Negro who would in time inherit this New Spain and guide it through the
troubled years that followed independence from the mother country into
the turbulence of the present century.

Today the course of history still lies upon the country in full view.
Ancient pyramids and temple centers and long-abandoned villages and
home sites once again are scenes of human activity as tourists view the
ruins and archaeologists probe the stones to seek more clues of early
life-styles. Ancient native languages can still be heard in areas where
Spanish, though mother tongue to many millions now, remains the
foreign tongue for some. The countryside reflects the old and new in
other ways. Digging stick and ox-drawn wooden plow still are often used
to prepare the land for planting although tractors and other modern
farm machinery can be found in growing numbers. Small plots of maize
and smog-producing factories stand side by side. Village life continues
many patterns of colonial and pre-Hispanic traditions even while new
roads, new schools, and new manufactured goods bring hinterland and
bustling urban center a little closer. Closer, but still far from full accord,
for one of the most urgent problems of our times lies in the great
economic and political gap between the growing numbers of poverty-
stricken *campesinos* or countrymen (and their lower-class urban counterparts) and the wealthy metropolitan elite of the cities.

FIGURE 1.3 With oxen and wooden plow a Mexican countryman cultivates
soil that yielded crops long before the distant colonial cathedral was erected.
Reprinted, by permission, from Eyler N. Simpson, *The Ejido, Mexico's Way Out*
(Chapel Hill, N.C.: The University of North Carolina Press, 1937).

Heartland and Frontiers

Through virtually all its history the central focus or heartland of Middle American culture history has been located in the densely populated highlands and immediately adjacent lowlands of central and southern Mexico and in portions of the interior uplands and Pacific plains of Central America. These are the regions where indigenous peoples evolved high levels of cultural complexity during the centuries prior to the Spanish conquest, where Hispanic settlements and colonial life-styles were most successfully established during the colonial period, and where the centers of national life are located today.

Foremost among these upland masses is the cool though somewhat dry Mexican central highlands, composed of a series of fertile upland basins and valleys separated from each other by volcanoes and rugged mountains which tower thousands of meters over the high valleys and also surround the entire complex on east, west, and south. The heart of this highland in turn is the Basin of Mexico where Mexico City is located today. In centuries long past the basin contained a series of shallow lakes, now drained, that once provided resources for Pleistocene hunters and gatherers. Later it saw the rise of the pyramids and marketplaces of Teotihuacán, the gleaming structures of the Mexica capital, Tenochtitlán, and the colonial palaces and churches and modern thoroughfares of Mexico City and its environs.

The headwaters of important rivers have cut deep, narrow valleys in the central highlands. Two major rivers flow from the more northern sections: the Lerma-Santiago, flowing through the broad, richly productive alluvial plain known as the Bajío en route to the Pacific, and the Río Pánuco leading from the highlands to the Gulf of Mexico. From the south tributaries conjoin to form the Balsas River which races through a low depression toward the Pacific Ocean with additional tributaries (the Tepalcatepec) reaching into western uplands long the homeland of the Tarascan Indians.

Throughout much of Middle America's culture history the highlands have been tied by important links of trade and exchange to adjacent lowland areas. The warm, fertile basin of Morelos and the adjacent lowlands of the Balsas River system, located on the slopes and at the base of the escarpment formed by the lofty volcanoes that delineate the southern rim of the central highlands, compose one such lowland region that has been associated over the centuries with the central mountain basins. Another lowland region lies to the east, where the highlands again sharply descend via deep valleys to the narrow Gulf coast of central Veracruz.

The hot, dry lowland depression formed by the Balsas River system is also an important complement to the rough, eroded mountains and valleys of the southern Mexican highlands. The latter are noteworthy for, among other things, the imposing ruins of the ancient Zapotec Indian

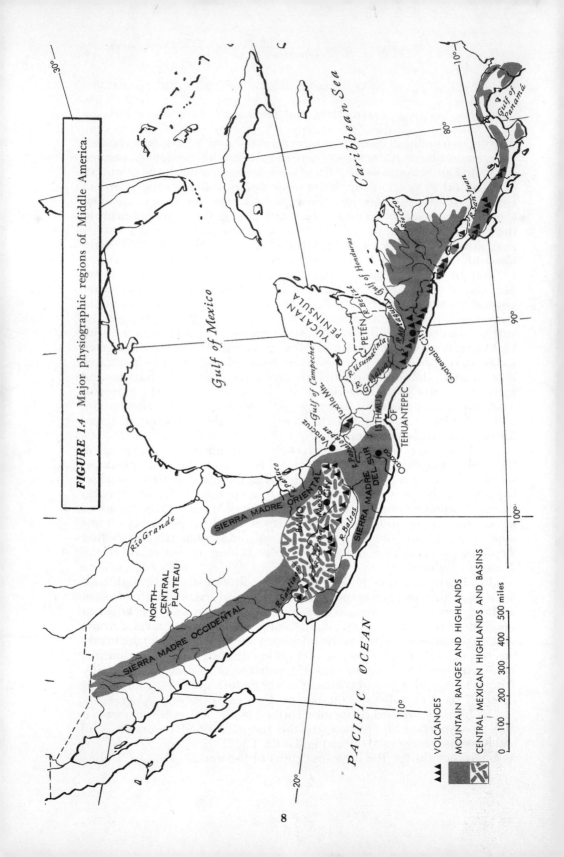

FIGURE 1.4 Major physiographic regions of Middle America.

VOLCANOES

MOUNTAIN RANGES AND HIGHLANDS

CENTRAL MEXICAN HIGHLANDS AND BASINS

0   100   200   300   400   500 miles

8

center, Monte Albán, built on a mountain top not far from Oaxaca City, the principal urban center of the southern highlands. Today these highlands still remain a center of "Indian" culture. They also produce the headwaters of the winding Papaloapan River system which enters the Gulf of Mexico in southern Veracruz through marshy lowlands that are part of the complex of jungle, savannah, river, and swamplands bordering the Bay of Campeche where long before the birth of Christ unknown peoples of the Olmec culture built early temple centers such as La Venta to the glory of their rulers and their gods. For millennia these lowlands have formed an important symbiotic region with the southern highlands, too.

Across the low, hot, forested isthmus of Tehuantepec yet a third highland region rises in the Mexican state of Chiapas and northwestern Guatemala. Here, in the isolation of remote, rugged, but well-watered mountains and steep, small valleys Maya-speaking populations still follow that blend of pre-Columbian, colonial, and nineteenth-century traditions that we term "Indian" today.

Tradition-oriented Maya peoples also continue to live in the volcanic highlands that lie west of Guatemala City. The Guatemalan capital itself neatly sits in an upland valley between two more lowland regions that again have long been bound to the highlands: the Pacific coastal plain and piedmont, and the lowlands adjoining the Gulf of Honduras, readily accessible by the Motagua River.

Tributaries of yet another mighty waterway, the Río Usumacinta, also link the Chiapas-Guatemalan highlands with a major lowland bloc. En route to the coastal swamps and lagoons of Tabasco and western Campeche, the Usumacinta passes through the western borders of the vast tropical lowlands of the Guatemalan Petén. Although they fell outside the heartland focus during the colonial period and remain frontiers today, during the pre-Hispanic era the Petén and the flat, riverless peninsula of Yucatán to the north saw the growth, florescence, and eventual decline of the lowland Maya capitals—Tikal, Uaxactun, Altar de Sacrificios, Chichén Itzá, Mayapán, and many others.[1]

The topography of Central America south of Guatemala continues the pattern of interior uplands with small intermontane valleys and plateaus surrounded by mountains and volcanic arcs, the whole bounded by narrow, relatively dry Pacific coastal plains and humid, rain-soaked tropical Caribbean lowlands.[2] A variety of indigenous peoples and cultures evolved in these uplands and lowlands with orientations to both Mexico-Guatemala and South America, although they failed to reach the levels of

[1] Angel Palerm and Eric R. Wolf, "Ecological Potential and Cultural Development in Mesoamerica," in *Studies in Human Ecology*, ed. A. Palerm et al., Social Science Monographs no. 3 (Washington, D.C.: Pan American Union, 1957), pp. 1–37; Robert C. West, "The Natural Regions of Middle America," in *Handbook of Middle American Indians*, ed. Robert Wauchope (Austin: Univ. of Texas Press, 1964), 1:363–83.

[2] Gilbert J. Butland, *Latin America, A Regional Geography*, 2nd ed. (London: Longmans, Green, 1966); West, "Natural Regions of Middle America," 1:363–83.

cultural complexity attained by the "high" cultures to the north and south prior to the Spanish conquest. Similarly, while conquering Spaniards generally found central and southern Mexico and portions of the temperate Guatemalan highlands to be congenial regions for the transplanting of Hispanic life-styles, for various reasons their colonies fared less well in lower Central America where they also chose sections of the uplands and of temperate western or Pacific plains for settlements. Thus Hispanic Central America south of Guatemala became somewhat peripheral to the capitals of the colonial heartland in Mexico-Guatemala, just as the native peoples of the region were more or less marginal or tangential to pre-Columbian heartland centers.

The heartland territories of Middle America (broadly speaking, the densely populated highlands and adjacent lowlands reaching from central Mexico through Guatemala to the Pacific slopes and uplands of lower Central America) are bounded on the north and southeast by more sparsely settled frontier regions that to greater or lesser extent have remained beyond the heartland focus over the centuries. The northern frontier can be said to range from the present boundary between the United States and Mexico south until it merges with the basins of central Mexico. Most of this vast hinterland is a semidesert plateau that grows increasingly arid from south to north. The northern tableland, in turn, is bounded on the east and west by wooded mountain ranges, the steep Sierra Madre Oriental and the lofty, deeply dissected Sierra Madre Occidental, respectively, which separate the dry central scrublands from the steppe and grasslands of the Gulf Coastal plain and the fertile river valleys of the narrow Pacific littoral.

In pre-Hispanic times this great northern desert was roamed by small, mobile bands of hunter-gatherers whose parched environs generally made the planting of the earth a hopeless task. The Spaniard, too, found settlement more difficult, except for mining towns and administrative centers whose dauntless residents resolutely endured the hardships of frontier life in search of the rich ores that still lie beneath the wastes in bountiful supply. Eventually the sheep and cattle of rich *hacendados* also found sufficient grazing lands across the hinterland where, after many decades of desperate defensive battle, the nomadic bands slowly receded before the halting but inexorable advance of Hispanic culture.

In striking contrast to the northland, the southeastern frontier includes the tropical forests and savannahs of the Caribbean lowlands from Panama through eastern Honduras and, since the advent of the colonial period, British Honduras, the Petén, and the eastern regions of the Yucatán peninsula. Because most sections of these hot and humid tropics were also inhabited by hostile Indians and there were no precious metals to repay the efforts of those who would venture to subdue them, most of this isolated territory, although officially claimed by Spain, was never effectively conquered by Spanish forces. Its native peoples saw instead the encroachment of English-speaking settlers: Europeans, North Americans, and Antillean Negroes oriented first toward lumbering and profitable contraband trade with Hispanic colonists across the mountains to the west and then, in later centuries, turning tropical forest and river lands into vast banana plantations.

In the following chapters we will examine Middle America's heartland and frontiers in more detail. We will trace the origins and development of agriculture, the extension of far-flung trade networks, and the growth of complex sociopolitical organizations as revealed by archaeological investigations of the long millennia of human occupation prior to the coming of the Spaniards. We will then consider the conquest and colonization of the realms of native rulers by newcomers from across the "Ocean Sea," the methods by which the native population and the natural resources of the land were controlled and exploited by the Spanish Crown and by the colonists themselves, and the rise of a new society formed by the interrelations of Spanish landowners-merchants-miners, Indian laborers, and Negro slaves and freemen. Finally, we will discuss some of the major problems facing the contemporary republics of Middle America as the provinces of the former Viceroyalty of New Spain strive to reorganize colonial economic and sociopolitical patterns so as to become viable nation-states in the twentieth century.

2

Early
Hunters and Gatherers

Pleistocene Origins

Although the circumstances surrounding the origins of man in the New World are only imperfectly understood, it is now firmly accepted by virtually all serious scholars that man first entered the New World from Asia, by way of the so-called Bering Strait Land Bridge. The term "bridge" is something of a misnomer here, for the passage at its greatest width extended almost 2,000 km (kilometers)—the width of the continental shelf which connects northwest North America with northeast Asia.

Today this extensive plain is submerged beneath the waters of the north Pacific Ocean. However, during the Pleistocene or Ice Age of the last million or so years, the vast amounts of water locked into continental ice sheets thousands of meters thick sufficiently lowered the sea level so that at various times North America and Asia became, in effect, one continent through the connecting platform of the Bering passage. It was during such periods that plants, then animals, and, eventually, man made their slow, centuries-long journeys across the passageway from Asia to the Western Hemisphere, eventually to reach the farthest corners of the new continent.

Just when this gradual peopling began is not definitely known, although it is agreed that early man began to populate the New World sometime during the last major glacial period, the Wisconsin, which may have begun 65,000 or 70,000 years ago. However, the earliest definitely accepted archaeological evidence for man's existence in the New World is dated by radiocarbon at a mere 11,000 to 12,000 years ago (it may be as much as 15,000 years old).[1]

Even though most of the material relating to early man is found in North America, a scattering of stone tools have been discovered in various parts of Mexico and Central America and in the highlands and plains of South America. For example, at the Tequixquiac site in the Basin of Mexico nearly 20 implements of chipped stone and polished bone definitely made by man have been unearthed together with a wealth of fossil bones of various large Pleistocene mammals, including mammoth, mastodon, horse, bison, camel, ground sloth, and various carnivores. The bone artifacts are mainly awls fashioned from splinters, while the stone tools include a variety of scrapers, blades, small knives, and points. These tools may prove to be more than 12,000 to 15,000 years old.[2] Another site yielding substantial evidence of early man in Middle America is located at Hueyatlaco at the Valsequillo Reservoir in the Atoyac River valley near Puebla, Mexico where a sequence of ancient artifacts again has been recovered in association with bones of extinct Pleistocene game animals.[3]

We also may have skeletal evidence of early man in the remains of the so-called "Tepexpan Man," found at what had been the edge of a deep swamp along a now dry section of Lake Texcoco in the Basin of Mexico. The bones of several mammoths, which were also discovered in the area, suggested to the original investigators that the marsh had been a hunting area, and Tepexpan Man the victim of an accidental death. The skeleton was originally thought to belong to the period from 10,000 to 9000 B.C., but critics have pointed out that the find may have really been an intrusion, that is, a burial of a later time which was dug into the earlier Pleistocene materials. On the other hand, more recent analysis indicates that Tepexpan Man, known now to have been a woman about 30 years old, may in fact be contemporary with the Pleistocene mammalian fossils.[4] We probably will never know with total certainty.

"Tepexpan Man," like others of her time, subsisted at least in part on the large Pleistocene animals which roamed the cool, wet grasslands and woodlands of the continent until 10,000 to 9,000 years ago. It is very

[1] C. Vance Haynes, Jr., "The Earliest Americans," *Science* 166 (1969):709–15; Alex D. Krieger, "Early Man in the New World," in *Prehistoric Man in the New World*, ed. Jesse D. Jennings and Edward Norbeck (Chicago: Univ. of Chicago Press, 1964), pp. 23–81.

[2] H. Marie Wormington, *Ancient Man in North America*, rev. ed. (Denver: Denver Museum of Natural History, 1957), pp. 199–202; Luis Aveleyra Arroyo de Anda, "The Primitive Hunters," in *Handbook of Middle American Indians*, ed. Robert Wauchope (Austin: Univ. of Texas Press, 1964), 1:396–401.

[3] Cynthia Irwin-Williams, "Associations of Early Man with Horse, Camel and Mastodon at Hueyatlaco, Valsequillo," in *Pleistocene Extinctions*, ed. Paul S. Martin and H. E. Wright, Jr. (New Haven: Yale Univ. Press, 1967), pp. 337–47.

[4] Helmut De Terra, Javier Romero, and T. Dale Stewart, *Tepexpan Man*, Viking Fund Publications in Anthropology no. 11 (New York: Wenner-Gren Foundation for Anthropological Research, 1949); Wormington, *Ancient Man*, pp. 238–41; Alex D. Krieger, review of De Terra, Romero, and Stewart, *Tepexpan Man*, in *American Antiquity* 15 (1950):343–49.

likely, however, that Pleistocene peoples also obtained much of their everyday food from smaller game and also from various wild plants. Although big game hunting has left the firmest archaeological remains, the extent of dependence on large game probably varied considerably from locality to locality, and for many people the killing of an elephant or bison may, in fact, have been a relatively infrequent event rather than a consistent source of food.

Dramatic evidence of a late Pleistocene big game kill in Middle America can be seen at the site of Santa Isabel Iztápan, not far from Tepexpan, where two skeletons of imperial mammoths and a few flint and obsidian tools were found imbedded in deposits of fine green muck along the former shores of what had been a shallow, marshy lake. The remains of both huge animals indicated that they had been killed at the site, probably by being driven into the marsh until they became mired and trapped in the lake bottom mud. The nature of the disarticulated skeletons and the deep cuts found on the bones suggest that the animals were butchered on the spot and the meat chopped off, probably to be carried back to waiting families at a home camp. The deposits containing the mammoths have been dated by radiocarbon at about 9,000 years ago.[5]

A glimpse at late Pleistocene home scenes, perhaps similar to those to which the Santa Isabel mammoth hunters returned after their successful kill, is afforded by information from cave and surface sites in the Sierra de Tamaulipas (Diablo complex and Lerma phase) in northeast Mexico and from the Valley of Tehuacán (Ajuereado phase), Puebla, in the central highlands, some 240 km southeast of Mexico City, where excellent preservation conditions have made possible highly informative reconstructions of the way of life of the early inhabitants.[6]

At both locales the small size of the earliest occupation zones, which date from approximately 12,000 to 10,000 years ago, implies that small family groups probably camped together, sometimes in the shelter of caves, and moved their camps seasonally in an annual round in search of a variety of wild plants and game. No bones of large Pleistocene animals have been found at any of these sites, suggesting that only the meat was brought back to the camp from a kill site of the sort described above. Bones of smaller animals (horses, antelope, jack rabbits, foxes, skunks, squirrels, turtles, lizards, quail, etc.) were found, however. In fact, analysis of refuse deposits from Lerma sites at Tamaulipas indicates that over one-half of the food supply consisted of small and medium-sized game, including modern species of deer and beaver.

    [5] Luis Aveleyra Arroyo de Anda, "The Second Mammoth and Associated Artifacts at Santa Isabel Iztápan, Mexico," *American Antiquity* 22 (1956):12–28.
    [6] Richard S. MacNeish, "Ancient Mesoamerican Civilization," *Science* 143 (1964):531–37; idem, *Preliminary Archaeological Investigations in the Sierra de Tamaulipas, Mexico*, Transactions of the American Philosophical Society, vol. 48, pt. 6 (Philadelphia, 1958); idem, "Speculation about How and Why Food Production and Village Life Developed in the Tehuacán Valley, Mexico," *Archaeology* 24 (1971):307–15.

Desert Culture Adaptations

Beginning about 11,000 years ago and continuing for perhaps 6,000 years (until approximately 2500 B.C.), the cool, wet climate characteristic of the Pleistocene gradually became significantly warmer and dryer. As the climate changed, lakes and ponds dried, grasslands became more desertlike, and woodlands shrank in extent. Contemporaneous with the start of these climatic and environmental adjustments, and possibly in some manner influenced by them, many species of big Pleistocene game animals rather quickly became extinct.[7]

As the large herbivores and the carnivores and scavengers dependent on them disappeared, generations of early man throughout the Americas undoubtedly found it necessary to make new adaptations for subsistence, although it is quite likely that the extinction of Pleistocene large game did not alter the basic life-style of these hunters and gatherers as much as we might initially think. As we noted above, it is quite likely that large game provided only part of the subsistence base during the Pleistocene, and that hunting of smaller game together with gathering of plant materials also furnished important food resources. To the extent that the ensuing warm period and big game extinctions required major economic adjustments by early man, the changes probably entailed increasing, rather than completely new, emphasis on hunting small mammals (which generally did not become extinct), fishing, and collecting wild plants for basic foods and raw materials.

We see evidence of these subsistence adaptations in the Tehuacán sequence in Puebla (El Riego phase) and in the Valley of Oaxaca. Analysis of the abundant plant and animal remains preserved in caves in these valleys has indicated that literally hundreds of plant species were collected by the peoples inhabiting these regions 9,000 to 7,000 years ago. Included among the food plants were annual grasses such as wild maize and foxtail, various fruits including wild onions, acorns, and pinyon nuts, several varieties of pigweed or amaranth, avocado, wild squashes, and chili peppers, and maguey, organ cactus, and prickly pear. There are also sizeable deposits of white-tailed deer and cottontail rabbit remains, in addition to a variety of other species of small game which in general indicate a continuum in the type of small game hunting seen in late Pleistocene levels at the same sites.

These food resources probably were utilized according to an annual seasonal cycle essentially based on the relative abundance of wild foods available during the rainy season (May to September) as contrasted to that of the dry season (October to March). During the rainy period, when

---

[7] Paul S. Martin and H. E. Wright, Jr., eds., *Pleistocene Extinctions* (New Haven: Yale Univ. Press, 1967).

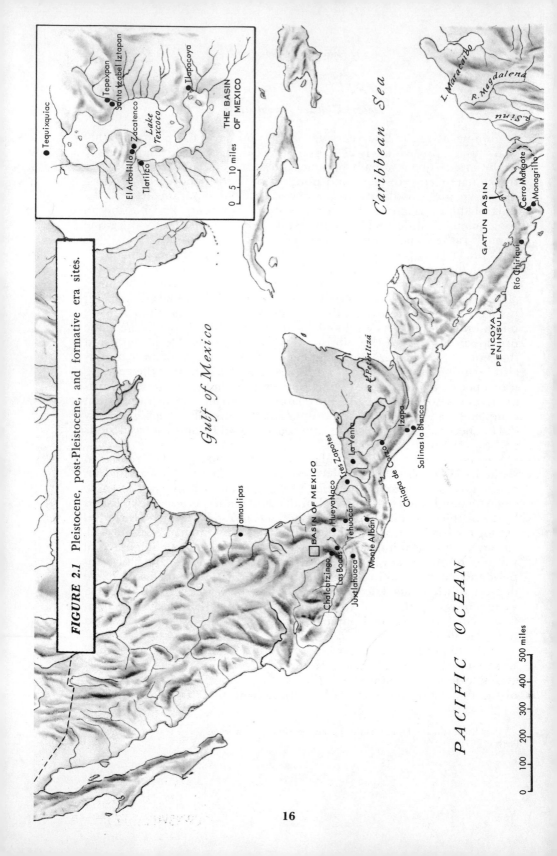

FIGURE 2.1 Pleistocene, post-Pleistocene, and formative era sites.

THE BASIN OF MEXICO

Tequixquiac
Tepexpan
Santa Izabel Iztapan
Tlapacoya
Zacatenco
Lake Texcoco
El Arbolillo
Tlatilco

0 5 10 miles

Caribbean Sea

L. Maracaibo
R. Magdalena
R. Sinu
GATUN BASIN
Cerro Mangote
Monagrillo
Río Chiriquí
NICOYA PENINSULA
Salinas la Blanca
Izapa
Chiapa de Corzo
L. Peténitzá
La Venta
Tres Zapotes
Hueyatlaco
Tehuacán
Monte Albán
Juxtlahuaca
Las Bocas
Chalcatzingo
BASIN OF MEXICO
Tamaulipas

Gulf of Mexico

PACIFIC OCEAN

0   100   200   300   400   500 miles

16

foodstuffs were freely available and, in their abundance, required many hands to help in gathering, larger groups of people, perhaps related family units, came together in larger camps. During the dry period, when wild food resources were less readily obtained, the camps split into smaller bands which scattered widely to hunt deer and to gather the now reduced plant resources.[8]

Farther to the south, in Guatemala, the lowlands of Yucatán, and the rest of Central America, there is virtually no information available for this time period. However, lithic evidence of early occupation, beginning at about 8,000 years ago, has been found in upland rock shelters in the canyon of the Río Chiriquí in western Panama.[9] In addition, at the Cerro Mangote site in the Parita Bay region of the Pacific coast of Panama excavations of coastal shell middens dated at about 7,000 years ago have indicated an economy based largely on fishing and the gathering of shellfish such as oysters, crabs, and small bivalves. Deer and small mammals, turtles, birds, and fish were also consumed.[10] It is quite possible that similar adaptations to sea and coastal resources were employed elsewhere along the Pacific, and probably also the Atlantic, littorals of Middle America during these millennia, paralleling the growing dependence on plants which we have seen in the Mexican highlands.

[8] Kent V. Flannery, "Archaeological Systems Theory and Early Mesoamerica," reprinted in *Prehistoric Archaeology,* ed. Stuart Struever (Garden City, N.Y.: Natural History Press, 1971), pp. 80–100.

[9] Olga Linares de Sapir and Anthony J. Ranere, "Human Adaptation to the Tropical Forests of Western Panama," *Archaeology* 24 (1971):346–55.

[10] Charles R. McGimsey, "Cerro Mangote: A Preceramic Site in Panama," *American Antiquity* 22 (1956):151–61.

3

Origins
of Agriculture

Concepts and Processes

For thousands of years the post-Pleistocene way of life remained essentially unchanged, at least from the point of view of daily routine for generation after generation of Middle American hunters and gatherers. The seasonal movement from one camp to another, and the dependence on fish, wild game, and especially on collected wild plants continued without much variation. Very gradually, however, a major change did occur. The period from approximately 7000 to 1500 (±500) B.C. also witnessed the origins and increasing utilization of domesticated plants —the beginnings of agriculture.

Middle America, particularly the highlands of Mexico and Guatemala, is one of the four or five primary centers of plant domestication in the world. Here maize, squashes (including pumpkins), beans, chili pepper, amaranth (in the pigweed family), and an array of other plants were gradually brought under cultivation. In the botanical sense, the term *domestication* essentially refers to the loss of the ability of the plant species to reproduce itself, and the dependence on a human agent to effect reproduction through the planting of seeds or cuttings. The process by which this change occurs basically entails altering the genetic makeup of the species in such a way that natural reproduction is no longer possible.

Genetic alterations are obtained by modifying the natural selective pressures operating on the wild species so that genetic combinations that generally would not survive under natural conditions are not removed from the plant population, but instead survive, along with the usual plant forms, to add increased diversity to the gene pool. Then a new selective agent, man, either knowingly or, more likely, by accident gradually chooses by selective harvesting those plant characteristics which, while not beneficial to the plant under natural conditions, ultimately make the plant more useful to human beings. The most important improvement from the point of view of human utilization is to reduce the plant's ability to readily lose its mature seeds when a strong puff of wind or a blow from a stone knife suddenly shakes the stem or shatters the brittle pod. A wild plant that was unable to disperse its seeds would soon perish under natural conditions, but this same handicap is an advantage to the gatherer who wishes to harvest the seeds for food, and who will be more successful if fewer fall to the ground in the process.

Under what conditions can these alterations in natural selection and, ultimately, in plant genetics take place? One procedure is to provide the plant species with "improved" conditions in which to grow more easily. Here again man very likely also was involved. By trampling the area around his camp and/or opening a clearing by fire man alters the ecology of a locale. The disturbed, open soil along his pathways provides another niche where plants may find extra growing room. The rubbish heap or midden at a human camp site, a refuse pile rich in nitrogen, provides another disturbed area of great potential where uneaten seeds casually tossed aside may take root, or where very ordinary weeds, such as amaranth, may find excellent growing conditions. Protection and occasional tending by the camp inhabitants would assist such plants to naturalize to the new locations, and more desirable plant characteristics could easily, indeed virtually automatically, be selected for in the process of harvesting.[1]

Plants may also be conveyed to new areas or ecological niches by human agents as they move from place to place trading or following the food quest. In this context it is important to note that all the major regions of primary plant domestication, including Middle America, exhibit great ecological variability in relatively close range. Highlands and lowlands lie in close proximity; mountain slopes and adjacent valley basins provide a diversity of microclimates as they are affected by sun, rain, and wind in varying degrees, depending on their elevations and the angle of their exposure to the elements. This diversity not only provided man with a considerable range of wild foods within a relatively small area, but also encouraged exchange of goods and resources between regions and, concomitantly, the movement of wild plants to areas outside their original ecological zone where different selective pressures could exist.[2]

[1] J. G. Hawkes, "The Ecological Background of Plant Domestication," in *The Domestication and Exploitation of Plants and Animals,* ed. Peter J. Ucko and G. W. Dimbleby (Chicago: Aldine, 1969), pp. 17–29; Edgar Anderson, "Man as a Maker of New Plants and New Plant Communities," in *Man's Role in Changing the Face of the Earth,* ed. William L. Thomas, Jr. (Chicago: Univ. of Chicago Press, 1956), 763–77.
[2] Michael D. Coe and Kent V. Flannery, "Microenvironments and Mesoamerican Prehistory," *Science* 143 (1964):650–54.

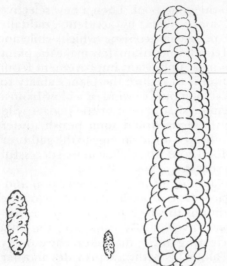

FIGURE 3.1 A cob of the earliest known maize dating ca. 5000 B.C., left, sketched actual size; right, compared with a modern ear of hybrid maize. The kernels of this early maize were small, hard, and capable of exploding when heated—a kind of popcorn.

We can best illustrate some of these points by examining the history of a primary Middle American food staple, domesticated maize. In fully domesticated forms of maize the individual kernels or seeds are not encased in glumes or chaff, as is the case with other cereals. Instead the kernels are firmly attached to a central cob, and the entire ear is tightly enclosed by modified leaf sheaths or husks so that cultivated maize is unable to disperse its seeds. However, careful analysis of remains of cobs and kernels of primitive varieties of maize recovered from archaeological sites indicates that earlier forms of maize kernels and cobs were not enclosed by long, restricting leaf sheaths. Instead individual kernels were covered separately by protective pods or floral bracts (glumes or chaff) and were easily dispersed by the fragility of the rachis or central core to which they were attached. Fully domesticated forms of maize have lost the glume or pod characteristic as a result of a rather simple genetic change. The ears are now tightly and permanently enclosed by husks and thus cannot disperse their kernels.[3]

Archaeological Evidence

Both archaeological and botanical evidence indicate that the Mexican-Guatemalan area was a major zone of plant domestication, not only for maize, but also for several varieties of beans, squashes and pumpkins, amaranth, and chili pepper, to name the most important Middle American cultigens. Climatic conditions suitable for domestication of these

[3] Paul C. Mangelsdorf, "Ancestor of Corn," *Science* 128 (1958):1313–20; Paul C. Mangelsdorf, Richard S. MacNeish, and Walton C. Galinat, "Domestication of Corn," *Science* 143 (1964):538–45.

types of plants, however, occur within an extensive upland area reaching from southwestern United States through highland Mexico and Guatemala as far south as Costa Rica. Throughout this range, in addition to ecological diversity, an arid to subhumid climate without frosts and with sufficient rain during the growing season is found. Archaeological evidence also supports this view of a large "natural zone" generally suitable for plant domestication since there is evidence that various cultigens first appeared in widely separate localities within this zone. Indeed, the domestication of diverse varieties in different locales and the exchange of information and cultigens between regions very likely played an important role in the overall evolution of domestic plants.

Direct archaeological evidence of plant domestication in Middle America is best observed in the same sequences at Tamaulipas in northeast Mexico and at Tehuacán, in the state of Puebla, where in the Lerma and Ajuereado-El Riego phases we saw evidence for the post-Pleistocene adaptation to small game and local plant utilization as noted in the previous chapter.[4] One of the most striking characteristics the data indicate is the gradualness of the domestication process and the relatively slight effect on human life-styles in the early stages of this process. In fact, it required close to 5,000 years for the cumulative effects of plant domestication and associated technologies and activities, such as permanent storage facilities and protection of land and resource areas, to culminate in the establishment of permanent village-farming communities, the emergence of which about 2000 to 1500 B.C. marks a significant turning point in Middle American culture history. Between that turning point and the earliest evidence for incipient plant domestication and cultivation, about 7000 B.C., lies a long period of gradual genetic changes in plant varieties, improvement in plant types, and slow yet constant increase in the use of domestic plants as part of the subsistence base. The data summarized in Table 3.1 illustrate the gradualness of this process, and also indicate that no single center predominated in the domestication process as a whole.[5]

In spite of these initial efforts at cultivation which seem so significant in retrospect, the annual subsistence cycle and accompanying round of

[4] There is good reason to think that similar experiments in plant domestication were also underway in other mountain valleys within the natural zone. The Valley of Oaxaca also shows indications of incipient plant domestication. The Upper Grijalva Basin in interior western Chiapas may be another such locale. Richard S. MacNeish, *Preliminary Archaeological Investigations in the Sierra de Tamaulipas, Mexico,* Transactions of the American Philosophical Society, vol. 48, pt. 6 (Philadelphia, 1958); idem, "Speculations about How and Why Food Production and Village Life Developed in the Tehuacán Valley, Mexico," *Archaeology* 24 (1971):307–15; Kent V. Flannery, Anne V. T. Kirkby, Michael J. Kirkby, and Aubrey W. Williams, Jr., "Farming Systems and Political Growth in Ancient Oaxaca," *Science* 158 (1967):445–54. Cf. Kent V. Flannery, "The Origins of Agriculture," in *Annual Review of Anthropology,* vol. 2, ed. Bernard J. Siegel (Palo Alto: Annual Reviews, Inc., 1973), 271–310.

[5] The early occurrence of bottle gourds at Tamaulipas is also noteworthy since bottle gourd is not edible, but makes a handy household utensil. Thus incipient domestication did not necessarily involve food resources alone.

TABLE 3.1
TEHUACÁN AND TAMAULIPAS SUBSISTENCE TRENDS COMPARED

TEHUACÁN

Cultigens	Subsistence Trend (H / Ag / G)	Phase	Date
Squash, Chili, Amaranth, Avocado, Cotton, Maize, Beans, Gourd, Sapote	(29) / (40) / (31)	AJALPAN	1000
			1500
		PURRON	2000
Squash, Chili, Amaranth, Avocado, Maize, Beans, Gourd, Sapote	(25) / (25) / (50)	ABEJOS	2500
			3000
Squash, Chili, Amaranth, Avocado, Maize, Beans, Gourd, Sapote	(34) / (14) / (52)	COXCATLAN	3500
			4000
			4500
			5000
Squash, Chili, Amaranth, Avocado	(54) / (6) / (40)	EL RIEGO	5500
			6000
			6500
			7000 BC

TAMAULIPAS

Phase	Subsistence Trend (H / Ag / G)	Cultigens
GUERRA / ALMAGRE	(10) / (30) / (60)	Cotton, Chili
FLACCO	(15) / (20) / (65)	Amaranth — Bean, Maize, Squash, Gourd
LA PERRA	(12) / (8) / (80)	Bean, Maize, Squash, Amaranth
OCAMPO		Bean, Squash, Chili, Gourd
NOGALES	(25) / (5) / (70)	Squash, Chili, Gourd
INFIERNILLO	(40) / (60)	

NOTE: H = % hunting; Ag = % horticulture; G = % wild plant utilization.

SOURCE: Adapted from *The Prehistory of the Tehuacán Valley* by Richard S. MacNeish, vol. 1, p. 301, fig. 186 (University of Texas Press, 1967) and from "Preliminary Archaeological Investigations in the Sierra de Tamaulipas, Mexico" by Richard S. MacNeish, *Transactions of the American Philosophical Society*, vol. 48, pt. 6 (1958): 151, fig. 48, by permission of the University of Texas Press, the American Philosophical Society, and Richard S. MacNeish.

activities changed but slowly. The fullest interpretation of the annual round derives from the Tehuacán sequence.[6] The caves, rock shelters, and open sites of the Coxcatlán phase indicate that, as in the earlier El Riego phase, nomadic bands moved about in an annual hunting and gathering cycle, breaking into smaller units during the dry season and coalescing into larger groups to reap the richer resources of the rainy period. The larger size of the occupation sites suggests, however, that the wet season macrobands were somewhat larger than before and stayed together in one place a bit longer, possibly to tend plants and then to utilize the fruits of their efforts at incipient cultivation, before dispersing for the dry season. It also has been estimated that the population of the Tehuacán Valley during later El Riego and early Coxcatlán may have numbered as much as four times that of the preceding Ajuereado and early El Riego phases. This is a very important point, for increasing population pressure on existing wild resources probably was one of the basic human factors intertwined with the evolution of domesticated plants.

The following Abejas phase reveals not only dry season hunting camps but also larger settlements composed of five to ten pit houses located on river terraces in the valley and possibly occupied fairly constantly throughout the year. This pattern obviously implies increased sedentism, probably through more balanced and more efficient food production, and, in fact, archaeological data also show a definite increase in number of types of domesticants, particularly the addition of beans and of varieties of hybrid maize. The appearance of hybrid maize is particularly significant since hybrids produce stronger stalks and larger ears with more kernels and thus are considerably more productive than more primitive varieties.

The Purrón phase, which succeeds Abejas, is most notable for the occurrence of some of the earliest ceramics yet to appear in Middle America—very crude, crumbly pieces of gravel-tempered, poorly fired pottery based on the same forms as the stone bowls and neckless globular jars which characterized previous periods.[7] In addition the Purrón phase very likely saw a continuation in population growth, sedentism, and utilization of cultivated resources. All these factors are seen to even better advantage in the following Ajalpán phase, when small villages housed several hundred inhabitants who now depended primarily, though not entirely, on agricultural activities for subsistence, emphasizing particularly maize, chili, beans, and squash.

[6] Richard S. MacNeish, "Ancient Mesoamerican Civilization," *Science* 143 (1964):531–37; idem, "Speculations about How and Why Food Production and Village Life Developed," 307–15; idem, "The Scheduling Factor in the Development of Effective Food Production in the Tehuacan Valley," in *Variation in Anthropology*, ed. Donald W. Lathrap and Jody Douglas (Urbana: Illinois Archaeological Survey, 1973), pp. 75–89.

[7] Cf. Charles F. Brush, "Pox Pottery: Earliest Identified Mexican Ceramic," *Science* 149 (1965):194–95.

Seed Crops and Root Crops

Before leaving the subject of early agriculture, we should note some additional characteristics of the foods so slowly domesticated during the millennia prior to 1500 B.C. To begin, the native Middle American highland crops which we have been discussing comprise what is known as a seed crop complex, in contrast to a vegetative or root crop complex.[8] These complexes differ in several important respects. Plants with edible roots or tubers, such as sweet potatoes, manioc, yams and yautia, and also the pejibaye or peach palm (which can be included as part of this complex), are propagated by planting slips and cuttings, or by tending root sprouts (in the case of the palm), and often are harvested at irregular intervals as they are needed. In general they cannot be readily stored for any length of time for future use, although by means of a complicated procedure the so-called "bitter" variety of manioc can be processed into flat, unleavened bread and flour which can be kept indefinitely. In contrast, seed crops—maize, beans, squashes, chili peppers, and amaranth—are propagated by the annual sowing of seeds, and then harvested, selected, and resown the following year or season. Furthermore, seed crops can be easily stored for considerable periods.

Seed crops and root crops also differ in nutritional balance and in the freedom they permit from dependence on wild food resources. The primary or staple seed crops with which we have been concerned comprise a fairly well-balanced diet. Maize provides protein and much carbohydrate, that is, sugars and starches, while beans are high in proteins, oils, and fats. Squashes (and pumpkins) also were probably first collected and then cultivated for their protein-rich seeds rather than for their starchy, sugary flesh. Indeed, wild varieties of squash contain very little flesh; the development of "pulp" is a consequence of domestication. Chili peppers, used as condiments, are a valuable source of vitamins and also aid in the digestion of plant foods, which are high in cellulose. A diet combining all these cultigens contains most of the nutrients essential for human health and requires only minor additions of animal proteins to be nutritionally well balanced.

In contrast, root crops are predominantly composed of starches and sugars and, with the important exception of the pejibaye palm, are low in vegetable proteins, oils, and fats. As cultigens they cannot provide a complete diet in themselves, but must be supplemented, either by a heavy intake of animal proteins, for example, game or fish, or by high-quality vegetable protein. Consequently, it is not surprising to find that seed

---

[8] Hawkes, "Ecological Background of Plant Domestication," pp. 17–29; Carl O. Sauer, *Agricultural Origins and Dispersals*, 2nd. ed. (Cambridge: The M.I.T. Press, 1969), chaps. 3, 4, supp. no. 1; David R. Harris, "Agricultural Systems, Ecosystems, and the Origins of Agriculture," in *The Domestication and Exploitation of Plants and Animals*, ed. Peter J. Ucko and G. W. Dimbleby (Chicago: Aldine, 1969), pp. 3–15.

FIGURE 3.2   Maize has long provided a staple food
for many Middle Americans. Here village farmers
of the Petén tend their milpa or maize field. Courtesy of Ruben E. Reina.

crops, which can be easily stored in large amounts if necessary and which
provide a well-rounded diet with only minimal supplementation from
wild food resources, rather than root crops, which can present a storage
problem and do not allow as much freedom from dependence on wild
resources, formed the essential subsistence base underwriting the large
populations, residential stability, and complex sociopolitical organizations characteristic of the heartland of Middle America from 1500 B.C. to
the present day.

Nonetheless, root crops were cultivated to a considerable extent in the
lowlands of Middle America. Unfortunately, archaeological and botanical
details regarding the evolution of root crop cultivation in these areas are
virtually unknown. Although lowland Middle America possibly may be a
place of origin of domesticated roots, a more prevalent opinion holds that
important root cultigens, especially manioc, probably evolved in riverine
and coastal areas of northern South America.[9] The presence of root crops
in lowland Middle America, then, is viewed as a spread west and north
from South America.

To date direct archaeological evidence of culture patterns in lowland

[9] Sauer, *Agricultural Origins*, chap. 3; Harris, "Agricultural Systems," pp. 3–15; Donald W.
Lathrap, *The Upper Amazon* (New York: Praeger, 1970), pp. 47–60.

FIGURE 3.3 Tubers of "sweet" manioc are still a staple in lowland Middle America. Unlike "bitter" varieties, "sweet" manioc does not require complicated processing to remove poisonous hydrocyanic acid. After scraping or peeling the brown outer surface it may be boiled, baked, or roasted like a potato. Photograph by Mary W. Helms.

Middle America during this period of incipient agriculture is rather scant. Nowhere are there definite indications either of permanent sedentary residence or of agricultural complexes. However, a few sites in Veracruz and on the Pacific coasts of Guerrero, Chiapas, and Guatemala suggest at least a semisedentary mode of settlement in which subsistence was based on the highly productive exploitation of tropical forest, tidewater river, lagoon, and estuary resources, including crabs, mollusks, fish, turtles, birds, and perhaps an occasional deer or tapir.[10] There is the possibility, too, that root crops, particularly manioc, were cultivated. It also has been suggested that by 2000 B.C. a primitive form of pod corn reached the alluvial coasts of Mexico and Guatemala, since even at this early date dried

[10] Michael D. Coe, *La Victoria, an Early Site on the Pacific Coast of Guatemala,* Papers, Peabody Museum (Cambridge: Harvard University, 1961), vol. 53; Dee F. Green and Gareth W. Lowe, *Altamira and Padre Piedra, Early Preclassic Sites in Chiapas, Mexico,* Papers, New World Archaeological Foundation no. 15 (Provo, Utah: Brigham Young University, 1967); Michael D. Coe and Kent V. Flannery, *Early Cultures and Human Ecology in South Coastal Guatemala,* Contributions to Anthropology (Washington, D.C.: Smithsonian Institution, 1967), vol. 3.

maize kernels were probably being traded by highland peoples for such coastal products as seashells, feathers, and especially salt which was crucial to the diet of plant-eaters.[11]

With respect to the lowlands of Yucatán and the Petén, analysis of a pollen core drilled into the bottom of Lake Petenxil has indicated that by 2000 B.C. maize was being grown near the margins of the lake.[12] More information concerning this early incipient agriculture is desperately needed, but it does appear that these lowlands were marginal to the development of seed crop cultivation in highland Mesoamerica. Whether or not root crops were utilized at this time we do not know.

Events in lower Central America are also virtually unknown. In the previous chapter we noted a dependence on sea and coastal resources by the early inhabitants of the Cerro Mangote site in the Parita Bay region of the Pacific coast of Panama. The next Parita Bay phase, Monagrillo, dating ca. 2100 B.C., indicates essentially the same subsistence pattern.[13] Shell heaps along the shoreline have yielded primarily oyster and *Tivella* shells, along with remains of deer, turtles, fish, and freshwater crabs. Monagrillo is most significant, however, for the occurrence of ceramic wares—primarily plain, thick bowls and beakers, which were probably modeled after previous stone containers, as in the Purrón phase at Tehuacán.

In summary, by the end of the period of incipient agriculture it is likely that several modes of subsistence were utilized in Middle America. In addition to the gathering of rich coastal and marine resources along the lowland littorals of the Pacific, the Gulf of Mexico, and, probably, the Caribbean, it is quite possible that incipient cultivation of root crops was also under way in these lowland areas. Another agricultural complex based on the cultivation of seed crops was evolving in the temperate zones of the Mexican highlands and also may have been established in similar zones in Guatemala and in the interior highlands of Central America. Relatively late in this period primitive forms of domesticated seed crops, such as maize, may have reached some of the lowland coasts. Here and there small bands of nomadic and seminomadic hunters and gatherers probably continued to subsist entirely on wild resources.

[11] Coe and Flannery, *Early Cultures*, p. 104.

[12] Matsuo Tsukada, "The Pollen Sequence," in *The History of Laguna de Petenxil*, Connecticut Academy of Arts and Sciences, Memoirs, vol. 17 (1966), pp. 63–66.

[13] G. R. Willey and C. R. McGimsey, *The Monagrillo Culture of Panama*, Papers, Peabody Museum (Cambridge: Harvard University, 1954), vol. 49, no. 2.

4

Villages
and Elite Centers

Formative Life Styles

A subsistence base which rests on food production differs from one based
solely on utilization of wild resources in several very important respects.
As it is mastered, agriculture reduces the seasonal variation characteristic
of dependence on wild foods. Agriculture is also a potentially more
productive form of subsistence base than is hunting and gathering, not
only in terms of absolute increase in food supply but also in its higher
productivity relative to the amount of human energy expended. Efficiency is further increased as improved cultigens with higher yields
evolve.

In Middle America the gradual development of larger, more productive maize hybrids after 3000 B.C. may well have been the most significant
factor underlying the farming way of life. Correlating with this break-
through in plant genetics was a notable expansion in population size and
density. Settled village life now emerged over much of Middle America as
numerous hamlets and villages containing anywhere from a dozen to
several hundred households appeared.

A number of new household crafts also materialized. Cloth of agave
and cotton fibers woven on belt looms and ceramics became common-
place. Indeed, the period of the village-farming community or the
Formative, as it is commonly known to the anthropologist, is identified
archaeologically by the appearance of pottery bowls, plates, jars, and
bottles, supplementing containers of stone, wood, and gourd. Small
female figurines, many only 7 or 10 cm (centimeters) long, handmade of

FIGURE 4.1 Formative villages and hamlets may have looked much like this lowland Maya village in southwest British Honduras. The windowless walls of the rectangular or oval houses of the early farming communities were constructed of poles in the lowlands or of split stone and adobe or wattle-and-daub in the colder highlands. Courtesy of the Field Museum of Natural History.

clay and occurring by the thousands, arc also highly characteristic of the Middle American Formative. The significance of these tiny objects is uncertain. Perhaps they depict family ancestors, or served as curing or fertility figures, or both. Other figures represent warriors, masked shamans, and dancers.

This general life-style developed in some regions as early as 2500 B.C. and certainly was widespread by 1500 to 1000 B.C. Yet it should be noted that virtually all substantive information concerning the Middle American Formative is obtained from sites located between central Mexico and western Salvador and Honduras. While village communities and an agricultural subsistence base probably existed in lower Central America by at least 1000 B.C., there is virtually no direct archaeological information available other than scattered finds. Recently, however, fossil pollen of cultivated maize dated at about 1100 B.C. was found in core sediments taken from the Gatun Basin in Panama.[1] Evidence is correspondingly scant in northern Mexico. It is possible, though, that by 1000 B.C. small, fairly permanent, semiagricultural communities existed in the mountain valleys and foothills of the Sierra Madre Occidental and perhaps along the lower courses of streams flowing from the mountains to the Pacific. Nonetheless, hunting and gathering continued to provide basic subsistence needs for most of the north.

[1] Alexandra S. Bartlett, Elso S. Barghoorn, and Rainer Berger, "Fossil Maize from Panama," *Science* 165 (1969):389–90.

FIGURE 4.2   Clay figurines from Tlatilco, a large Formative village in the Basin of Mexico. Though standing in a simple pose, there is a sense of animation in the tiny feminine figures which are only 8 to 11 cm high. Note detailed headdress and hair styles. Courtesy of the Field Museum of Natural History.

Within the prevailing village-farming framework there was also considerable diversity, most notably in agricultural techniques, in the amount of hunting, fishing, and gathering complementing cultivation, and in the form of settlement pattern. Indeed, virtually every village may have developed particular and unique adaptations to specific local environmental conditions. In the Tehuacán Valley, for example, where the onset of the Formative era technically can be associated with the Purrón phase (2300–1500 B.C.) if the appearance of pottery is taken as a guide, agriculture continued to be substantially supplemented with wild foods. One hundred to 300 persons inhabited small villages during the rainy season, from May through October, while they planted and harvested a wide range of foods on the alluvial plain of the Río Salado. However, abundant remains of white-tailed deer together with many projectile points and obsidian scrapers indicate that in the dry season, November through February, when agriculture was not feasible, some of the population dispersed to hunting camps in wooded slopes and thorn forest above the valley floor where deer were abundant. In April and May various wild fruits were ready to be collected in the uplands, prior to the return to the villages on the valley floor for spring planting. A variety of small game also was available and utilized on a year-round basis.[2]

[2] Michael D. Coe and Kent V. Flannery, "Microenvironments and Mesoamerican Prehistory," *Science* 143 (1964):650–54; Kent V. Flannery, "Archaeological Systems Theory and Early Mesoamerica," reprinted in *Contemporary Archaeology,* ed. Mark P. Leone (Carbondale: Southern Illinois Univ. Press, 1972), pp. 222–34; MacNeish, "The Scheduling Factor in the Development of Effective Food Production in the Tehuacan Valley," pp. 75–89.

In contrast, excavations at the site of Salinas La Blanca, located on the banks of the Naranjo River on the Pacific coast of Guatemala (see Figure 2.1), have indicated quite a different form of adaptation during the early Formative (Cuadros phase, 1000–850 B.C.). Subsistence in this humid lowland emphasized maize possibly cultivated year-around along the fertile banks of the river and on alluvial flats, supplemented by resources of the marine estuary and lagoon, most notably fish, mangrove oysters, marsh clams, and crabs. In response either to the rich coastal and riverine resources or to the feasibility of continuous agricultural activity, or to both, virtually no hunting was done. The villagers also apparently lived permanently throughout the year in small villages averaging 3 to 20 families located near the estuaries and lagoons, rather than seasonally dispersing to camps farther afield, as at Tehuacán.[3]

Several agricultural techniques probably were practiced in Middle America by this time, too. The procedures used by riverine-estuary peoples to cultivate the rich alluvial soils of river levees are not well understood though we can note that enrichment of the soil through periodic flooding would have permitted fairly permanent plots. A more characteristic technique, termed *swidden,* has been more thoroughly studied. Swidden is a form of "slash and burn" cultivation which basically entails cutting several acres of forest or woodland brush, firing the debris after it has dried, and then planting seeds or tubers in holes punched into the ash-covered soil with a digging stick or a *coa,* a digging stick with a triangular blade. After two or three years the plot is abandoned, frequently owing to the difficulties of clearing weed growth. A new clearing is then cut, and the cycle is continued. After some years, perhaps 5 or 8 or 12 depending on the region, the first field has regrown a brush cover and can be recut, fired, and planted again. It is important to note, however, that this system, which can be highly productive and capable of supporting sizable populations, obviously requires relatively large areas of land in order to operate effectively. It is, in other words, an extensive rather than intensive form of land use.[4]

While swidden may have been the most common agricultural technique employed during the Formative, particularly in the more humid lowlands, it was not the only procedure utilized at this time. There is growing evidence, especially from the drier highlands, of a more intensive form of dry farming with fallowing, as well as indications of simple irrigation and terracing. We can see these several systems in operation in the Valley of Oaxaca which, by virtue of its size, fertile soils, and favorable climatic conditions, held great agricultural potential.

During the early period of village-farming in Oaxaca, about 1500 to 600 B.C., most settlements were located in or near a zone of rich alluvial soils, part of an old river flood plain, where the water table lies a mere 3 m

[3] Coe and Flannery, "Microenvironments and Mesoamerican Prehistory," pp. 650–54.

[4] Eric R. Wolf, *Sons of the Shaking Earth* (Chicago: Univ. of Chicago Press, 1959), chap. 4; Angel Palerm, "The Agricultural Basis of Urban Civilization in Mesoamerica," reprinted in *Man in Adaptation: The Cultural Present,* ed. Yehudi A. Cohen (Chicago: Aldine, 1968), pp. 348–61.

FIGURE 4.3 Swidden agricultural techniques are still practiced in portions of Middle America. Here debris burns as a milpa (maize field) is cleared in the Petén (a); Miskito Indians of eastern Nicaragua plant beans with the aid of digging sticks in a slashed but unburned field (b); rice is planted in holes made by digging sticks in a field that has been both slashed and burned (c). a: courtesy of Ruben E. Reina; b, c: photographs by Mary W. Helms.

below the surface. At the present time the Zapotec Indians resident in the valley practice a form of rudimentary water control, sometimes known as "pot-irrigation," when cultivating fields in the high water table area. Pot-irrigation involves digging a series of shallow wells along the edges of the field, drawing water from each well in a large container, and individually watering each plant. By means of this simple system contemporary farmers can realize as many as three harvests a year. Archaeologists have excavated a similar well which appears to date from the early village-farming period, strongly suggesting that, in addition to dry farming techniques, simple water control was practiced by the ancient Zapotec who inhabited the valley during the Formative.[5]

During later stages (600–200 B.C.) of the Formative, population grew and expanded beyond the high water table alluvium and into the piedmont or foothills of the mountains surrounding the valley. Most settlements now are located on perennial streams at points where water could be most effectively directed into small canals for distribution to nearby fields. Remains of one such irrigation system actually have been found on a hillside below a spring particularly rich in travertine (a concretionary limestone). Deposits of dissolved travertine "fossilized" the irrigation canals, revealing to modern excavators that a series of stone terraces were irrigated by means of small channels which led the water along the tops of the terraces to the fields.[6]

Since the area in which small-scale canal irrigation is practicable in the

[5] Kent V. Flannery, Anne V. T. Kirkby, Michael J. Kirkby, and Aubrey W. Williams, Jr., "Farming Systems and Political Growth in Ancient Oaxaca," *Science* 158 (1967):445–54.
[6] Ibid.

Oaxaca Valley is limited, villagers today augment their water-control farming by cultivating the nearby hillsides under a simple dry farming and fallowing technique known as *tlacolol* or *barbecho*. Formative agriculturalists very likely did the same, not only here, but over large sections of the Middle American highlands, wherever cool and temperate conditions prevailed. Tlacolol is basically another variant of "slash and burn" and thus is similar to swidden except that tilling is generally done with the hoe rather than with the digging stick. Two systems of fields are usually involved, one of which is planted while the other lies fallow for a relatively short period (in comparison with swidden), perhaps two or three years, before it is cleared, burned, and planted in turn and the first allowed to fallow for a comparable period. Ironically enough, although this strategy does not require as much land as swidden due to the shorter fallow period, in itself tlacolol generally is not as productive as lowland swidden because it encourages erosion on the hillsides where it is used. Therefore tlacolol is frequently combined with a more intensive form of cultivation, such as some form of water-control farming, in what is known as the infield-outfield system. Infield-outfield incorporates an intensely cultivated, often irrigated, core area with a more extensively cultivated hinterland. Productivity may exceed that of either tlacolol or swidden. The later Formative farmers of the Valley of Oaxaca probably used such a system to some extent.[7]

The Valley of Oaxaca also offers an informative glimpse of the trade in basic subsistence products and raw materials which moved over virtually the entire Middle American region during the Formative. This trade, a major factor underlying future cultural development, was grounded in the great diversity of resources characteristic of Middle America, both within single valleys or coastal strips and between major highland-lowland blocks. Thus throughout the entire area there was a busy exchange of such items as cotton, salt, and obsidian. Peoples of the Oaxaca Valley in the early Formative also imported marine pearl oyster and *Spondylus* shell from the Pacific and *Neritina* and freshwater mussels from the Gulf Coast, all to be made into ornaments. An edible mollusk was also obtained from the Chiapas-Guatemala shore. In turn the valley populations may have exported mica and small "mirrors" of magnetite and related iron ores, important ceremonial materials in demand by Olmec peoples of the southern Gulf Coast, whom we shall consider shortly.[8]

In considering both trade and agriculture it is noteworthy that human labor provided the primary form of energy available for work. Nowhere in Middle America were large animals domesticated to serve as beasts of burden or as pullers of wagons and plows. Instead, all during the pre-

---

[7] William T. Sanders and Barbara J. Price, *Mesoamerica* (New York: Random House, 1968), pp. 123–25 and 145–51; Eric R. Wolf, *Peasants* (Englewood Cliffs, N.J.: Prentice-Hall, 1966), pp. 19–25; Palerm, "Agricultural Basis of Urban Civilization," pp. 348–61.

[8] Flannery et al., "Farming Systems and Political Growth," p. 451; Kent V. Flannery and James Schoenwetter, "Climate and Man in Formative Oaxaca," *Archaeology* 23 (1970):144–52.

Columbian period human porters laboriously carried goods over the difficult terrain, although transportation by boat along rivers and sea-coast was also common. Similarly, agriculturalists cultivated small plots with hoe and digging stick instead of with animal-drawn plows. The only fauna domesticated were several breeds of dogs (including a barkless strain), turkeys, and, particularly in the Central American lowlands, the Muscovy duck.

The Rise of the Elite

The pattern of life of the village-farming community has continued to exist even to the present day, unchanged in many essentials from the life-style instituted so long ago. While it has endured much in the past four millennia, the Middle American rural village continues as a viable unit, often standing protectively between the wider world and the in-habitants dwelling within. Concurrently, the simple farming community has also long been part of more complex forms of sociocultural organiza-tion. This development is first noted archaeologically by the elaboration of some villages into ceremonial or elite centers characterized by distinc-tive mounds and buildings. These centers were inhabited by specialized craftsmen and politico-religious leaders who, because of their high social positions, performed little or no agricultural work but instead depended for their subsistence on contributions of food and services from nearby farming communities. In turn, the agricultural village itself no longer formed the largest social unit, but became part of a wider network of communities oriented toward a common focal point: the ceremonial center and its elite residents.

The processes contributing to the elaboration of the elite center were undoubtedly many-stranded and complex, and very likely the particular factors involved varied from region to region depending on the local situation. For example, pressures underlying the rise of centralization in lowland areas where swidden agricultural techniques or cultivation of river levees predominated may have differed somewhat from compul-sions in highland regions where agriculture rested on tlacolol and simple irrigation. Similarly, the factors responsible for the initial development of elite centers in any region need not be identical to those underlying the emergence of later centers in the same area. But in all regions at least two important independent variables probably contributed one way or another to the rise of elite centers: population growth as agriculture proved increasingly successful, and ecological diversity in terms of natural resources and/or agricultural potential.

As population increased general disputes and quarrels and the pres-sure for agricultural lands undoubtedly intensified, too, probably en-couraging families to leave their original village and settle farther away where land was more readily available or where disputes could be avoided. Yet ties with the parent community may well have continued. The original village, after all, was the home and burial place of the ancestors, whose remains validated and legitimized their descendants' rights to cultivate and defend the land, and ceremonial rites and commemorative events periodically could draw the scattered populace together and reassert the ritual primacy of the parental center and the kinship ties between families and villages.

As population continued to expand there would come a time when the area would be populated to capacity in terms of the productivity of the agricultural techniques employed, and prime agricultural lands could not be available to all. Some would be forced to utilize other resources, including more marginal agricultural terrain. The lands of greatest productivity—for example, a riverine flood plain which might yield two or even three crops per year—would become most valued, and that village or group of people, probably a family unit or lineage, which controlled this prized land would be in a position to make access to it by others contingent on some form of payment or obligation to them. In other words, differential access to restricted resources is another factor with potential to create inequalities between groups of people and between villages, inequalities now of a sociopolitical nature.

Sociopolitical inequalities can also be stimulated by heightened pressures for recognized authorities to adjudicate and prevent serious internal conflict, particularly of the sort associated with increasing utilization and elaboration of irrigation systems. Resolution of disagreements over individual and family rights to crucial water sources and control of water distribution could stimulate centralization of authority, and continued management and regulation of land and water resources could further consolidate the power and status of an administrative elite.

A community emerging as a ritual center and as the seat of powerful resource holders or authorities for conflict resolution could also serve as a central market where villagers from outlying settlements might bring their produce for exchange with that from other sections. Here the natural diversity and varying productivity of surrounding regions once more become significant. In a valley such as Tehuacán, for example, which included cultivable river plains, wooded hillsides, and savannahs rich with game and wild plants, the rise of elite centers on the fertile alluvial plain very likely facilitated exploitation and exchange of the fruits of this diversity either by marketing or by distribution of goods by the elite.[9]

Elite centers appear by approximately 1000 B.C., if not earlier. They are represented archaeologically by flat-topped, pyramid-shaped platforms constructed of earth or stone and often faced with sun-hardened clay or stone slabs. Elite residences or a small temple of poles and thatch origi-

[9] Cf. Sanders and Price, *Mesoamerica*, pp. 42–44 and 128–34; Gordon R. Willey, "Mesoamerica," in *Courses Toward Urban Life*, ed. Robert J. Braidwood and Gordon R. Willey, Viking Fund Publications in Anthropology no. 32 (New York: Wenner-Gren Foundation for Anthropological Research, 1962), pp. 94–96.

	WESTERN MEXICO	NORTHERN FRONTIER		CENTRAL MEXICO	OAXACA	GULF COAST	MAYA HIGHLANDS		MAYA LOWLANDS		LOWER CENTRAL AMERICA
		West	East	Basin of Mexico			Guatemala Highlands	Guatemala Coast	Petén	Yucatán	

POST-CLASSIC — 1500, 1000

CLASSIC — 500

AD/BC

FORMATIVE — 500, 1000, 1500, 2000

INCIPIENT AGRICULTURE — 2500, 3000, 3500, 4000

Tzintzuntzán — Casas Grandes — Tula — Tenochtitlán — Teotihuacán — Mitla — Monte Albán — Tres Zapotes — La Venta — Chiapa de Corzo — Izapa — Salinas La Blanca — Tikal — Uaxactún — Mayapán — Chichén Itzá (Toltec) — Sitio Conte — Venado Beach — Monagrillo

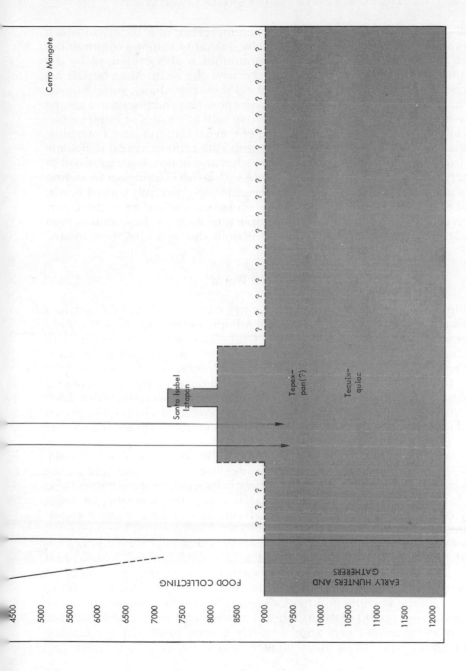

FIGURE 4.4 Chronological chart of major cultural eras and sites mentioned in text.

nally stood on the platform base. The emergence of a society in which power and social prestige are unequally distributed among communities and among members of single communities is also evidenced by the nature of the grave furniture interred with the dead. Most burials associated with the early Formative period show few, if any, social distinctions. The deceased was wrapped in a sleeping mat and placed in a simple grave, often under the house floor, along with a few pots or implements, occasionally with a jade bead, symbol of eternal life. But later Formative burials, particularly those associated with elite centers, reveal that some individuals were now accorded great riches and honor, were wrapped in finery, and were buried in special tombs with lavish offerings of food, fine ornaments in profusion, elaborate headdresses, carefully carved bowls, and even sacrificed retainers! The careful treatment accorded these persons is in sharp contrast with the simple interment of the common man and reveals that significant social distinctions also separated them in life.

The Olmec World

Many, but by no means all, of the early elite centers are located in a crescent-shaped region of tropical lowlands extending from southern Veracruz–western Tabasco on the Gulf Coast across the Isthmus of Tehuantepec and along the Pacific coasts of Chiapas and Guatemala. Three sites on the southern Gulf Coast—La Venta, Tres Zapotes, and the Río Chiquito or San Lorenzo group—reveal the greatest elaboration of the early elite center complex. In overall terms these sites date from 1200 B.C. to about 100 B.C., but the peak of development falls within the period 900 to 600 B.C. when it is believed the major ceremonial center at La Venta was at its height.[10]

The monumental sculptures, mounds, and carvings found at La Venta, Tres Zapotes, and San Lorenzo are identified archaeologically as the Olmec style or tradition. The term Olmec in its archaeological context also includes the art forms and general style expressed in smaller material objects associated with these sites and found at a number of other sites in central and southern Middle America. The dominant motif expressed in bas reliefs, figurines, and large sculptures is that of a "werejaguar," an anthropomorphized feline depicted as a combination of human and jaguar. The human element is frequently represented as an infant and combines the chubby face, short wide nose, and thicker lips of a young child with the snarling mouth of a jaguar. Sometimes an indentation or cleft is shown on top of the bald head, which is often elongated. Another common theme portrays an elaborately garbed adult with an aquiline nose and, frequently, a small, pointed beard.

[10] Michael D. Coe, *America's First Civilization* (New York: American Heritage, 1968); Ignacio Bernal, *The Olmec World* (Berkeley: Univ. of California Press, 1969); Phillip Drucker, R. F. Heizer, and R. J. Squier, *Excavations at La Venta, Tabasco*, Bureau of American Ethnology Bulletin no. 170 (Washington, D.C.: Smithsonian Institution, 1955).

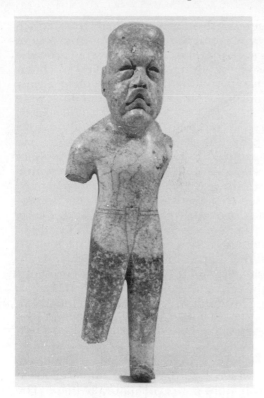

FIGURE 4.5 This Olmec standing male figure of jadeite 30 cm tall shows the infantile features and down-turned, snarling mouth characteristic of the man-jaguar motif in Olmec sculpture. Note also the bald, elongated head. The child born of a woman and a jaguar was an important theme in Olmec symbolism. Courtesy of the Art Institute of Chicago.

The significance of the Olmec motifs, particularly the werejaguar theme, is by no means certain. A widespread and probably ancient concept among indigenous peoples of South and Central America identifies the jaguar with humans, specifically with shamans or religious practitioners. This identification is often based at least in part on the mythical belief that the earliest ancestors of mankind were both human and animal in the same form. The shaman-jaguar symbolizes this ancient mystical solidarity. In more formal Mesoamerican religious tradition the jaguar is commonly associated with rain and crop fertility and also takes the guise of an underworld force, at times expressed in earthquakes. These various attributes are combined in the concept of the jaguar as symbol of sacred-secular power.[11]

The major sites of the Olmec heartland are situated in a hot, wet tangle of lowland swamps and jungles where a network of several river systems enters the Gulf of Mexico, in the vicinity of the Tuxtla Mountain range. This is an area rich in natural resources. The jungle must have teemed with wild game and fowl, and the rivers, lagoons, and sea provided an abundance of fish, shellfish, turtles, and aquatic fowl. Nonetheless, ag-

[11] Peter T. Furst, "The Olmec Were-Jaguar Motif in the Light of Ethnographic Reality," reprinted in *Contemporary Archaeology*, ed. Mark P. Leone (Carbondale: Southern Illinois Univ. Press, 1972), pp. 333–53; Wolf, *Sons of the Shaking Earth*, pp. 70–73.

riculture formed the basis of Olmec subsistence (although from an agricultural point of view the area in general suffers from an excess of water). The pattern of rainfall is such that two crops a year were probably harvested from cultivated areas of higher and dryer ground in Olmec times, as they are today. In all likelihood the banks of the many rivers, which were constantly renewed with rich silts by periodic flooding, were also cultivated.[12]

The variety and abundance of local resources undoubtedly supported a sizeable population and, in fact, dozens of sites have been located, although most have yet to be archaeologically explored. The major Olmec center, and the most impressive site, is La Venta, situated today on some 5 km² of raised land in the midst of a great mangrove swamp near the Tonalá River. La Venta was constructed along an axis oriented 8° west of true north-south, a feature which probably reflected even at this early date the pre-Columbian belief in the symbolism and ritual significance of the cardinal directions. The main structure is a pyramid 32 m high constructed of earth and clay in the shape of a fluted cone with a truncated top. This is a highly unusual pyramid form, and it may represent a deliberate attempt to duplicate the configuration of volcanic cinder cones such as those in the nearby Tuxtla Mountains. It is easy to imagine that in their fiery splendor volcanoes may have evoked not only wonder and awe, but perhaps a desire to emulate such power among the rulers of La Venta.[13]

To the north of the pyramid lie long mounds of specially selected red, orange, yellow, and white clays which must have been imported from sources beyond the island, for clay does not occur naturally there. The mounds lead to a ceremonial court or plaza enclosed by 2-m (7 ft.) columns of prismatic basalt weighing between 680 and 1,040 kg (1,500 and 2,300 lb.) apiece, which also were brought to the site from outside sources.[14] Excavations among these mounds, platforms, and plazas have brought to light additional evidence of the wealth and power which the inhabitants of La Venta enjoyed. Some of the mounds revealed rich burials with offerings of obsidian, amber, amethyst, turquoise, and especially serpentine and jade exquisitely carved into small engraved celts (ax-shaped implements), elegant figurines, earplugs, beads, and other ornaments. Indeed, Olmec lapidaries produced the finest jade work of pre-Columbian Middle America. No craftsmen of later eras ever exceeded or even duplicated their mastery in carving the blue-green stone

---

[12] Philip Drucker and R. F. Heizer, "A Study of the Milpa System of La Venta Island and Its Archaeological Implications," *Southwestern J. of Anthro.* 16, (1960):36–45; R. F. Heizer, "Agriculture and the Theocratic State in Lowland Southeastern Mexico," *American Antiquity* 26 (1960):215–22.

[13] R. F. Heizer and Philip Drucker, "The Fluted Pyramid of the La Venta Site," *Antiquity* 42 (1968):52–56.

[14] For a full description of the La Venta site see Drucker, Heizer, and Squier, *Excavations at La Venta.*

FIGURE 1.6 A massive Olmec stone head from the site of Tres Zapotes. This monolith stands 1.47 m high and weighs 7.8 tons, making it one of the smaller colossal heads. Reprinted by courtesy of the University of California Archaeological Research Facility from C. W. Clewlow, R. A. Cowan, J. F. O'Connell, and C. Benemann, *Colossal Heads of the Olmec Culture* (Contributions of the University of California Archaeological Research Facility no. 4, 1967), pl. 11.

that was the most precious substance known to ancient Middle Americans.[15]

Olmec rulers also had use for concave mirrors, worn as chest ornaments, made of carefully ground and polished pieces of iron-rich ores such as hematite, ilmenite, or magnetite. These mirrors can reflect images on a blank surface, and one can imagine that they were used by Olmec leaders in mysterious rites designed to impress onlookers with proper awe and respect.

Perhaps these noble rulers are the personages represented by four colossal basalt heads found at La Venta which weigh between 12 and 24 tons apiece and stand about 2 to 3 m (6 to 9 ft.) high. The sculptures may be either portraits of actual Olmec chieftains or representative of rulers in a general sense. Each head wears a characteristic form of headgear not

[15] Charles Wicke, *Olmec: An Early Art Style of Pre-Columbian Mexico* (Tucson: Univ. of Arizona Press, 1971); M. W. Stirling, "The Olmecs, Artists in Jade," in *Essays in Pre-Columbian Art and Archaeology,* ed. S. K. Lothrop et al. (Cambridge: Harvard Univ. Press, 1961), pp. 43–59.

unlike a modern football helmet, which possibly depicts a helmet worn for a ceremonial Middle American ball game well known from later periods of pre-Columbian history (see pp. 64–65). The basalt blocks used in these sculptures, as well as in the columns surrounding the ceremonial court and in other monoliths, were all laboriously transported to La Venta from the Tuxtla Mountains.[16]

One of the most important Olmec discoveries, Stela C, does not come from La Venta, but from Tres Zapotes, and belongs to the late stages of Olmec activity, after the abandonment of La Venta about 600 or 500 B.C. A stela is a flat, rectangular stone frequently carved or inscribed in some manner which, particularly during the Classic Maya era, was often set upright behind a low flat stone altar. At least 18 stelae have been found at various Olmec sites, many carved with a jaguar mask or with the open mouth of a feline within which appear human figures. However, Stela C, which depicts an Olmec-derived werejaguar mask on one side, reveals on the other a date carved in the notation of a calendrical system known today as the Long Count which was used by the Classic era Maya and other lowland peoples. The Stela C date is one of the earliest Long Count inscriptions known and the oldest Olmec date on record.[17]

The Long Count is so called because it begins with a fixed date in the past, just as our own calendrical system is based on the birth of Christ. In the Maya calendar this starting point is termed 4 Ahau 8 Cumku and is equivalent to a day in the year 3113 B.C. by our calendar, according to the Goodman-Martinez-Thompson correlation.[18] (This is not to say that the Long Count was invented on this date. Rather, this was the date that was agreed upon much later as the starting point for calculations.) Calendrical calculations were expressed through time periods of varying length. Individual days, called *Kins,* were counted and combined to form larger segments of time based on units of 20. Thus, 20 *Kins* formed a *Uinal* or month; 18 *Uinals* composed a *Tun* or a year (a departure from the vigesimal system to conform with the solar year); 20 *Tuns* formed a *Katun;* and 20 *Katuns* constituted a *Baktun,* or 144,000 days. Three signs were used to write numbers: a dot for one, a horizontal bar for 5, and a glyph in the shape of a stylized shell for zero. For example, the number 18 would be indicated thus:[19]

•••
═══════

[16] C. William Clewlow et al., *Colossal Heads of the Olmec Culture,* Contributions of the University of California Archaeology Research Facility no. 4 (Berkeley, 1967).

[17] Michael D. Coe, "Cycle 7 Monuments in Middle America: A Reconsideration," *American Anthropologist* 59 (1957):597–611.

[18] One of the major concerns of Middle American archaeologists has been to correlate Long Count dates with those of the Christian calendar. Two major correlations have been advanced: the Goodman-Martinez-Thompson (G-M-T) and the Spinden. We are following the G-M-T correlation throughout most of our discussion since radiocarbon dates have best upheld this scheme so far. However, the matter is by no means firmly settled.

[19] For a general discussion of hieroglyphic writing, arithmetic, and astronomy among lowland peoples with emphasis on the systems used by the Maya see Sylvanus G. Morley, *The Ancient Maya,* 3rd ed., rev. G. W. Brainerd (Stanford: Stanford Univ. Press, 1956), chap. 12.

FIGURE 4.7 Inscription from Stela C, Tres Zapotes. Reading from top to bottom the bars and dots indicate 16 (*Katuns*), 6 (*Tuns*), 16 (*Uinals*), 18 (*Kins*). From "Cycle 7 Monuments in Middle America: A Reconsideration," Fig. 1, by Michael D. Coe. Reproduced by permission of the author and the American Anthropological Association from the *American Anthropologist* 59:598, 1957. Not for further reproduction.

On Stela C the largest unit, the *Baktun* number, unfortunately has been broken off at the top of the stone, but the date is reconstructed as 7 *Baktuns*, 16 *Katuns*, 6 *Tuns*, 16 *Uinals*, 18 *Kins;* or, as it is usually written, (7).16.6.16.18. This notation records a time period equivalent to 1,125,688 days since the base date 4 Ahau 8 Cumku, or a day in the year 31 B.C. in the Christian calendar.[20] Additional glyphs on other monuments

[20] Coe, "Cycle 7 Monuments in Middle America," pp. 597–611.

in the Olmec area also suggest a form of writing; as we shall see below, however, writing and calendrics appear at an even earlier date at Monte Albán in the Valley of Oaxaca.

The representation of calendrical notations and glyphs, the delicate crafting of jade and serpentine, and the skilled carving of monumental sculptures, together with the tremendous amount of sheer labor that must have been expended to transport multi-tonned basalt blocks to Olmec elite centers and to build mounds and pyramids, signify that Olmec society was highly organized under a powerful leadership capable of mobilizing and directing considerable numbers of workers. These rulers very likely served as high priests, and while strictly secular affairs must have fallen under their control, they probably derived much power from their positions as intermediaries between gods and men, particularly as they assumed responsibility for the divine intercession (combined with detailed climatic and astronomical knowledge) necessary to assure abundant harvests for the populace. In a more prosaic context, the economic basis underlying the power of the Olmec elite may have centered on possession and control of the highly productive natural river levees.

The elite were supported by a lower stratum of commoners, village-dwelling agriculturalists who contributed produce, time, and labor for their rulers' needs and for the building and maintenance of the ceremonial centers. We know virtually nothing of these humble laborers, for while house sites are abundant in the Olmec area, very few have been excavated and preservation is poor in the damp and acid soil.

Yet even more distant contacts were required to maintain Olmec society. Olmec-style rock carvings, cave paintings, and small portable objects such as ceramics and figurines are found in central Mexico, Guerrero, the Valley of Oaxaca, Chiapas, and along the Pacific coastal plain of Guatemala as far as El Salvador and even to Costa Rica. This material has been interpreted as indicative of military conquests, colonization, proselytizing missionaries, or trade contacts. Since proselytism in general was not a feature of Middle American religions, missionary activity per se is not a satisfactory explanation. In later eras of Middle American culture history, military activities, colonization, and trade were often combined, and there is evidence suggesting warlike events in scenes of combat on a monument at Tres Zapotes and in carvings at La Venta which depict human figures bound by cords, perhaps captives.[21]

There is good reason to doubt, however, whether Olmec society in spite of its splendor was sufficiently powerful and organizationally complex to actually conquer more distant peoples. Instead, essentially peaceful trade and interregional exchange are the most defensible theories at present to explain Olmec presence beyond the Gulf Coast heartland. Through such trade precious necessities such as obsidian and important ceremonial

[21] Coe, *America's First Civilization;* Bernal, *Olmec World;* Sanders and Price, *Mesoamerica,* pp. 117–22; Gordon R. Willey, "The Early Great Styles and the Rise of the Pre-Columbian Civilizations," *American Anthropologist* 64 (1962):1–14.

materials, including serpentine, jade, and iron-rich ores, could be obtained. Some commerce may have been conducted by professional Olmec traders. Exchange also may have occurred within ceremonial contexts featuring interchange of key resources as gifts between Olmec rulers and leaders of distant elite centers.

It is quite conceivable, too, that such high-level exchanges held important political implications in the sense that contact with a highly ramified society such as the Olmec must have been could have stimulated similar sociopolitical elaborations elsewhere. The diffusion of Olmec symbolism, such as the werejaguar motif, could have occurred as part of this process as status-seeking local leaders attempted to emulate the prestigeful behavior of their highly regarded Olmec contemporaries.[22]

One of the Olmec trade routes led from the Gulf Coast through Puebla into the highlands of central Mexico, then down through Morelos into Guerrero and the Balsas drainage. Figurines, ceramics, and a few small stone sculptures in the Olmec style have been discovered at various locations here, often at entrances to major passes or valleys, suggesting something on the order of protective way-stations on trade or travel routes.

In the Basin of Mexico the sites of Tlatilco and Tlapacoya, which lie near the entrances to major passes leading to Puebla and to Morelos, may be a case in point. A number of Formative era communities—Tlatilco, Tlapacoya, Zacatenco, and El Arbolillo are among the best known—have been located in the basin adjacent to hilly terrain and the lake system, where the diverse resources of the hills, plains, and lakes would be readily available. Tlatilco, a very large village on a small stream not far from Lake Texcoco, and Tlapacoya, located on the lake shore in the southeast part of the basin, give evidence of Olmec influence in burial offerings and occupational refuse, suggesting that these communities actually may have been inhabited by Olmec persons.[23] It is important to note, however, that most of the material relating to the Basin of Mexico Formative is distinctly local and non-Olmec in style and manufacture.[24]

Other Olmec sites, again possible trade depots or perhaps politico-religious centers, stand at entrances to passes through the hills in Puebla and Morelos (e.g., Chalcatzingo and Las Bocas) and lie along rivers near valleys leading from Morelos south into Guerrero where Olmec figurines, beads, masks, pectorals, and ornaments are particularly frequent. Cave

[22] Michael D. Coe, *The Jaguar's Children: Pre-Classic Central Mexico* (New York: Museum of Primitive Art, 1965); Robert H. Cobean et al., "Obsidian Trade at San Lorenzo Tenochtitlán, Mexico," *Science* 174 (1971):666–71; Kent V. Flannery, "The Olmec and the Valley of Oaxaca: A Model for Interregional Interaction in Formative Times," in *Dumbarton Oaks Conference on the Olmec*, ed. Elizabeth Benson (Washington, D.C.: Dumbarton Oaks Research Library and Collection, 1968), pp. 79–117.

[23] The Olmec objects may represent portable trade items, too, perhaps received in exchange for obsidian from sources in the basin and in Hidalgo to the north.

[24] Coe, *Jaguar's Children;* Michael D. Coe, *Mexico* (New York: Praeger, 1962), pp. 70–81; Paul Tolstoy and Louise I. Paradis, "Early and Middle Preclassic Culture in the Basin of Mexico," *Science* 167 (1970):344–51.

paintings in Olmec tradition deep in the recesses of Juxtlahuaca Cave attest further to Olmec influence in Guerrero, where Olmec individuals may have searched particularly for deposits of jade.[25]

Another major Olmec route extends across the Isthmus of Tehuantepec into the Central Depression (Grijalva Basin) of Chiapas and along the Pacific coastal plain of Chiapas and Guatemala into El Salvador and even distant Costa Rica. Olmec materials along the Pacific Coast may be indicative once again of a search for jade and also for obsidian from the Guatemalan highlands.

Olmec symbolism and iconography also reached the Valley of Oaxaca. Here Olmec motifs in figurines and ceramics first precede and then are contemporaneous with the early periods of the major ceremonial center of the valley, Monte Albán. Monte Albán originated about 900 B.C. atop a high hill some 450 m above the valley floor. A large central square, also oriented along a north-south axis, was slowly fashioned from the summit rock until in its final form it covered some 15 acres. A variety of platforms, pyramids, and temples were gradually constructed along its sides. One of the earliest temple platforms, the Temple of the Dancing Figures, contains a series of rectangular stone slabs on which ornamented nude males are depicted in varied positions of motion and distortion (hence the name of dancing figures or *danzantes*). However, these unusual figures probably are not ordinary dancers. They may portray religious functionaries engaged in an ecstatic ritual dance or, more likely, they may represent captured or slain enemies dishonored by forced nudity or mutilation. Interestingly enough the droop of the mouths is very reminiscent of Olmec style and nine of the figures have the peculiar elongated head shape often found on Olmec carvings.[26]

Many of the *danzantes* are accompanied by still undeciphered hieroglyphs and occasionally by numbers, possibly indicating the names of the men portrayed and dates. This evidence of writing and of calendrics predates the glyphs and Long Count notation on Stela C at Tres Zapotes and suggests that the Zapotec of early Monte Albán may have been among the first to originate writing and calendrics in Middle America. The calendrics inscribed here, however, are not in the Long Count, but may refer instead to a simpler system, known to scholars as the *Calendar Round*. The Calendar Round reckoned time in terms of a great cycle comprised of a 260-day fortune-telling and ceremonial year combining 20 named days with 13 numbers, which intermeshed with a 365-day solar or calendar year composed of 18 months with 20 days each plus 5 highly unlucky extra days. The great cycle resulting from the coordinating of these two shorter cycles was completed every 52 solar years. The basic difference

[25] Bernal, *Olmec World;* Coe, *America's First Civilization;* David Grove, "Chalcatzingo, Morelos, Mexico: A Reappraisal of the Olmec Rock Carvings," *American Antiquity* 33 (1968):486–91.

[26] John Paddock, "Oaxaca in Ancient Mesoamerica," in *Ancient Oaxaca,* ed. John Paddock (Stanford: Stanford Univ. Press, 1966), pp. 83–242; Alfonso Caso, "Sculpture and Mural Painting of Oaxaca," in *Handbook of Middle American Indians,* ed. Robert Wauchope (Austin: Univ. of Texas Press, 1965), 3:849–55.

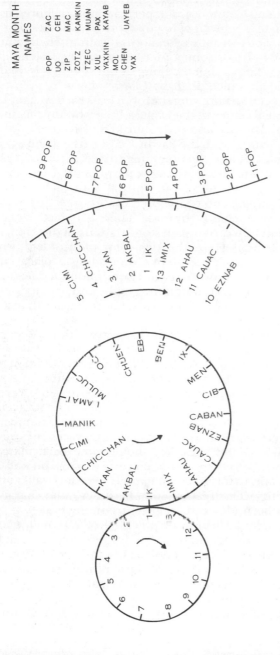

MAYA MONTH
NAMES

POP	ZAC
UO	CEH
ZIP	MAC
ZOTZ	KANKIN
TZEC	MUAN
XUL	PAX
YAXKIN	KAYAB
MOL	
CHEN	UAYEB
YAX	

A

B

FIGURE 4.8 (*a*) Schematic representation of the intermeshing of 13 numbers with 20 named days to form a 260-day Sacred Year. Each day in the Sacred Year was identified by a number and a name. Using Maya day names, day 1 Ik will be followed by 2 Akbal, etc. (*b*) The 260-day Sacred Year combined with the 365-day Solar Year (18 months of 20 days each plus a period of 5 unlucky end-of-year days) eventually to form the 52-year cycle of the Calendar Round. A day calculated within this cycle now is identified by its Sacred Year and Solar Year position, that is, 1 Ik 5 Pop, 2 Akbal 6 Pop, etc. Adapted, by permission of the publishers, from Michael D. Coe, *The Maya* (New York: Frederick A. Praeger, Publishers, 1966), fig. 8 and fig. 10, and from Sylvanus G. Morley, *The Ancient Maya*, 3rd ed., rev. by George W. Brainerd (Stanford University Press, 1956), fig. 20, copyright © 1946, 1947, 1956 by the Board of Trustees of the Leland Stanford Junior University.

between the Calendar Round and the Long Count is that the Calendar Round, in contrast to the Long Count, was not permanently anchored in time. A Calendar Round date is equivalent to our shorthand notation of, say, '70, which has the obvious weakness of not indicating whether it refers to 1570, or 1870, or 1970, or some other century. The Calendar Round eventually was widely known, but the Long Count system was used only by various lowland peoples including the Classic Maya.[27]

Monte Albán must have been an imposing site, even in its earliest stages. While not the only ceremonial center in the Oaxaca Valley by any means, it quickly became the administrative and ceremonial focus for the valley and for a broad region stretching from the Pacific Coast to the Tehuacán Valley. Most of the peoples of this territory may have accepted the influence of the rulers of Monte Albán willingly, perhaps for economic advantages and social prestige accruing from contacts with such an important center. But if the *danzantes* do represent slain captives, they may indicate that these ties also were achieved by force. There is, in fact, strong evidence for military conquests in carvings on stone slabs from the Monte Albán II period (300–100 B.C.). Here the depiction of upside-down human heads with closed eyes, of "hill glyphs" indicating a place, of glyphs probably giving the name of the place, and inscriptions of dates all suggest the successful use of force, although the glyphs and inscriptions have also been interpreted in terms of religious symbolism rather than as evidence of military activity.[28]

Since in its early stages Monte Albán was contemporary with La Venta, it indicates that major centers were evolving from the Formative base in regions other than the southern Gulf Coast. (We shall note additional important Formative centers in the discussion of Classic cultures.) Although the presence of Olmec symbolism suggests that Olmec elite were in contact in some manner with the elite of Monte Albán, the Oaxacan center was basically a local development. For example, there are a number of architectural features here which also occur in earlier Oaxacan sites but are not found at the major Olmec sites. We should note particularly attempts to combine the so-called *tablero,* a sunken vertical panel on walls, with the *talud,* or sloping plane, to form a combination of vertical walls and sloping surfaces on buildings. This feature soon becomes quite characteristic of central and southern Mexican architecture in general.

Undoubtedly the economic (agricultural) potential of the Valley of Oaxaca with its large flat floor, high water table, low erosion rate, and frost-free flood plain was a major factor underwriting the rise of Monte Albán. We have already noted the variety of agricultural techniques, including dry farming and pot irrigation and canal irrigation and terracing, by which this potential was exploited and expanded. The natural resources of the valley formation together with these diverse agricultural

---

[27] Morley, *Ancient Maya.*
[28] Paddock, "Oaxaca in Ancient Mesoamerica"; Jorge R. Acosta, "Preclassic and Classic Architecture of Oaxaca," in *Handbook of Middle American Indians,* ed. Robert Wauchope (Austin: Univ. of Texas Press, 1965), 3:814–36.

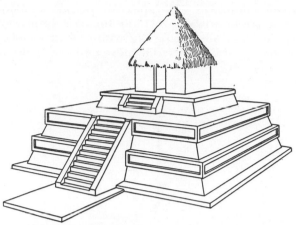

FIGURE 4.9 Reconstruction of structure A-7 from the highland Guatemala site of Kaminaljuyu shows a thatch-roofed temple surmounting a low platform pyramid built in *tablero-talud* style. Sloping planes (*talud*) are interrupted by vertical rectangular moldings with inset panels (*tablero*). Reprinted, by permission of the Carnegie Institution of Washington, from A. V. Kidder, J. D. Jennings, and E. M. Shook, *Excavations at Kaminaljuyu, Guatemala,* fig. 108, Carnegie Institution of Washington Publication no. 561, 1946.

techniques stimulated Monte Albán's emergence from the village-farming base and then furnished the agricultural support necessary to maintain the activities of skilled craftsmen and an administrative elite. So successful was this growth that by the start of the Christian era Monte Albán and the Oaxaca Valley formed the dominant political entity in the southern highlands of Mexico.

Also by this time fundamental characteristics of Middle American civilization can be discerned. The simple village-farming way of life was rapidly being transformed into a more complicated pattern. Resting on an agricultural subsistence base exploited by a diversity of techniques, a complex form of society had evolved typified by social differentiation between a ruling elite and a supporting base of common men. Writing and calendrics had been developed, probably in conjunction with the elaboration of organized religion and a specialized priesthood. The expression of religious ritual and of symbolism in iconography was common, and representations of supernatural concepts regarding rain, the power of fertility and regeneration, and life and death can be seen in the Olmec werejaguar and related motifs. Basic architectural features including burial mounds, stone-faced and stepped platform pyramids, and planned plazas or squares with an orientation toward the cardinal points were increasingly widespread. Full-time craft specialists and interregional trade and commerce flourished, forming the basic impetus, along with shared ideologies and increasing agricultural proficiency, for the emergence of states and the related achievements of civilization characteristic of the Classic era.

5

Tikal
and Teotihuacán

Mesoamerica
and the Classic Era

In studies of Middle American prehistory the term "Classic" has held a number of distinct connotations which in sum render it rather imprecise. It has been applied in a stylistic sense to the culmination or fruition of art forms in stone, painting, cloth, clay, and mosaics, and especially in architecture. The term is then readily extended to define the period or developmental stage in a given region when these arts reached their peak. In this context "Classic" refers not only to achievements in art and architecture, but also to related sociocultural developments including the rise of urbanism and of states, the elaboration of more intensive agricultural techniques, particularly irrigation, to support a steadily increasing population, and the growth of interregional trade. It also has been traditional to view the Classic era as a time of peace when theocratic rulers maintained their positions through an intense religiosity shared with all the populace. This assumption now is being challenged by evidence indicating that while religion was indeed a basic integrative social force, control of secular, even militaristic, power was also important for those who ruled.

Finally, the Classic era has been defined chronologically, although this is probably the least useful of all its designations. In temporal terms the Classic becomes that period of time, approximately A.D. 250 to 900, when the lowland Maya of the Guatemalan Petén and adjacent regions carved dates in the Long Count on stelae and other monuments. These centuries generally correlate with the flowering of Maya arts and architecture and with sociocultural growth. But in areas outside the Maya lowlands comparable developments do not always occur within the same chronological period. In the central Mexican highlands, for example, the Classic age may be said to start several centuries earlier, about the beginning of the Christian era, and to end at times varying from A.D. 700 to 1200 depending on what region is considered.

In the following pages we will use the term "classic" primarily in the sense of a developmental stage. As such, however, it is applicable only to select cultures within certain areas of Middle America, specifically to societies included in the region or culture area traditionally known to anthropologists as Mesoamerica. The boundaries of this unit varied over time, but in general they can be placed at the Panuca-Lerma drainage on the north and somewhat to the east of the Ulua River and Lake Yojoa in Honduras. Territories beyond this sphere, both to the north and to the south, are excluded from this formulation because the pre-Hispanic societies located in them either did not share as fully in a common Mesoamerican cultural tradition or failed to achieve levels of sociocultural development comparable to those societies included within the framework of "Mesoamerica." We will examine these frontiers in Chapter 7. Our concern here is with several of the distinct regional centers which evolved within the Mesoamerican sphere during the Classic era. Foremost among these were Teotihuacán, located in the central Mexican highlands, and Tikal, the greatest of the Maya lowland settlements. The growth and interrelationships of these and other highland and lowland societies form the framework for the cultural dynamics of the Mesoamerican Classic era.

Irrigation
and the Rise of the State

The most influential society in Mesoamerica during the Classic era was Teotihuacán, centered in an immense urban metropolis of the same name located in a valley on the east side of the Basin of Mexico (see Figure 5.1). The rise of this great state, its organizational format, and the scope of its influence bring to the forefront a number of important topics. The emergence of urbanism is one of these considerations. Urbanism was one of two polar types of settlement pattern characteristic of pre-Hispanic Mesoamerica. The other, exemplified at La Venta, was a dispersed plan of scattered residences located in the general vicinity of an elite center. This mode of habitation, which is commonly associated with swidden agricultural techniques, typified the Maya lowlands and we will consider it in more detail below. Urbanism, in contrast, occurred most commonly in the arid highlands of Mesoamerica in conjunction with subsistence techniques based on irrigation.

By "urban" we mean in general a tightly compacted, nucleated settlement pattern with a large population numbering in the thousands and

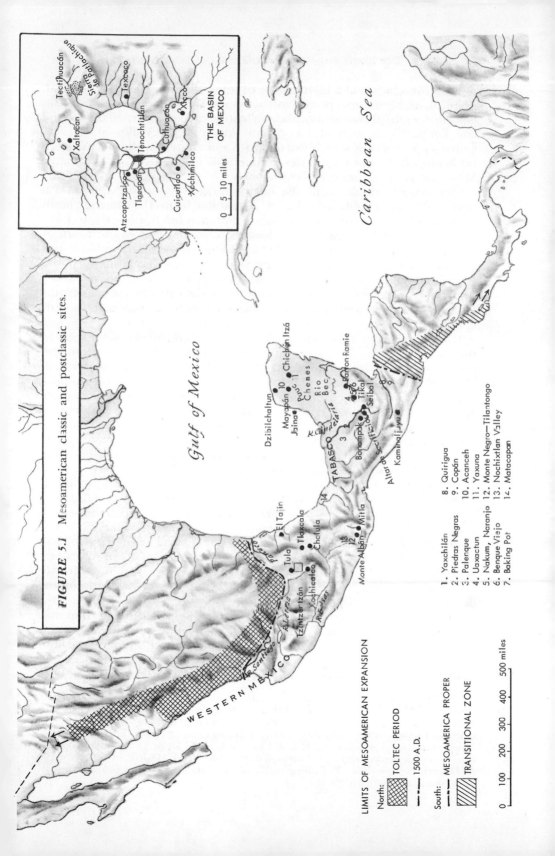

FIGURE 5.1 Mesoamerican classic and postclassic sites.

THE BASIN OF MEXICO

0   5   10 miles

Tecfihuacán
Sierra de Patlachique
Texcoco
Xaltocan
Tenochtitlán
Culhuacán
Xico
Atzcapotzalco
Tlacopan
Cuicuilco
Xochimilco

Caribbean Sea

Gulf of Mexico

WESTERN MEXICO

R. Santiago
R. Lerma
Izintzuntzán
Xochicalco
R. Balsas
Tula
El Tajín
Tlaxcala
Cholula
Mitla
Monte Albán

Dzibilchaltun
Mayapán 10
Isina
Chichén Itzá
Punc T
Chenes
Rio
Bec
Balton Ramie
Tikal
Seibal
Bonampak
R. Usumacinta
Altar de Sacrificios
R. Chixoy
Kaminaljuyu
TABASCO
R. Candelaria

1. Yaxchilán
2. Piedras Negras
3. Palenque
4. Uaxactun
5. Nakum, Naranjo
6. Benque Viajo
7. Baking Pot
8. Quirigua
9. Copán
10. Acanceh
11. Yaxuna
12. Monte Negro—Tilantongo
13. Nochixtlan Valley
14. Matacapan

LIMITS OF MESOAMERICAN EXPANSION

North:
TOLTEC PERIOD
1500 A.D.

South:
MESOAMERICA PROPER
TRANSITIONAL ZONE

0   100   200   300   400   500 miles

tens of thousands and a high degree of internal differentiation in social, political, and economic power and activities. Initial stages of population growth, social differentiation, and nucleation can be discerned during the late Formative at such sites as Monte Albán in the Valley of Oaxaca, Cuicuilco in the Basin of Mexico, and Kaminaljuyú in the Guatemalan highlands. But the first full development of urban life in pre-Hispanic Mesoamerica took place at Teotihuacán.

One major variable in the rise of urbanism here was the agricultural potential of the Teotihuacán Valley. The valley forms the drainage basin of the Río de San Juan which, in pre-Columbian times, flowed into Lake Texcoco, one of the chain of shallow lakes on the floor of the Basin of Mexico. Like the basin, the Teotihuacán Valley is bordered by hills and mountains. The solid rampart of the Sierra de Patlachique stands to the south and southeast, while to the north a string of isolated volcanoes dominates the landscape. But to the northeast the valley lies open to plains leading to Tlaxcala and Puebla and, ultimately, to the lowlands of the Gulf Coast.

Water is the most important single factor affecting human settlement in the valley. The surrounding mountains reduce rainfall to one of the lowest yearly averages in the entire Basin of Mexico. The annual rainfall also fluctuates greatly from year to year and droughts are not uncommon. The limited availability and dependability of precipitation, in turn, place serious restrictions on agriculture. The most favorable sections for rainfall-dependent maize cultivation are limited to the southern sections of the valley, in the low ridges and foothills of the Patlachique range, where rainfall is heaviest. (Similar moisture problems throughout the Basin of Mexico make the southern part of the basin in general most favorable to rainfall-dependent maize cultivation.) However, agricultural yields and crop security in the Teotihuacán Valley (and the Basin of Mexico in general) are vastly improved by irrigation. Determination of the antiquity of irrigation systems in both the valley and the basin is a major archaeological problem, but in all likelihood water control was practiced by the late Formative. Moreover, it can be convincingly argued that the rise and florescence of the city of Teotihuacán was directly interrelated with the economic advantages and sociopolitical conditions inherent in the application of irrigation in this dry valley.

In light of what we have just summarized it is not surprising to find that the vast majority of the Formative village-farming settlements in the Teotihuacán Valley were located in the south, scattered about on the hilly slopes of the Patlachique range where tlacolol was probably the predominant agricultural technique.[1] By 500 B.C., however, there are indica-

---

[1] Unless otherwise specified, discussion of the Valley of Teotihuacán and the form and functioning of the society that evolved there is derived from William T. Sanders, "The Cultural Ecology of the Teotihuacán Valley" (Department of Sociology and Athropology, The Pennsylvania State University, 1965); William T. Sanders and Barbara J. Price, *Mesoamerica* (New York: Random House, 1968); William T. Sanders, "Hydraulic Agriculture, Economic Symbiosis and the Evolution of States in Central Mexico," in *Anthropological Archeology in the Americas,* ed. B. J. Meggers (Washington, D.C.: The Anthropological Society of Washington, 1968), pp. 88–107.

tions of a gradual shift to the alluvial plain of the valley floor and a growing tendency for villages there to become more densely settled, more nucleated. By 300 to 200 B.C. small elite centers appear in the valley; they are located on tops of small hills in the river delta and on the summits of foothills at the edge of the plain, although most of the population continued to live in ordinary hamlets.

In spite of this growth, during the Formative era the Teotihuacán Valley lagged behind other sections of the central Mexican highlands both culturally and demographically. For example, southern Puebla and Morelos, on the southern escarpment of the central plateau, contain a number of more substantial Formative sites, and in the southern and western territories of the Basin of Mexico sizable remains of terraced earth platforms and ceremonial plazas indicate that social differentiation and a more complex social system were further evolved here than in the Teotihuacán Valley. It was not until the beginning of the Christian era that the scene shifted to the heretofore marginal Teotihuacán Valley where, through the development of intensive agriculture probably based on irrigation and a high level of sociopolitical organization, a supremacy of population and social organization was achieved that lasted for the next seven centuries.

The focal point of this growth was the city of Teotihuacán itself, strategically located on the alluvial plain midway along the length of the valley adjacent to some 80 permanent springs. By 200 B.C. a nucleated town stood at this spot, and during the next three centuries (Tzacualli phase), when as much as 50 percent of the valley population gradually came to reside here, the early phases of an urban metropolis can be discerned. During the Classic era of Teotihuacán supremacy (A.D. 200–700), at least 60 percent and, toward the end of the era, as high as 90 percent of the valley population was concentrated in this one community. Estimates of absolute population figures for Teotihuacán vary somewhat due to difficulties in interpreting the archaeological data, but during the height of its glory about A.D. 500 (Xolalpan phase) 60,000 to 125,000 or more persons may have lived in the city; an overall average of about 100,000 persons is a fairly conservative estimate.[2]

The ceremonial, political, and economic core of the metropolis was a carefully planned complex of avenues, markets, paved plazas, pyramids, and other structures covering about 2.6 km[2]. The main avenue of the city and the major north-south thoroughfare, the so-called Street of the Dead, was a broad, paved avenue 55 m wide lined with more than 100 pyramids, temples, and residences which ran from the Pyramid of the Moon in the city center to well beyond the southern limits. Other major avenues trended east and west, again beginning from points in the city center. Most buildings were oriented along the north-south axis, as were additional streets which were spaced at regular intervals, thus giving an orderly appearance even to the most crowded areas. The sense of order is

[2] René Millon, "Teotihuacán," *Scientific American* 216 (1967): pp. 38–48; idem, "Teotihuacán: Completion of Map of Giant Ancient City in the Valley of Mexico," *Science* 170 (1970):1077–82.

FIGURE 5.2   View of Teotihuacán. The broad Avenue of the Dead was lined by more than 100 temples, shrines, and elite residences. The massive structure to the left is the monumental Pyramid of the Sun. In the foreground stands the somewhat smaller Pyramid of the Moon. In the background lie the Ciudadela (left) and the Great Compound (right). Reprinted from René Millon, "Teotihuacán: Completion of Map of Giant Ancient City in the Valley of Mexico," *Science* 170: 1077–82 (4 December 1970). Copyright 1970 by the American Association for the Advancement of Science. Courtesy, René Millon, all rights reserved.

further emphasized by the fact that many of the residential structures that surrounded the city center were carefully constructed within a grid of 57-m square city blocks; many of the cement-paved streets also seem to repeat multiples of the 57-m unit. Even the river which ran through the center of the metropolis was canalized so as to conform to the grid plan.[3]

The heart of the city focused on two immense enclosures standing opposite each other, one to the east and one to the west of the Street of the Dead, and known today as the Ciudadela or Citadel and the Great Compound, respectively. The Great Compound, composed of two broad raised platforms flanking a large plaza, may have been a major market place, one of several in the city. The Ciudadela, with its clusters of rooms and temple structures enclosed by massive stone-faced embankments,

---

[3] Millon, "Teotihuacán"; idem, "Teotihuacán: Completion of Map."

FIGURE 5.3 Detail of the Temple of Quetzalcóatl, Teotihuacán. This elaborately sculpted and painted façade was preserved intact by a larger temple later superimposed over it. Projecting heads of Quetzalcóatl, the Feathered Serpent, alternate with portrayals of Tlaloc. Representations of water and the stylized body of the serpent lie between them. Courtesy of the Field Museum of Natural History.

may have availed as a politico-religious center. Perhaps this was the residence of the supreme ruler(s) of Teotihuacán.

Within the Ciudadela stands an elegant six tiered step pyramid, the Temple of Quetzalcóatl. Along with other temples, civic buildings, and palaces of Teotihuacán the Temple of Quetzalcóatl is constructed with the talud-tablero architectural motif. On the ornately carved and brightly painted façade, sculpted portrayals, replete with shining obsidian eyes, of what may be Tlaloc, the rain god (or perhaps it is Xiuhcóatl, emblem of drought), alternate with Quetzalcóatl, the Feathered Serpent, symbol of divine wisdom and the principal character in the pantheon of pre-Columbian Mexico, who through blood sacrifice imparted life to man and gave him the first maize for his sustenance. These are two of the many gods venerated by Mexicans during and after the Classic era which are represented in paintings and images from Teotihuacán. A Sun God, Moon Goddess, Water Goddess, old Fire God, a bird-butterfly deity, and Xipe Totec, symbol of the annual renewal of nature, are similarly portrayed. It is noteworthy that most of these deities are in some fashion symbolic of a concern with growth and agriculture.[4]

[4] Wigberto Jiménez Moreno, "Mesoamerica Before the Toltecs," in *Ancient Oaxaca*, ed. John Paddock (Stanford: Stanford Univ. Press, 1966), pp. 38–44; Eric R. Wolf, *Sons of the Shaking Earth* (Chicago: Univ. of Chicago Press, 1959), chap. 5.

FIGURE 5.4 Fragment of a wall fresco, Teotihuacán style. The walls of the more elaborate residences of Teotihuacán were often painted with many-colored frescoes depicting the gods, priests, animals, fruits, and flowers. Courtesy of the Art Institute of Chicago.

Along the Street of the Dead stand dozens of other buildings, including the residences of the elite. These structures, resplendent in gleaming white stucco, were flat-roofed masonry compounds composed of dozens of one-story rooms commonly arranged around a sunken central court which was open to the sky and often contained an altar. Since the individual rooms were without windows, groups of rooms were lighted and aired by smaller sunken patios. Rainwater was carried off by drains in the house court pavement which connected to an underground city drainage system built beneath the streets.

Ordinary Teotihuacanos of lower social position lived in thousands of residential buildings which surrounded the city center on all sides. Groups of residential buildings often were set apart from surrounding structures so as to form a neighborhood or ward. Neighborhoods sometimes were inhabited by craftsmen practicing a common specialization such as working in obsidian or precious stones or making pottery. Still other groups of buildings are correlated with ceramics from other areas of Middle America, especially from the Gulf Coast, Yucatán, and Guatemala, suggesting foreign enclaves, perhaps merchants' quarters.[5]

[5] Millon, "Teotihuacán," pp. 38–48; idem, "Teotihuacán: Completion of Map," pp. 1077–82.

The residences comprising the neighborhood groups were crowded complexes of one-story rooms, porches, patios, access ways, and small temples which formed "apartment compounds." A typical compound consisted of several apartments, each composed of groups of rooms surrounding a light and airy patio with its own drainage system, grouped around one or more central courtyards where small ceremonial platforms stood. The entire complex was secluded from the narrow street by high windowless walls broken only by a few narrow gates which to those approaching from the outside must have presented a forbidding appearance—a guise quite in contrast with the open, bright, patioed interior.

A conservative estimate suggests that 12 to 60 persons may have inhabited an apartment compound depending on its size. In all likelihood these residents were related in some manner. The location of one or more small temples within a compound suggests common ritual activities, probably also reflecting common kinship ties. We have already noted a tendency for common occupation. This organization of apartment compounds and then neighborhoods in terms of common interests and activities may have been a major factor in city government. Such groups probably promoted considerable social solidarity among themselves and could have provided a cohesive intermediate level between the individual and the state.[6]

Although the tens of thousands of persons resident in Teotihuacán were highly differentiated in terms of social and economic activities, most of the population of the main city and of a series of immediately adjacent smaller communities probably worked to greater or lesser extent as agriculturalists, cultivating the rich alluvial plain and nearby hillsides. But to achieve sufficient productivity to feed a metropolis the size of Teotihuacán a method of cultivation more intensive and more productive than tlacolol must have been utilized. Very likely some form of irrigation was the answer.

Until relatively recently this idea did not seem plausible. Scholars had long thought that irrigation evolved much later in Middle America, not long before Mexica (Aztec) times, some 500 years after the decline of Teotihuacán. Within recent years, however, evidence has accumulated which strongly suggests that intensive agriculture was in fact practiced in various highland areas of Mesoamerica as early as the Formative era. The probable utilization of "pot-irrigation" in the Oaxaca Valley during the Formative is a case in point. Studies in the Tehuacán Valley also indicate that irrigation ditches, dams, and terraces were in use by at least the late Formative.[7] This material lends support to the possibility of simple irriga-

[6] Ibid.; Sigvald Linné, *Archaeological Researches at Teotihuacán, Mexico,* Ethnographical Museum of Sweden Publication no. 1 (Stockholm, 1934); idem, *Mexican Highland Cultures,* Ethnographical Museum of Sweden Publication no. 7 (Stockholm, 1942).

[7] Richard S. MacNeish, "Speculations about How and Why Food Production and Village Life Developed in the Tehuacán Valley, Mexico," *Archaeology* 24 (1971):307–15; Melvin L. Fowler, "A Preclassic Water Distribution System in Amalucan, Mexico," *Archaeology* 22 (1969):208–15; Barbara J. Price, "Prehispanic Irrigation Agriculture in Nuclear America," *Latin American Research Review* 6 (1971):3–60.

FIGURE 5.5 Ceramic censor top, 37 cm high, of
Teotihuacán style, illustrates the grace and elegance
of Teotihuacán sculpture and ceramics. The portrait-
like face of an old man, perhaps representing the old
fire god, is surrounded by a plumed headdress containing emblems of Quetzalpapalotl, a bird-butterfly
diety. Heavy-beaked quetzal heads are portrayed at
the throat and the middle of the forehead, while a
forward-curling spiral representing a butterfly pro-
boscis rises above the upper plumes. Courtesy of the
Art Institute of Chicago.

tion efforts in the Basin of Mexico, perhaps even in the Teotihuacán
Valley, during the Formative era.

If irrigation were coming into use, it also would have generated change
and adjustment in activities other than the strictly economic. As we noted
in the previous chapter, the allocation of land and water resources holds
potential for serious social conflict. The necessity for ways and means to
resolve this conflict may be one factor facilitating the rise of political
centralization. Increasing control of water-land distributions in order to
avoid additional disputes, together with organization of labor to expand
and maintain the irrigation systems, may further strengthen the central

authority and develop mechanisms of cooperation and integration which will tie smaller, formerly autonomous communities into larger, increasingly centralized sociopolitical structures.

Concurrently the central authority also obtains control of an effective weapon with which to guarantee compliance with its decisions: the capability of withholding water from recalcitrant parties. As the system grows, the governing body of a society based on hydraulics, such as Teotihuacán probably was, can become extremely powerful and can gain command over great numbers of people. All who reside within its territories fall under its direction no matter who they are. Official laws are promulgated and offenders are judged in formal courts. Censuses may be taken and corvée labor, tribute, and taxes demanded to support the needs of government. A professional military stands ready to enforce sanctions, if necessary. In other words, a state evolves.

The origins and early growth of the city of Teotihuacán can be readily understood in these terms. The shift of population from the hills to the alluvial plain was probably a response to growing pressure on tlacolol, which proved increasingly insufficient to meet subsistence requirements. Population concentration at a single strategic point on the valley floor where permanent springs and tributary streams fed into the Río de San Juan points in the direction of irrigation and the concomitant development of political controls. As Classic Teotihuacán expanded, much of the valley population fell under its sway, and the alluvial plains and lower piedmont slopes of the valley were probably integrated into a single, highly productive hydraulic network under the control of the city authorities.

Given an irrigation system postulated as capable of feeding tens of thousands of persons, it would seem that some indication of its existence would be found archaeologically. In fact, there is considerable evidence for pre-Columbian irrigation in the Teotihuacán Valley. Unfortunately it is not easy to correlate the terraces, dams, and canals with periods of cultural development since the same irrigation system has been in continuous use since pre-Hispanic times. Thus, while there is a strong likelihood that systems of intensive agriculture were developed on the alluvial plain and piedmont slopes of the Teotihuacán Valley in late Formative and Classic times, there is no direct evidence to date to substantiate this hunch.[8]

While agriculture probably kept most Teotihuacanos employed, tens of thousands, perhaps 25 percent of the city population, worked at various nonagricultural crafts. More than 500 craft workshops have been found in archaeological surveys of the metropolis. Most of these are obsidian shops, for the valley held major deposits of the volcanic stone which was in demand all over Middle America as cutting and scraping tools and for projectile points. Deposits of high-quality obsidian north of the Basin of Mexico were also controlled by Teotihuacán, and mass production of

[8] Sanders, "Cultural Ecology of the Teotihuacán Valley," pp. 146–53.

blade implements and trade in obsidian became a major component of Teotihuacán's economy. There were other craft specialties, too, including manufacture of pottery and figurines (now mold-made, rather than handmade) and work in precious stones, basalt, and slate. Additional shops crafted items of perishable materials such as cloth, leather, feathers, and wood, which have left only slight archaeological traces. Craftsmen connected with municipal constructions as plasterers, masons, carpenters, and painters also must have lived and worked in the city, and there undoubtedly were large numbers of persons engaged in marketplace and long-distance trade.[9]

Much trade and commerce must have been conducted at Teotihuacán's bustling markets. The city's location on a major highland-lowland route linking the Valley of Mexico with the Valley of Puebla and, ultimately, with the lowlands of coastal Veracruz, would have forced much long-distance commerce to pass through the metropolis, no doubt adding significantly to its coffers with taxes and tribute. Judging from discoveries of grave goods, diverse foreign resources flowed into the city to be fashioned into offerings to the gods and into luxury apparel and ornaments for the elite. Shells from the coasts, precious stones from Guerrero, mica from Oaxaca, feathers from the colorful birds of tropical lowlands, and cotton from Morelos or Veracruz were all imported, and finely crafted ceramics, obsidian tools, and other items were traded out. Cylindrical slab-legged tripod vessels decorated with carving or with painted scenes were particularly widely traded, as was Thin Orange ware, probably produced in southern Puebla from an exceptionally fine clay that could be formed into unusually hard, thin-walled vessels of a bright and pleasing color. Trade and commerce became increasingly important in the later stages of Teotihuacán's growth, and undoubtedly many Teotihuacanos were fully occupied in providing services for the throngs of visiting merchants, traders, and peddlers attracted to the city's markets as well as for pilgrims from near and far attending religious affairs.

From a local standpoint there must have been considerable exchange of goods and services among the various craft groups, agriculturalists, and other specialists of the city and also between city peoples and those from surrounding regions of the Basin of Mexico as well as from Tlaxcala, western Puebla, and Morelos. Even though much of Teotihuacán's basic subsistence was obtained (presumably) from a highly productive, intensive agricultural base, it is likely that the valley's irrigation system was not sufficiently productive to support the city at its height. Thus many essential products including food had to be obtained by trade, tribute, or governmentally directed production activities from other sections of central Mexico. Such economic interdependence would have contributed significantly to the integration of Teotihuacán society, and political con-

---

[9] Millon, "Teotihuacán," pp. 38–48; idem, "Teotihuacán: Completion of Map," pp. 1077–82.

trol of crucial trade would further stimulate the growth and expansion of this powerful state.[10]

In sum, the city of Teotihuacán emerges not only as an agrarian center, but also as a major market and trade depot and as a focus for religious and political activities. The complexity of its occupational specializations, its high population density, overall great size, and tightly organized and highly integrated social, economic, and political system combined to make the metropolis the most highly urbanized center of its time and the capital of a strong state. Teotihuacán's supremacy, in turn, identified central Mexico and particularly the Basin of Mexico as the most influential sphere, the heartland, of Mexico and Mesoamerica. It has retained this position ever since.

As Teotihuacán evolved its sphere of influence gradually widened until at the height of its powers (Tlamimilolpa-Xolalpan phases, A.D. 200–500) its presence was recognized over a considerable portion of Mesoamerica. For the most part this contact is represented materially by the widespread presence in archaeological sites of Teotihuacán-style artifacts and ceramics, especially Thin Orange ware and the cylindrical tripod vase, by artistic motifs in murals, and occasionally by architectural styles. Like much of the Olmec influence which we examined earlier, Teotihuacán's impact generally takes the form of a blend with regional traditions rather than a direct imitation or duplication of Teotihuacán ways. There is, however, a notable exception to this statement at the Maya site of Kaminaljuyú in highland Guatemala.

Teotihuacán's foreign affairs are thought to have concerned the acquisition by trade, perhaps in some cases backed by military pressures, of various resources, both staples and luxury items, which were needed at home. Thus the state's control over the Basin of Mexico and most of the central highlands probably reflected primarily the need for a wider area to supply basic food staples for the general populace. In all likelihood, however, Teotihuacán's interest in more outlying regions such as the Gulf Coast of Mexico, the Valley of Oaxaca, and the Guatemalan highlands was not centered on staples but on precious, otherwise unobtainable, luxury items.

For example, contacts with the contemporary cultures of the Gulf Coast of Mexico may have reflected a symbiotic relationship based on exchange of regional products between a major highland city and important lowland centers. Generally speaking the Gulf Coast held closer cultural ties with the Maya lowlands to the southeast than with the highland Mexican cultures to the west. Nonetheless, decorative scroll motifs characteristic of the coast appear in Teotihuacán ceramics and murals, and many Teotihuacán elements appear in Gulf Coast art and ceramics. Even more significant is occasional evidence of tablero-talud construction in coastal

[10] Cf. Jeffrey R. Parsons, "Teotihuacán, Mexico, and its Impact on Regional Demography," *Science* 162 (1968):872–77.

architecture (Matacapan site) which may signify actual "colonization" by Teotihuacanos, perhaps in a manner comparable to that indicated at Kaminaljuyú, which we shall examine shortly.[11]

The Gulf Coast Classic is identified archaeologically in terms of stonework and ceramic styles. Yet there is also evidence of sociopolitical growth and organization at several important centers, chief of which is El Tajín. This site, still largely unexcavated, is located in a small valley near Papantla in northern Veracruz where over 100 acres of major buildings indicate a center of considerable significance.

El Tajín is perhaps most noteworthy to date for the variety of materials commonly associated with the ritual ball game characteristic of Mesoamerica during the pre-Columbian period.[12] Although a number of regional variations are found, the game essentially was a competitive team sport centering on a bouncing ball of solid rubber (or stone or wood) 15 to 20 cm in diameter. Ideally players could touch the ball only with the buttocks, hips, or waist, which were safe-guarded by heavy padding and protective pieces. Elbows, knees, and hands were also padded for protection when the player fell to the ground in his efforts to deflect the heavy, zooming ball. Ballplaying was rough, and if through fatigue or inexperience a player misjudged, an unexpected blow to a vital part could prove fatal.

Games were played in formal paved courts usually constructed in elite centers. The courts vary in design, but many are shaped like a capital I. A narrow alleylike playing area 30 to 38 m long bordered by low, often sloping side walls opened on either end to a rectangular space where the ball was not to go. Stone markers were set into the floor of the court along the major axis or at the ends, or were positioned on the walls.[13]

The ball game had both a secular, sporting aspect and religious significance. It was played by commoners and by the nobility who also employed professionals in their service. Heavy betting, to which Mesoamericans were strongly addicted, was frequent. Even the gods played ball, according to traditions, settling disputes and achieving aggressive ends through the outcome of the game. Similarly, among mortals the game contained a heavy element of intense competition and aggression and perhaps was a way of channeling hostilities. Judging from the carved reliefs on stelae and ball court walls, human sacrifice was also involved. Ballplayers, possibly of the losing team, are shown decapitated or dismembered, and it is thought that this judgment was related to ritual efforts to ensure the fertility and fruitfulness of the earth.

A magnificent masonry ball court, complete with what appear to be

[11] Michael D. Coe, "Archaeology of Veracruz and Tabasco," in *Handbook of Middle American Indians,* ed. Robert Wauchope (Austin: Univ. of Texas Press, 1966), 3:704–5.

[12] Theodore Stern, *The Rubber-Ball Games of the Americas* (Seattle: Univ. of Washington Press, 1945).

[13] During the Postclassic vertical-walled courts were preferred, and stone rings or hoops were set as goals in the center of the walls about 2½ m above the floor. If a player succeeded in putting the ball through the ring—a highly unusual event because of the close fit of ball and ring—the game was automatically won then and there.

FIGURE 5.6 Fallen ballplayer carved on a limestone wall panel from the Usumacinta River area, 45 cm long, 26 cm high. Note the ball and the heavy waist padding worn by the player, who may be awaiting the determination of his fate by the elaborately costumed figure to the left. Courtesy of the Art Institute of Chicago.

grandstands for spectators, graced the large plaza at Monte Albán during the Classic, along with beautifully stuccoed and painted platforms, pyramids, and temples built over earlier Formative structures in a constant program of renewal and enlargement. The increasing number of sites in the Valley of Oaxaca also indicates steady population growth. A considerable populace lived in the immediate vicinity of Monte Albán, although the center retained more of an administrative and ceremonial flavor and was not as urban as Teotihuacán. Nonetheless, at the height of its development, late in the Classic era, Monte Albán included not only the original mountain top but also some 39 km² of nearby hills. The tops and slopes of this entire range are terraced, and numerous house platforms can be recognized. Monte Albán's regional influence continued to be widely felt, too, not only in the rest of the valley but also throughout the extensive territory included in the present-day state of Oaxaca.[14]

Classic Monte Albán is also famous for the elaborate tombs which have been discovered in platform terraces or under patios. These burial sites were originally graced by carved and painted lintels and walls finely frescoed in Teotihuacán style. Innumerable pottery urns containing powerfully modeled figures of gods (or priests costumed as gods) richly dressed with elaborate headdresses, heavy necklaces, and large earplugs have been unearthed, too. Cocijo, the Zapotec version of the rain god, is

[14] John Paddock, "Oaxaca in Ancient Mesoamerica," in *Ancient Oaxaca,* ed. John Paddock (Stanford: Stanford Univ. Press, 1966), pp. 83–242.

FIGURE 5.7 Zapotec effigy funery urn, 34 cm high by 30 cm wide by 20 cm deep. The frontal position of the figure with hands on knees is standard form for these urns. The figures frequently represent gods or, as seems to be the case here, priests dressed as deities. Courtesy of the Art Institute of Chicago.

represented here, as are Pitai Cozobi, god of abundance and maize, the Feathered Serpent, a Butterfly God (derived from Teotihuacán), a Bat God (possibly a guise of Pitai Cozobi), and the old Fire God, among others. The effigy urns, which were themselves offerings to the deceased or to the gods, often contained additional gifts of obsidian blades or carved jades.[15]

Teotihuacán themes are also discovered in pottery shapes, and the occurrence of Thin Orange ware further indicates that some form of contact existed between these two great Classic centers. Nonetheless, Teotihuacán's influence at Monte Albán is predominantly stylistic, in themes on frescoes and in ceramics, and there is no archaeological evidence of more direct interaction such as is found in another highland area of Mesoamerica at the (probably) Maya site of Kaminaljuyú.

[15] Frank Boos, *The Ceramic Sculptures of Ancient Oaxaca* (South Brunswick, N.J.: A. S. Barnes, 1966).

The ruins of Kaminaljuyú lie on the outskirts of modern Guatemala City toward the western edge of a broad valley surrounded by hills and volcanoes and strategically located on the continental divide between waterways flowing toward the Pacific lowlands to the south and the Motagua River valley to the north (see Figure 5.1). The site itself is rapidly being overrun by the expanding modern city, but excavations among the 200 or so mounds still extant have revealed a sequence of events of considerable significance.[16]

The earliest materials date from the middle Formative when a village-farming culture was distributed over most of the arable land and clay temple mounds were constructed in the large, centrally located town that was gradually emerging to preeminence. Population growth continued until, several hundred years later (Miraflores phase), Kaminaljuyú had become a major center.

During the Miraflores period brightly plastered, terraced temple-pyramids were constructed to receive the remains of deceased rulers covered with cinnabar and impressively interred with sacrificed retainers and literally hundreds of precious objects in roofed burial chambers. Elegant ceramic vessels, bowls of marble and of grey-green schist, vases of green and of black stone, jade ornaments, obsidian flakes, thin sheets of mica, and stingray spines (used ceremonially for sacrification and for drawing blood from the tongue, nose, ears, and genitals as a penitential offering to the gods) have been recovered. (More riches than these were buried originally, but the tombs were looted before they could be archaeologically studied so we have only a glimpse of the wealth they once contained. Similarly, cotton textiles and elaborately carved wooden objects have been lost by disintegration through the passage of time.) Since much of this material, including many pottery vessels, shells, and stingray spines, does not occur or was not made locally, the grave goods also indicate that the lords of Kaminaljuyú had established far-flung contacts during the Miraflores period, around 300 B.C.

The culmination of Formative growth at Kaminaljuyú was reached about A.D. 400 when the center entered a period of renewed greatness identified archaeologically as the Esperanza phase of the early Classic era. At this time Kaminaljuyú fell under the control of Teotihuacán, some 1,000 km away. This turn of events is evidenced in the contents of more richly stocked tombs which contain Teotihuacán luxuries including Thin Orange ware and the highly characteristic three-footed cylindrical covered jar painted in pastel tones to show designs and personages characteristic of Teotihuacán. Even more significant is the talud-tablero motif

---

[16] Information concerning Kaminaljuyu is drawn primarily from Alfred V. Kidder, Jesse D. Jennings, Edwin M. Shook, *Excavations at Kaminaljuyu, Guatemala*, Carnegie Institution of Washington Publication no. 561 (Washington, D.C., 1946); Edwin M. Shook and Alfred V. Kidder, *Mound E-III-3, Kaminaljuyu, Guatemala*, Carnegie Institution of Washington Contributions to American Anthropology and History no. 53 (Washington, D.C., 1952); Sanders and Price, *Mesoamerica*.

which is found at some of the pyramids built during this period but is not at all characteristic of Maya architecture.[17]

What was Teotihuacán seeking so far from home? Perhaps the contact between these two centers dealt with religious interests or possibly trade was the major attracter. Located in the highlands between the Pacific coastal plain and the Guatemalan lowlands, Kaminaljuyú undoubtedly had long been a busy market center for regional products, some of which could be exchanged with Teotihuacán. The existence of buildings in Teotihuacán style, however, strongly suggests that these foreigners were actually on the spot commanding sufficient power to direct the local labor forces to build in their own style. This in turn implies that Kaminaljuyú was actually colonized and ruled by people from Teotihuacán. Why?

One provocative reconstruction of events suggests that during the late Miraflores phase Kaminaljuyú probably exchanged a variety of products with Teotihuacán but perhaps was of most interest to Mexican merchants because of its proximity to a large obsidian source at nearby El Chayal and to the Pacific lowlands which, it is postulated, were rich in cacao. In later centuries these Pacific coast lands, then called Xoconusco, were dominated by the Mexica (Aztecs) because of the cacao they produced, which was used as a form of currency and as a luxury beverage, *chocolatl*. Early Classic Teotihuacanos may have similarly valued the purplish beans and traded with Miraflores Kaminaljuyú for this resource and for obsidian, perhaps maintaining a permanent colony of resident merchants in the city for these ends. As time went on Teotihuacán's contact probably became increasingly political, and soldiers and priestly rulers eventually assumed direct control of the city and possibly of the trade routes, too.[18]

Problems and Processes
in the Central Maya Lowlands

Another major question still to be fully answered regarding the cultural dynamics of the Classic era concerns the relationships between Mesoamerican highland centers, especially Teotihuacán, and Maya areas other than the Guatemalan highlands. More specifically, to what degree or in what manner did contacts with highland cultures play a role in the development, florescence, and ultimate decline of the Classic era cultures of the Guatemalan Petén and adjacent lowlands of Guatemala, Chiapas, Tabasco–southern Campeche, British Honduras, and western Honduras? The companion piece to this question of cultural interrelationships concerns the nature of the adaptation of lowland Maya culture to the natural environment of the region. Here, too, are many still-

---

[17] In addition there are no more indications of the Maya Long Count or of large-scale stone sculptures such as were found during the Miraflores period, and Tlaloc, probably patron of Teotihuacán, is represented on painted ceramics and in sculpture.

[18] Sanders and Price, *Mesoamerica*, pp. 168–69.

unresolved issues, most of which focus on the agricultural potential of the area and the form of social organization supported by this base.

Topographically the Petén and adjacent regions are characterized primarily by rolling uplands predominantly covered today by vast tropical forests inhabited by a variety of birds and animals. The forests alternate with open savannah, a few lakes, and large, flat swampy sections known as *bajos* which abound with aquatic wildfowl. The area is partly drained by rivers and streams, a few of which are permanent, most notably the Río Usumacinta in the west and the Belize River system in the east. Most of the interior waterways, though, are intermittent, holding water only during the rainy season. After heavy rains water also stands on the clay surface of the bajos. Throughout the dry months of February into May, however, the bajos and most streams and rivers become completely dry. The availability of water in dry season is an important limiting factor determining modern settlement patterns for the small population that inhabits parts of the Petén today. It must have posed similar or even greater problems for the ancient Maya who populated the area in far greater numbers.

Many important Classic Maya centers are located near the major rivers (see Figure 5.1). Piedras Negras and Yaxchilán stand along the banks of the Río Usumacinta while Palenque and Bonampak are situated slightly to the west along smaller tributaries. At the point where the Usumacinta junctions with two major headwater tributaries, the Río de La Pasión and the Río Salinas-Chixoy, stands the site of Altar de Sacrificios. Seibal is located still farther inland along the Pasión. Similarly to the west a practically continuous strip of settlements borders the Belize River system in British Honduras.

Other major centers are situated between the river systems on sections of higher ground in the tropical forest often near large bajos. Uaxactún, Naranjo, Nakum, and Tikal, the largest site of all, are so located in the heart of the Petén. Farther south at least two important sites deserve mention: Quirigua along the Motagua River and Copán in western Honduras.

Except for ceramics, the early stages of cultural development in this broad region are not well known. It is noteworthy, however, that the earliest occupations known to date (ca. 800 B.C.) are at riverine sites such as Altar de Sacrificios and Seibal on the Usumacinta system and Barton Ramie on the Belize, suggesting a riverine-estuary subsistence base utilizing fish and shellfish, river levee agriculture, and various plant and animal resources from inland forests and bajos. A subsistence pattern of this sort would be somewhat comparable to the early Formative adaptations indicated at Salinas La Blanca (Cuadros phase) on the Pacific coast of Guatemala.

This postulated similarity with Pacific coastal Guatemala also rests on the fact that the earliest ceramics associated with Barton Ramie, Altar de Sacrificios, and Seibal can be related to pottery of the Cuadros phase at Salinas La Blanca. Ceramic associations can also be discerned between the early Usumacinta occupations and the Mexican Gulf coast lowlands. Thus the overall picture indicates that the earliest lowland Maya were predominantly a riverine-oriented people with cultural affinities with the lowlands of the Guatemalan Pacific coast and the south Gulf coast of Mexico.[19]

By the fifth century B.C. village-farming communities, whose inhabitants probably cultivated the soil by swidden techniques, were established in the interior reaches of the Petén. A few centuries later some of these sites, such as Tikal and Uaxactún, evidence modest ceremonial structures in the form of platforms built with masonry blocks and lime plaster. Burials in which the deceased is accompanied by ceramics, various necklaces, pendants, and other ornaments made of shell and jade, and sometimes by stingray spines, which must have been imported from areas outside the Petén, also attest to the rise of an elite and give indications of long-distance trade.[20]

Building continued apace at Tikal and similar centers in the last centuries before Christ as new platforms were constructed over the burned and razed remains of older ones. By now platforms and terraces support fairly elaborate buildings, and the corbeled vault, a hallmark of Classic Maya architecture, is found in the construction of burial chambers. Expansion and growth continued into the Classic era (A.D. 250–900) when centers such as Tikal reached their height.

The growth of elite centers in the Maya lowlands has raised questions concerning the factors that underwrote this development. One area of investigation has considered the fertility and agricultural potential of tropical forest soils when cultivated by swidden techniques. Could this form of agriculture have sustained a population density of sufficient size to have built, maintained, and supported a center like Tikal? The answers are by no means conclusive, although it is increasingly apparent that the Petén and adjacent areas are more suitable for swidden agriculture than was long thought, and that swidden, with supplementary hunting, gathering, and fishing, was sufficiently productive to have supported the growing elite centers during the Formative era.[21]

However, another problem emerges regarding the type of settlement pattern and sociopolitical organization associated with swidden techniques. Because it requires fallowing and plot rotation, swidden tends to encourage a dispersed rather than a centralized settlement pattern. It is difficult to visualize the development of centralized political controls under such conditions, particularly since, in contrast to the highlands,

[19] Dennis E. Puleston and Olga S. Puleston, "An Ecological Approach to the Origins of Maya Civilization," *Archaeology* 24 (1971):330–37. Cf. D. W. Sedat and R. J. Sharer, *Archaeological Investigations in the Northern Maya Highlands*, Contributions of the University of California Archaeology Research Facility no. 16 (Berkeley, 1972), pp. 23–35.

[20] William R. Coe, "Tikal, Guatemala, and Emergent Maya Civilization," *Science* 147 (1965):1401–19.

[21] Don E. Dumond, "Swidden Agriculture and the Rise of Maya Civilization," *Southwestern J. of Anthro.* 17 (1961):301–16; U. M. Cowgill, "An Agricultural Study of the Southern Maya Lowlands," *American Anthropologist* 64 (1962):273–86.

there are relatively few topographical barriers in the lowlands to limit population movement and to stimulate the demographic pressures which seem to be a major condition leading to centralization in the highlands. Similarly the absence in the lowlands of the high degree of ecological diversity associated with highland ecology reduces the need for centers to facilitate exchange of local resources.

Yet perhaps demographic pressure and resource redistribution were components after all in the complex of processes that generated the rise of elite centers in the Petén. With respect to population pressure it is feasible to suppose that populations would tend to cluster around those areas —rivers perhaps, or uplands near lakes and bajos—where a diversity of wild resources, good soils, and adequate water could be most readily exploited. Under the growing press of population, leaders of centrally located villages might gradually assume important roles in intercommunity political and managerial activities. Organization and control of crucial *long-distance* trade with far-off highlands and seacoasts in order to exchange local forest products for necessary yet locally unavailable household items such as salt, obsidian, and hard grinding stones (which archaeological data show to have been imported), followed by the local redistribution of these goods, could also have encouraged the rise of a more powerful elite. The largest or perhaps the oldest community in the area could rise to prominence via religious leadership, too.[22]

In all likelihood a mix of demographic, economic, and religious pressures such as these played a role in the evolution of Tikal and similar lowland centers during Formative centuries. But new questions arise with respect to the Classic era when building programs and population densities grew to heights that require additional explanatory factors in order to be understood. Before entering this thicket, however, let us look briefly at some of the glories of the lowland Maya Classic era, using Tikal as our type site.

The Maya Classic era is commonly divided into two parts, Early (A.D. 250–600) and Late (A.D. 600–900), on the basis of a number of contrasts including ceramic styles and evidence of increasing population pressure, social stratification, and militarism during the Late Classic. There are also indications of Teotihuacán contact toward the end of the Early Classic, but an absence of this influence during the Late Classic, after the destruction of Teotihuacán about A.D. 700 (see below). We will consider the nature of this interaction between the central Mexican highlands and the Maya lowlands further on in the discussion. We note here only that during the three centuries of the Late Classic, perhaps partly in response to the removal of Teotihuacán's influence, lowland Maya civilization reached its greatest achievements in architecture, arts and crafts, and calendrics.

[22] William L. Rathje, "Praise the Gods and Pass the Metates: A Hypothesis of the Development of Lowland Rainforest Civilizations in Mesoamerica," in *Contemporary Archaeology*, ed. Mark P. Leone (Carbondale: Southern Illinois Univ. Press, 1972), pp. 365–92.

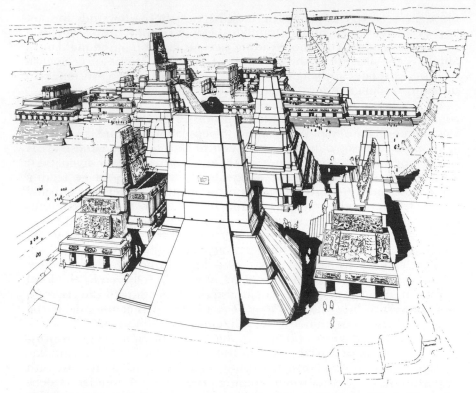

FIGURE 5.8 Artist's reconstruction of the Great Plaza at Tikal. Note the elaborately decorated roof combs rising from the rear of the temple structures atop the platform pyramids. These temples convey an impression of elegant, soaring height which stands in strong contrast with the sense of ponderous, gigantic mass produced by the pyramids of Teotihuacán. Reprinted, courtesy of the Tikal Project, University Museum, University of Pennsylvania, from William R. Coe, *Tikal* (University Museum, 1967), p. 26.

During the Classic era Tikal became the major lowland Maya center.[23] To date 16 km² of the site have been mapped, and over 3,000 separate constructions have been located. Temples and shrines, ceremonial platforms, residences of various sizes, ball courts, terraces, causeways, plazas, and water reservoirs have been identified, along with hundreds of burials and ritual caches of objects and over 200 stelae and altars.[24]

[23] Discussion of the ruins of Tikal rests heavily on William R. Coe, *Tikal: A Handbook of the Ancient Maya Ruins,* University Museum (Philadelphia: University of Pennsylvania, 1967).

[24] Some of the stelae are plain, but many are elaborately carved, usually showing a standing personage richly dressed in attire symbolizing power and authority. It was once thought these figures depicted gods or priests in the guise of gods, but some scholars now feel that most portray real individuals, probably members of ruling elites. Tatiana Proskouriakoff, "The Lords of the Maya Realm," *Expedition Magazine* 4 (1961):14–21.

The heart of Tikal as it is observed today, and as it stood during the Late Classic when it reached its final grandeur, is formed by an elaborate complex of buildings arranged in various compounds. Although scholars do not always agree as to what functions are indicated by the various buildings, it is thought that in general they provided facilities for religious ceremonies and rituals, for market and administrative activities, and in some cases may have served as either permanent or temporary elite residences.

The focal point of Classic Tikal is the Great Plaza, a paved area of 2½ acres bounded on the east and west by two of the five great temples of the site, Temple I, known today as the Temple of the Giant Jaguar, and Temple II, the Temple of the Masks, respectively. Temple I provides a good illustration of the type of temple constructed by the Maya. Its solid substructure, a pyramid platform with nine terraces mounted by a sloping, heavily plastered stairway, rises above a large vaulted burial chamber dug into the foundation core where a richly accoutered man of obviously high status was interred. At the platform summit a temple with three narrow, dark rooms spanned by high corbeled vaults was built. Another important individual was buried deep beneath the floor at the center of the rear room. An elaborately decorated roof comb, once brightly painted, rises over all to surmount even the surrounding forest.

To the north of the Great Plaza stands the huge platform of the North Acropolis where, in its final form, about a dozen temples stood on the platform base. On the south side of the Great Plaza lies the so-called Central Acropolis, which in its latest stage consisted of six rather small courts surrounded by long, low, multiroomed buildings connected by an intricate system of stairways and passageways. The windowless rooms sometimes contain benches perhaps originally seats or thrones or sleeping platforms. In some sections remains of carved friezes can still be seen.

Today these buildings are labeled "palaces" to distinguish them from the temples, but the term is somewhat misleading since their function is not well understood. Perhaps they provided places of temporary retreat where priests could undergo ritual fasting and spiritual cleansing. Conceivably they were the permanent homes of the ruling elite and their families, although a darker, danker place to live would be hard to imagine. Possibly they functioned as administrative buildings where scribes and judges held forth, or where high-ranking officials met with their advisors and assistants. At present the most acceptable explanation favors combined functions of residence and administration. East of the Great Plaza stands the so-called Market Place, a quadrangle of long low buildings with numerous doors and rooms, which may have been a place of exchange.

On all sides this central complex is surrounded by additional ruins. Outlying temples and building complexes are linked to each other and to the Great Plaza and East Plaza by causeways, raised roads paved with plaster and flanked by parapets or walls punctuated by periodic exits. Small ceremonial and administrative nuclei and numerous house mounds stretch farther still, although there is a marked drop-off in the density of ruin mounds as one moves away from the center.

Quite unlike the tight, compact, careful patterning of apartment compounds at Teotihuacán, at Tikal and elsewhere throughout the Maya lowlands the stone and rubble house mounds on which the pole, mud, and thatch homes of the populace stood are scattered about the countryside in a seemingly random fashion with considerable breathing space between house sites. Actually, this form of settlement pattern is not as casual as it seems, but reflects a definite preference for elevated, relatively level terrain suitable for house construction, the availability of a water supply, and proximity to well-drained and fertile soils.

Usually four or five house platform mounds are arranged around a small plaza forming a compound or cluster, and a hamlet composed of several clusters occupies a single elevated area. In all likelihood each plaza group or cluster housed an extended family, while a hamlet may have contained a patrilineal lineage, that is, several extended families related through the male line.[25]

Since the dispersed settlement pattern characteristic of Tikal stands in definite contrast with the tightly nucleated pattern at Teotihuacán, there is considerable debate whether Tikal is a true preindustrial city, or whether it should be considered instead primarily as a large ceremonial and administrative center, a sort of immense version of La Venta. Supporting arguments have been marshalled for both points of view. Much of the problem is based on differences of opinion as to what constitutes the critical components in the definition of "urban." In terms of overall settlement pattern it is apparent that the densely populated, nucleated structure of Teotihuacán is not found at Tikal. Nor does the population density of Tikal, which may have reached 600 persons per square kilometer in the central core area (a total sustaining population of 45,000 to 50,000 has been suggested for Tikal at its height, although some investigators feel this figure is too large), approach that of Teotihuacán which attained approximately 4,500 persons per square kilometer in Xolalpan times. Consequently, to those who view nucleation and population density as critical factors in the definition of "urban," Tikal is not in the same category as Teotihuacán.[26]

Others have argued, however, that nucleation is a relative matter; they point out that the central zone at Tikal indicates a population density six times that of the surrounding territory. Furthermore, population density and pressure can be influenced to some extent by topography. The urban nucleation at Teotihuacán is possible at least in part because of the flat valley floor on which the city is situated, while at Tikal high ground

---

[25] William R. Bullard, Jr., "Maya Settlement Patterns in Northeastern Petén, Guatemala," *American Antiquity* 25 (1960):355–72; Gordon R. Willey et al., *Prehistoric Maya Settlements in the Belize Valley*, Papers of the Peabody Museum (Cambridge: Harvard University, 1965), vol. 54. See also Joyce Marcus, "Territorial Organization of the Lowland Classic Maya," *Science* 180 (1973):911–16.

[26] Cf. Sanders and Price, *Mesoamerica*, pp. 144–45 and 162–66.

suitable for building is not as continuous because of the bajos. In this view, the basic criteria for an urban setting focuses on social and economic variation in a context of relatively dense population. In these terms it can be argued that while those living on the periphery of Tikal were probably full-time agriculturalists, the population density of the central section was such that a great many persons must have been occupied in more specialized activities. Whether the population of Tikal was as economically and socially diversified as that of Teotihuacán then becomes a crucial question which we cannot definitely answer as yet. But there are growing indications, both direct and inferential, that Tikal was considerably diversified. Evidence of trade in a variety of nonperishable items and probably of perishable ones, too, suggests specialization in crafts and commerce. Very likely professional experts worked in architecture, carving and painting, calendrics, and general administration. Furthermore, a complex system of social stratification evolved in the Late Classic. Thus, while Tikal hardly seems as "urban" as Teotihuacán, it may have attained a degree of population density, nucleation, and socioeconomic differentiation that sets it apart from the category of "elite center" per se.[27]

Another problem still unresolved concerns the nature of the subsistence base which underwrote Tikal society during this time. While swidden agriculture augmented with local hunting and gathering may have maintained the growing centers during the Formative era, there is reason to wonder whether slash-and-burn could have supported population densities of the size calculated for a major center such as Tikal during the Classic, and particularly the Late Classic era. Consequently, we must consider the possibility, indeed probability, that alternate agricultural techniques were utilized by the Classic Maya. This is not to say that swidden was abandoned. On the contrary, slash-and-burn agriculture probably continued to provide a significant percentage of basic subsistence needs. But it is not clearly understood whether more intensive swidden methods were implemented, such as better weeding or shorter fallow periods, or whether additional agricultural techniques such as terracing or irrigation were added to this base. Similarly, questions have been raised concerning the types of foods that were exploited. Heretofore much emphasis has been placed on the role of maize as the principal food, but scholars are beginning to feel that maize was likely only one of several staple crops on which the Maya depended.

Although a number of theories have been advanced regarding agricultural techniques and food diversity, to date all are hindered by a dearth of positive evidence and remain in the nature of hypotheses. One hypothesis notes the close association of groves of ramón (breadnut) trees, which produce an edible nut, with house ruins in some areas of the Petén and suggests that with only a little effort a highly nutritious food would have been available virtually at the doorstep. It also has been suggested that

[27] William Haviland, "Tikal, Guatemala, and Mesoamerican Urbanism," *World Archaeology* 2 (1970):186–99; idem, "A New Population Estimate for Tikal, Guatemala," *American Antiquity* 34 (1969):429–33.

root crops and the pejivalle palm were major staples. Heavy dependence on root crops, of course, requires supplementary protein and fats. The game, fish, and wildfowl resources of the forests, rivers, lakes, and bajos would have been essential in this respect, and there is evidence of increased reliance during the Classic on seafoods traded into the interior from the coasts.[28]

However, swamps, lakes, and other water-logged areas may have been equally significant for their agricultural potential. It is possible, although as yet there is no firm evidence, that these areas were intensively cultivated by some method still unrecognized. Preliminary reports of apparently pre-Columbian ridged fields and canals from the Candelaria region of western Yucatán and from British Honduras are tantalizing in this respect. Intensive ridged-field cultivation, in which low ridges, mounds, or platforms of earth are built up on seasonally flooded or water-logged terrain, is known from lowland tropical savannahs of South America. Perhaps similar techniques were practiced by the lowland Maya.[29]

Possibly basic economic needs were met at least in part by trade and commerce and/or tribute demands from more distant regions. Again there is very little data indicating the importation of basic subsistence resources from outside the area, although, as we have mentioned above, substantial amounts of shellfish, dried fish, and other marine resources apparently were obtained from the coasts of Yucatán, probably in exchange for inland agricultural products. Nonetheless, during the Classic era the lowland Maya were involved with other Mesoamerican societies, particularly with Teotihuacán and with the Teotihuacán outpost at Kaminaljuyú. Strongest evidence for interaction between these highland societies and the peoples of the Petén is found at Tikal about A.D. 500 when Teotihuacán was at its height (Xolalpan phase) and when Kaminaljuyú was flourishing under Teotihuacán control (Esperanza phase).

On an early Classic stela, No. 31, at Tikal is carved a Maya personage flanked by two standing warriors wearing Mexican dress and carrying spear-throwers and shields of a Teotihuacán type. From burials of the same period come ceramic forms, including the cylindrical tripod vase and Thin Orange ware, that also indicate some manner of contact with Teotihuacán traditions. Finally, we find definite evidence of Teotihuacán influence in the architecture at Tikal: three platform structures dating about A.D. 600 contain moldings in the tablero-talud style.

How is this data to be interpreted? Conceivably Teotihuacán and Tikal were directly linked by trade. Clear evidence here is scant although green obsidian flakes and clay earspools from central Mexico are found in burials at Tikal, and sherds of Tzakol ware (characteristic of the early lowland Classic) have been found in a section of Teotihuacán. There also

[28] Bennet Bronson, "Roots and the Subsistence of the Ancient Maya," *Southwestern J. of Anthro.* 22 (1966):251–79; Frederick W. Lange, "Marine Resources: A Viable Subsistence Alternative for the Prehistoric Lowland Maya," *American Anthropologist* 73 (1971):619–39.

[29] Alfred H. Siemens and Dennis E. Puleston, "Ridged Fields and Associated Features in Southern Campeche," *American Antiquity* 37 (1972):228–39; William M. Denevan, "Aboriginal Drained-Field Cultivation in the Americas," *Science* 169 (1970):647–54.

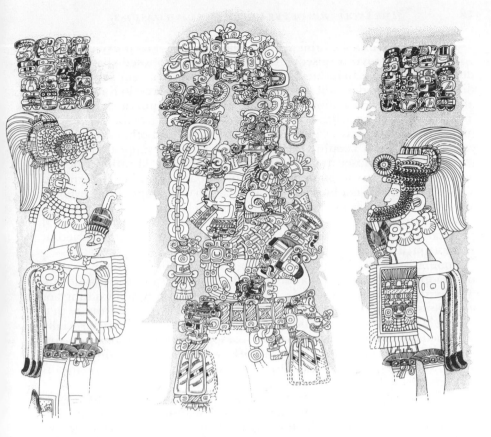

FIGURE 5.9 Figures on Stela 31, Tikal. The two warriors flanking the elaborately carved central figure carry spear-throwers and shields and may portray
persons from Teotihuacán. One shield carries the face of Tlaloc, the rain god,
believed to have been a principal deity of Teotihuacán. Reprinted, courtesy of
the Tikal Project, University Museum, University of Pennsylvania, from William
R. Coe, *Tikal* (University Museum, 1967), p. 49.

may have been a brisk market at Teotihuacán for perishable luxury items
from the lowlands such as salt, bright feathers from tropical birds, jaguar
pelts, cotton textiles, objects of rare lowland woods, and copal, a resin
obtained from various tropical trees and widely used throughout
Mesoamerica as incense at religious rituals. It seems more plausible,
however, given the distances and primitive forms of transportation involved, that highland-lowland exchange was conducted not with distant
Teotihuacán but with the Guatemalan highlands. Again feathers, pelts,
copal incense, rare woods, even lime may have gone to the highlands,
together with other lowland products including vanilla, rubber,
dyewoods, flint points, pottery, and wax and honey of the stingless bee. In
return the highlands could have supplied obsidian, jade, hematite, pyrite,
and marine materials from the Pacific.[30]

[30] J. Eric Thompson, *Maya History and Religion* (Norman: Univ. of Oklahoma Press, 1970),
chap. 5.

Undoubtedly much of this Guatemala highland–Petén exchange involved Kaminaljuyú. Consequently it has been proposed that the evidence of Teotihuacán influence at Tikal does not represent Teotihuacán directly, but instead is indicative of Teotihuacán's interest in Kaminaljuyú and the Guatemalan region. In this same vein, Teotihuacán's interest in Tikal may have been of a general diplomatic nature with a view to protecting Kaminaljuyú's interests, mercantilistic and otherwise, and by extension, those of Teotihuacán.[31] The overall picture appears similar to the situation proposed for Kaminaljuyú during the Miraflores period before the actual assumption of control by Teotihuacán. The presence of a few buildings in Teotihuacán style at Tikal further suggests that eventually a corps of ambassadors, probably acting as both diplomats and merchants, actually came to reside at the center, perhaps anticipating gradual political inroads here analogous to what already had been achieved at Kaminaljuyú.

Comparisons with Teotihuacán may also shed some light on the nature of sociopolitical integration among the lowland Maya of the Classic era. The existence of centers such as Tikal and of burials revealing a range of variations in wealth items interred with the deceased clearly indicate that Classic Maya society was politically centralized and to some extent socially stratified. Questions remain as to how sociopolitical integration was maintained, and how categories of social differentiation were defined. Once again, although guidelines can be suggested, the situation is by no means well understood.

At Teotihuacán social stratification and the evolution of a state probably were interwoven with the managerial demands of an intensive hydraulic system that underwrote the subsistence base. As the city grew, craft specialization and market exchange of diverse regional products facilitated and increased economic interdependence among the various social and economic units. The population of Tikal, in contrast, depended heavily on swidden for subsistence. This cultivation technique does not usually require managerial control and often produces a centrifugal effect on settlement pattern by encouraging scattered residences. Nor do we have any direct evidence for other, more intensive forms of agricultural activity which might have required centralized administrative controls.[32]

With respect to trade and exchange as an integrative mechanism, the Maya lowlands in themselves do not contain as high a degree of natural ecological diversity as that which characterizes the highlands and made the marketplace there such a vital center. On the other hand, as we have seen, Tikal may have contained a market place of sorts where necessary material items could have been redistributed. But the integration fostered

[31] Sanders and Price, *Mesoamerica*, pp. 145 and 168–69.

[32] It is entirely possible that growing population pressure on available land resources favored increasing regulation of the swidden cycle and of land reallocation by central authorities. The extreme concern with time and calendrics among the Maya elite may reflect to some extent the need for careful interdigitating of the agricultural cycle with the annual climatic cycle so as to obtain maximum agricultural benefits.

by redistribution at Tikal was probably of a different order than that obtained by market exchange at Teotihuacán.

Redistribution at Tikal and other Maya centers was primarily concerned with the circulation of elite or luxury resources (rather than basic subsistence items), which were often obtained by long-distance (rather than regional) trade. This redistribution was directed by an elite which focused its activities at the ceremonial-administrative centers. The hierarchy of elite, in turn, controlled the various sociopolitical positions necessary for the functioning of ceremonial, political, and economic life.

The steps in the sociopolitical hierarchy are illustrated by the settlement pattern itself. In addition to major centers such as Tikal, Uaxactún, Naranjo, Yaxha, and the many others, medium-sized centers with several pyramid platforms, perhaps a "palace," a water reservoir, and a few plain stelae dotted the hilltops of the landscape along with even smaller settlements containing only one or just a few small platforms and buildings arranged around plazas and lacking stela-altar complexes. The priestly and administrative hierarchy of the smaller and medium centers provided a series of intermediate steps linking the rural populace, whose house platforms were scattered about the surrounding countryside, first to a local center and then to a larger regional sphere under the direction of a still more prestigeful and powerful elite. The ordinary man with his family and neighbors contributed time, goods, and periodic labor to the support of the local and regional centers of his area.[33]

Analysis of burials suggests further that during the early Classic era Maya society allowed considerable sociopolitical mobility. Positions of prestige, power, and authority within the ceremonial-administrative hierarchy were probably open to any adult who could accumulate sufficient wealth to maintain his post. As the Classic era progressed, however, there is increasing evidence, again from burial data, that sociopolitical mobility yielded to sociopolitical stratification and that access to positions of political and religious authority was obtained less by achievement and more by ascription. Wealth and power were increasingly limited to a smaller segment of society, a hereditary ruling elite which became self-perpetuating, a unit in itself. An individual's genealogical position, the accident of his birth, was now a major criterion for high sociopolitical status. Wealth was probably still a necessary prerequisite for office, but wealth also came to be increasingly limited to those of high birth and the proper family ties. Consequently, during the Late Classic Maya society came to be highly stratified, with a ruling elite separated from the rest of society by virtue of wealth, power, authority, and control of the crucial trade and exchange networks that provided the prestigeful wealth-items and status symbols essential for those in high positions.[34]

The sagacious conduct of intraregional political affairs undoubtedly

[33] Bullard, "Maya Settlement Patterns," pp. 355–72; Marcus, "Territorial Organization," pp. 911 16; Gordon R. Willey, "The Structure of Ancient Maya Society," *American Anthropologist* 58 (1956):777–82.

[34] William Rathje, "Socio-political Implications of Lowland Maya Burials: Methods and Tentative Hypothesis," *World Archaeology* 1 (1970):359–75.

also strengthened the power of the ruling elite. Among the glyphs carved on stelae and other monuments at various major sites are so-called "emblem glyphs," signs which occur repeatedly at one place and only occasionally or not at all at other sites. Scholars believe that these glyphs represent identification symbols signifying a particular elite center or a ruling lineage. When the glyphs for one center are portrayed at other locations, as, for example, the emblem glyph of Tikal frequently appears at Naranjo and among a group of sites in the Río Pasión Valley, it may indicate a degree of political linkage or overlordship. Thus a certain amount of integration may have obtained at least among the higher levels of the various ruling hierarchies of the Maya lowlands during the Late Classic era, although no single unifying government arose.[35]

It has been persuasively argued, too, that the increasing stratification of Late Classic Maya society reflected a delayed response to interaction between Maya leaders and the more powerful and more highly organized polity of Teotihuacán at the end of the Early Classic period. Perhaps in answer to various diplomatic and/or commercial pressures from Teotihuacán (which could have included a hint of force), Maya society evolved a more highly structured and organized ruling strata than might otherwise have emerged under local pressures alone.[36] This is an intriguing hypothesis, not only for its insights into the nature of Maya sociopolitical organization, but also for the clues it offers concerning another major problem, the decline of Classic Maya civilization.

The End of the Era

The truly impressive achievements of Mesoamerican peoples during the Classic era came to equally impressive ends between A.D. 700 and 1000. Teotihuacán was the first to fall. The destruction by fire of civic and ceremonial buildings in the city center at the end of the seventh century has been attributed by some scholars to internal upsets. Others have stressed military conquest perhaps, judging from ceramic evidence, by peoples from the northern frontier, the Toltecs of Tula in southern Hidalgo, who eventually replaced Teotihuacán as the leading central Mexican state in the early Postclassic era.

Why would Teotihuacán have been susceptible to outside pressures and what internal difficulties might the city have encountered? It has been suggested that a decline in rainfall in the central plateau or deforestation and erosion of the surrounding hills may have induced significant changes in the natural ecology of the valley which could have posed serious agricultural problems and tensions within the city itself, perhaps facilitating external conquest. It is also quite possible, indeed probable, that Teotihuacán's downfall was the result of too much, yet too imperfect, success. At the height of its power the state of Teotihuacán had flung

[35] Marcus, "Territorial Organizations," pp. 911–16.
[36] Sanders and Price, *Mesoamerica*, p. 205.

contacts and influence far and wide. Perhaps the political structure coordinating this growth reached too far and grew too large, became overextended and lost a crucial measure of flexibility rendering it unable to continue effective control of its farthest frontiers or to satisfactorily compete with changing frontier societies, themselves emerging to new political heights. On these sociopolitical borders, where controls are weakest, uprisings against the central authority are most likely to successfully occur.

The location of Tula and the Toltecs in a hinterland just beyond the Basin of Mexico is very suggestive in this respect. At Teotihuacán's height of power the people of Tula probably were loosely tributary to this state, but then became politically independent, as did, it seems, a number of former tributary areas outside the Teotihuacán Valley itself. There is also reason to think that critical changes in trade patterns were occurring among societies to the south and east. Concurrently, the data indicate increasing militarism at the city of Teotihuacán itself, perhaps for defensive purposes. Ultimately the heart of the capital was fired, its ruling hierarchy destroyed, and its influence in Mesoamerica effectively halted. As its political leaders fell, centrally directed municipal activities undoubtedly collapsed and many people left the now disfunctional city. The former metropolis gradually disintegrated into a complex of rural and semiurban communities, and the Teotihuacán Valley became a distinctly marginal region during the succeeding Postclassic.[37]

The collapse of Teotihuacán produced a power vacuum in central Mexico lasting several hundred years. During this time various smaller states on the peripheries of the Basin of Mexico, now freed from Teotihuacán's overwhelming influence and control, competed vigorously with each other for domination of the region. This period of political fragmentation and shifting trade and economic alignments, when growing states such as Xochicalco in Morelos, Cholula in Puebla, and Tula in Hidalgo jockeyed for economic and political power, was finally submerged under the unifying hand of the Toltecs of Tula.[38]

Teotihuacán's fall directly correlates with renewed florescence in other areas as well. The last centuries of Classic lowland Maya society, for example, saw the highest development of calendrics, sculpture, architecture, ceramics, and painting, all after Teotihuacán contact had disappeared. Similarly, the Veracruz coast culture centered at El Tajín reached new heights of power and expansion until this capital, too, was destroyed by fire about A.D. 1200. The fall of Teotihuacán also may have been involved in some manner with the final events at Monte Albán, which was

[37] Don E. Dumond and Florencia Muller, "Classic to Postclassic in Highland Central Mexico," *Science* 175 (1972):1208–15; Sanders, "Cultural Ecology of the Teotihuacán Valley"; Malcolm C. Webb, "The Significance of the 'Epi-Classic' Period in Mesoamerican Culture History," mimeographed (1973).

[38] Pedro Armillas, "Northern Mesoamerica," in *Prehistoric Man in the New World,* ed. Jesse D. Jennings and Edward Norbeck (Chicago: Univ. of Chicago Press, 1964), pp. 310–12; Michael D. Coe, *Mexico* (New York: Praeger, 1962), pp. 130–32; Webb, "Significance of the 'Epi-Classic' Period."

deserted by at least A.D. 1000 and possibly as early as the eighth century. In contrast to Teotihuacán, however, no human enemy destroyed the mountain center. It simply was abandoned and fell into ruin, although it continued to be used as a necropolis.

The abandonment of Monte Albán has been similarly interpreted in terms of a social order which became overextended and/or failed to adjust to changing times. The latter years of the Classic era in the Valley of Oaxaca saw considerable population growth to the extent that the agricultural potential of the valley was probably exploited to its utmost. Continued deforestation of hillsides for a millennium or more may have produced serious soil erosion, aggravating the agriculture problem. During the Late Classic society possibly became increasingly stratified, too (a situation not unlike that of the lowland Maya), and the ruling elite more self-contained and removed from contact with the rest of society, although not necessarily coercive. The leadership also may have grown too rigid and conservative, content to try to solve current difficulties with traditional remedies well validated, to be sure, by their success in earlier times, but not necessarily applicable to later issues brought about by increasing population pressures on limited agricultural resources. In short, the inability of a traditional elite to cope with new problems may underlie the ultimate abandonment of Monte Albán and, by implication, the fall from power of traditional leaders.[39]

The beginning of the end of Classic lowland Maya civilization in the Petén and adjacent areas becomes apparent by the first decades of the ninth century A.D. with a definite reduction in craft activities, in building, and in the carving and erecting of dated stelae at major ceremonial centers. By A.D. 900, when the last dated stelae were erected, many of the major sites had been completely abandoned. In contrast with the Valley of Oaxaca and Teotihuacán, analysis of house mounds further indicates a sharp decline in overall population by the early decades of the tenth century, although not total abandonment as has often been claimed.

A variety of explanations have been advanced to explain this change, but we still do not know what really happened.[40] There is no evidence for catastrophic natural disasters such as earthquake and epidemics of malaria as some investigators have suggested. Similarly, explanations which emphasize agricultural deterioration through erosion or the spread of savannahs have been seriously criticized, although persuasive arguments have been advanced for the spread of uncultivable grasslands in place of fertile forest through unsuccessful attempts to intensify swidden techniques in the face of serious overpopulation.

Yet while it is possible, indeed even probable, that the high population

[39] Paddock, "Oaxaca in Ancient Mesoamerica."

[40] George Cowgill, "The End of Classic Maya Culture: A Review of Recent Evidence," *Southwestern J. of Anthro* 20 (1964):145–59; Gordon R. Willey and J. Sabloff, "The Collapse of Maya Civilization in the Southern Lowlands," *Southwestern J. of Anthro.* 23 (1967):311–36; Gordon R. Willey and D. B. Shimkin, "The Collapse of Classic Maya Civilization in the Southern Lowlands," *Southwestern J. of Anthro.* 27 (1971):1–18.

densities of the Late Classic placed a serious strain on the subsistence base and that this pressure provided a significant component to the final complex of events and processes, other factors undoubtedly were involved. For example, we have seen evidence of increasing social stratification during the Late Classic which we have attributed at least in part to interaction with Teotihuacán. After Teotihuacán's fall, and the removal of pressures and support from this power, Maya society may have been top-heavy with administration requiring, in turn, more support from local resources and manpower than could readily be obtained, especially in the face of heavy population and, possibly, a strained agricultural system. Concurrently the upper levels of the sociopolitical hierarchy may have become too conservative, rigid, and inflexible to respond adequately to new problems, not only internal but external.

The turbulent centuries following the destruction of Teotihuacán give evidence of change and population movement in various regions of Mesoamerica, including possibly (the dating is quite uncertain) an intrusion of peoples with Mexican language and culture, known collectively as the Pipil, into highland and Pacific coast Guatemala, and movement of Mexican or Mexican-influenced peoples up the Usumacinta River to the Río Pasión during the ninth century A.D. Evidence for this latter encroachment is found in carvings on stelae and in the appearance of foreign ceramic styles and figurines, many of which portray non-Maya costuming and depict warriors with spears and shield, at a series of Classic Maya sites along the Usumacinta and Pasión rivers including Altar de Sacrificios and Seibal. Thus it has been suggested that over a period of some 100 years a series of foreign intruders presented additional problems for the Maya power hierarchy, already top-heavy and beset with intrasocietal difficulties.

Finally we may consider whether the disruptions and reorientations among Mexican peoples might have affected the lowland Maya by disrupting crucial trade routes. Certainly invasions along the Río Usumacinta would have severed ties between the Chiapas uplands and the rest of the lowlands. Furthermore the central Mexican states which succeeded Teotihuacán did not utilize the former trade connections through Kaminaljuyú, but instead developed a trade network linked to Veracruz (El Tajín) and Yucatán, a route which bypasses the Petén. Conceivably this readjustment deprived the elite of the Petén centers of access to important foreign materials, thereby placing yet another strain on Petén society by preventing high-ranking rulers from fulfilling certain ceremonial and redistributive obligations to the society that supported them.[41]

As a general conclusion, then, it appears that Teotihuacán, Monte Albán, and lowland Maya society of the Petén all in one way or another became politically too overextended or institutionally too rigid to ade-

[41] Malcolm C. Webb, "The Petén Maya Decline Viewed in the Perspective of State Formation," in *The Classic Maya Collapse*, ed. T. Patrick Culbert (Albuquerque: Univ. of New Mexico Press, 1973), pp. 367–404.

quately cope with changing times. Population pressure probably was one of the major factors requiring new adjustments, especially as it affected the subsistence base. A top-heavy, perhaps unduly conservative, administrative elite, which then placed disproportionate demands on already strained economic resources, would have increased the tensions on the system. Under these conditions, any of several additional pressures such as frontier revolt, foreign invasions, shifting trade alignments, and even several years of poor agricultural yields could have provided the final set of problems that could not be overcome without cultural reorientations that were beyond the capabilities of traditional systems.

6

The Heritage
of
Teotihuacán

The Character of the Postclassic

The culture pattern that arose in Mesoamerica after the decline of the major Classic centers traditionally has been described as strongly militaristic, secular, and "action-oriented," in contrast with a presumably more peaceful, theocratic, and intellectual Classic era. Fortified cities now appear, powerful gods of war replace, or at least share honors with, the more pacific deities of earlier times, and interregional ties based on exchange of diverse resources through generally peaceful trade are augmented to a significant degree by bonds expressed in tribute payments reflecting the fortunes of war and conquest.

To some extent, however, these stylistic contrasts may be more apparent than real, for when viewed developmentally the Classic is seen to evolve directly into the Postclassic in economic and sociopolitical terms. For one thing, the Classic era no longer appears as peaceful as once was thought. Murals and carvings of warriors armed with spear-throwers, shields, and spears are associated with Teotihuacán; clay figures of warriors are known from the Gulf Coast by Late Classic times; and scenes of bound captives and of lance-brandishing conquerors are found at Monte Albán. In the lowland Maya area the famous murals painted on three walls of a room at the Late Classic site of Bonampak depict in vibrant detail a successful raid against a neighboring group, the triumphal cele-

85

brations following victory, and the miserable end of the unfortunate captives.[1]

On the other hand virtually no fortifications are found during most of the Classic, and the deities associated with the era are represented as a peaceful lot. Of course, absence of fortifications and of representations of gods of war does not necessarily indicate total peace, but it does suggest that the Classic era may have been *relatively* more peaceful overall than was the succeeding Postclassic, or that raids and warfare were not yet accorded the high ideological honors which they received during later centuries.

This gradation from relative peace to increased emphasis on war may well reflect another characteristic shared by both the Classic and Postclassic (although again in significantly varying degrees): the presence of states. It was during the Classic era that the first Mesoamerican states, Teotihuacán and, possibly, Monte Albán, evolved. We have traced the general outline of this growth at Teotihuacán, noting its early development in the Teotihuacán Valley and then following its expansion beyond the confines of the valley itself as more distant peoples and places came to feel the weight of its economic, political, and military power. However, the growth and expansion of a state may stimulate similar reactions in the societies it contacts. The increasing stratification of Classic lowland Maya civilization may be one case in point. The smaller states—Xochicalco, Cholula, and Tula (see Figure 5.1)—which jostled for position in central Mexico after Teotihuacán's power was broken are probably other examples of "secondary" stratified societies which developed state forms of sociopolitical organization, including a professional military force, as a result of interaction with, or absorption into, an earlier state, in this case Teotihuacán.

Therefore it is no accident that evidence of warfare increases during the later centuries of the Classic era, when the number of states (and competition for supporting resources) was rapidly growing. This process continued throughout the Postclassic when the culture history of Mesoamerica reflects the rise and fall of numerous aggressive states, some large, many small. The clashes and pressures accompanying the growth, expansion, and decline of these strongly competitive stratified societies explain to a great extent the widespread concern with militarism so characteristic of the time.

Also associated with the proliferation of states during the Postclassic era is the adoption of irrigation practices in virtually all areas of Mesoamerica where water-control agriculture is feasible. As we might expect, the implementation of irrigation reflected and also fostered rapid population growth and encouraged more complex forms of settlement pattern, especially urbanism, and elaboration in sociopolitical organization including

---

[1] Concerning primary versus secondary states in Mesoamerica see William T. Sanders and Barbara J. Price, *Mesoamerica* (New York: Random House, 1968), p. 235; concerning Bonampak see K. Ruppert, J. Thompson, and T. Proskouriakoff, *Bonampak, Chiapas, Mexico,* Carnegie Institution of Washington Publication no. 602 (Washington, D.C., 1955).

FIGURE 6.1 This 31-cm clay figure of a warrior is in the Jaina style and derives from Campeche in Yucatán. The Island of Jaina, off the west coast of the peninsula of Yucatán, was used as a necropolis and ceremonial center during the Classic and Early Postclassic eras. Quantities of realistically modeled figurines have been obtained from burials. Courtesy of the Art Institute of Chicago.

warfare. These developments were particularly significant in heretofore marginal areas of Mesoamerica which up to now had remained more or less at Formative levels of village and elite center integration. Events in western and north-central Mexico exemplify this growth particularly well.

As we noted in Chapter 5, rainfall agriculture becomes increasingly precarious towards the northern reaches of the central Mexican highlands. Teotihuacán was located in an area dryer and more frost prone than more southern regions, and while rainfall agriculture was possible, agriculture became measurably more secure with irrigation. Still farther to the north, however, where rainfall is very scant and irregular, it becomes virtually impossible to conduct rainfall agriculture with any degree of security. In these regions irrigation is a necessity for permanent, settled agricultural life. Comparable conditions occur to the west and northwest of the central core, in areas too distant to receive rain from the Gulf of Mexico.

Much of this northern and western hinterland is drained, however, by major river systems—the Panuco flowing to the east and the Lerma-Santiago flowing through the west. During the Postclassic the smaller streams and tributaries of these rivers were effectively tapped for irrigation by colonists from the wetter areas to south and east. Water-control agriculture then contributed substantially to population growth and to the subsequent cultural florescence. The highest cultural achievements attained in these border areas are associated with the Tarascan polity, primarily centered at Tzintzuntzán on the shores of Lake Pátzcuaro in central Michoacan, and with the evolution of the Toltec state focused at the capital city of Tula in southern Hidalgo. From here for over 300 years (from about the ninth to the late twelfth centuries) the Toltecs held sway over much of northern Mesoamerica.

The Toltecs
and Their Contemporaries

The rise of the Toltecs of Tula can also be considered as part of a periodic cycling, of a dynamic process of expansion and eventual retreat, which characterized the northern frontier of Mesoamerica during the Postclassic and perhaps to some extent also occurred during the Classic. The natural ecology of the northern frontier creates a delicate balance in the agricultural potential of the outer border zone, particularly along the eastern slopes and foothills of the Sierra Madre Occidental and on the southern edge of the great northern plateau. Here a belt of woodland and savannah meets the arid steppe and desert of the northern tableland. Here marginal farmers, who supplemented hunting and gathering with minor agriculture, precariously existed between the more highly developed agrarian societies of Mesoamerica to the south and the predominantly nomadic hunters and gatherers, collectively known to us as Chichimecs, who roamed the dry plateau.[2]

As the Tula Toltec, themselves a northern frontier people, adopted irrigation and rose to be a formidable political power, they pushed the agricultural Mesoamerican frontier into this border zone, attempting to stabilize and defend it both militarily and with colonies of agricultural settlers (see Figure 5.1). To this end marginal farmers (also sometimes termed Chichimecs) and hunting-gathering Chichimecs were trained and organized as auxiliary troops and encouraged to settle in outlying areas. This tutoring in agricultural, military, and political techniques, however,

[2] Angel Palerm and Eric R. Wolf, "Ecological Potential and Cultural Development in Mesoamerica," in *Studies in Human Ecology*, ed. A. Palerm et al., Social Science Monographs no. 3 (Washington, D.C.: Pan American Union, 1957), pp. 2–6.

also provided the organizational base by which these Formative-level farmers and hunter-gatherers were able to coalesce into larger, potentially militant, tribal confederacies. Then in the twelfth century when, for reasons not yet understood, the central Toltec power had become weak and disorganized, the Chichimecs of the outer frontier, no longer under effective Toltec control, abandoned their precarious efforts to achieve a settled, agricultural life-style and reverted to more nomadic patterns of hunting, gathering, and raiding other outlying agricultural villages. This upset on the frontier not only reflected, but also probably hastened, the ultimate disruption of the Toltec state itself. Eventually the socioeconomic upheavals caused by the political collapse of Tula allowed Chichimec raiders to penetrate portions of the central Mexican highlands considerably south of the savannah-steppe divide. Once well within the precepts of Mesoamerican tradition, however, the mobile "barbarians" quickly acculturated to settled, agrarian Mesoamerican ways and were absorbed within the cultural mainstream.[3]

It is tempting to interpret the political growth of the Toltecs themselves in terms of a comparable acculturative process. We intimated in the previous chapter that the Toltecs acquired a high degree of political sophistication by virtue of their experiences on the northern frontier of Teotihuacán's domain, where they could have learned techniques of irrigation and terracing and may have been organized administratively by Teotihuacán along lines suitable for incorporation within its political sphere. Eventually, when Teotihuacán's power declined, the Toltecs emerged with a state organization of their own.

There has been considerable confusion in the past as to just who the Toltecs really were and where Tula or Tollán, their capital city, was located. It is now virtually certain, however, that the capital of the Toltec state was located in southern Hidalgo. Today it lies on the outskirts of the modern city of Tula, where numerous pyramid-platforms, mounds, and plazas, still only partially excavated, indicate a city of some size, although not nearly as large as Teotihuacán.

The ruins of the site are particularly noteworthy for their indications of militarism.[4] For example, in front of Pyramid B, a five-stepped pyramid-platform, stand remains of a colonnaded hall with vividly painted bas-reliefs depicting spear-carrying warriors. The roof of the temple sanctuary which once stood on the platform was supported by a series of large columns carved in the form of immense warriors or portraying figures of warriors in low relief. Around the base of Pyramid B four rows of reliefs repeatedly present the image of Quetzalcóatl peering

[3] Paul Kirchhoff, "Civilizing the Chichimecs," in *Some Educational and Anthropological Aspects of Latin America*, Latin-American Studies no. 5 (Institute of Latin-American Studies, University of Texas, 1948), pp. 80–85.

[4] Pedro Armillas, "Northern Mesoamerica," in *Prehistoric Man in the New World*, ed. Jesse D. Jennings and Edward Norbeck (Chicago: Univ. of Chicago Press, 1964), pp. 314–18; Gordon R. Willey, *An Introduction to American Archaeology* (Englewood Cliffs, N.J.: Prentice-Hall, 1966), 1:153–56; B. Dutton, "Tula of the Toltecs," *El Palacio* 62 (1955):195–251; Eric R. Wolf, *Sons of the Shaking Earth* (Chicago: Univ. of Chicago Press, 1959), pp. 111–22.

out from between the jaws of a feathered monster and a series of coyotes, jaguars, and eagles, the latter eating bleeding hearts. The eagle, coyote, and jaguar are associated with military orders during the Postclassic. The eagle, symbol of the sun, is also linked with human sacrifice, and there are indications that such sacrifice, an integral part of the ritual life of the Postclassic (and perhaps of earlier periods), may have been conducted at Tula. This practice, which seems so barbarous to us, was an act of highest honor and devotion for pre-Columbian Mexicans. Only by continued penance and blood sacrifice could the life and movement of the sun, indeed of the very universe, and thus of the mortals dependent on it for warmth, light, and life be sustained from day to day. Similar sacrifices for thanksgiving and renewal were also made to many other deities.

Very little can be said concerning the nature of Toltec society and the extent of the state. There is much confusion and uncertainty, attributable to frequently contradictory myths and semilegendary accounts about the Toltec rulers recorded by members of the Mexica (Aztec) aristocracy after the Spanish conquest. To the Mexica the Toltecs were a nation of tall, strong, superior people, wise and experienced in matters of government, and builders and craftsmen par excellence, and while the stories recounting their political rise and fall undoubtedly contain an element of truth, there are obvious embellishments and allegorical elaborations which confuse the actual picture.

The accounts do indicate, however, that the growth of the Toltec state was beset with difficulties. The Mexica myths recount an apparent power struggle between several factions with the leading protagonists portrayed in ethical and religious terms. On the one hand was a peace-loving priest-king, the fair-skinned, dark-bearded, gentle Topíltzin, who probably was a real person, but who also was identified with the deity Quetzalcóatl. His opponent was the fierce warrior Tezcatlipoca, also the patron god of warriors. After a series of confrontations, Topíltzin-Quetzalcóatl and his followers, defeated by evil and shameful trickery perpetrated by Tezcatlipoca and his group, left the city and, after harrowing experiences, reached the Gulf Coast where, in one version of the myth, Topíltzin-Quetzalcóatl immolates himself and becomes the Morning Star, while in another he sets off across the waters to the east, promising to return.[5]

Under the control of the aggressive Tezcatlipoca faction, the Toltec state reached its highest grandeur. Although the extent of Tula's tributary domain is not actually known, it probably included a large portion of central and north-central Mexico, from northern Veracruz, the Bajío (Querétaro and Guanajuato), and Hidalgo to Michoacan. Evidence of Toltec contact is also found throughout western Mexico from Sinaloa and Chihuahua south to Guerrero. Warrior-merchant colonies moved to the south and east, too, and Toltec influence is noted as far away as northern

[5] Michael D. Coe, *Mexico* (New York: Praeger, 1962), pp. 135–38; but see Robert Chadwick, "Native Pre-Aztec History of Central Mexico," in *Handbook of Middle American Indians*, ed. Robert Wauchope (Austin: Univ. of Texas Press, 1971), 11:474–504.

Yucatán. These far-flung contacts are indicated archaeologically by (among other things) distinctive ceramics such as Mazapán ware, which appears over a wide area of central Mesoamerica, and a distinctive glazed Plumbate ware widely traded and imitated, which also serves as a horizon marker for the Early Postclassic in general.

The appearance of Mazapán and Plumbate ceramic styles in Michoacan provides the first good evidence linking western Mexico with the main-stream of Mesoamerican tradition.[6] Although western Mexico in general is poorly understood archaeologically, what is known indicates that much of this often arid land was significantly set apart from the developmental currents of Mesoamerica until the Late Classic–Early Postclassic expansion of irrigation when the region became a Mesoamerican frontier and felt the influence of Tula.[7]

The fullest information from western Mexico concerns the Postclassic when the region reached its highest development in terms of population growth and ceremonial center construction. Particularly noteworthy is the rise of Tarascan society, centered in the basin of Lake Pátzcuaro in the mountainous country on the western extension of the Central Plateau. Fish and wild fowl were abundant and lake shores were intensely culti-vated with a variety of simple irrigation techniques. Good farming was also possible in portions of the surrounding mountains, while a variety of lowland products were available from the Balsas River depression to the south.

The fishing and farming Tarascans first come to our attention during Toltec times when, according to legend, the populations of the Pátzcuaro Basin were united under the rule of Chichimecs recently arrived from the northwest. Over succeeding centuries, and particularly after the fall of Tula, the Tarascan polity, with a capital at Tzintzuntzán, gradually was extended over the mountainous portions of Michoacan, Jalisco, and Colima.[8]

Just as the locus of Early Postclassic events in central Mexico shifts from the Basin of Mexico to more northern (and western) frontiers, so the major Postclassic developments in the Maya lowlands unfold in the Yucatán Peninsula, north of the Petén Maya area. Here again availability of water is a major factor determining the location of human settlements.

[6] Typically included in this frontier region are the present-day states of Michoacan, Jalisco, Colima, Nayarit, Sinaloa, and sometimes Guerrero.

[7] Prior to this time western Mexico's external ties appear to have been oriented more toward southern Central America, Colombia, Ecuador, and Peru. However, settlement pattern, figurines, and pottery give evidence of significant contact with Classic Mesoamerica, particularly Teotihuacán, by A.D. 600. See Clement W. Meighan, "Prehistory of West Mexico," *Science* 184 (1974):1254–61.

[8] The Tarascans are also famous for their elaborations of metallurgical techniques, which had been introduced to Mesoamerica from the Andean area by the Early Postclassic. The Tarascans produced ornaments of gold and copper, various copper implements, and thin, T-shaped pieces of hammered copper possibly used as a form of money. Technology in general, however, was not significantly affected by metallurgy. Armillas, "Northern Mesoamerica," pp. 318–20; Dan Stanislawski, "Tarascan Political Geography," *American Anthropologist* 49(1947):46–55; Meighan, "Prehistory of West Mexico," p. 1259.

FIGURE 6.2 A pair of dancing warriors, 20 cm and 21.5 cm high, from Colima, western Mexico. Clay figurines of many styles have been recovered from burials in western Mexico. Such figures may have been interred as guardians or attendants of the dead. They frequently provide useful ethnographic details of dress and other aspects of material culture. Courtesy of the Art Institute of Chicago.

The low, flat limestone bed underlying the Yucatán Peninsula becomes increasingly porous toward the north, and surface waters are quickly absorbed into subsurface drainage systems. Consequently, there are no surface streams in the northern regions. Water must be obtained instead from catch pools, artificial wells, or sinkholes (*cenotes*) formed by the caving in of the limestone surface. Similarly the tropical forest and savannah vegetation characteristic of the Petén is replaced by dry forest and then by dry scrub bush to north and northwest.

Contrary to previous opinion northern Yucatán was continually populated during the Formative and thereafter. Furthermore, generally speaking there has been more population stability and cultural continuity here than in areas farther south, for there are no major breaks in the archaeological record comparable to the decline of elite centers in the Petén at the end of the Classic era. To date the fullest developmental sequence is at the large site of Dzibilchaltún situated in the far northwestern corner of Yucatán; it was inhabited without interruption since the Formative era (see Figure 5.1).

By the Late Formative elite structures appear, not only at Dzibilchaltún, but also at Yaxuná and Acanceh,[9] and during the Classic era such characteristic Maya features as stelae, the corbeled vault, monumental sculpture, calendrics and hieroglyphic writing, and plastered causeways occur. To be sure these features were not as elaborately and carefully crafted as those in the Petén, but they do indicate the steady development of the same Maya culture pattern in both regions.[10] As the Classic era draws to a close, however, the reconstruction of events grows more complicated, not so much in terms of what happened, but with respect to *when* these incidents occurred and how they are to be understood in relation to developments elsewhere in Mesoamerica. Let us note, first of all, the major points in question.

At a number of sites in several areas of the peninsula noticeable changes occur in architectural style, both in basic construction techniques and in façade decoration which becomes very elaborate and superficial. For example, the so-called Río Bec style found in southeast Campeche is characterized by high towers in the shape of small temple-pyramids placed on rather ordinary palace platforms. The towers, however, are completely solid, with impossibly steep stairways and false doorways at the summit. In northern Campeche, in the Chenes area, elaborately ornamented façades predominate, as they do in the Puuc Hills, too, where pyramids and multistoried palaces are flamboyantly faced with carved mosaic ornamentation in the form of veneer masonry. This thin stone veneer is placed over a basic concrete mass, which replaces the true masonry construction of Classic era architecture when walls were built of large stone blocks that actually bore the weight of the structure. Elegant vaulting appears, too, but constructed now of concrete and only faced with stone veneer, rather than being actually vaulted. Furthermore the practice of erecting stelae with Long Count dates declines and disappears; as we shall see, this presents a frustrating problem in dating.[11]

Elements of the Puuc style are also found farther east at Chichén Itzá where, however, they are quickly overwhelmed by a wealth of architectural, ceramic, and artistic evidence signifying an influx of Mexican influences into Yucatán and particularly linking Chichén Itzá with Tula. For example, in addition to such fundamentally Maya characteristics as vaulting, styles of molding, and elaborately carved stone mosaic façade ornamentation, Chichén Itzá architecture now evidences extensive use of columns rather than walls as roof and vault supports and widespread application of the feathered serpent motif in bas-reliefs, carvings, and

[9] E. Wyllys Andrews, IV, "Dzibilchaltun: A Northern Maya Metropolis," *Archaeology* 21 (1968):36–47; idem, *Excavations at Dzibilchaltun, Northwestern Yucatan, Mexico*, Proceedings of the American Philosophical Society (Philadelphia, 1960), 104:254–65.

[10] There is even occasional evidence of Teotihuacán in the north, for example, in the tablero-talud motifs and in various sculpted figures at the site of Acanceh.

[11] J. Eric S. Thompson, *The Rise and Fall of Maya Civilization*, 2nd ed. (Norman: Univ. of Oklahoma Press, 1966), pp. 83 and 85; E. Wyllys Andrews, "Archaeology and Prehistory in the Northern Maya Lowlands: An Introduction," in *Handbook of Middle American Indians*, ed. Robert Wauchope (Austin: Univ. of Texas Press, 1965), 2:288–330.

FIGURE 6.3 This elaborate façade at Uxmal in the province of Yucatán illustrates the use of thin, carefully cut veneer masonry set in flamboyant, highly conventionalized latticelike designs and frets and in serpent motifs that characterize the Puuc style of façade ornamentation. Courtesy of the Field Museum of Natural History.

murals. Mexican deities including Quetzalcóatl and Texcatlipoca are well represented, although Maya deities remain, too. Bas-reliefs depicting Toltec warriors and priests and prowling felines and eagles offering hearts to the sun god are common, as are characteristic Toltec statues, quite prevalent at Tula, known as "Chacmools," figures of reclining humans holding on their stomachs shallow bowls or disks which may have served as receptacles for the hearts of sacrificial victims. Human sacrifice probably was conducted at Chichén Itzá, for a long platform carved on all sides with depictions of human skulls on stakes is associated with the site. In Postclassic Mexico these platforms, called *tzompantli,* supported great racks on which the heads of victims were displayed.[12]

The Temple of the Warriors is particularly Toltec in form and has a close counterpart in the smaller Pyramid B at Tula. Furthermore, the interior walls of the Temple are covered by a set of murals which are not only decorative but record the defeat of a group of Maya by Mexicans.

[12] Thompson, *Rise and Fall,* pp. 116–39; Willey, *Introduction to American Archaeology,* 1:165–67 and 177 note 116.

FIGURE 6.4 A design from a gold disk from the Sacred Cenote at Chichén Itzá showing two Mexican warriors (right) wielding spears and spear-throwers against two hapless Maya warriors wearing feather capes. Scenes on other disks portray the retreat of the Maya warriors before pursuing Mexicans. Reprinted from *The Ancient Maya*, 3rd ed., fig. 57a, by Sylvanus G. Morley, revised by George W. Brainerd with the permission of the publishers, Stanford University Press. Copyright © 1946, 1947, 1956 by the Board of Trustees of the Leland Stanford Junior University.

Another set of frescoes in another temple also shows a defeat, ending with the sacrifice of the unfortunate Maya leaders under the watchful gaze of the Feathered Serpent. Similar scenes of conquest appear on golden disks recovered from the famed Sacred Cenote at Chichén Itzá where, according to Spanish sources, human sacrifices and gifts of jades, precious metals, and other objects were offered to the rain gods in time of drought.[13]

While there is some debate as to how this material should be interpreted, the most generally accepted explanation proposes that Mexican authority was established over the local Maya population at Chichén Itzá and, on the evidence of ceramics, perhaps also at Dzibilchaltún. In general, though, direct evidence of foreign influence is not widespread in the Yucatán Peninsula. On the other hand, most of the Río Bec, Chenes, and Puuc sites were abandoned close to the beginning of the Toltec period at Chichén Itzá; there may be some relationship between these events.[14]

Quite possibly Chichén Itzá became an outlying link in the economic-

[13] A. M. Tozzer, *Chichén-Itzá and its Cenote of Sacrifice*, Memoir of the Peabody Museum, vols. 11 and 12 (Cambridge: Harvard University, 1957).

[14] Thompson, *Rise and Fall*, p. 115. .

political network of the Toltec state. If so, the Mexicans in control need not have been Toltecs from Tula, but could have come from elsewhere in the Mexican highlands where Tula held sway. Perhaps the foreigners in residence were not Mexicans per se but a highly Mexicanized Maya group such as sea-going Chontal-speaking Maya from the Tabasco area, long an important trade frontier for Mexican peoples, which may have been a jump-off point for the Late Classic non-Maya incursions into the Usumacinta River system, too.[15]

Nor is it clear when this period of foreign influence occurred. The answer to this question depends on how the preceding Puuc–Río Bec–Chenes period is related to the Classic era of the Petén. Two main interpretations have been advanced (see Figure 6.5). In one view the Puuc materials *directly correlate* with the Late Classic of the Petén and end at approximately A.D. 900, when the Late Classic is terminated according to the Goodman-Martinez-Thompson correlation. In another interpretation, the Puuc *follows* the Petén Classic, that is, becomes the earliest stage of the Postclassic in the north. However, this second view requires that a great deal of material, including the Puuc–Río Bec–Chenes florescence and the Toltec phase at Chichén Itzá, be crammed into a relatively short period of some 300 years between the end of the Classic in the Petén (as dated by the Goodman-Martinez-Thompson method) and the beginning of the Late Postclassic in the northern region (that is, the period following Toltec Chichén Itzá) which is fairly well correlated with Christian calendar dates and begins about A.D. 1200.

This problem raises the issue of the correlation of the Maya and Christian calendars, a matter of fundamental importance for interpretations of Mesoamerican culture history in general and one which has yet to be satisfactorily resolved. The basic difficulty lies in determining the Christian date of the Spanish conquest in terms of Maya calendrics. At first glance this would not seem much of a problem; all that is required is the date of the conquest in terms of the Long Count. Unfortunately, by the time of the Spanish conquest the Maya were no longer using the Long Count, but had turned to an abbreviated method of recording dates, the so-called Short Count, which fails to directly provide all the information given in Long Count inscriptions, information needed for scholars today to establish dates in terms of the Long Count's fixed starting point. Instead, notations are provided for only part of a date with the assumption that the viewer could supply the rest, which, of course, a contemporary Maya could have done. Consequently it is necessary for archaeologists to determine by other means what the full Long Count date would be for the Short Count dates and then to correlate this information with the Christian calendar.

So far two major correlations have been advanced, the Goodman-Martinez-Thompson and the Spinden systems. The Goodman-Martinez-Thompson (G-M-T) correlation associates the Christian year 1539 with the projected Long Count date 11.16.0.0.0, while the Spinden

<hr>

[15] Wolf, *Sons of the Shaking Earth*, pp. 124–25; Thompson, *Rise and Fall*, pp. 116–20.

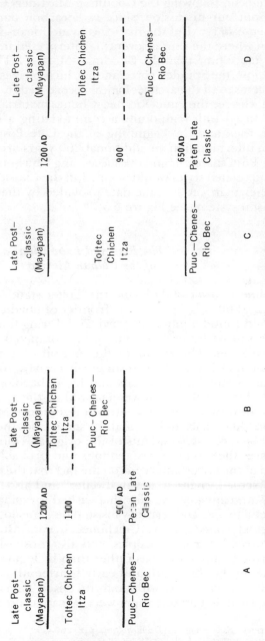

FIGURE 6.5 Four interpretations of the northern Yucatán Early Postclassic. Figure C is the least likely possibility.

correlation relates 1539 with the projected Long Count date 12.9.0.0.0. We have been following the Goodman-Martinez-Thompson correlation throughout our discussion, since radiocarbon dates have best upheld this scheme so far. But the matter is by no means fully settled, and in a situation where the flow of events is interpreted in such a manner as to require more time than the Goodman-Martinez-Thompson correlation would allow, the Spinden correlation, which pushes all dates back by 260 years, seems to fit the archaeological record better. This is the argument of those who see the Puuc–Río Bec–Chenes materials as Early Postclassic, but are faced with temporally accommodating a great deal of activity between then and the beginning of the Late Postclassic. By using the Spinden interpretation an additional 260 years are gained to accommodate the Puuc materials and the succeeding Chichén Itzá period, since the Puuc and related styles would begin, and the Classic era end, at about A.D. 650 rather than A.D. 900, the date provided by the Goodman-Martinez-Thompson system (see Figure 6.5).[16]

The Rise and Expansion of the Culhua Mexica

The political power of Tula and the Toltec state was effectively broken about A.D. 1200. The agricultural frontier of northern Mesoamerica now contracted considerably southward, and during the thirteenth and fourteenth centuries lesser states once more competed for supremacy in the central plateau. The events of this period of confusion and political fragmentation are hard to distinguish clearly. According to the data afforded by historical accounts and by archaeology this was a time of considerable population movement and of the appearance of "Toltec" domains in various areas of central and southern Mesoamerica, as far as highland Guatemala and beyond. In some cases these post-Tula Toltecs seem to be direct descendants of the original Toltec power elite, but in other cases the ties are more tenuous and probably often unreal.

Much of the uncertainty rests on the fact that the term "Toltec" came to signify "settled, civilized, urban dweller" and also "legitimate ruling authority," and any political elite that wished to validate a claim to rightful rule over a people and territory insisted on genealogical connections with the original Toltec royalty. (Chichimec, in contrast, carried the connotation of unsettled, rough peoples, and also those who proudly and arrogantly rule by force of arms rather than by legitimate right.) Thus, for example, in the thirteenth and early fourteenth centuries a number of small "Toltec" city-states with doubtful ties to Tula appear in the basin of Mexico. Included among them were Azcapotzalco, headquarters of the

[16] Andrews, *Excavations at Dzibilchaltun*, pp. 260–65; Willey, *Introduction to American Archaeology*, 1:137–38; Gordon R. Willey, "An Archaeological Frame of Reference . . . ," in *Desarrollo Cultural de los Mayas*, ed. Evon Z. Vogt and Alberto Ruz (Universidad Nacional Autonoma de Mexico, 1964), pp. 157–59.

Tepanec, who controlled the western and northwestern section of the basin; Xaltocan, from which the northern part of the basin was directed; and Acolhua, on the eastern shore of Lake Texcoco. But the Toltecs of Xicco and of Culhuacán, who dominated the southwestern section of the basin, may have held legitimate claims to the original Toltec traditions.[17]

While "Toltec" dynasties jockeyed for power and authority proud "Chichimecs" also moved into central Mexico, gradually settling down to sedentary Mesoamerican life, mixing with Toltec domains, and adding their considerable political sophistication and military prowess to the struggle for power. In this fashion Chichimecs gained ascendancy over the important Acolhua domain at Texcoco and also moved into northern Puebla where they fused with Toltecs and the local population to found another major center at Tlaxcala. Tlaxcala became an important focal point for trade and exchange between the central highlands and the Gulf lowlands where Chichimecs, who may have been responsible for the burning of El Tajín, also established control over the local population.

Among the groups competing for position in the Basin of Mexico were the Tenochca or Culhua Mexica, more commonly, though less accurately, known as Aztecs, a Nahuatl-speaking people who possibly originated as a semiagricultural frontier group with experience as auxiliaries in the armies of the Toltecs of Tula, although ceramic evidence suggests a more localized derivation from earlier central highland cultures. At any rate, about the middle of the fourteenth century the Culhua Mexica were established in the Basin of Mexico under the protection of the Toltec-derived state of Culhuacán. On islands in the western marshes of Lake Texcoco they built their settlement, Tenochtitlán, which was closely affiliated with another island city, the nearby trade center of Tlatelolco. During the late fourteenth and early fifteenth centuries the Mexica continued to serve as mercenaries, now for the Tepanec kingdom of Azcapotzalco, which gradually attained political and economic control of the Basin of Mexico first by defeating the other small states and then by expanding east and south until it had acquired mastery of the basic economic core of central Mexico.[18]

After the death of the Tepanec ruler in 1427, the Mexica began their rise to prominence by filling the power vacuum created by the ultimate defeat of the Tepanec by the forces of a tripartite alliance composed of the Mexica of Tenochtitlán, the Acolhua of Texcoco, and the state of Tlacopan, part of the former Tepanec domain. This Triple Alliance succeeded in organizing a fairly stable political unit, divided the Basin of Mexico among themselves, and united forces for external conquests.

During the next 30 years the Mexica and their allies embarked on an ambitious expansion program. Under the leadership of the king of Texcoco they reunited the lands of the former Tepanec state, thereby achieving control of the economic core of central Mexico. The Mexica of

[17] Wolf, *Sons of the Shaking Earth*, pp. 123–28.
[18] Armillas, "Northern Mesoamerica," pp. 320–25; Friedrich Katz, *The Ancient American Civilizations* (New York: Praeger, 1972), chap. 10.

FIGURE 6.6 Quetzalcóatl, creator of mankind, culture hero, deity, and symbol of divine wisdom was a principal character in the myths and philosophy of Mesoamerica. Here he is graphically portrayed as the Feathered Serpent in an Aztec-style lava sculpture 14 cm high from Tula, Hidalgo. Courtesy of the Field Museum of Natural History.

Tenochtitlán then further consolidated their own position by gaining effective de facto ascendancy over the other members of the alliance. The governments of Tlacopan and Texcoco, although still independent allies of Tenochtitlán, became subservient to Mexica leadership, particularly in matters of war policy. The Mexica then extended their rule throughout much of central and southern Mexico, pushing the Mesoamerican boundary back toward the north and ultimately assuming domination over much of the territory from the Huastec south to the present Mexican-Guatemalan border (see Figure 6.8).[19]

The growth and expansion of the Mexica state was grounded basically in the successful exploitation of the natural resources and agricultural products of the Basin of Mexico and immediately surrounding areas. The lake system of the basin was of critical importance in this regard. For one thing, the lakes were the scene of *chinampa* agriculture, the most productive agricultural technique devised in pre-Columbian Mesoamerica. Chinampas, the so-called "floating gardens," were in reality quite stable artificial islands and peninsulas formed by draining the swamps and lake shores via a system of canals. Mud dug from the canals was piled between them and layers of water vegetation were added to build long, narrow, rectangular plots separated from each other by waterways. By applying mulches of lake bottom mud and vegetation and by using seed beds the highly fertile chinampas could be made to yield three to four harvests annually. In addition to chinampas, slopes of the surrounding hills and mountains were terraced and, in some sections, irrigated either by flood-

[19] Alexander Moore, "The Aztec 'Empire' as a Federative Monarchy" (unpublished manuscript, 1969).

water or by water carried by canals and aqueducts. The plains between the foothills and the lakes were also intensively cultivated.[20]

The high agricultural productivity attainable by terracing, irrigation, and chinampa cultivation permitted in turn the high population density characteristic of the Basin of Mexico and adjoining areas in the fifteenth and early sixteenth centuries. Within the basin much of this population was concentrated in two or three major political, religious, and commercial foci, each composed of a large urban center containing tens of thousands of persons surrounded by smaller towns with perhaps 3,000 to 6,000 people, and by still smaller dependent rural settlements. Tenochtitlán-Tlatelolco was the largest of the capital cities with a population conservatively estimated at 60,000 to 120,000 inhabitants or more. Three large masonry causeways connected Tenochtitlán-Tlatelolco to a cluster of large towns on the western lakeshore, including Tlacopan and Azcapotzalco. On the opposite side of the lake stood the city of Texcoco, likewise surrounded by towns and rural villages. A third population cluster may have focused on Xochimilco, which, like Tenochtitlán, owed its population growth largely to the evolution of chinampa agriculture. Politically, this basin population was divided among some 60 semiautonomous tributary states of various sizes, each governed by a hereditary ruler to whom tribute in corvée labor, goods, and military service was paid by the population under his control, and who in turn owed similar annual tribute to one of the three major powers—Texcoco, Tenochtitlán, or Tlacopan.[21]

Equally important for the support of these large population clusters was the fact that the lake system provided an efficient transportation route within the basin, making it possible to easily transport the diverse produce from hillside terraces, plains, and chinampas to urban centers, and welding the basin into a single economic region. Thus lime, nopal, maquey products, and obsidian from the drier northern section, lumber, wood products, and wild foods from forested upper mountain slopes, maize, amaranth, beans, chili, tomatoes, and a wide range of other agricultural products from the lower piedmont and plain, and fish, waterfowl, and agricultural produce from the open lakes and chinampas could all be found in the markets of Tenochtitlán, along with village craft specialties such as mats and baskets, salt, and ceramics from a number of lakeside communities.[22]

In addition to the products of the Basin of Mexico, many basic subsistence resources were obtained from the intensely cultivated and heavily populated valleys and plains of adjacent Puebla, Morelos, Toluca, and southern Hidalgo. Some of these lands, particularly the upper and middle Balsas River system, provided ready access to important lowland

[20] Michael D. Coe, "The Chinampas of Mexico," *Scientific American* 211 (1964):90–98; Pedro Armillas, "Gardens on Swamps," *Science* 174 (1971):653–61; Angel Palerm, "The Agricultural Basis of Urban Civilization in Mesoamerica," reprinted in *Man in Adaptation: The Cultural Present,* ed. Yehudi A. Cohen (Chicago: Aldine, 1968), pp. 348–61.

[21] Sanders and Price, *Mesoamerica,* pp. 151–60.

[22] Ibid., pp. 191–93.

FIGURE 6.7 Diorama of market activity at Tlatelolco, the trade center for Tenochtitlán. The bustle of commerce and the diversity of foods and crafts exchanged here during the hegemony of the Mexica and their allies probably was very similar to that found in the markets of Teotihuacán 1,000 years earlier. Courtesy of the Field Museum of Natural History.

resources such as cotton, cacao, and various tropical fruits and root crops which were otherwise unavailable in the highland basins, but which were essential to the support of the growing highland states. The frost-free climate of this low-lying southern escarpment, together with hydraulic agriculture, also made it possible to grow maize year-round, again supplementing the more limited and more hazardous agriculture of the highlands. Thus it is not surprising to find that the societies of these rich valleys and plains were integral parts of the growing Mexica empire.

Yet the armies of the Triple Alliance ventured still farther afield to

FIGURE 6.8 The Mexica empire and frontier regions (facing page). Adapted in part from "Port of Trade Enclaves in Aztec and Maya Civilizations," p. 118, by Anne M. Chapman, in *Trade and Market in the Early Empires*, ed. Karl Polanyi, Conrad M. Arensberg, and Harry W. Pearson, copyright 1957 by The Free Press, a Corporation, by permission of Macmillan Publishing Co., Inc., and from *The Extent of the Empire of the Culhua Mexica* by R. H. Barlow, University of California Press Publications in Ibero-Americana vol. 28, 1949 (originally published by the University of California Press; reprinted by permission of The Regents of the University of California).

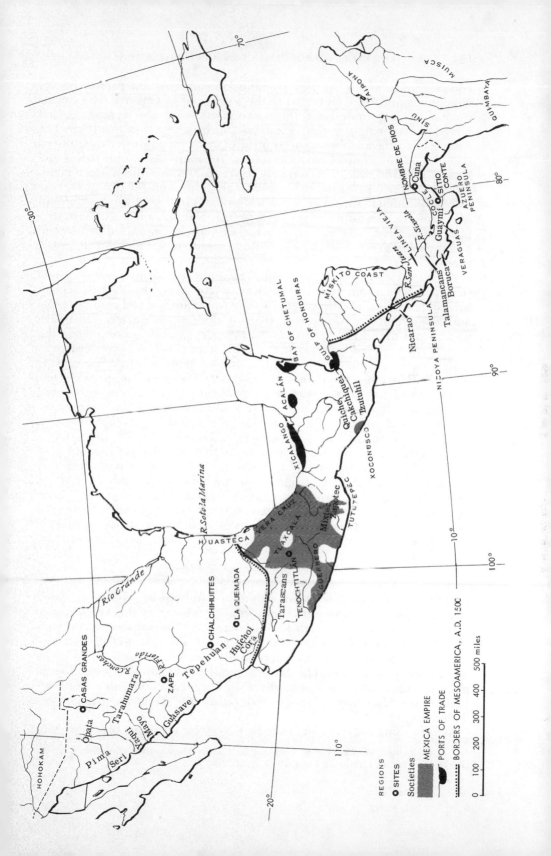

REGIONS
○ SITES
Societies

MEXICA EMPIRE
● PORTS OF TRADE
⋯⋯⋯ BORDERS OF MESOAMERICA, A.D. 1500

0   100 200 300 400 500 miles

conquer towns and territories from the Río Panuco to the Pacific coast of Guatemala and from Veracruz to the west coast of Oaxaca. The fundamental motives underlying these conquests were also economic, and aimed at acquiring strategic resources which were either insufficient or completely unavailable on the central plateau through the exacting of tribute and the control of trade routes. In many cases local rulers and sociopolitical organizations were allowed to function without much political interference provided tribute was paid, although Mexica governors were appointed to supervise tax collections and soldiers from the Basin of Mexico were garrisoned at strategic points. The so-called Mexican "empire," therefore, was in reality a rather loosely organized federation embracing a great diversity of semi-independent ethnic and linguistic groups.

A wide variety of goods flowed into the capital city from the 38 tributary provinces which composed the Mexica domain. Annual payments of basic subsistence items including maize, beans, amaranth, dried chili peppers, and maguey honey, along with items of clothing, pottery bowls, native paper, and the like, were required from the provinces composing the central core and those closest to it. More distant provinces were primarily obligated to provide more exotic high-status items and raw materials to Tenochtitlán, items used not in the everyday life of the common people, but reserved for the support and enhancement of the elite or for the conduct of religious ritual. For example, the tribute demanded from the northernmost provinces included live eagles and deer, while the lowland domains in Veracruz furnished, among other things, liquid amber, richly decorated mantles, jade beads, quetzal feathers, lip plugs of crystal and of light amber mounted in gold, loads of cacao, gold headbands and diadems, gold shields, feather standards, rubber balls, and ocelot skins. Similarly from the southern provinces of Oaxaca and Guerrero came richly decorated quilted mantles, gold strips, bowls of gold dust, strings of jade beads, deer and jaguar skins, sacks of cochineal, and rich feathers.[23]

Lands Beyond the Realm

A glance at Figure 6.8 will show that although large areas of central and southern Mexico became tribute-paying provinces of the Mexica, substantial regions remained outside such controls. The important commercial state of Tlaxcala in the central plateau, though surrounded and subject to serious pressures, successfully resisted invasion, as did the Tarascans, to the west. The Mexica armies were also prevented from gaining control of all of Oaxaca where the Zapotec, allied with a neighboring people, the Mixtec, seriously defeated the Mexican armies near Tehuantepec.

We are using the term Mixtec to refer collectively to peoples of various

[23] R. H. Barlow, *The Extent of the Empire of the Culhua Mexica,* Ibero-Americana no. 28 (Berkeley: Univ. of California Press, 1949).

ethnic background but general linguistic similarity who inhabited the highlands and the semitropical lowlands of the western third of the modern state of Oaxaca and adjacent portions of Guerrero and Puebla, particularly the rugged upland section of Oaxaca known as the Mixteca Alta. Here excavations at various sites, including Monte Negro-Tilantongo and Coixtlahuaca, and surveys of the Nochixtlán Valley have indicated a long period of demographic and cultural growth from the Formative on.[24]

Prior to approximately A.D. 700 the peoples of the Mixteca living closest to the Valley of Oaxaca occupied a somewhat inferior and peripheral position vis-à-vis the Zapotec centered at Monte Albán, although both groups were culturally quite similar, while the northern Mixteca may have been associated with Teotihuacán. From the Late Formative there also was more or less continual social and economic interaction with southern Puebla, including the Tehuacán region and Cholula. The so-called Mixteca-Puebla artistic style, which grew out of this exchange during the interim between the fall of Teotihuacán and the rise of Tula, produced some of the finest sculpture, ceramic, lapidary, and mosaic work of the Postclassic era.

By the beginning of the Postclassic the Mixtec began to develop politically and soon emerged as the dominant force in the region.[25] Yet the Mixtec themselves probably were never permanently unified under a single ruler, although such prominent and powerful leaders as the famous "Eight-Deer Tiger-Claw" are known to have reigned among them.[26] Instead these peoples were organized into a number of small states, some comprising one or more of the communities of a single valley, others combining several adjoining valleys. Each state was governed by powerful lineages which controlled the most productive lands and provided a hereditary ruler and a corps of noble retainers, advisors, and assistants. In return for leadership and protection, the common folk paid tribute to the elite, provided labor for their fields and homes, and served as soldiers in time of war. There was in fact considerable warfare (generally in the nature of raids) among the various Mixtec communities or valley-states regarding boundary disputes, to obtain captives for sacrifice, perhaps over questions of royal succession, and to broaden the range of tribute-paying domains. Expansion was also effected and the gains of warfare consolidated by intermarriage among royal families, and in this manner the lineages of the Mixtec aristocracy became closely interrelated.

Through royal intermarriage Mixtecs also obtained some measure of political control over the Valley of Oaxaca by the Late Postclassic. To be sure Zapotec peoples continued to occupy traditional Zapotec territory, including the Oaxaca Valley, with little acceptance of Mixtec customs in

[24] Ronald Spores, "Settlement, Farming Technology, and Environment in the Nochixtlan Valley," *Science* 166 (1969):557–69.

[25] Information on the Mixtec is derived largely from Ronald Spores, *The Mixtec Kings and Their People* (Norman: Univ. of Oklahoma Press, 1967).

[26] Coe, *Mexico*, pp. 149–50; J. C. Clark, *The Story of "Eight Deer" in Codex Colombino* (London, 1912).

spite of growing Mixtec political influence. However, Mixtec occupation is revealed at the vast majority of Zapotec sites dating from this period, including Mitla, the fortified hilltop which had become the new Zapotec religious center, and at deserted Monte Albán. At Monte Albán the Mixtecs reused the ancient tombs of Zapotec rulers to bury their own royal dead, and it is from one of these crypts, Tomb 7, that some of the finest of all pre-Columbian treasure has been recovered, revealing that the Mixtecs were also master craftsmen in metallurgical and lapidary skills.[27]

After various campaigns, the armies of the Triple Alliance succeeded in conquering the Mixteca Alta and most of the adjacent lowlands and imposed Mexican garrisons and a schedule of tribute payment. They also gained control of much of the Zapotec area. However, as a result of a subsequent Mexican-Zapotec alliance, bolstered by the timely marriage of the Zapotec king to a near relative of the Mexica ruler, the Mixtec were forced to retreat from Zapotec territory and by the time of the Spanish conquest the Zapotec had reasserted local control in the Valley of Oaxaca.

As Figure 6.8 indicates, the lands east of the Oaxaca Valley fell beyond the effective limits of the Mexica empire, and rulers here did not pay tribute to the allies. However, a string of Mexican garrisons was located in this uneasy hinterland to protect Mexican armies and traders passing through en route to the southernmost of the Mexica territories, the tribute-paying province of Xoconusco on the Pacific coast of Guatemala, and to the important trading centers of Xicalango in southern Veracruz-Tabasco.

Xicalango and to some extent Xoconusco are examples of what have been termed "ports of trade." A port of trade was a relatively neutral area, purposefully kept safe and peaceful by the major political powers, usually located between major ecological zones on lagoons and rivers of gulf areas where important transportation routes, generally waterways, converged. In addition, the territory of the port of trade was often a region where cacao (widely used as currency) grew. The specific function of the towns and cities in these sectors was to provide services and warehouses for foreign traders who convened to exchange goods, again usually high-status items and raw materials associated with the elite of their respective polities.[28]

The Mesoamerican ports of trade were situated south of the Mexican provinces and on the edges of Maya territories (see Figure 6.8). Xicalango, a major center where routes from the Basin of Mexico, the southern Maya highlands, and the Bay of Honduras converged, provided the main link between Mexican and Maya areas. The Bay of Chetumal

[27] Alfonso Caso, "Reading the Riddles of Ancient Jewels," *Natural History* 32 (1932):464–80.

[28] The following discussion is based primarily on Anne C. Chapman, "Port of Trade Enclaves in Aztec and Maya Civilizations," in *Trade and Market in the Early Empires*, ed. K. Polanyi, C. M. Arensberg, and H. W. Pearson (Glencoe: The Free Press, 1957), pp. 114–53. See also Frances F. Berdan, "Ports of Trade in Mesoamerica: A Reappraisal" (mimeographed, 1973).

and the Gulf of Honduras, where four large rivers lie in close proximity, similarly linked Mesoamerica with lower Central America. The commercial center of Acalan on the Candelaria River served as a major interior crossroads between the Gulf of Mexico and the Gulf of Honduras.[29]

Transactions at the ports of trade were generally conducted between professional long-distance traders, frequently with the aid of local "go-between" merchants. Among the Mexica the occupation of long-distance trader, called *pochtecatl* (plural, *pochteca*) in Nahuatl, was passed on from father to son, and the pochteca constituted a tightly knit organization in Mexican society.[30] Since the pochteca traded almost exclusively with peoples beyond the frontier of the Mexican state, much of their time was spent away from the capital cities of the Basin of Mexico on arduous, perilous journeys by foot and by canoe to the warehouses and meeting places of the distant ports of trade.

Pochteca activities may also have assisted the expansion of the Mexica empire. These traders apparently operated as state agents to provide estimates of the tribute possibilities of an unconquered region. Entering enemy territory disguised as a native and with command of the local language, the pochtecatl sat in the market place, ostensibly to trade in such common goods as knives and combs of flint, but in reality watching, listening, and asking questions to obtain vital information for the lords of Tenochtitlán. Once the territory was conquered and subject to tribute, the pochteca usually ceased to trade there.[31]

The Mexica "empire" was less than 100 years old at the time of the Spanish conquest and probably had not reached its peak of political integration and stabilization by 1521. Continued advance may well have been anticipated, particularly to the south where, except for Xoconusco, the southern Maya highlands and the rest of Central America lay unconquered.[32] Very likely highland Guatemala was particularly ripe for control since in the Late Postclassic this region was a land of conflict where a number of small, warring states (Quiché, Cakchiquel, Tzutuhil, Mam, Pokomam, Kekchi, etc.) competed for control of various resources and for political supremacy.

This turmoil is reflected in changing Postclassic settlement patterns. Although in some areas of Guatemala the Maya population continued to live in scattered valley hamlets and villages, elsewhere these small communities were crowded onto hillslopes close to larger centers situated on high summits or ridges surrounded by deep ravines and further shielded by fortifications. According to local histories the ruling elite ensconced in many of these mountain centers claimed a Mexican, specifically Toltec, ancestry. This assertion is further substantiated by the Mexican architec-

[29] France V. Scholes and Ralph E. Roys, *The Maya Chontal Indians of Acalan-Tixchel,* Carnegie Institution of Washington Publication no. 560 (Washington, D.C., 1948).

[30] Jacques Soustelle, *The Daily Life of the Aztecs* (Stanford: Stanford Univ. Press, 1961), pp. 59–65 and 85–86.

[31] Chapman, "Port of Trade Enclaves," pp. 124 and 141.

[32] Doris Stone, *Pre-Columbian Man Finds Central America* (Cambridge, Mass.: Peabody Museum Press, 1972), chaps. 3 and 4.

tural style of the temple-pyramids, apartment or barracks buildings, and ball courts associated with many of the hilltop forts.[33] We need not take the historical accounts for literal truth and should remember that "Toltec" often was used by non-Tula peoples to mean simply "sophisticated city-dweller" and "legitimate ruler." It does appear, however, that many of the Postclassic village-farming Maya, most notably the Quiché, Cakchiquel, and Tzutuhil, were controlled by elite groups of Mexican origin, whose appearance in Guatemalan culture history at this time may be related to the disruptions in Mexico at the end of the Toltec era. Eventually, however, the Mexican overlords gradually became acculturated to local languages and traditions, so that the native rulers who shortly were to face the advancing Spanish conquistadors appear as distinctly Maya in the chronicles of the conquest.

Warfare between small competing states also characterized the last century (1440–1541) of pre-Hispanic Maya culture in the Yucatán peninsula. It may account for the development of fortified communities in the northern Maya lowlands, most notably at Mayapán in northwest Yucatán, which for some 200 years (from about 1200–1440) was the center of a state that controlled much of northwest and north-central Yucatán. As was the case with Chichén Itzá, there is considerable uncertainty as to just who were the rulers of Mayapán. Once again the ruling elite are portrayed as culturally distinct from the local Maya and there are suggestions of Mexican connections in family names as well as indications of ties with the Mexicanized Maya of the Tabasco regions.

Archaeological investigations have revealed Mayapán to be a walled enclosure encompassing some 5 km² and containing a small ceremonial center and over 2,000 house mounds where 10,000 to 12,000 persons may have lived. There is no evidence of planning in this settlement pattern. Rather, the house mounds are tightly aggregated in a haphazard manner, as if a once dispersed population were simply drawn together into closer quarters. Consequently, here again there is considerable discussion as to whether Mayapán represents a true urban settlement with a fully diversified population reflecting a heterogeneous society, or whether it should be viewed instead as a large ceremonial center inhabited primarily by elite residents and their retainers.[34]

Mayapán also raises a number of other questions concerning archaeological interpretations of cultural processes in general and

[33] Edwin M. Shook and Tatiana Proskouriakoff, "Settlement Patterns in Meso-America and the Sequence in the Guatemalan Highlands," in *Prehistoric Settlement Patterns in the New World,* ed. G. R. Willey (New York: Wenner-Gren Foundation for Anthropological Research, 1956), pp. 93–100; R. M. Adams, "Changing Patterns of Territorial Organization in the Central Highlands of Chiapas, Mexico," *American Antiquity* 26 (1961):341–60; Stephan F. de Borhegyi, "Settlement Patterns of the Guatemalan Highlands," in *Handbook of Middle American Indians,* ed. Robert Wauchope (Austin: Univ. of Texas Press, 1965), 2:59–75.

[34] There is also a difference of opinion as to whether the fortified and nucleated form of settlement at Mayapan reflects Mexican influence, or whether it represents an indigenous response to growing militarism. H. E. D. Pollock et al., *Mayapan, Yucatan, Mexico,* Carnegie Institution of Washington Publication no. 619 (Washington, D.C., 1962); Andrews, "Archaeology and Prehistory in the Northern Maya Lowlands," 2:322–27.

Mesoamerican culture history in particular. The material culture associated with the ruins at Mayapán indicates a return to earlier Classic Maya building techniques utilizing masonry instead of the cement-veneer construction characteristic of the Early Postclassic. Nonetheless, although the general Classic method is reasserted, the actual construction is frequently inferior, revealing cruder stonework and liberal use of plaster to provide a handsome exterior while hiding basically poor masonry. Buildings are smaller and less resistant to the ravages of time. Similarly, although stelae are raised once more, the carving is cruder and stucco is often applied to delineate final features. Ceramics likewise indicate a return to basic Maya techniques, but are much softer and coarser than earlier wares. This material frequently has been interpreted as indicative of a general resurgence of Maya culture patterns and organizational forms after the Mexican interlude at Chichén Itzá, but as a return that does not replicate former levels of skill and sophistication.

The question has been raised, however, whether this apparent decadence in art and architecture really reflects a comparable decline in sociopolitical sophistication and complexity, or whether the peoples of the time simply put their time and energy into activities other than well-constructed monumental architecture and elaborate stonework that are not recorded in the archaeological record. Recording written matter and calendrics on lime-sized bark paper, for example, would be just as functional as carving stone, perhaps more so, although less likely to survive archaeologically, and plastered buildings would be highly impressive at the time of their intended use even if less durable over long periods. Perhaps the increase in warfare and an elaboration of political activities among competing states consumed more of the effort of the elite so that shortcuts were applied in other areas which had been accorded more attention in Classic times. In short, although archaeological data suggest an interpretation in terms of a decline in arts, architecture, and, by association, in sociopolitical forms, this view may not be an accurate description of Postclassic Yucatecan society in general.[35]

In the middle of the fifteenth century Mayapán was burned and its former domain fragmented through civil war. Yucatán was now divided into about 16 small, militant, competing polities centered in fortified towns. In spite of political fragmentation, however, the peninsula of Yucatán, together with adjacent lands along the coast of the Gulf of Mexico and the Caribbean Sea, remained an economic entity unified by common commercial interests and by linguistic similarities. Within the peninsula itself fish, salt, pottery, canoes, dyes, copal, wooden idols, game, fruits, maize, and cacao were exchanged locally, while the ports of trade at Chetumal, the Bay of Honduras, Acalan, and the Xicalango region linked Yucatán with the rest of Mesoamerica. Through these long-distance trade centers a variety of other goods were obtained. Cotton cloth, slaves acquired in wars and raids, salt, flint implements, and honey from Yucatán

---

[35] Charles J. Erasmus, "Thoughts on Upward Collapse: An Essay on Explanation in Anthropology," *Southwestern J. of Anthro.* 24 (1968):170–94.

were exchanged for cacao and for ornaments of gold and copper, obsidian knives, points, and earplugs, skeins of dyed rabbit fur for use in weaving, and various medicinal herbs brought to Xicalango by Mexica pochteca. A variety of precious and semiprecious stones, obsidian, fine feathers, and cacao were acquired from the southern Maya highlands, again by way of Xicalango and through the Gulf of Honduras. The Gulf of Honduras also afforded an entryway to the Honduranean highlands (famed for gold and precious feathers), to the Pacific coast of Nicaragua (for valuable red shells), and, by way of the Caribbean coast, to even more distant lands of lower Central America.[36]

[36] Ralph L. Roys, *The Indian Background of Colonial Yucatán,* Carnegie Institution of Washington Publication no. 548 (Washington, D.C., 1943).

7

The Far Frontiers

Lower Central America

By the sixteenth century A.D., Mesoamerican culture patterns were firmly established as far south as northwest Honduras and El Salvador west of the Lempa. They also extended, though with less intensity, into a transition zone including El Salvador east of the Lempa, southwest and central Honduras as far as the Aguan River and the headwaters of the eastern tributaries of the Ulua, the Pacific coast and slopes of western Nicaragua, and the Nicoya Peninsula and adjacent mainland of northwest Costa Rica (see Figure 5.1). Beyond this periphery the predominant societies shared major linguistic and ethnological characteristics with peoples of South America rather than with Mesoamerica, although trade contracts with Mexican and Maya centers probably long existed, and, as we shall see, there is evidence of small enclaves of Mesoamerican peoples living within this region.[1]

The pre-Columbian culture history of lower Central America is not well known. Except for northeast Costa Rica, virtually no significant archaeological work has been conducted in the central highlands of Nicaragua, Costa Rica, or Panama or on the slopes and plains of the Caribbean watershed. Only the narrow Pacific coast is known archaeologically to any extent, and even here sites with stratigraphic sequences are

[1] Doris Stone, "The Eastern Frontier of Mesoamerica," *Amerikanistische Miszellen* 25 (1959):118–21; Angel Palerm and Eric R. Wolf, "Ecological Potential and Cultural Development in Mesoamerica," in *Studies in Human Ecology*, ed. A. Palerm et al., Social Science Monographs no. 3 (Washington, D.C.: Pan American Union, 1957), pp. 6–9.

few. Nonetheless, it is clear that no large elite centers or urban communities were constructed in these regions during the pre-Columbian centuries. No Teotihuacáns, Tulas, or Tikals evolved.

Most research to date has focused on Panama, and several outstanding regions and sites should be briefly mentioned. The widely traded polychrome plates, bowls, and jars from the Asuero Peninsula and the province of Coclé show masterful decorative styles, with some affinities with northern South American ceramics. Many examples of these wares along with celts, chipped blades, metates, bone points, spear throwers, traces of bark cloth and woven textiles, and ornaments of semiprecious stone, bone, and shell were discovered in graves at the well-known Sitio Conte in Coclé (see Figure 6.8), particularly in association with burials of high-ranking persons. But the most outstanding grave goods from Sitio Conte are the many pieces of hammered and cast gold jewelry: decorative disks to adorn clothing, helmets, nose and ear ornaments, rings, bracelets, arm and leg bands, breastplates, necklaces of hollow beads, and a variety of pendants. Similar artifacts, particularly pendants in the shape of men and of various animals, are associated with rich graves farther west, in Veraguas, and are made of a gold-copper alloy known as *tumbaga*.[2]

These and other masterpieces of metallurgical skill would seem to indicate that Panama was once a center for work in precious metals. This generally has been assumed and may be true. However, it is noteworthy that historical documents from the Spanish conquest do not present reliable evidence of smelting, casting, or other techniques of metalworking among Panamanian peoples, although gold occurred naturally in the country. Consequently, while simple skills such as gold hammering probably were practiced in Panama, it is possible that most of the more elaborate Panamanian gold pieces were actually crafted elsewhere, probably in Colombia, where gold hammering and annealing were practiced as early as 500 B.C. and where a variety of metallurgical techniques, including smelting, various types of casting, and work in tumbaga came to be highly refined by craftsmen of the Quimbaya, Sinú, and Tairona cultures. In fact, the metalwork recovered from even the early levels of Sitio Conte includes traded pieces in Quimbaya and Sinú styles, and Sinú and Quimbaya pendants are also found in Veraguas.[3]

Judging from the archaeological distribution of lower Central American gold, ceramic, and lapidary pieces during the Classic and Postclassic eras, trade was widespread not only among the various Central American regions and with northern South America, but also between lower Central

[2] Samuel K. Lothrop, *Coclé, An Archaeological Study of Central Panama*, pts. 1 and 2, Memoirs, Peabody Museum, vols. 7 and 8 (Cambridge: Harvard University, 1937–42); Samuel K. Lothrop, *Archaeology of Southern Veraguas, Panama*, Memoirs, Peabody Museum, vol. 9 (Cambridge: Harvard University, 1950).

[3] William C. Root, "Pre-Columbian Metalwork of Colombia and Its Neighbors," in *Essays in Pre-Columbian Art and Archaeology*, S. K. Lothrop et al. (Cambridge: Harvard Univ. Press, 1961), pp. 242–57; Dudley T. Easby, Jr., "Early Metallurgy in the New World," *Scientific American* 214 (1966):72–83.

FIGURE 7.1 Two examples of gold pieces from Panama. The delightful 8.25-cm frog from Venado Beach was worn as a pendant. It was fashioned by lost wax hollow core casting. The 6.7-cm standing male figure in Coclé style is also of cast gold. Courtesy of the Art Institute of Chicago.

America and Mesoamerican states. For example, disks of sheet gold from Panama have been discovered as far away as central Mexico and Yucatán, where they have been dredged from the depths of the Sacred Cenote at Chichén Itzá. In fact, cast gold and tumbaga objects from lower Central America compose two-thirds by weight of all the gold recovered from this famous well. Coclé gold pieces and pendants of agate carved from rough stone occurring in northern Colombia have been found in Oaxaca and Michoacan, too. A tumbaga bead in the Coclé style also was recently recovered from an offering cache at Altun Ha, British Honduras, which dates about or before A.D. 500, indicating that trade and contact between these regions was in effect by the Early Classic.[4]

Perhaps some of these items passed through the major trade center in the Linea Vieja area of northeast Costa Rica (Figure 6.8). Pottery, jade, and gold artifacts both of imported and locally copied foreign styles are particularly common at the many Linea Vieja sites. For example, jade pieces show relationships to styles characteristic of Nicoya and northern Honduras, of Panama and the northern Andes, and even of the West

[4] Samuel K. Lothrop, *Metals from the Cenote of Sacrifice, Chichén Itzá, Yucatán*, Memoirs, Peabody Museum, vol. 10 (Cambridge: Harvard University, 1952); D. M. Pendergast, "Tumbaga Object from the Early Classic Period, Found at Altun Ha, British Honduras," *Science* 168 (1970):116–18.

Indies and Peru. Gold pieces copied from Panamanian objects and in Tairona and Quimbaya styles have been unearthed, while ceramic wares indicate affinities with both Mesoamerican and northern South American pottery.[5]

Unfortunately, little can be said concerning the cultural dynamics that generated this activity. As we noted in Chapters 3 and 4, lower Central America probably shared with Mesoamerica in a common Formative base, although evidence from Monagrillo, in Panama, indicates that fish and shellfish were important adjuncts to whatever agriculture may have been practiced. By the beginning of the Christian era the available data from Nicaragua, Costa Rica, and Panama reveal small permanent villages where cultigens probably provided the main food staples, with fishing and hunting as important supplements. This picture remains essentially unchanged until about A.D. 500.[6]

Between A.D. 500 and 800, the number of known sites attests to a definite population increase. Carved jade, agate, opal, and other semi-precious stones and sophisticated goldwork indicate access to the artistry of skilled craftsmen. Individual and communal graves, the resting places of chiefs and members of the nobility who are often accompanied by sacrificed retainers, also have been unearthed, again in Panama (Venado Beach, early Sitio Conte), indicating that definite distinctions in social rank were recognized. After A.D. 800, tall stone columns and statues, earth and stone mounds (sometimes arranged around plazas), elaborately carved stone metates, and ornaments of gold and jade are widespread in Pacific coast Nicaragua, Costa Rica, and Panama. The archaeological record also reveals that a rather high level of social stratification and complexity had developed in some areas of lower Central America by the time of the Spanish conquest, although no overall sociopolitical unity was achieved.

The limited information available in accounts of native customs written by Europeans in the years immediately following the conquest verifies this general picture. We find essentially three culture patterns in lower Central America in the early sixteenth century: rank societies of Panama and Costa Rica, Mesoamerican-influenced peoples of Pacific Nicaragua and Nicoya, and tribal societies of the extensive Caribbean lowlands of eastern Nicaragua and Honduras.[7] Panama was divided into numerous small, centralized chiefdoms, each composed of ruling chiefs with authority in matters of war and religion, nobles who served as warriors or religious

[5] Samuel K. Lothrop, "Jade and String Sawing in Northeastern Costa Rica," *American Antiquity* 21 (1955):43–51; Doris Stone and Carlos Balser, "Incised Slate Disks from the Atlantic Watershed of Costa Rica," *American Antiquity* 30 (1965):310–29.

[6] This discussion rests heavily on Claude F. Baudez, "Cultural Development in Lower Central America," in *Aboriginal Cultural Development in Latin America*, ed. B. J. Meggers and C. Evans, Smithsonian Miscellaneous Collections (Washington, D.C.: Smithsonian Institution, 1963) 146:45–54.

[7] Carl O. Sauer, *The Early Spanish Main* (Berkeley: Univ. of California Press, 1966); Doris Stone, *Pre-Columbian Man Finds Central America* (Cambridge, Mass.: Peabody Museum Press, 1972).

functionaries and lesser administrators, commoners who attended to basic subsistence activities, and war prisoners. All lived either in dispersed villages or in palisaded settlements of up to 1,500 persons. The Guaymí (as they are called today) in western Panama and the Cueva-Cuna to the east are the best-known descendants of these peoples. Warfare and palisaded villages were also characteristic of much of Costa Rica where the Güetar and those known collectively today as the Talamancans and the Boruca composed a number of small, centralized societies. The Costa Rican chiefdoms, however, probably were not as highly stratified as those in Panama.

Many of the Panamanian and Costa Rican rank societies included within their domains portions of seacoast, coastal lowlands, rivers, and in some cases central highlands, which in sum would have provided access to the resources of diverse ecological zones. Not surprisingly there is also evidence of exchange of a wide range of goods, including shells, gold figures, cotton, salt, salted fish, wild game, agricultural produce, feathers, etc. In all likelihood, therefore, the rise of centralized societies in lower Central America can be understood in the familiar terms of differential control of basic resources and exchange of regional specializations, facilitated and increasingly necessitated by growing population pressure in a small and rugged area with only limited room for territorial expansion. Perhaps, too, contacts between these Central American societies and neighboring peoples in northwest South America, where some societies were becoming even more centralized and stratified, further stimulated comparable developments in Central America.[8] It is tempting to speculate that the intersocietal exchanges of various high-status items, such as ornaments of gold and semiprecious stones, noted in the archaeological record represent such contacts, which could have occurred either as trade or as formal exchanges between leaders of the various elite groups anxious to bolster and validate their respective positions through prestigeful connections and alliances with the rulers of other centralized societies.

In northwest Costa Rica and Pacific coast Nicaragua society was also composed of chiefs and nobility, commoners and war prisoners. However, Mexican languages (Nahuat and various Chorotegan-Mangue dialects) were spoken at the time of conquest, and we find characteristic Mesoamerican communities with houses in the vicinity of central plazas where temples and dwellings for the elite stood on low earth mounds. Markets where cacao beans, maize, and cotton cloth served as money were located in the principal towns.

Although the archaeology of Nicoya indicates ties with Mexico and the Maya areas from the Formative through the Postclassic eras, the Chorotegans and the Nahuat-speaking Nicarao encountered by the Spanish here and in western Nicaragua were not the original inhabitants of the area, although the Chorotegan apparently had inhabited the region for some time. The Nicarao, however, were relative newcomers.

[8] Cf. Gerardo Reichel-Dolmatoff, *Colombia* (London: Thames & Hudson, 1965).

FIGURE 7.2 Effigy jar, Nicoya Peninsula, Costa Rica, A.D. 500 to 800. This stocky 23-cm figure of light orange clay painted with red-orange, black, and grey paint offered the potter a broad field in which to display the effects of polychrome painting, a technique that was handsomely mastered in lower Central American ceramics. Courtesy of the Field Museum of Natural History.

There is much diversity of opinion concerning the interpretation of the semilegendary histories of these people and the correlation of developments in these Mesoamerican frontiers with events in the heartland to north and west.

In general, during the Late Classic and the Postclassic eras peoples speaking Mexican languages and with Mexican customs moved into highland Guatemala, El Salvador, western Nicaragua, and Nicoya. We have briefly encountered some of these groups before in the "Pipils," who are found in highland Guatemala at the end of the Classic, and in the Mexican ancestors of the ruling elite of the Postclassic Maya states of Quiché, Tzutuhil, and Cakchiquel. Similar peoples, including the Nicarao and Chorotegans, all of whom are also confusingly termed "Pipils" (a term that probably meant "princes" or "nobles") in the early historical documents, appear in El Salvador, western Nicaragua, and Nicoya. Although details of population movements and the identity of the various groups are still poorly understood, the arrival of "Pipils" in these southern and eastern hinterlands corresponds in general to major periods of sociopolitical change in Mexico, particularly the interim after the fall of Teotihuacán and the similar period of reorientation which followed the decline of Tula.[9] As we shall see below, the latest Mexicans to arrive in lower Central America may be associated with the expansion of the Mexica empire.

Across the Nicaraguan central highlands, in the extensive Caribbean lowland plain of eastern Nicaragua and eastern Honduras, we find a culture pattern that may be somewhat indicative of the life-style of Formative Central America. Here, on the Miskito Coast, there are no indications of permanent villages and a centralized society. Instead, according to historical accounts, egalitarian family groups lived seminomadically in small, temporary settlements along the coast and rivers. Each village-kinship unit was politically autonomous. Above the local level linguistic commonality provided a point of identification, and linguistic differences comprised the major distinction between groups, who frequently warred against each other. As far as has been determined these tribes, as well as the people of Panama and of Costa Rica (including probably Nicoya and also lower Nicaragua prior to the advent of Mesoamericans) spoke languages and dialects related to Chibchan, a language family of northwest South America.[10]

Among these Caribbean lowland tribes, as among the other peoples of lower Central America, subsistence was based on hunting, fishing, and swidden agriculture. Sweet manioc and other cultivated tubers, pineapples, and the fruit of the pejibaye palm were widely consumed, as were peppers and varieties of beans. Maize was an important foodstuff, too, although it did not carry the same significance in lower Central America as it did in Mesoamerica. In fact, among Caribbean lowland peoples the cultivation and use of maize may have been a relatively late development.[11]

Given the widespread utilization of sweet manioc in lower Central America and the occurrence of such culture traits as bark cloth, hammocks, and excessive intoxication on ceremonial occasions, it is likely that the basic pre-Columbian culture pattern of the region once had ancient Formative affinities with certain tropical forest peoples of South America.[12] Similarly, after the rise of centralized societies, the stratified

[9] Stephan F. de Borhegyi, "Archaeological Synthesis of the Guatemalan Highlands," in *Handbook of Middle American Indians,* ed. Robert Wauchope (Austin: Univ. of Texas Press, 1965), 2:38–41.

[10] M. W., "The Mosquito Indian and His Golden River," in *A Collection of Voyages and Travels,* ed. A. Churchill (London, 1732), 6:285–98; John Esquemeling, *The Buccaneers of America,* ed. H. Powell (London, 1893).

[11] Doris Stone, "Date of Maize in Talamanca, Costa Rica: An Hypothesis," *J. Soc. des Américanistes* 45 (1956):189–94.

[12] Anne C. Chapman, "An Historical Analysis of the Tropical Forest Tribes of the Southern Border of Mesoamerica" (Ph.D. diss., Columbia University, 1958).

cultures of Costa Rica and Panama again form part of a wider geographical and cultural sphere oriented toward South America which included, in addition to lower Central America, the coastal plains and highlands of northwest Venezuela, northern Colombia, and Ecuador. This culture sphere has been termed the Intermediate Area, which refers to the fact that these lands and peoples are situated geographically between the high-culture areas of Mesoamerica and those of the central Andes. Furthermore, one of the most perplexing questions for students of pre-Columbian culture history concerns why the centralized societies of Costa Rica, Panama, and adjacent northwest South America evolved so slowly in comparison with cultures of Mesoamerica and Peru, and why they did not achieve the state level of sociopolitical organization characteristic of these centers.

The various explanations that have been advanced can be placed into two general categories. On the one hand are those considerations that emphasize either directly or indirectly the isolation of the Intermediate Area from the influences of neighboring high-culture centers. For example, the fact that Olmec stylistic motifs do not occur in much of lower Central America may indicate that, in spite of a common village-farming Formative base, lower Central America failed to share in the wider interactions and associations that brought the various regions of Mesoamerica into mutually stimulating contact at this time. Similarly, judging from archaeological materials recovered to date, the isthmian area apparently was bypassed by a series of contacts between Mesoamerica and the Andean regions of South America from Formative times through the Postclassic; the contacts were presumably effected by sea rather than by overland routes.[13]

The other line of argument emphasizes local ecological conditions rather than contact problems. In spite of the ecological diversity of the region, there are no arid or subhumid uplands or lowlands in lower Central America comparable to those regions in Mesoamerica where systems of hydraulic agriculture were developed on a scale sufficient to influence the evolution of states. Consequently, as far as can be determined from the literature, only extensive forms of cultivation were used.[14]

Both categories of explanation may be relevant to the ultimate solution of the problem. Apparently local conditions were not conducive to the evolution of primary states, and distances may have been too great to effect the intensity of contact necessary for the development of secondary states through interaction with existing states in the Andes or in Mesoamerica. Perhaps, though, if the European discovery and explora-

[13] Gordon R. Willey, "The Early Great Styles and the Rise of the Pre-Columbian Civilizations," *American Anthropologist* 64 (1962):1–14; Michael D. Coe, "Archaeological Linkages with North and South America at La Victoria, Guatemala," *American Anthropologist* 62 (1960):363–93.

[14] William T. Sanders and Barbara J. Price, *Mesoamerica* (New York: Random House, 1968), pp. 172–73; Gordon R. Willey, *New World Archaeology in 1965*, Proceedings of the American Philosophical Society (Philadelphia, 1966), 110:144–45.

tion of the "New World" had been delayed a few centuries, lower Central America might have been increasingly drawn toward the wider Mesoamerican sphere. In the historical literature of the conquest there are scattered references to small enclaves or colonies of Mesoamericans located on the Nicaraguan east coast at the mouth of the Río San Juan, in the Sixaola River basin in the Talamancan plain of southeast Costa Rica, and at Nombre de Dios on the Caribbean shore of Panama. It has been suggested that these (and possibly other) enclaves represented outposts of a still-expanding Mexican "empire" which eventually might have incorporated more of Central America under its trade and tribute structure if the Spanish conquest had not intervened.[15] While actual incorporation of distant Central America into Mexican political organizations may be questioned, trade and exchange networks may well have continued and flourished.

The Far North

Although both lower Central America and northern Mexico were situated adjacent to the high-culture areas of Mesoamerica, the culture patterns and cultural dynamics of these two hinterlands differed greatly. These contrasts basically reflect sharp distinctions in natural ecology which promoted contrasting patterns of interaction with Mesoamerica.[16]

In some ways, however, northern Mexico and lower Central America are comparable. In both regions there is a dearth of archaeological material leaving great gaps in our understanding of pre-Columbian cultural developments. Both territories also indicate significant relationships with neighboring cultural traditions other than Mesoamerica: lower Central America with northern South America as the Intermediate Area, and northern Mexico with southwestern United States as the "Greater Southwest." In both cases, however, local, indigenous adaptations conditioned the basic form of local cultures.

We have already noted some of the salient geographical and climatic features of the Gran Chichimeca, as northern Mexico has sometimes been called. The dry, desert scrub and mesquite grasslands of the vast northern plateau are flanked on east and west by strips of savannah and forested mountain ranges beyond which lie dry coastal plains. Much of this territory was not suited for pre-Columbian agriculture because of the alkaline soils and generally scant and highly irregular pattern of rainfall. Consequently, the dominant pre-Hispanic culture pattern was that of seminomadic bands of hunters and seasonal gatherers who lived in caves, brush shelters, or skin-covered huts and existed on small game, fish, wild fowl, and wild plants, and whose meager material culture has not left many archaeological traces.

[15] Stone, *Pre-Columbian Man,* pp. 186–208.
[16] Palerm and Wolf, "Ecological Potential and Cultural Development," pp. 2–5; Pedro Armillas, "Review of *Handbook of Middle American Indians,* vols. 2, 3, 4," *American Anthropologist* 71 (1969):1198–1202.

In select areas, however, where rainfall and streams were more abundant, hunting and gathering was supplemented with horticulture and the seminomadic pattern altered toward a more settled village-farming orientation. Conditions most favorable for agriculture occur in southern Tamaulipas in the east, and, in the west, along the long, narrow strip of foothills between the western edge of the interior desert and the eastern slopes of the Sierra Madre Occidental, and along the lower courses of the streams which cross the Pacific coastal plain from the western slopes of the Sierra Madre.

In these areas simple agricultural efforts probably date from the Formative. Indeed, as we have seen, the caves and rock shelters of southern Tamaulipas have provided some of the earliest evidence of plant domestication and incipient agriculture known from Middle America. After 3500 B.C. such characteristic Middle American cultigens as beans, squash, and varieties of maize are also found in southwestern United States, and by the beginning of the Christian era clay figurines and pottery appear here, too; all of this indicates contacts with Formative cultures of Middle America. Although these materials probably diffused to the Southwest by a number of routes and at different times, the eastern mountain slopes and foothill corridor of the Sierra Madre Occidental almost certainly were involved. This supposition, in turn, suggests (although definite proof is lacking) that by the Late Formative scattered settlements of village-farmers existed on these foothills and slopes.

We noted in Chapter 6 the tenuous nature of such agricultural efforts unless irrigation is utilized. However, in the wake of the spread of irrigation, as early as the Mesoamerican Classic era, the settled, agrarian lifestyle characteristic of central Mexico developed successfully along this northern corridor and along the Pacific Coast as far as northern Sinaloa. Even more important for the establishment of an agrarian culture pattern in these regions was the support and control concomitant with the expansion of the Toltec state during the Early Postclassic when portions of the north can be considered a sociopolitical as well as an economic frontier of Mesoamerica.

The Chalchihuites culture of Durango, Zacatecas, and northern Jalisco, which dates from A.D. 250 to 1350 with the principle period of occupancy after A.D. 900, provides some indications of the life-style of these frontier farmers. Scattered at intervals along the eastern foothills of the Sierra Madre Occidental are fortified hilltop civic-ceremonial centers (La Quemada, Shroeder, the type site of Chalchihuite, and Zape are particularly notable) with masonry buildings, platform-pyramid mounds, colonnaded courts, and an occasional ball court (Figure 6.8). Smaller valley settlements cluster nearby, and terraced hillsides may give some indication of the nature of the agricultural base. Similar, though smaller and less elaborate, sites are situated on hills or hill slopes in the high mountains. A variety of artifacts including ceramics, clay figurines, stone and carved shell ornaments, mosaic mirrors, incense burners, obsidian flake blades, and cast copper bells used as beads also indicate affinities with central and western Mexican cultures.[17]

Furthermore, from about A.D. 500 or 600 to 1100 or 1200 new Mesoamerican traits appear in portions of the North American Southwest, particularly in the Hohokam culture of southern Arizona. Ceramic designs and motifs, shell carving, and a wide variety of stone objects suggest relationships particularly with Chalchihuites and contemporary cultures of the Pacific coast of Sinaloa. The appearance of ball courts, platform mounds of earth and adobe, various ceramic forms and motifs, copper bells, carved stone figures, cultivated cotton, loom weaving, mosaic mirrors or plaques inlaid with iron pyrite crystals, etc. reflect more widespread Mesoamerican traits. Some of these features undoubtedly were introduced as trade items, while others are local copies of Mesoamerican forms. Certain ceremonial activities and religious beliefs may have been introduced from the south, too. In general, this material indicates that Mesoamerican contact extended to the Southwest during Late Classic and particularly during Toltec times, and once again the longitudinal mountain valleys and foothills of the Sierra Madre Occidental provided a major route for culture transmission, although later, after A.D. 1200, contacts between the Southwest and Mesoamerica seem to have involved Sinaloan cultures west of the Sierra.[18]

Unfortunately, it is difficult to detail more precisely the exact points of contact between the Mesoamerican Chalchihuites frontier and the Southwest, for the intervening mountains, valleys, and desert basins of Sonora and Chihuahua are poorly known archaeologically. It is apparent, however, that this area presents a meeting and mingling of Mesoamerican and Southwest traditions, so that we can see a virtual continuum of sedentary agricultural life-styles stretching from central Mexico into the Southwest by at least A.D. 1000.

One village-farming culture pattern found along the sierra and reaching to the east into the desert basin of central Chihuahua was based, probably rather precariously, on riverine floodwater irrigation. Small villages are located at intervals along river terraces above the flood plains of the Río Florida and Río Conchos, southern tributaries of the Río Grande. Pit houses grouped around plazas, ceramic motifs, and other artifacts suggesting Southwest orientations are characteristic. More to the north, as the foothills of the Sierra Madre corridor fade into the mesquite grassland characteristic of the Chihuahua desert, a general pattern of

[17] R. H. Lister and A. M. Howard, "The Chalchihuites Culture of Northwest Mexico," *American Antiquity* 21 (1955):123–29; J. Charles Kelley, "Settlement Patterns in North-Central Mexico," in *Prehistoric Settlement Patterns in the New World*, ed. G. R. Willey (New York: Wenner-Gren Foundation for Anthropological Research, 1956), pp. 128–39.

[18] Albert H. Schroeder, "Unregulated Diffusion from Mexico into the Southwest Prior to A.D. 700," *American Antiquity* 30 (1965):297–309; Albert H. Schroeder, "Pattern Diffusion from Mexico into the Southwest after A.D. 600," *American Antiquity* 31 (1966):683–704; Erik K. Reed, "The Greater Southwest," in *Prehistoric Man in the New World*, ed. Jesse D. Jennings and Edward Norbeck (Chicago: Univ. of Chicago Press, 1964), pp. 175–91.

terraced hillsides below groups of small, crude, masonry hilltop structures may extend as far as the desert basins of northwest Chihuahua. However, platform-pyramids and elaborate stone masonry are missing now, as are such Mexican items as obsidian blades and certain ceramic forms. Instead, high in the cliffs of deep gorges and canyons of the sierra and outlying hills are large, often multiroomed cliff dwellings of stone masonry and adobe which resemble the "apartment" dwellings characteristic of the Southwest. In nearby valleys are terraces, probably used for agriculture. In the adjacent river valleys and extending east into the desert basins compact house ruins of adobe and stone are set on low hills near streams. Of these the site of Casas Grandes is the most elaborate and best known, and here, too, we may see something of the interaction linking Mesoamerica and the Southwest.[19]

Casas Grandes lies along the upper reaches of the Río Casas Grandes in the most fertile of the mountain valleys of the northern Sierra Madre. The early periods of the site correspond to the general pattern of multiroomed house clusters around a central court. During the eleventh century, however, Casas Grandes becomes increasingly Mesoamerican, with platform mounds and a ball court added to the Southwest-style apartment building complex. Possibly Casas Grandes became a Toltec outpost and regional trade center linking the Southwest and Mesoamerica. After about A.D. 1200 the community expanded rapidly until it boasted several thousand inhabitants, including craftsmen in shell work, turquoise, and copper. The surrounding valley, which was intensively farmed, was also carefully defended with outposts and communication towers. Shortly after A.D. 1300, however, the defenses failed and Casas Grandes was sacked and burned, perhaps by raiding bands of desert hunters and gatherers. In fact, most of the Mesoamerican-oriented cultures of northern Mexico disappeared during the fourteenth century, and the Mesoamerican frontier retreated to southern Zacatecas.[20]

Consequently, by the time of Spanish contact most of the north once more lay beyond the borders of Mesoamerican sociopolitical organization. Linguistic ties remained, however, for in contrast with lower Central America, where language provides a major basis for distinguishing Mesoamerican from non-Mesoamerican cultures, the major language families represented in northern Mexico are also found in Mesoamerica. These included Uto-Aztecan, to which Nahuatl, the language of the Mexica, belongs, and Otomanguean, an ancient Mesoamerican language family including, among others, the Zapotec, Mixtec, and Chorotegan languages.

[19] Kelley, "Settlement Patterns in North-Central Mexico," pp. 128–39; J. Charles Kelley, "North Mexico and the Correlation of Mesoamerican and Southwest Cultural Sequences," in *Men and Cultures,* Selected Papers, 5th International Congress of Anthropological Sciences, ed. A. F. C. Wallace (Philadelphia: Univ. of Pennsylvania Press, 1960), pp. 566–73.

[20] C. C. DiPeso, "Cultural Development in Northern Mexico," in *Aboriginal Cultural Development in Latin America: An Interpretive Review,* ed. B. J. Meggers and C. Evans, Smithsonian Miscellaneous Collections (Washington, D.C.: Smithsonian Institution, 1963), 146:1–16.

In subsistence economies and political organization, the peoples of northern Mexico formed self-sufficient and autonomous tribes and bands at the time of European contact. Very little can be said concerning the life-style of the small bands of wandering hunters and gatherers of the northeast, for most of these groups became extinct soon after contact and the historical accounts available to us are as scanty as the archaeological remains of the region. More information is available, though, for the northwest where the various peoples can be roughly grouped in terms of general geographical location and economic adaptation to coast and mountains (see Figure 6.8).

The most densely populated areas were located along the coastal flood plains of southern Sonora where the Mayo and Yaqui enjoyed especially favorable agricultural conditions. Along the desert coasts to north and south, however, seminomadic bands of hunters, gatherers, and fishermen, known collectively as the Guasave and Seri, practiced no agriculture at all. Farther inland a series of tribes (e.g., Huichol and Cora) who supplemented hunting and gathering with agriculture lived in the foothills and along the upper drainage systems of the major rivers flowing from the Sierra Madre to the Pacific. Still farther east in the mountain valleys and ridges of the Sierra Madre proper were such groups as the Tarahumara, Tepehuan, and Concho who ranged over a wide territory, living in widely scattered farmsteads or in caves excavated in cliffs. These people also tilled the soil but relied heavily, too, on hunting and gathering and moved seasonally from summer locations on mountain ridges, where small fields were tended, to winter shelter in lower altitudes. Finally, to the north and west were groups of Pima and the Opata, who practiced agriculture on the alluvial plains of intermontane basins until contact with Hispanic conquistadors set in motion an irreversible train of events that significantly altered their lives and the lives of all other indigenous Middle Americans.[21]

[21] Ralph Beals, *The Comparative Ethnology of Northern Mexico before 1750*, Ibero-Americana no. 2 (Berkeley: Univ. of California Press, 1932), pp. 93–225; Edward Spicer, *Cycles of Conquest* (Tucson: Univ. of Arizona Press, 1962).

part two

THE VICEROYALTY

OF

NEW SPAIN

8

The Spanish Legacy

The Reconquista

Before tracing the course of Middle American culture history after the
discovery of the lands of the "Indies" by Spain in the early sixteenth
century, it will be useful to review briefly some of the events and processes
that underlay the formation of the Spanish state and gave rise to a
distinctly Spanish culture. We can best begin with the years A.D. 711 to 718.
During this time much of the Iberian Peninsula was conquered by Muslim
armies sweeping in from North Africa, and most of the Christianized
peoples of Hispania, as well as thousands of Hispanic Jews, were incorporated into the life of the Muslim-controlled territory, now known as
Al-Andalus. Only in the Cantabrian Mountains of the far north did bands
of Christians remain outside Muslim political domination.

After an initial period of strong dynastic rule Al-Andalus fragmented
into numerous small, rival Muslim kingdoms. This divisiveness prepared
the way for the *reconquista* and the gradual reestablishment of Christian
control in the peninsula. From approximately A.D. 850 to 1250 armed
knights, rough shepherds, and soldier-peasants slowly and fitfully removed the skillfully cultivated land, enormous commercial wealth, and
heterogeneous peoples of Al-Andalus from Muslim suzerainty and returned them to the hands of various Christian nobles, churchmen, and
royal rulers. By 1250 only the small, mountainous kingdom of Granada in
the extreme south of the peninsula remained in Muslim hands. Most of

FIGURE 8.1 Iberian Peninsula, A.D. 1500.

Hispanic Iberia now was divided politically between the Christian king doms of Castile and Aragon (Portugal likewise began its separate course).[1]

The centuries of the reconquista posed numerous problems of control and organization for the rulers of the Christian kingdoms. Newly won frontiers had to be administered and defended. Services rendered in the cause by nobles, churchmen, and ordinary soldiers had to be rewarded. In some areas repopulation was necessary, although elsewhere Muslim and Jewish inhabitants stayed behind to share with the Christians in the processes of reorganization.

To provide for the government and defense of recaptured territories and as recompense for services, grants of recovered land, cities and towns, castles, revenues, and privileges were conferred by the kings of the realms to knights and nobles, to high churchmen and the churches and monasteries under their charge, and to religious-military orders and their directors. These recipients in turn bestowed grants and donations from their holdings to still others of lesser social station. The grants and donations varied greatly with respect to the conditions specified in their titles, but all required recognition by the recipient of the dominion of the overlord and the obligation that the former serve the latter with military service and other duties.[2]

If the grants rewarded the recipient with jurisdiction over towns he received rights to tributes and services from the inhabitants and, in some cases, usufruct of lands for a specified period of time, often the lifetime of the recipient or of the sovereign. In other cases the crown granted recovered lands with full rights of ownership and inheritance. For example, when the reconquista regained the rich lands of Andalusia, the king of Castile assigned the great estates of the Muslims to nobles, churchmen, and the religious-military orders, who in turn were free to maintain, sell, or exchange them as they wished. As a result of such land grants the church and the military orders acquired extensive holdings. The great landed estates or latifundia of the nobles grew, too, protected against fragmentation by the practice of entailed inheritance, that is, the passing on of an estate unbroken to the oldest son.

As the Muslim threat receded, the various grants and donations also provided the nobility and church with wealth and power to effectively challenge the growing control of the ruling houses of Castile and Aragon. Faced with this threat to their desired supremacy the sovereigns in turn sought support from the towns and cities. During the reconquista, particularly in depopulated frontier areas of the north, old and new municipalities were organized and recognized as separate legal entities. Charters granted by the king or another powerful lord stated the citizens'

---

[1] H. B. Johnson, Jr., "Introduction," in *From Reconquest to Empire*, ed. H. B. Johnson, Jr. (New York: Knopf, 1970), pp. 5–12; Jaime Vicens Vives, *Approaches to the History of Spain*, 2nd ed. (Berkeley: Univ. of California Press, 1970).

[2] Robert S. Chamberlain, *Castilian Backgrounds of the Repartimiento-Encomienda*, Carnegie Institution of Washington Contributions to American Anthropology and History vol. 5 (Washington, D.C., 1939).

obligations, which included payment of tribute, military service, and hospitality to the monarch in his travels through the realm. However, the artisans, farmers, craftsmen, and merchants of the towns generally enjoyed a great deal of freedom in determining their own affairs. The municipal officials were local men, elected by the heads of families and landowners, who received remuneration by keeping the fines paid for infractions of rules and by charging for their services.[3] The crown itself also granted special privileges and immunities from general laws and taxes to the municipalities as incentives for the establishment of communities in the often dangerous frontier and to gain a block of supporters to balance the growing arrogance of the rival nobility.

As a result of these advantages, by the thirteenth century the municipal burghers possessed considerable power in their own right. Consequently, during succeeding decades the crown, reversing its previous position, now moved to establish greater administrative and judicial control over local government (which also had become notably corrupt). *Corregidores* (royal agents) and other royal representatives were sent to towns where they first served alongside the regularly elected officeholders, but then gradually replaced them. By the late fifteenth century and the reigns of the "Catholic monarchs," Ferdinand of Aragon and his wife, Isabel of Castile, municipal affairs were thoroughly supervised and controlled by crown officials.

Building a Nation

The marriage in 1469 of Ferdinand and Isabel, which linked the royal houses of Castile and Aragon, was a significant step toward the eventual political unification of a virtually reconquered Spain. But unity did not come easily. Then as now the broken topography of the peninsula and the generally poor transportation and communication systems encouraged regionalism rather than centralization. Regional rather than national loyalties continued to be preeminent for many people, who identified themselves as Catalan or Asturian as readily as Spanish. Even in royal matters Castile and Aragon, though nominally united, continued separate governments.[4]

In their efforts to obtain a paramount position for the thrones, both Ferdinand and Isabel faced the problem of the nobles, who were veritable sovereigns over their own manorial tenants and were anxious to secure a dominant political status vis-à-vis the crown in order to consolidate their economic advantages. Many lords were securely ensconced with private armies on stoutly defended estates. However, by granting titles, assuring continued social prestige, and conferring various tax exemptions Fer-

[3] John P. Moore, "The Urban Heritage," reprinted in *From Reconquest to Empire*, ed. H. B. Johnson, Jr. (New York: Knopf, 1970), pp. 148–64.
[4] J. H. Elliott, *Imperial Spain, 1469–1716* (London: Edward Arnold, 1963); Jaime Vicens Vives, *An Economic History of Spain* (Princeton: Princeton Univ. Press, 1969).

dinand and Isabel lured numerous noble families into establishing a second residence in the cities where, presumably, they would fall more firmly under royal control. Nonetheless, through their extensive lands and privileges consolidated by intermarriages among their families, the nobles continued to form the social and economic elite of the country and to wield formidable political influence.[5]

It was also necessary for Ferdinand and Isabel to curb the immensely powerful church if they were to succeed in their efforts to insure the primacy of the crown. The church, whose bishops were also members of the nobility, was by now extremely wealthy in landed estates, over which it held full secular powers, and in important privileges, particularly tax avoidance. Since the church was far too influential for Ferdinand and Isabel to directly attack its secular powers, the monarchs attempted to achieve their aims by gaining control of appointments of bishops. But this was a prerogative which the Papacy also wished to claim, and Ferdinand and Isabel were soon engaged in a bitter defiance of Rome. Eventually the Catholic monarchs succeeded in obtaining a papal bull giving the crown the highly unusual right to royal patronage over all major ecclesiastical benefices in the recently conquered (1492) kingdom of Granada. Strengthened by this political gain, Ferdinand and Isabel were soon able to have their own nominees appointed to bishoprics in general and gained a measure of control over the wealth of the church.[6]

Christianity also served the interests of the crown as ideology. The Catholic faith had long provided a common unifying standard among the diverse peoples of Christian Spain, particularly during the earlier centuries of the reconquista when, with crusaders' zeal, the Christian armies had rallied, not only with the sword, but also with the battle cry of their patron saint, Santiago, St. James the Greater. Now once again, through the Inquisition, religion became a powerful uniting force, this time in the service of nationalism, and particularly in Castile.

As part of the program to purify the faith and strengthen the body politic the non-Christian minorities, in spite of their numerous and invaluable social and economic services as skilled artisans, farmers, miners, financiers, and managers, were given the choice of either conversion to Christianity or expulsion from the country. In 1502, after much bloodshed, unconverted Muslims were exiled from Castile and, later, from Aragon. A similar fate awaited the Jews, who for centuries had engendered the hatred of nobles and bishops and of the common people because of their role as rich moneylenders and tax collectors. In 1492 they, too, were given the choice of conversion or exile. Some elected to stay, but many thousands left.[7]

Thus at the beginning of the sixteenth century, having achieved significant checks on the divisive powers of the municipalities, the nobility, the church, and non-Christian minorities, Spain stood at the threshold of

[5] Elliott, *Imperial Spain*.
[6] Ibid.
[7] Ibid., pp. 95–99 and 299–303.

political and ideological accord. This unity was further consolidated during the next 100 years under the guidance of two great Spanish Hapsburg kings, Charles I (or, as Emperor of the Holy Roman Empire, Charles V), grandson of Ferdinand and Isabel, and his son, Philip II. This century was to see great libraries and universities flourish and to witness the greatest painters, novelists, and dramatists in Spanish history. It was also to be an age when the riches of a vast New World were to flow in a seemingly endless stream back to the mother country, now the heart of a great empire.

At the Crossroads

Nonetheless, in spite of growing national unity and pride, in the early decades of the sixteenth century the vast majority of the Hispanic population lived in poverty in an economically backward Spain. The seignorial patterns derived from the traditions of conquest and lordship which had guided her through the centuries of the reconquest continued to predominate, even as the Mediterranean and northern Europe became increasingly capitalistic and industrial.

In the heterogeneous social and economic world of the reconquista Jews, Muslims, and Christians had more or less divided the economic needs of the kingdoms among themselves. The Muslims were highly skilled agriculturalists, craftsmen, and artisans. Diplomatic and commercial dealings, tax collecting, money lending, medicine, and a wide variety of crafts were the province of the Jews. Many Christians, however, spurned the manual labor and money matters associated with non-Christians, preferring whenever possible the mobile life of fighters and shepherds, although in actuality many also tilled the soil. As the reconquista continued, some achieved the economic advantages and social prestige of administrators and landowners, too.[8]

Sheep-raising was an ancient tradition among the Hispanic Christians. As the reconquista opened new lands to the south, shepherds of Galicia and Asturias expanded their flocks in the broad pasture lands of central Castile and Aragon and in Andalusia. Unfortunately, this expansion of sheepherding also interfered greatly with agricultural efforts. In spite of a pressing need for grain, during the reign of Ferdinand and Isabel agriculture was virtually paralyzed as more and more land was removed from cultivation and restricted to pasturage.[9]

The Castilian sheep industry produced high-quality wools, and during the fourteenth and fifteenth centuries a thriving, highly lucrative export

[8] Vicens Vives, *Economic History;* Americo Castro, *The Structure of Spanish History*, trans. E. L. King (Princeton: Princeton Univ. Press, 1954); Thomas F. Glick and Oriol Pi-Sunyer, "Acculturation as an Explanatory Concept in Spanish History," *Comparative Studies in Society and History* 11 (1969):136–54.

[9] Elliott, *Imperial Spain*, pp. 106–9; Vicens Vives, *Economic History;* see also Charles J. Bishko, "The Peninsular Background of Latin American Cattle Ranching," *Hisp. Amer. Hist. Rev.* 32 (1952):491–515.

trade was established with the developing textile industries of Flanders and Italy. At the same time, although returns were high, relatively little capital was invested in the development of Spanish industry and commerce. Those individuals who acquired wealth preferred to use their income to strengthen their own economic and social positions instead. Similarly, rather than encouraging the growth of a sound agricultural and industrial economy at home, the crown of Castile bowed to its own pressing fiscal needs and continually emphasized the more immediate, but also more transient, rewards available from sheep-raising and the sale of wool to foreign markets. This seemingly short-sighted utilization of immediate wealth for immediate purposes with little long-range planning and investment was a policy that the crown had encouraged previously when it had consumed the rich lands and material wealth of Al-Andalus during the reconquista. It would take the same attitude toward the huge, but again fleeting, fortune in gold and silver soon to flow from the Americas.

The wealth from wool realized by the crown, the nobles, and other sheep owners also attracted Italian merchant-bankers eager to take advantage of new commercial opportunities and to exploit the rich luxury market that wool sales made possible. This orientation of Mediterranean (predominantly Italian) merchants towards Castile was part of a general reorganization of Mediterranean business from its traditional focus on the eastern Mediterranean to new potentialities in the western Mediterranean. By the mid-fifteenth century the traditional Italian commercial relations with the Byzantine Empire were less profitable as a result of various political readjustments. Concurrently significant adjustments occurred in the availability of gold, a crucial medium of exchange in the Mediterranean and European business worlds, which also caused realignments in commercial activity.

During the last centuries of the Middle Ages much of the gold available to Europe was carried across the Sahara from the interior of West Africa to coastal ports of North Africa whence it moved into the commercial cities of Italy and into the Muslim kingdoms of Al-Andalus. As Mediterranean trade expanded gold was in ever-greater demand, and by the fifteenth century the need had become critical. In the mid-fifteenth century Portugal effectively upset the traditional overland gold route by contacting the rich "Gold Coast" of West Africa directly by sea. European merchants, including those of Italy and of Castile, were hard hit by Portugal's new controls and the resulting collapse of the North African route and were shortly seeking new sources of wealth themselves. Castile eventually remedied this situation somewhat in the sixteenth century with the discovery of precious metals in the New World.[10]

Those who were to conquer Spain's New World and produce this new flood of wealth took with them to the frontiers of the Indies the seignorial

[10] E. W. Bovill, *The Golden Trade of the Moors*, 2nd ed. (London: Oxford Univ. Press, 1970); Johnson, *From Reconquest to Empire*, pp. 12–24; Charles Verlinden, "Italian Influences in Iberian Colonization," *Hisp. Amer. Hist. Rev.* 33 (1953):199–211.

social and economic traditions developed during the centuries of the Spanish reconquista.[11] In these new lands, as in Spain, social rank and hierarchy were to be of fundamental importance, and the winning of wealth and social position by bold conquest would be valued above that achieved by the settled, more mundane development of craft and agrarian skills. The challenge of a new frontier once more would allow full range to dreams, and sometimes actualities, of fortuitous social climbing in which an ordinary citizen, if he could obtain a horse and a sword, could become a noble gentleman and join the lesser aristocracy, perhaps eventually to boost his social fortunes still further by acquiring land and livestock and receiving tribute from a subordinate manorial peasantry. In like manner not only the dreams but also the ideals of the nobility would be shared by virtually all Hispanic men regardless of original station in life. The conquest and colonization of New Spain owed much to the popular beliefs that seemingly impossible feats in fact could be accomplished through sheer physical courage and will and that personal honor and dignity should be defended at all costs. These were values and attitudes which sixteenth-century Spain, particularly Castile, inherited from the centuries of the reconquista and then imbued in the new conquistadors who headed west to claim another land for God and king.

[11] Claudio Sánchez-Albornoz, "The Continuing Tradition of Reconquest," in *From Reconquest to Empire,* ed. H. B. Johnson, Jr. (New York: Knopf, 1970), pp. 41–54.

9

Exploration
and Conquest

The Early Spanish Main

In the early sixteenth century the dynamism of a Spain well on the way to political unity, fresh and restless from the conquest of the last Muslim state, and filled with the self-righteous zeal of renewed religious purity spilled over to the unknown lands which the voyage of Columbus had revealed to the west. Broadly viewed, this expansion, part of a general European growth, was the culmination of many pressures—economic, political, and ideological—which in sum turned continental Europe from its traditional southern orientation toward the Mediterranean and the Levant to face a broader western horizon across the Ocean Sea. It is no accident that the nations of the Iberian Peninsula, facing the commercial Mediterranean on one side, but also with a tradition of maritime experience on the stormy Atlantic on the other, played early pivotal roles in this new orientation and expansion.[1]

Spain's main observation post toward the Atlantic was the port of Seville, by the fifteenth century a vigorous polyglot commercial community and port. From here she engaged in her first step in overseas colonial ventures by acquiring possession of the Canary Islands which then became the jumping-off point for ships destined for the Indies to the west.

The focus of the first three decades of Spanish exploration in the Indies, from Columbus's first sighting of the Bahama Islands on October 12, 1492 until Cortés's entry into Tenochtitlán in 1519, lay in the islands

[1] J. H. Parry, *Europe and a Wider World, 1415–1715*, 3rd ed. rev. (London: Hutchinson, 1966); idem, *The Age of Reconnaissance* (Cleveland: World, 1963); Carlo M. Cipolla, *Guns, Sails and Empires* (New York: Pantheon, 1965).

and immediately adjacent mainland of the Caribbean Sea, the region commonly known to English speakers as the Spanish Main. The driving force behind virtually all Spanish activities in this region during this time was a single-minded obsession with discovering gold. Whatever other objectives may have motivated Columbus's voyages, there can be no doubt that he sought the precious metal. The following decades would see thousands of footloose adventurers and fortune hunters continue the search. Some were destined to die of hunger and disease. Others eventually returned to Spain disillusioned or disaffected. But still others met with great success and avariciously exploited both the human and natural resources of the islands and mainland shores.

The first New World settlements and the first gold rush occurred in the island grandly named by Columbus *La Isla Española* (later known as Hispaniola) where in 1496 the harbor town of Santo Domingo was successfully established as a base of operations.

Although the Spaniards did not realize it until far too late, the real wealth of Española lay not in its gold, but in its native populace. From the first days of conquest the indigenous Arawak provided for the Spaniards' needs with food, personal service, and gold, at first voluntarily, but soon by forced labor. However, the unaccustomed hard labor in the gold fields, disease, mistreatment, and malnutrition due to disruption of traditional hunting and fishing patterns rapidly took a toll of Indian lives, and the island's native population quickly declined. To meet the constant demand for labor, and in the continued search for new sources of gold, slave-hunting expeditions visited virtually all the Caribbean islands from the Bahamas to the Bay Islands of Honduras to Curaçao, shipping cargo after cargo of natives to Santo Domingo and also to newly discovered gold fields in Puerto Rico and Cuba.[2]

For awhile personal fortunes were realized from gold, four-fifths of which could be kept by the entrepreneurs while one-fifth, the "royal fifth," reverted to the crown. In actuality, though, both gold and natives were limited in quantity. After 1510 the gold return began to fall. By 1520 the gold placers were essentially exhausted and the native populace of the Caribbean islands also was virtually extinct. If the Spanish settlements on Española and the other major islands—Cuba, Jamaica, and Puerto Rico—were to continue, a new labor force and economic base had to be established.

The problem of labor was met by importing African slaves, increasingly sold in southern Europe in the fifteenth century and introduced into Española for use in the mines as early as 1501.[3] By 1518 importation of Negro slaves to the New World on a large scale was underway. The problem of a new economic base was solved by exploiting several new resources, primarily animal products and sugar cane. The export of hides, tallow, dried meat, and lard offered a substantial source of income,

---

[2] Discussion of the Spanish Main rests heavily on Carl O. Sauer, *The Early Spanish Main* (Berkeley: Univ. of California Press, 1966).

[3] Ruth Pike, "Sevillian Society in the Sixteenth Century: Slaves and Freedmen," *Hisp. Amer. Hist. Rev.* 47 (1967):344–59.

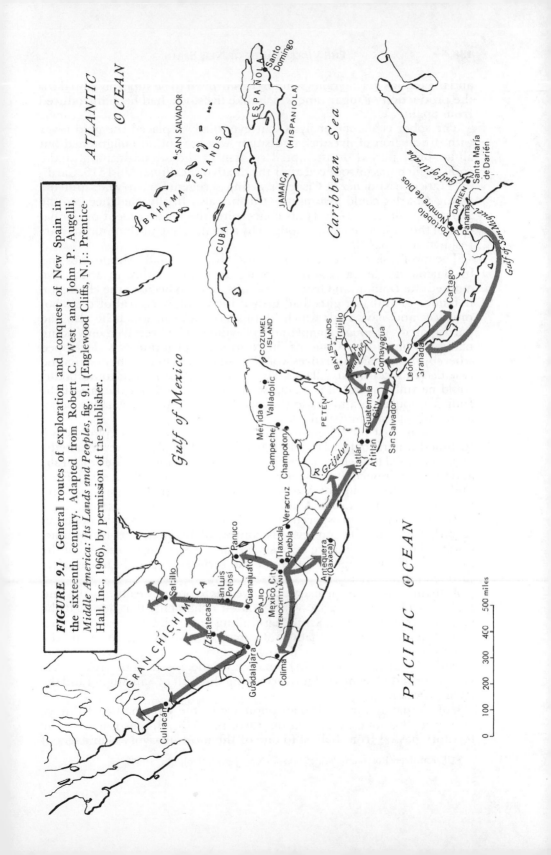

FIGURE 9.1 General routes of exploration and conquest of New Spain in the sixteenth century. Adapted from Robert C. West and John P. Augelli, *Middle America: Its Lands and Peoples*, fig. 9.1 (Englewood Cliffs, N.J.: Prentice-Hall, Inc., 1966), by permission of the publisher.

and the islands' fertile valleys and basins proved to be superbly suited for the production of sugar cane which, like livestock, had been introduced from Spain.

The sober economic analysis that eventually replaced the gold fever with production of livestock and sugar was part of an enlightened but all-too-brief period of attempted reform in the administration of the Indies which was introduced after the death of Ferdinand in 1516. Cardinal Francisco Ximenez de Cisneros, acting as regent for two years until the young Charles could assume the throne, also finally paid heed to the growing number of complaints concerning the mistreatment of the natives of the Indies which were lodged by a small group of Dominican friars resident in Española.

The most insistent protests were raised by Antonio de Montesinos and by Bartolomé de Las Casas, a young adventurer who, in 1522, also entered the Dominican Order. Las Casas, later to become the champion defender of Indian rights, had grown increasingly critical of the labor practices and slave raids which he observed and in which he also had participated. Although complaints to Ferdinand had received only nominal attention, under Cisneros, in contrast, a program was developed whereby the remaining natives would be relieved from further labors and resettled in free Indian villages. Unfortunately, before this undertaking could be fully instituted a smallpox epidemic wiped out the last of the Indian population and made the question of reforms in native policy academic, at least in Española.

The same lust for adventure and wealth that brought explorers and fortune-hunters to the islands of the Spanish Main also drew them to the adjacent mainland where operations centered about the Gulf of Urabá and the lands immediately to the west, known as Darién (Figure 9.1). Here under the supervision of Vasco Núñez de Balboa the first successful mainland settlement, Santa María del Antigua del Darién, was founded in 1510. Santa María prospered under Balboa's direction. Although his record is not entirely spotless, his control of his men and his conduct toward the native populace were such that the Spaniards resident at the town were freely supplied with food and services and could move safely throughout the area.[4]

As in the islands, the primary objective was to obtain wealth. To this end Balboa, seeking the source of the golden ornaments that adorned the natives, moved west from Santa María along the Caribbean coast and then turned inland, where his native informants spoke of a great sea on the other side of the cloud-covered range that rose from the interior. Consequently, in September of 1513 Balboa made his famous trek to the viewpoint at the top of a ridge overlooking the Gulf of San Miguel and the Pacific Ocean.

Unfortunately for the Indian populace of the Panamanian Isthmus, known at this time as Castilla del Oro, in 1513 administration of the territory passed from Balboa to one of the most unsavory characters of

---

[4] Cf. Kathleen Romoli, *Balboa of Darien* (New Jersey: Dolphin, 1953).

FIGURE 9.2 Balboa and his men first hear of the existence of the Pacific Ocean from the son of a Panamanian chief who has also presented the Spaniards with rich gifts of golden ornaments. From Theodoro de Bry, *India Occidentalis,* vol. 4, pl. XXI, 1594, reproduced in C. L. G. Anderson, *Old Panama and Castilla del Oro* (Boston: The Page Company, 1914), opposite p. 162.

the time, Pedro Arias de Ávila, better known as Pedrarias. Pedrarias quickly upset the peaceful relations with the natives, permitting murderous and destructive raids for gold ornaments and slaves. He also abandoned Santa María and, in 1519, established a new seat of government on the Pacific at a site on the Bay of Panama. A trail across the interior mountains linked the new town of Panama with the port of Nombre de Dios on the Caribbean.

As a result of continuing hostilities, the indigenous population of the Panamanian Isthmus quickly declined. As agriculture also ceased, the cultivated open savannahs that had covered extensive portions of the isthmus prior to contact gradually became overgrown with bush and then with trees. Much of the once prosperous province reverted to tropical forest, relatively uninhabited except for a few groups of Guaymí and Cueva-Cuna about whom we shall have more to say in later chapters.

By 1519 both the islands and mainland rim of the Spanish Main had fallen into a decline. In little more than one generation of Spanish occupation gold and natives both had been exhausted. Restless adventurers from Cuba had begun the entry into Mexico, and the first indications of Peru were reported by a party moving south from the isthmus. Men and capital were leaving the worked-out regions of former wealth for the new lands of greater promise. From now on Española and the other Caribbean islands and the Isthmus of Panama would be quiet backwoods areas, distant from the new centers of conquest and colonization. To be sure, the narrow crossing from Nombre de Dios, later replaced by Portobello, to the town of Panama would provide the link between Spain and Peru. But the isthmian region would flourish only periodically, when fleets from Spain would dock, and men and supplies destined for the south would be transported by mule train and fleets of canoes across the narrow width of land to resume their journey over the Pacific, while riches and passengers bound for Spain would pass in the opposite direction. During the long months between arrivals and departures of the fleets the isthmian towns would be inhabited by a relative handful of Spaniards, while the intervening distances fell under the control of rough predatory bands of escaped Negro slaves who sought refuge in the mountain fastnesses and terrorized travelers.

The Fall of Tenochtitlán

Most of the coast of Yucatán was discovered in 1508 by two adventurers, Yáñez Pinzón and Días de Solís. Yucatán again was skirted in 1517, and in 1518 an expedition under the direction of Juan de Grijalva ran out the coast of the Gulf of Mexico as far as the Río Panuco, returning with rich gifts of gold, silver, gems, textiles, and featherwork, and with tales of even greater riches farther to the west. Grijalva's expedition sparked still another venture, in 1519, captained by the dashing, valiant, and resourceful Hernán Cortés.[5]

Outfitted with 11 ships, 16 horses, and some 500 men, Cortés first landed at Cozumel Island off the east coast of Yucatán and then at the mouth of the Río de Tabasco, renamed Grijalva, where hostile natives engaged the Spaniards in fearful combat. Encouraged by his eventual victory and with his party sustained by gifts of food, women (including the famous Doña Marina), and golden ornaments, Cortés proceeded by ship to Veracruz (San Juan de Ulua).

Among the first matters of business was the formal founding of a town, Villa Rica de Vera Cruz, complete with governing council (*cabildo*) and magistrates. This seemingly optimistic move served two purposes. As had been the case in Española and in Darién (in turn based on precedent established during the Spanish reconquista), formal establishment of a settlement, no matter how roughly built, signified legal possession of the territory and the presence of the Crown of Castile. But Cortés made further use of the powers invested in what was now an independent

[5] Sauer, *Early Spanish Main*, pp. 129–30, 166–68, and 214–17.

Castilian municipality legally falling under direct protection of the crown: he had the newly appointed council or *cabildo* elect him governor and commander of New Spain. This move gave Cortés full legal authority and responsibility, subject only to the crown itself, for his decisions and actions in the new territory. He then destroyed the ships, saving only the rigging, sails, anchors, and other useful items. With this means of immediate retreat removed, Cortés and his followers were fully committed to their endeavor.[6]

Meanwhile, news of the latest "floating mountains" and foreigners to arrive from the east had reached Tenochtitlán. An incredulous and distressed Moctezuma, ruler of the Triple Alliance, immediately ordered the preparation of elaborate costumes and ornaments: lavish apparel of quetzal feathers, gold, silver, and jade of a quality fit for the gods, for such he suspected the light-skinned, bearded beings to be. The ancient Toltec myth of the exile of Topíltzin-Quetzalcóatl had prophesied the eventual return of the unfortunate hero-deity to reclaim his rightful lands and power. Now Moctezuma, mindful of the prophecy, sent ambassadors of highest rank to the coast to convey the precious gifts to the strangers and ascertain the situation. His apprehension was not much appeased by their report. The strangers, he learned, rode a species of huge, antlerless "deer" and were accompanied by large, fierce dogs. They had a contraption that spat fire and evil-smelling smoke with a deafening roar and shot out a deadly ball of stone. The newcomers were also extremely interested in gold.[7]

The presentation of Moctezuma's rich presents had, in fact, greatly excited the Spaniards' cupidity. Cortés soon learned that most of the wealth at Tenochtitlán had been obtained as tribute reluctantly paid by peoples such as the Totonac of Veracruz, where he was now located. Though fearful of the possible consequences, these tribute-payers were not disinterested in the possibility of striking a blow against their Mexica overlords. Accompanied by hundreds of native nobles, retainers, and porters to carry the baggage, guns, and munitions, Cortés and his party now moved inland toward the fortresses of Tlaxcala, which was defiantly maintaining its independence from Mexica control. Here again, after several days of battle, Cortés found willing allies. Accompanied by Tlaxcalans, the band of Spaniards then crossed the remaining mountains to the Basin of Mexico and the bustling, teeming city of Tenochtitlán where, on November 8, 1519, they were formally greeted with flowers and rich gifts by the highly apprehensive Moctezuma.

Rising from the waters of the great lake, the white-washed towers, temples, and general buildings of Tenochtitlán appeared to the amazed

[6] The formal establishment of Veracruz as an independent Castilian municipality and the declaration of the cabildo also were calculated to sever Cortés from his subordination to the Governor of Cuba, who had authorized his expedition to trade and search for wealth, but who had not included rights to conquest and settlement.

[7] Bernal Diaz del Castillo, *The Bernal Diaz Chronicles; The True History of the Conquest of New Spain*, trans. and ed. Albert Idell (Garden City, N.Y.: Doubleday, 1956); Miguel Leon-Portilla, *The Broken Spears* (Boston: Beacon Press, 1962).

Spaniards to be of another world, as indeed they were. They marveled at the lake and the network of canals filled with a multitude of produce-laden canoes approaching and leaving the city; at the causeways which were broad enough to allow the passage of several horsemen riding abreast; at the diversity of produce and crafts in the crowded, humming marketplaces; at the gleaming temple-pyramids and palaces of the city center where the newcomers were housed.

The Spaniards were well aware of their limited numbers, of their potentially helpless position in an island city that could easily become a trap, and of the uneasy tension surrounding them. After an anxious week they decided to strengthen their position by seizing the emperor, Moctezuma, himself. This bold stroke appeared to be successful. Moctezuma ordered that gold, royal finery, and all manner of precious things be brought as tribute to the powerful Spanish ruler to whom he now reluctantly declared submission.

Some five months after his arrival in the city, Cortés found it necessary to return to the coast for several weeks, leaving Pedro de Alvarado in charge of the forces at Tenochtitlán. Alvarado, as ruthless as he was handsome, permitted a surprise attack and massacre against Mexica warriors as they were celebrating a sacred festival (with Alvarado's prior permission). Consequently, when Cortés returned he found the Spaniards under siege within their palace quarters by enraged Mexicans who hoped to avenge their loss by starving the foreigners to death. During the savage attack that followed many Spaniards and the emperor Moctezuma were killed.

The situation was critical, and the only hope of survival lay in retreat. On the night of June 30, 1520 the Spaniards and their Tlaxcalan auxiliaries began to leave the city across the western causeway leading to Tlacopan. Alerted by the noise of the attempted crossing, the Mexica warriors swiftly attacked by canoe along the waterway, and before the *noche triste,* the Night of Sorrows, ended, three-fourths of the Spanish contingent was lost.

The survivors withdrew with difficulty to the safety of Tlaxcala, there to rest and to augment their forces with supplies, horses, and men newly arrived from Cuba. Using the rigging, sails, iron ware, and other materials saved at Veracruz, they also prepared 13 brigantines for use on Lake Texcoco, for it was now apparent that it would be necessary to control the waterways if the city were to be taken. By the end of May, 1521, the ships had been launched, and the final phase of the conquest of Tenochtitlán was begun.

In the interim following the Night of Sorrows an epidemic of smallpox, heretofore unknown in Mexico, struck Tenochtitlán, killing vast numbers. In spite of the ravages of the plague, when Cortés renewed his attack the desperate valor of the defending Mexica was such that, in spite of good assistance from the Tlaxcalans and support by the brigantines, the Spaniards were able to win the city only after long and bloody battle and by systematically reducing the central core of the metropolis to rubble.

Surrender of Cuauhtemoc + defeat of city

After nearly three months of ceaseless combat and house-to-house destruction, many of the remaining populace, ill and starved, swarmed across the lake in a desperate bid for survival. Among them was Cuauhtemoc, the last ruler of the Mexica empire, who was seized and surrendered to Cortés on August 13, 1521. The shouts and cries and din of battle that had continued unabated for over 90 days now ceased, and Tenochtitlán lay quiet in defeat.[8]

Mainland Expansion

With the fall of Tenochtitlán and the surrender of Cuauhtemoc, the Spaniards gained control of the heart of the Mexica empire. Now from all directions came envoys from native rulers to view the destroyed city and, with rich gifts, to pay their respects to the foreigners who were shortly to become the new rulers of the land. Similarly, bands of Spaniards were dispatched by Cortés to gain the subordination of major native cities and to seek the sources of Mexica gold. In this way various Spanish communities, new centers for expansion, were also established during the first years of the conquest; Colima, Antequera (Oaxaca City), Puebla, and Pánuco were a few of those founded at this time (Figure 9.1).

For the most part these early explorations and the subsequent colonization were oriented toward and most successful in the highly organized, densely populated, sedentary agricultural sphere of Mesoamerica, which is to say, central and southern Mexico and the Pacific side of northern Central America. Here the Spaniards found various forms of material wealth. In some areas, such as Oaxaca and Colima, gold, silver, or copper were discovered. Elsewhere even if precious metals were lacking Indian labor was abundant. There were large stretches, too, that were favored by a temperate climate which the Spaniards found suitable for European forms of agriculture and animal husbandry. In contrast, the more sparsely populated lands beyond the high-culture area of Mesoamerica generally were explored and conquered at a much slower pace. Some areas, particularly semiarid portions of northern Mexico, the humid, low-lying east coast of Central America, the swampy and forested Petén, and the interior and east coast of Yucatán, were really not effectively conquered at all.

Generally the conquistadors behaved with some restraint towards the natives they encountered, with, unfortunately, a few notable exceptions. The exploration and conquest of Guatemala by Pedro de Alvarado is one of these. With a large party of Mexica and Tlaxcalan auxiliaries, Alvarado

---

[8] Many factors contributed to the defeat of Tenochtitlán and the fall of the Mexica empire. For additional details see Percy Ashburn, *The Ranks of Death: A Medical History of the Conquest of America* . . . (New York: Coward-McCann, 1947); R. M. Denhardt, "The Equine Strategy of Cortés," *Hisp. Amer. Hist. Rev.* 18 (1938):550–55; C. Harvey Gardiner, *Naval Power in the Conquest of Mexico* (Austin: Univ. of Texas Press, 1956); Charles Gibson, *Spain in America* (New York: Harper & Row, 1966), pp. 35–36.

and his party moved south across the Isthmus of Tehuantepec into the highlands of Chiapas and Guatemala early in 1524. In spite of heavy depopulation and devastations caused by epidemics of cholera and small-pox which preceded him, he encountered stout resistance, particularly from the Cakchiquel and Quiché. Finally, however, with the burning of Utatlán, the Quiché capital, and the capture of Atitlán, the main Cakchi-quel redoubt, native resistance was effectively broken, although revolts erupted periodically thereafter. After these defeats Alvarado established his capital, Santiago de Los Caballeros de Guatemala (la Ciudad Vieja) at a former Cakchiquel town and continued his subjugation of the highlands. From this base he also explored to the south, founding the Spanish town of San Salvador in 1525 and moving into adjacent regions of northern Honduras.

Honduras was a region of considerable interest to the Spaniards since this mountainous country was rumored to be rich in gold and copper. Consequently, while Alvarado was battling his way through Guatemala, Cortés dispatched Cristobal de Olid by sea from Veracruz to the north coast of Honduras with instructions to explore this territory. Olid, how-ever, was fatally stabbed at dinner by rival conquistadors soon after his arrival. The successful plotters then established a new settlement, Trujillo, which for a decade or so was the only permanent Spanish community in Honduras. Similar rivalries for wealth and authority among conquistadors and colonists, exacerbated by the remoteness of the province from other centers of colonization and by stout Indian resis-tance, delayed further colonization of Honduras for several decades. But by 1540 placer mining of gold and vein mining of silver had begun near newly founded highland towns such as Gracias a Dios and Comayagua, and there was hope, never to be realized, that Honduras might become the major commercial center for all of Central America.[9]

The exploration and colonization of Nicaragua and Costa Rica was part of a general exploratory move that originated not from Mexico but from Panama (see Figure 9.1). In 1522 two conquistadors, Gil Gonzalez Dávila and Andrés Niño, had sailed north along the Pacific coast and briefly explored Nicoya and western Nicaragua. A year or so later Francisco Hernández de Córdoba conquered the Pacific plain of Nicaragua and established two major settlements, Granada and León, in the vicinity of the Nicaraguan lakes. From these bases additional explorations moved north into El Salvador, where Alvarado's settlers were encountered, and into Honduras, where they became embroiled in the complicated rivalries for Olid's claims. As in Honduras, settlement of western Nicaragua was seriously hampered for many years by political machinations between various factions of rival conquistadors and colonists. These rivalries,

[9] Robert S. Chamberlain, *The Conquest and Colonization of Honduras, 1502–1550* (New York: Octagon Books, 1966). For information on the conquest of Guatemala see Pedro de Alvarado, *An Account of the Conquest of Guatemala in 1524*, trans. S. J. Machie (New York: The Cortes Society, 1924).

FIGURE 9.3 Panorama of Trujillo from a seventeenth-century print. Reprinted, by permission of the Carnegie Institution of Washington, from Robert S. Chamberlain, *The Conquest and Colonization of Honduras, 1502–1550*, fig. 5 (Carnegie Institution of Washington, Publication no. 598, 1953).

however, did not deter the slaughter and enslavement of the once-numerous native populace.[10]

Nicaragua was also the jump-off point several decades later for explorations into Costa Rica, which had been bypassed by the Spaniards in the earlier years of conquest and colonization, although their diseases already had seriously reduced the warlike Güetar and many Talamancan groups. Following false rumors of rich gold deposits, exploratory parties finally moved into the mountainous interior of Costa Rica in the 1540s and again in 1560 to 1562. In 1563 the city of Cartago was permanently founded on a mountain-ringed highland basin, the *meseta central* or central plateau.

By the second half of the sixteenth century the main exploration of

[10] Hubert Howe Bancroft, *The Works of Hubert Howe Bancroft*, (San Francisco: The History Co., 1886), 7: chaps. 14, 20, and 21. Concerning the controversial Bancroft see Howard F. Cline, "Hubert Howe Bancroft, 1832–1918," in *Handbook of Middle American Indians*, ed. Robert Wauchope (Austin: Univ. of Texas Press, 1973), 13:326–47.

Central America was essentially completed. Although virtually all the territory of the Caribbean lowlands remained unconquered, major settlements had been established on the temperate plains and highland plateaus of the west. Here the native population was more or less subjugated, and the search was well underway for gold and silver. Gold-rich mountain streams were discovered in the north-central Nicaraguan highlands and, in Honduras, in the Olancho Valley, especially the Río de Guayape area. Large veins of silver were also located near Comayagua in the Tegucigalpa district of central Honduras. For a time these gold and silver deposits provided a substantial share of the mineral wealth of New Spain. By the end of the sixteenth century, however, the gold placers in Nicaragua were substantially depleted. Although the silver mines of Honduras continued to produce sporadically for the duration of the colonial period, the real mineral wealth of New Spain was not found here. It lay instead in the north, in the frontiers of the Gran Chichimeca.[11]

In contrast to the conquest of the settled populations of Mesoamerica, the three-pronged advance along the coastal plains and into the great central plateau of northern Mexico was slow and halting. Until 1540 little progress had been made, with the notable exception of the vicious conquest and subjugation of Michoacan, Jalisco, Nayarit, and Sinaloa in the 1530s by the infamous Nuño de Guzmán. During this campaign several towns were founded, including Culiacan and Guadalajara, which were to serve as jump-off points for further frontier expansion (Figure 9.1).

From approximately 1540 to 1600 the advance of the Spaniards into the northern plateau between the eastern and western Sierras was opposed by constant warfare with militant tribes of nomadic Chichimecs. However, in 1541 to 1542 the difficult defeat of a large group of Chichimec, stung to rebellion (the Mixton War) by the excesses of Guzmán's expedition, opened a route from Guadalajara into Zacatecas, leading in turn to the accidental discovery of vast silver deposits. By midcentury the resulting "silver rush" had opened a cart road, heavily defended against periodic Chichimec raids, between Zacatecas and Tenochtitlán-Mexico, the new capital that was rising from the remains of the Mexica metropolis. Over this road mining and settlers' supplies streamed in one direction, while in the other moved the flow of bullion that was to make New Spain the richest of Spain's colonies.

In 1563 extensive silver mines were opened in Guanajuato, and the Bajío was brought under Spanish control. By the end of the sixteenth century additional territory immediately to the north was similarly colonized, more silver deposits were opened, and the town of San Luis Potosí was founded. A series of rich lodes had also been located north of Zacatecas along the eastern foothills of the Sierra Madre Occidental as far as southern Chihuahua, and additional mines would be opened in coming centuries. By 1600 another line of silver and lead mines and associated Spanish settlements followed the grassy foothills of the Sierra Madre

[11] Robert C. West, "The Mining Economy of Honduras during the Colonial Period," in *33rd Int'l Congress of Americanists* (San Jose, Costa Rica, 1959), 2:767–77.

Oriental, with Saltillo as an important jump-off point. In short, by the end of the sixteenth century the great central plateau had been colonized at strategic points. In spite of these advances, however, other sections of northern Mexico, particularly portions of the coastal corridors of the northwest and the northeast and of the central desert, were not effectively colonized until much later, if at all.[12]

Devoid of gold, silver, and precious gems, much of the peninsula of Yucatán also was left unexplored and unpacified for many years while the Spaniards turned their interests to more rewarding areas. After the initial contacts in 1517 to 1519, Yucatán was ignored until 1527 when Francisco de Montejo landed on the mainland coast near Cozumel. Because of the nature of Maya sociopolitical organization at this time, Montejo and those who assisted him found conquest a difficult, at times seemingly impossible, undertaking. In contrast with the highly centralized Mexica empire where control of the key sociopolitical positions was accomplished by the capture of a single capital city, there was no single seat of native government in Yucatán. Instead, the political structure was fragmented among numerous small states. In the face of continuing guerrilla warfare, towns taken were hard to hold, and the Spaniards seemed unable to maintain a permanent foothold. Not until 1542 was a capital city, Mérida, finally established in the north, and only a few other Spanish towns were founded in the restless peninsula. Although the last great Maya uprising was finally subdued after hard campaigning in 1547, unrest continued for the remainder of the sixteenth century, and revolts erupted as late as the nineteenth century in the interior and eastern regions.[13]

[12] Philip Powell, *Soldiers, Indians and Silver* (Berkeley: Univ. of California Press, 1952).

[13] Robert S. Chamberlain, *The Conquest and Colonization of Yucatán, 1517–1550* (New York: Octagon Books, 1966).

10

Evolving
a Colonial Policy

Encomiendas and the New Laws

The decades succeeding the conquest of Tenochtitlán and the initial expansion of conquistadors throughout much of Mesoamerica were essentially a time of transition. Between 1521 and the beginning of the seventeenth century, Spanish interests in New Spain turned from the dramatic events of exploration and conquest to the more ordinary concerns of colonization. It was not long before the restless, indomitable, and fiercely independent conquistadors were replaced by steadier men and women whose tasks, though no less difficult, lay now in the more mundane affairs associated with the organization of a settled and viable Hispanic society. In this undertaking labor would be provided by the Indian, administration by the Spanish colonist, and a formal governing structure by the crown of Castile.

The most important institution during this transitional period was the *encomienda,* a system of control which allowed the relatively few thousand conquerors and settlers to effect the subordination of millions of conquered. In legal terms the encomienda was a grant bestowed either by the leader of a conquest expedition or, later, by representatives of the crown to former conquistadors, to leading colonists both lay and churchmen, and to virtually anyone else (including in some cases members of the Indian nobility) who had performed worthy service in the royal cause. The donation entrusted to the administration of the recipient a specified number of native families, generally inhabitants of one or more Indian communities, with the privilege to receive from them tribute in the form of labor, general services, and produce. In return, the *encomendero* was

148

obligated to "civilize" the natives under his charge by providing for religious instruction and discipline and was to furnish military service in the event of Indian uprisings and in the general defense.[1]

As we saw in Chapter 8, such grants were precedented in the various donations awarded in Spain during the reconquista. However, in contrast with many of the reconquista grants, encomiendas in the Indies did not confer legal ownership of land. Instead natives' traditional rights to land which they occupied and cultivated were to be respected, while lands which were not under Indian proprietorship and all subsoil rights were to be reserved to the crown. Nonetheless, in addition to their formal encomienda grants many encomenderos also claimed private land holdings which were worked by encomienda Indians.[2]

Because of the wealth and high social position which they conferred, encomiendas were highly desired, and claimants competed vigorously for the richest donations available in Mexico and Central America. The largest holding was awarded by Charles V to Cortés, who, as the newly titled Marques del Valle, acquired an encomienda encompassing the fertile Valley of Oaxaca and villages in Morelos, Puebla, and Veracruz—a total of 23 towns and over 200,000 Indians. Other large holdings involving tens of thousands of tributaries were granted in the densely populated basin and adjacent escarpment of central Mexico. But most encomiendas were much smaller, although grants of 2,000 or more tributary household heads were not uncommon. Some encomenderos acquired only a few poor hamlets with a mere handful of tributaries lost in the mountains.[3]

An encomienda frequently included one or more capital towns or elite centers where the hereditary native chiefs traditionally resided, together with subsidiary, dependent villages. Very often, too, the real work of labor direction and tribute collection was conducted by the local native aristocracy who had carried out such duties under the preconquest sociopolitical system and continued to be used in this capacity by the new Spanish overlords. The Spaniards themselves generally did not live in the native villages under their charge, but by royal order and their own self-regard as "superior" peoples in relation to the "inferior" native populace they congregated instead in the few widely spaced Spanish towns. From these more urban vantage points they administered the affairs of their rural holdings and in return received their livelihood from the food, firewood, textiles, and other products paid by their native tributaries.[4]

Most encomiendas remained significant to the end of the sixteenth

---

[1] Charles Gibson, *Spain in America* (New York: Harper & Row, 1966), chap. 3; Lesley Byrd Simpson, *The Encomienda in New Spain*, rev. ed. (Berkeley: Univ. of California Press, 1966); Charles Gibson, *The Aztecs Under Spanish Rule: A History of the Indians of the Valley of Mexico, 1519–1810* (Stanford: Stanford Univ. Press, 1964), chap. 4.

[2] Legal grants of unoccupied territory, called *peonías* and *caballerías*, were also awarded by the crown to ordinary foot soldiers and horsemen who did not receive encomiendas.

[3] Gibson, *Aztecs Under Spanish Rule*, pp. 61–68.

[4] Charles Gibson, "Spanish-Indian Institutions and Colonial Urbanism in New Spain," in *37th International Congress of Americanists* (Buenos Aires, 1969), 1:229–30; Dan Stanislawski, "Early Spanish Town Planning in the New World," *Geographical Review* 37 (1947):94–105.

century, although in more remote areas, such as Yucatán, they continued
to function for the duration of the colonial period. However, the encomienda as a dominant economic and especially sociopolitical institution
was undercut during the latter half of the 1500s by the crown's reaction to
the system and by catastrophic native depopulation.

The crown's concern was twofold. First and foremost was the growing
possibility that continued granting of encomiendas and their inheritance
in family lines would create a new colonial aristocracy which might effectively challenge the power of the crown. This problem only recently had
been somewhat ameliorated in Spain, and the crown had no intention of
allowing a similar threat to its control to develop in the Indies.

The crown's second problem involved the legal status of the Indians,
both those held in encomienda and others under direct crown control.
This concern also had political overtones and, in addition, reflected a
larger debate regarding the rights and abilities of the conquered native
populace in general.

In reference to encomiendas, the crown had been informed that the
Indians living under this system, instead of being protected and
"civilized," were often abused and virtually enslaved, especially by heavy
labor demands. However, from the onset of exploration in the New
World a royal tenet held that, with certain specific exceptions, the indigenous inhabitants of the new colonies were legally free subjects of the
crown.[5] As such they should not be bought and sold and were to be treated
humanely, although, like other free men, they were subject to payments
and labor for the public good. Therefore, concerned for the general
conditions of Indian life with particular reference to those living under
the encomienda system, and also with the political implications of the
encomiendas well in mind, Charles V in 1542 proclaimed the *Leyes Nuevas*
or New Laws. Among other provisions this legislation forbade enslavement of encomienda Indians and ordered the manumission of all enslaved natives whose owners did not possess legal title of possession (and
few did), regulated the amount of tribute required of Indians, and forbade the granting of new encomiendas and the inheritance of those
already existing.[6]

The colonists of New Spain, some 40 percent of whom in Mexico alone
were directly supported by encomienda income while many more benefited indirectly,[7] reacted so violently to these demands that the New Laws
were soon significantly modified. Inheritance of encomiendas by wife and
children was allowed, and loopholes were found to circumvent the prohibition of slavery. On the other hand, the Laws did reinforce royal

[5] Exceptions included rebellious natives taken in battle, cannibals, those who had committed criminal acts, and those who already were slaves within the native social system.

[6] Lewis Hanke, *The Spanish Struggle for Justice in the Conquest of America* (Boston: Little,
Brown, 1965), chap. 7; L. B. Simpson, "On the New Laws," in *Labor in the Spanish Indies*, ed. J.
F. Bannon (Boston: Heath, 1966), pp. 46–55.

[7] Charles C. Cumberland, *Mexico, The Struggle for Modernity* (London: Oxford Univ. Press,
1968), p. 71.

authority and in fact over the years many encomiendas gradually reverted to the crown as an aftermath of complicated inheritance regulations. In like fashion the enslavement of Indians was significantly reduced, and by the 1560s prohibition was generally effective in most areas, although enslavement of militant Chichimec continued on the northern frontiers.

In order to further assert imperial authority and limit the economic and political autonomy of the encomenderos another series of royal acts were promulgated after 1548 which effectively separated Indian labor from other forms of tribute and removed the regulation of vitally important labor forces from direct control by colonists, specifically encomenderos. Instead, from 1550 to the first half of the seventeenth century a system of state-directed labor service known as *repartimiento* was regularized. Under repartimiento a percentage (theoretically 4 percent) of the able-bodied tribute payers from an Indian town and its dependent villages formed a labor pool from which groups of workers were assigned on a rotational basis by a local state official to Spaniards who now had to make application for their services instead of enjoying direct access to native labor. There was little change, however, in the type of work done by native laborers who, as before, were consigned to heavy, unskilled jobs in the mines and in the construction of roads and municipal and church buildings, or served as field hands or as porters.[8]

The encomienda system in New Spain was also effectively undermined by tremendous demographic changes in the native population. In addition to the deaths caused by warfare, dislocation, and enslavement during the conquest years, epidemics of European diseases such as smallpox, measles, typhus, and what may have been a kind of influenza or typhoid fever devastated the Indian populace. Between 1519 and the beginning of the seventeenth century population losses of up to 90 percent occurred in some areas while other regions were completely depopulated. Absolute figures are somewhat tentative, but estimates suggesting a decline from about 25 or 30 million to about one million in Mexico during this time give an indication of the severity of the problem.[9]

This drastic contraction in Indian population reduced the amount of tribute obtainable from encomienda holdings, making them less profitable and thus less desirable as a source of income to colonists. On the other hand depopulation also placed a higher premium on available Indian labor and increased both the demand for repartimiento crews and abuses of the repartimiento system. The crown, recognizing that labor under repartimiento was still coercive and that there no longer were sufficient workers to meet all demands, gradually restricted the types of work for which the dwindling repartimiento crews could be assigned. By 1632 the

[8] Gibson, "Spanish-Indian Institutions," pp. 230–31; idem, *Aztecs Under Spanish Rule*, pp. 224–36.

[9] Gibson, *Spain in America*, p. 63; S. F. Cook and W. Borah, *The Indian Population of Central Mexico, 1531–1610*, Ibero-Americana no. 44 (Berkeley: Univ. of California Press, 1960).

job limitations had become so numerous that the repartimiento system was virtually terminated.[10]

The Labyrinth of Government

During the initial years of the new colony government was assumed by those locally on the scene—the conquistadors-encomenderos and the town councils or cabildos that they organized and on which they served. Each cabildo concerned itself with local matters of immediate interest, although as conquest turned to colonization the cabildo of Tenoch-titlán–Mexico City sought on some occasions to legislate for the entire colony. Indeed, during the first 50 years of settlement in New Spain the cabildos enjoyed their finest hour as effective instruments of secular authority. Membership at this time was highly esteemed and was determined by annual election from a slate composed of the heads of leading families. The elected officials included *alcaldes ordinarios* or magistrates, whose principal duties included jurisdiction in minor civil and criminal cases, and *regidores,* councilors who were concerned with such diverse matters as water supply, local taxes, garbage disposal, details of public ceremonies, military and police protection, impounding stray livestock, regulation of market prices, and general safeguarding of their own economic and political interests.[11]

As soon as the new colonies' viability became apparent, however, the Spanish monarchs acted to limit the influence of the cabildos (which also were dominated by encomenderos). Consequently, except for the most distant provinces where cabildos retained some degree of effectiveness, matters of local government were increasingly subsumed under royal authority, and the town councils became simply the receiving end of a chain of command that originated in distant Spain. In like manner, as we shall see, the crown maneuvered to control the activities of the church and to bring trade and commerce under its immediate direction. In other words, virtually all aspects of colonial life were soon subject to meticulous imperial administration.

This policy of centralization had begun with Ferdinand and Isabel, who vigorously attempted to implement a similar course among the Spanish kingdoms of the peninsula, but had been bitterly opposed by a number of well-entrenched power groups. To these embattled rulers the lands of the Indies offered pristine conditions for the realization of their ideals regarding proper government. Accordingly, the Catholic monarchs and their immediate successors acted with dispatch to limit the development

---

[10] Long after repartimiento had disappeared in other areas crews were assigned to the Desagüe General, an ambitious undertaking designed to drain the lakes in the central Basin of Mexico as a flood-control measure. See Gibson, *Aztecs Under Spanish Rule,* pp. 236–42.

[11] Clarence Haring, *The Spanish Empire in America* (New York: Oxford Univ. Press, 1966), chap. 9.

of any opposing power factions in Spanish America and to organize a chain of command which they could firmly control.[12]

The highest governmental position was, of course, the crown itself, specifically the crown of Castile, for from its inception the exploration and colonization of the Indies was considered a distinctly Castilian undertaking.[13] The crown would be advised in its colonial management by a specially appointed legislative and advisory body, the Council of the Indies, which was answerable to the monarch alone.

Although the council remained with the royal court and never was located in America, nonetheless it legislated all laws pertaining to the colonies, served as the highest court of appeals for colonial civil suits, controlled finance and trade, and supervised the church. The council also sent *visitadores* or inspectors to the Indies to investigate general conditions and particular problems, conducted the *residencia* or formal review of an official's conduct at the end of his term in office, and nominated the highest-ranking ministers to reside directly in New Spain: the *viceroy* and the *oidores* or judges of the *audiencias* or appellate courts.[14]

In many ways the viceroy and audiencias formed the equivalent on Spanish American soil of the crown and the Council of the Indies in the peninsula. The viceroy, as the highest official and direct representative of the crown, was responsible to no one save the king and the Council of the Indies. His numerous duties included responsibility for the welfare of the Indians, general supervision of treasury affairs, nomination of lesser officials, concern with military defense and civil order, and implementation of the rulings passed by the council and approved by the king. The viceroy's powers and responsibilities were further augmented by the fact that he could effectively reinterpret the content of royal legislation to make it more suitable for the colony and could refer orders which appeared inappropriate back to the council for reconsideration.[15]

More often than not some adjustment was necessary, for one of the major hindrances to the crown's realization of effective imperial rule was the distance, both geographic and conceptual, separating the Indies from Spain. Given the relatively infrequent sailing schedule and the duration of transatlantic crossings, two or three years could easily elapse between the time a letter was dispatched to Spain and, after due deliberations by the council, an answer received. Then, too, several exchanges might be

---

[12] The following discussion is derived from Gibson, *Spain in America*, chap. 5; Haring, *Spanish Empire;* R. M. Morse, "Toward a Theory of Spanish American Government," *J. of Hist. of Ideas* 15 (1954):71–78.

[13] Significant attempts were made to limit the settlement of the colonies to citizens of the kingdom of Castile and to channel the economic wealth of the Indies through the hands of Castilian merchants and entrepreneurs. The laws of the Indies also would be based primarily on the codes which guided Castile.

[14] Haring, *Spanish Empire*, chap. 6.

[15] Haring, *Spanish Empire*, chap. 7. Cf. Irving A. Leonard, *Baroque Times in Old Mexico* (Ann Arbor: Univ. of Michigan Press, 1959), chap. 1; Stanley J. Stein and Barbara H. Stein, *The Colonial Heritage of Latin America* (New York: Oxford Univ. Press, 1970), pp. 68–75.

necessary to settle the innumerable details of policy and to iron out misunderstandings which were frequently intensified by the council's misinformation regarding the realities of colonial life. Consequently, two sets of laws evolved: those formally enacted by king and council, and those by which the colonists actually guided their affairs. The viceroy stood at a major juncture in this legislative duality, for while awaiting guidance from abroad he also had to govern affairs as they stood, often by exercising his own judgment as to what aspects of existing formal legislation were applicable to the colonial situation and what de facto changes should be allowed.

In the exercise of his office the viceroy could be helped or hindered by the audiencias which, in addition to being appellate courts, were also viceregal advisory bodies. By 1550 four audiencias were recognized in the Viceroyalty of New Spain (Figure 10.1). One was centered in Santiago de Guatemala with jurisdiction over Central America from the Isthmus of Tehuantepec to Costa Rica.[16] Another was situated in Santo Domingo with jurisdiction over the Caribbean islands. A third, located in Guadalajara, held authority over the province of New Galicia. The fourth and most influential by virtue of its location in Mexico City maintained jurisdiction over Yucatán, Tabasco, and central and southern Mexico as far as the Isthmus of Tehuantepec.

Although their functions were initially judicial, the audiencias also served at times as executive and legislative bodies and gradually became powerful instruments of royal control. Not infrequently, however, the effectiveness of the audiencias and also of the viceroy was severely limited by conflicting spheres of influence. This was not coincidental. On the contrary, the crown took great care to develop an intricate system of overlapping authority and responsibilities at all stages of colonial rule under the theory that elaborate checks and balances would maintain the supremacy of the crown by assuring that no single colonial office or governing body could acquire ultimate decision-making responsibility. Unfortunately imperial control was achieved at the expense of effective colonial government.[17]

At the level of local government stood yet another combination of council and individual representative, the municipal cabildos and the district official known variously as the *corregidor, gobernador,* or *alcalde major,* who presided over their meetings. The local powers of the corregidor (and gobernador or alcalde major, whose duties all seem to have been essentially the same) were considerable. He was responsible for local law and order and for "justice" and general administration including tax and tribute collecting; he also directed the repartimiento. As with other royal officials, efforts were made to limit the possible abuse of this broad

[16] Panama was not included since it soon became part of New Granada and the Viceroyalty of Peru.

[17] Haring, *Spanish Empire,* chap. 7; Howard F. Cline, "Introductory Notes on Territorial Divisions of Middle America," in *Handbook of Middle American Indians,* ed. Robert Wauchope (Austin: Univ. of Texas Press, 1972), 12:17–31; J. H. Parry, *The Audiencia of Nueva Galicia in the Sixteenth Century* (Cambridge: Cambridge Univ. Press, 1948).

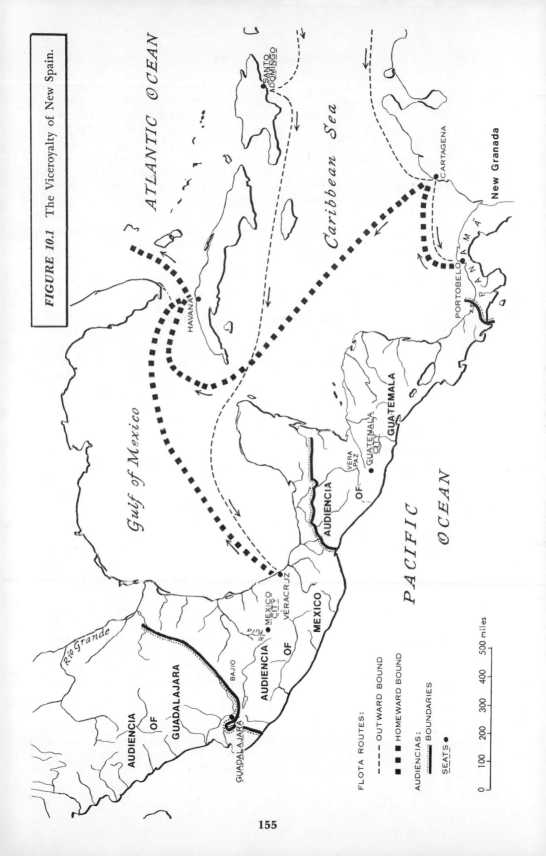

FIGURE 10.1 The Viceroyalty of New Spain.

ATLANTIC OCEAN

Caribbean Sea

Gulf of Mexico

PACIFIC OCEAN

SANTO DOMINGO

CARTAGENA

New Granada

PANAMA

PORTOBELO

HAVANA

GUATEMALA

GUATEMALA CITY

VERA PAZ

AUDIENCIA OF GUATEMALA

VERACRUZ

MEXICO CITY

Bajío

AUDIENCIA OF MEXICO

Río Grande

GUADALAJARA

AUDIENCIA OF GUADALAJARA

FLOTA ROUTES:
--- OUTWARD BOUND
■■■ HOMEWARD BOUND

AUDIENCIAS:
_____ BOUNDARIES

SEATS: ●

0 100 200 300 400 500 miles

155

range of power and authority by technically forbidding corregidors and similar officials to enter into commerce or other private business while in office, to marry within the district except by special royal permission, or to accept gifts or personal services from Indians. In actuality, however, the district officials were often too remote from higher viceregal or imperial authority for effective control. Consequently they enjoyed considerable leeway in the exercise of their office, and many became veritable local bosses, highhandedly exploiting natives and accruing personal advantages for themselves and their friends.

This self-serving attitude toward civil service derived in part from the reconquista when receipt of an exploitable public office was considered a reward and a spoil of war. More immediately, local graft and embezzlement by municipal officials helped to compensate for the frequent absence of fixed salaries.[18]

Mining, Merchants, and the State

The crown's policy of centralization for the Indies was also applied to trade and commerce. According to the mercantilist theories prevalent in Europe during the fifteenth and sixteenth centuries, economic relations between the mother country and her colonies were meant to enhance the profit, power, and prosperity of the former. The colony was to serve as a source of raw materials and of manufactured goods which were scarce or unavailable in Spain, was to provide a lucrative market for those products produced in Spain, and, most important, was to render tribute to the Spanish crown to defray Spain's expenses in Europe. Successful implementation of this economic strategy was thought to necessitate a monopolistic system of exchange between Spain and the Indies whereby privileged merchants in the colonies would deal only with select Spanish merchants and supply commodities only to Spain. However, for a number of reasons the actual application of the principle of monopoly was not successful, and the colonies were never financially profitable for Spain. Attempts to make them so helped only to further the economic ruin of the mother country and forced the colonists to take steps toward the development of a self-sustaining economy of their own.[19]

The central agency responsible for directing overseas trade and commerce was the House of Trade. Among other things, the House of Trade licensed ships, merchants, and emigrants bound for Spanish America and collected duties, taxes, and royal revenues returned to Spain by the colonies. It was also responsible for maintaining up-to-date navigational charts and the master map of the Indies and for training navigators for

[18] Haring, *Spanish Empire*, chap. 8; Gibson, *Aztecs Under Spanish Rule*, pp. 81–97.

[19] Gibson, *Spain in America*, pp. 101–6; Stein and Stein, *Colonial Heritage*, p. 46; Haring, *Spanish Empire*, chap. 16; Jaime Vicens Vives, *An Economic History of Spain* (Princeton: Princeton Univ. Press, 1969); J. H. Parry, *Trade and Dominion* (London: Weidenfeld and Nicolson, 1971), p. 25.

FIGURE 10.2　Early nineteenth-century view of Guanajuato, where rich silver veins yielded abundantly, particularly after the introduction of the patio process for refining silver by amalgamation with mercury. From H. G. Ward, *Mexico,* 2d ed., enlarged, vol. I (London: Henry Colburn, 1829), between pp. 120–21.

duty in these waters.[20] By its location in the port of Seville the House of Trade also effectively channeled the flow of trade through the hands of the wealthy and influential Castilian merchants of that city. These merchants were organized into a powerful, privileged guild which enjoyed royal favor and protection and a monopoly of legal trade privileges with America in return for capital for commercial activities.

During the early decades of colonial settlement virtually all material goods, including basic foodstuffs and manufactured items, were obtained from Spain. In return such items as sugar cane, dyes (indigo, cochineal, and dyewoods), hides, drugs and spices, and (most important of all) gold and vast quantities of silver were shipped to the mother country. In Europe the demand for precious metals was virtually inexhaustible as national economies expanded, while the Spanish crown carried the additional burden of financing the countless European wars in which Charles and his successor, Philip II, were involved as head of the Holy Roman

---

[20] Haring, *Spanish Empire,* chap. 16; Clarence Haring, "Trade and Navigation between Spain and the Indies: A Re-View, 1918–1958," *Hisp. Amer. Hist. Rev.* 40 (1960):53–62.

Empire. Consequently, although great amounts of wealth flowed into Seville from the Indies, both in coin and bullion and from the various taxes and fees the crown levied on steps in the refining, minting, and assaying of metal, more was always needed.

There were, of course, additional sources of royal revenue in the Indies. The tribute paid by all free adult male Indians furnished a respectable amount, a tithe of all agricultural and pastoral production was required, and the sale of public offices was encouraged.[21] State monopolies were placed on such diverse items as mercury and blasting powder (both critical to the mining process), salt, pepper, and stamped paper for legal documents. A number of taxes and duties also were levied on various commercial transactions as the crown sought to obtain sorely needed revenues.

To facilitate the collection of duties and to maintain control over commerce in general three Spanish American ports were officially designated as primary ports of entry for Spanish ships: Cartagena in Colombia, primarily a military base; Nombre de Dios (later replaced by Portobello) in Panama, for receipt of goods destined for Peru; and Veracruz in Mexico, the entryway to Mexico City and New Spain. Virtually all legal imports moved to these entry points. After a few weeks of furious trading when the fleet arrived, a select group of privileged colonial merchants (counterparts in the Indies of the merchants' guild of Seville) began the further slow dispersal of goods throughout the colonies. Generally, given the lack of good highways, the farther removed settlements were from these dispersal points the more difficult and expensive it was for them to obtain imported goods. Therefore, while communities in central Mexico were able to obtain supplies fairly readily, the Central American provinces and the more distant mines of northern Mexico stood at a considerable disadvantage.

The colonists' economic problems were compounded by the fact that as the Hispanic population of the Indies expanded during the latter decades of the sixteenth century, Spain was no longer able to provide sufficient quantities of luxury textiles, glass, paper, books, and other items necessary for an increasingly settled and civilized life. Although enormous quantities of wealth reached the mother country, Spain's fledgling industries were handicapped by the crown's expenditures in European wars, the system of latifundia, the monopolization of lands for sheep grazing, and a number of other factors. Goods were scarce both at home and abroad, and what supplies did arrive in Spanish America were prohibitively expensive as a result of numerous duties and taxations and because of a deliberate crown policy of undersupply at grossly inflated prices intended to maximize the profits accruing to Spain.[22]

Faced with these restrictions the colonists resorted to two main alterna-

---

[21] The directives for the freeing of Indian slaves issued in the New Laws may well have been determined at least in part by the fact that more free natives would mean more tribute. Gibson, *Spain in America*, pp. 106–8; Haring, *Spanish Empire*, chap. 14.

[22] Stein and Stein, *Colonial Heritage*, pp. 12–20; Vicens Vives, *Economic History*, pp. 411–55.

tives to obtain needed supplies: the development and expansion of local industry and trade with nations other than Spain. Textiles, wheat, oil and other foodstuffs, and various handicrafts which originally were imported came to be produced locally in increasing quantity after the midsixteenth century, so that by 1600 many of Spain's industries were paralleled in the Indies.[23] By the middle of the sixteenth century "illegal" commerce between Spanish colonists and English, French, and Dutch traders was also thriving, and contraband soon provided Spanish America with basic necessities. Contraband goods either were smuggled ashore at numerous isolated points along the undefended frontiers of New Spain or, with a few well-placed and readily accepted bribes, were easily entered through busy ports. Indeed, by the latter half of the seventeenth century illicit trade probably accounted for two-thirds of colonial commerce.

England, France, and the Netherlands were anxious to trade with the Indies on several counts. On the one hand they wished to obtain a share of Spanish American gold, silver, and raw materials to assist their own commercial and industrial expansion, and, on the other, harassment of Spain through her traffic with the colonies was a useful device within the context of European political maneuvering. With these goals in mind, English, French, and Dutch sovereigns also gave their blessing to freebooters who attacked the Spanish galleons on the high seas and turned the islands of the Bahamas and the Caribbean into veritable nests of piracy (see Chapter 13).

In response to this intervention Spain inaugurated the *flota* or convoy system for transoceanic travel. As early as 1525 Spanish ships laden with colonists and supplies bound for the Indies traveled together under armed escort. By midcentury a pattern was established whereby two fleets of some 60 or 65 ships departed Spain each year for the always hazardous two-month voyage. One fleet sailed in April or May bound for Veracruz; another departed in July-August with Portobello and Cartagena as its destination. Both fleets wintered over in the Caribbean and then, loaded with treasure, reassembled in the spring at Havana for the return trip (Figure 10.1).[24]

Non-Hispanic goods could also be obtained in the colonies through more official channels. Many of the supplies legally exported from Spain originated in other European countries. For many complex reasons Spain's home economy became increasingly upset, and the late sixteenth and first half of the seventeenth centuries were times of rampant inflation and commercial stagnation. It soon became cheaper for Seville's merchants to purchase many of the materials destined for the Indies (as well as for home consumption) from the growing industrial nations of north-

[23] Luxury textiles, particularly silks, were also obtained from the Philippines, and the Manila-Acapulco trade flourished, particularly around the turn of the seventeenth century. William L. Schurz, *The Manila Galleon* (New York: Dutton, 1939).

[24] Stein and Stein, *Colonial Heritage*, pp. 4–11 and 48–53; Philip A. Means, *The Spanish Main, Focus of Envy, 1492–1700* (New York: Scribner's, 1935); J. H. Parry, *Europe and a Wider World, 1415–1715*, 3rd ed. rev. (London: Hutchinson, 1966); Robert F. Marx, *The Treasure Fleets of the Spanish Main* (Cleveland: World Publishing, 1968).

ern Europe and from Italy rather than from Spanish industries. Consequently, while the House of Trade and thus the crown continued to collect the usual fees and duties and Spanish merchants still received income as shippers and expediters, much of the wealth earned from the sale of goods in the colonies was returned to foreign countries.[25]

In short, although she claimed the riches of the Indies for her own, Spain in effect became little more than a way station by means of which much of this wealth was channeled on to other European nations. Furthermore, while silver production in Spanish America continued throughout the colonial period, the seemingly inexhaustible flow of precious metal declined significantly by the midseventeenth century. As Spain fell into dismal economic ruin, Spanish America was forced to become increasingly self-sufficient and inward-oriented. The official trade continued, but to the increasing benefit of foreign rather than Spanish merchants. Spain's monopolistic structure remained intact, but monopoly no longer existed in fact.[26]

The Struggle for Souls

In the Indies, as in Spain, the institutions of church and state, religion and politics, were closely interwoven during the colonial era. The Spanish American clergy represented to those under their charge the temporal authority of the crown as well as the spiritual authority of Christian deities, while the crown encouraged clerical interests and enlisted the aid of the church to help effect royal policy. However, during the first 40 or 50 years of the colonial experience, religion as faith and ideology was uppermost, inspiring a vision of utopia among the first friars in the New World which, in its own way, was comparable to the imperial ideals of the crown and the dreams of wealth and adventure which motivated conquistadors and colonists during the Age of Conquest.

The utopian dream carried to New Spain by the first generation of Spanish clerics had its immediate genesis in the austerities advocated by fifteenth-century church reformers among the Franciscan, Dominican, and Augustinian Orders and also championed in the writings of various Renaissance humanists including Erasmus of Rotterdam and his friend, Sir Thomas More. Inspired by the virtues and nobility of the early days of the Christian faith, and repulsed by the worldliness, wealth, and general corruption of the contemporary church, these reformers urged a return to the principles which had guided the first Christians in their search for a perfect Christian life.[27]

[25] Stein and Stein, *Colonial Heritage*, pp. 17 and 45–46; Haring, *Spanish Empire*, chap. 16.

[26] Some of the factors involved in the decline of mining included greater production costs, heavier costs of local government, and labor shortages based on the severe depopulation of Indian laborers. Stein and Stein, *Colonial Heritage*, p. 38; D. A. Brading, *Miners and Merchants in Bourbon Mexico* (Cambridge: Cambridge Univ. Press, 1971), pp. 9–12; P. J. Bakewell, *Silver Mining and Society in Colonial Mexico* (Cambridge: Cambridge Univ. Press, 1971).

[27] George Kubler, "The Mendicant Contribution," reprinted in *From Reconquest to Empire*, ed. H. B. Johnson, Jr. (New York: Knopf, 1970), pp. 165–81.

The first friars in the Indies represented the more radical body of Mendicant reformers. They saw in the native populace of the New World a simple, uncorrupted, inherently noble people in an ideal setting in which to actualize their dreams of a return to the perfect Christian life. Of course, other Spaniards in the early decades of conquest viewed the indigenous population in a far different light, and although the general goal of Christianization was recognized by the conquistador-encomenderos, they did not wish to see their valuable tribute-payers and laborers become the exclusive property of idealistic missionaries. Not surprisingly, friars and encomenderos soon clashed head-on regarding treatment of the Indians.

As we have seen, the first disputations concerned the doomed natives of the Caribbean islands. The next centered on conditions on the mainland. The positions taken by the secular colonists were championed by Juan Ginés de Sepúlveda, a highly respected and learned scholar, who argued the case for the inherent inferiority of the pagan Indian and the doctrine of the "just war." This concept, developed during the European Middle Ages and put into practice during the crusades and the Spanish Reconquista, held that warfare was "just" if its aims were "just" and if it were conducted in a proper manner by legitimate authority. More specifically, a "just war" legitimized forced Christianization of non-Christian peoples by means of conquest and enslavement if the infidels refused to surrender and accept the faith peaceably. Proponents of this approach to the New World Indian also based their position on the Aristotelian doctrine which claimed that "rude" native beings were capable of only limited understanding and thus were inherently nonrational and inferior. Enslavement and obedience to "superior" civilized peoples (Christian Spaniards) was thus a natural and expectable condition for the Indian and, since he would be protected, Christianized, and civilized, one in his best interest.[28]

Once again the views of the Orders were put forth most aggressively and articulately by Bartolomé de Las Casas, who opposed the slaughter and enslavement of Indians on the grounds that they were not naturally inferior but, like Christians, were fully rational beings with souls who were also quite capable of being Hispanicized and of living as "superior" a life as Spaniards. As such, Indians were inherently free men with a right to human dignity and to all the guarantees of liberty and justice provided by the laws of Castile to subjects of the crown to which, in turn, all subjects then owed allegiance. Las Casas also argued that natives of the Indies could not be held accountable for initially refusing the Christian faith in the same manner as the Muslim of the reconquista since, unlike Moors who were long familiar with the tenets of Christianity yet deliberately chose to remain infidels, the Indians were ignorant of the "true faith" at the time of their conquest. Peaceful conversion rather than slaughter and slavery were, he felt, the only appropriate methods for Christianization under these conditions.[29] Vast quantities of ink were spilled over these and related questions in the first half of the sixteenth century, but while

[28] Hanke, *Spanish Struggle for Justice.'*
[29] Ibid.

philosophers, theologians, and other learned men heatedly debated the fine points of the issues, encomenderos, indignant at the "meddling friars," continued their exploitation of Indian labor, and Franciscan, Dominican, and Augustinian missionaries worked zealously to peaceably convert and "civilize" the native.

It was the practice for two or three of these energetic and intrepid friars to travel together unarmed to an Indian town and to begin their efforts with a baptism of as many as possible. Sometimes the friars met death at the hands of suspicious and defensive natives whose knowledge of Spaniards was predicated on less pleasant encounters with conquistadors and encomenderos. At other times the friars were more successful. Then a church and a monastery would be erected, frequently on the ruins of the native temples and often with the same stones in order to visually emphasize the replacement of the old religion by the new.

Very shortly the external forms of the Catholic religion, the rites and feast days of the church calendar with their panoply of attendant processions and celebrations, were solemnly observed and enjoyed by thousands of Indians. But the tenets of Christian faith were not as easily transferred. The vast majority of natives continued to hold to indigenous beliefs, but added and then inextricably interwove elements of Catholic Christianity with their own polytheistic world view to create, in effect, a wholly new religion.[30]

This religious syncretism occurred very quickly, in many areas within a generation or two, and was facilitated by similarities in cultural forms between Spanish Catholicism and the preconquest religions of Mesoamerica. For example, religious images, baptism, confession, the cross as a religious form, celebration of calendrically determined feast days, and fasting were common to both belief systems, although the content of these forms and the context within which they were used often differed greatly. Similarity in forms then led to ready combinations as, among other things, pre-Columbian religious shrines assumed Christian uses and identifications and native gods assumed the guise of Catholic saints or of the Virgin.[31]

In line with the utopian goal of establishing Christian communities and to facilitate missionary teaching, particularly in rural areas where Indians traditionally lived in scattered hamlets at some distance from the religious center, the natives were induced to congregate in new communities where an orderly arrangement of residential blocks and plazas centered around

[30] Robert Ricard, *The Spiritual Conquest of Mexico,* trans. L. B. Simpson (Berkeley: Univ. of California Press, 1966); Gibson, *Aztecs Under Spanish Rule,* chap. 5; Gibson, "Spanish-Indian Institutions," pp. 231–33.

[31] Most notable of these latter syncretisms was the reverence for the Virgin of Guadalupe, whose shrine was built immediately north of Mexico City on the spot where in preconquest times had stood a temple dedicated to Tonantzin, goddess of the earth and of fertility. Large pilgrimages to the traditional shrine of Tonantzin continued to be made after conquest to the Virgin of Guadalupe to whom traditional beliefs still clung. See Eric R. Wolf, "The Virgin of Guadalupe: A Mexican National Symbol," *J. of Amer. Folklore* 71 (1958):34–38. Cf. Munro S. Edmonson et al., *Nativism and Syncretism,* Middle American Research Institute Publication no. 19 (New Orleans: Tulane University, 1960).

FIGURE 10.3   A household shrine in the Petén, Guatemala. Offerings of maize kernels, food, and candles are placed before a saint's picture. Courtesy of Ruben E. Reina.

the church, monastery, and municipal buildings. These ecclesiastical *reducciones* or *congregaciones*, each named after a patron saint, were instrumental in introducing Hispanic customs and institutions in agriculture and political life as well as in religion, and the friars frequently became powerful voices in community affairs in general.

One of the most elaborate of the early community projects was organized by Bishop Vasco de Quiroga among Tarascans of Michoacan. From 1536 to 1565 Quiroga attempted to apply the ideals of the humanists to the organization and management of native communities in the Michoacan lake country, and his *pueblos* of Santa Fe became models for future missionary techniques.[32] A similar experiment was attempted about the same time but with less success by Las Casas and fellow Dominicans in a heretofore unconquerable region of Guatemala, known at first as *Tierra de Guerra*, Land of War, but after their ministrations renamed *Vera Paz*, True Peace. Las Casas was determined to silence his opponents

[32] F. B. Warren, "The Idea of the Pueblos of Santa Fe," in *The Roman Catholic Church in Colonial Latin America*, ed. R. E. Greenleaf (New York: Knopf, 1971), pp. 37–46.

by peacefully gaining the cooperation of rebellious natives and, contrary to the beliefs of the just war advocates, successfully converting them without resort to arms. His work made a definite impression even after the seemingly pacified inhabitants of Vera Paz finally rose in rebellion, murdered several friars, and returned to their traditional ways until militantly defeated by royal order.

The crown was among those who had watched the outcome of Las Casas's efforts with interest. Balancing religion with politics, the crown took something of a middle position between the demands of the friars and the arguments of the lay colonists. The New Laws sought to placate the former by officially outlawing slavery, while the recognition and official encouragement of the repartimiento took into account the need for Indian labor. This intertwining of religion and politics was a major characteristic of contemporary Europe and particularly of sixteenth-century Spain. The growth of a national identity under the Catholic monarchs had as its foil the antipathy of the Christian sectors of Spanish society toward Muslims and Jews. Under Charles V, Catholic Spain opposed Muslim Turks and, after subduing the brief Erasmian enthusiasm, spearheaded the counter-Reformation against Protestant developments in northern Europe. Imperial concern for the Christianization of the natives of the Indies was thus genuine and predictable, as was ecclesiastical concern for the implementation of crown policies.

The crown's religious obligations in Spanish America were all the weightier because of the royal patronage which a papal bull of 1508 had extended to the Indies from its original application to newly conquered Granada. Under this highly unusual arrangement, you will recall, the crown, as reward for efforts to propagate the faith (and for other more material favors to the Papacy), received the right to found missions, churches, and cathedrals; to nominate the recipients of all ecclesiastical offices, from Archbishop to the lowest parish priest; and in general to handle virtually all church matters, both great and small. In short, this privilege effectively placed the organization of the colonial church under the arm of the state which could veto papal bulls and briefs, decide which clerics should go to the Indies and which should be expelled, and allocate church revenues. Conversely, ecclesiastical influence was often felt in secular political affairs, and men of the cloth frequently held formal government office, including the post of viceroy.[33]

By managing the church the crown again hoped to limit the growth of an institution which otherwise might become sufficiently powerful to seriously challenge royal control. Ultimately the crown failed somewhat in this endeavor, largely because of long-standing traditions honoring ecclesiastical immunities which protected churchmen from many secular

---

[33] Gibson, *Spain in America*, chap. 4; Lesley Byrd Simpson, *Many Mexicos*, 4th ed. rev. (Berkeley: Univ. of California Press, 1967), chaps. 15 and 16; Stein and Stein, *Colonial Heritage*, pp. 75–76; Haring, *Spanish Empire*, chap. 10; J. Lloyd Mecham, "The Church in Colonial Spanish America," in *Colonial Hispanic America*, ed. A. C. Wilgus (New York: Russell & Russell, 1963), pp. 200–39.

FIGURE 10.4 Sandaled friar (left) and well-shod regular clergy represent the church in New Spain, an institution whose influence, both sacred and secular, reached virtually all sectors of society. Thousands of persons joined its ranks as ecclesiastics, and the numerous churches and cathedrals became the largest and most ornate structures in the land. From Brantz Mayer, *Mexico; Aztec, Spanish and Republican,* vol. II (Hartford: S. Drake and Company, 1852), opposite p. 250.

laws and judicial actions. Furthermore, by 1700 the church had become the largest landholder in the colonies and the major money-lending institution. As a result, its wealth and prestige became formidable and unassailable, and its ranks swelled with thousands of men and women who, by donning ecclesiastical garb, were guaranteed a measure of economic security and social prestige and a life free from demeaning manual labor.

In fact, by the latter half of the sixteenth century the ecclesiastical life-style in the Indies already had begun to deviate significantly from the utopian dreams of the first bare-footed friars. The Mendicants, however, did not relinquish their efforts willingly, and a bitter factionalism arose between the "regulars" or friars of the Mendicant Orders and the "seculars," especially the bishops, of the ecclesiastical hierarchy particularly over the issue of establishing secular dioceses in the missionlands. By this time the missionaries unquestionably enjoyed a high position and considerable influence among their native charges, and the crown (whose control over the regulars was somewhat tentative) was anxious lest they become too firmly established among the masses. Therefore, according to the imperial plan the regulars, who had arrived first in the Indies and had worked almost entirely with Indian communities, were to relinquish their missions to secular control after a designated period, usually 10 years. By this time it was judged that the work of conversion and "civilizing" should be completed and the natives should be ready to lead "useful" lives under the established episcopal structure of the church.

The regulars greatly resented this tactic. Among other things they did not enjoy seeing the fruits of their often difficult labors removed just as a measure of success was attained, not to mention the loss of property and income associated with monasteries. They also questioned the ability of seculars, who were few in number until after midcentury and who generally handled the Spanish congregations, to work with native converts.[34]

Unfortunately for the friars, the crown eventually decided in favor of the authority of the bishops, whom it could better control, over the Order clergy, whose subordination to the crown was less certain. Thus, except for the far frontiers where missions continued for several more centuries (see Chapter 13), by the late sixteenth century the official path of the church in the Indies was no longer that of zealous utopian missionizing, but that of the settled, established, realistically worldly ecclesiastical hierarchy.

In addition to its involvement in matters of high politics and finance, the established colonial church also assumed the vast responsibility for badly needed social services. The efforts of priests and nuns in education and charitable work contributed greatly to the profound influence that the church developed in the lives of both Indians and colonial Spanish Americans. Furthermore, in 1553 the University of Mexico was established by royal authorization primarily to prepare future churchmen. Here, as in other colonial universities, the curriculum centered on theology and canon law, but with additional chairs provided for medicine, astrology, and rhetoric. To prepare for the translation of the scriptures many scholarly clerics also became deeply involved in learning and recording native languages, literature, and pre-Columbian religions and sociopolitical forms, and much of our present knowledge of these matters is based on their records.[35]

In conclusion, during the somewhat chaotic sixteenth century in New Spain, as in the Indies in general, the groundwork was laid for three

[34] Gibson, *Spain in America*, pp. 77–78; Mecham, "Church in Colonial Spanish America"; A. Ennis, "The Conflict between the Regular and Secular Clergy," in *The Roman Catholic Church in Colonial Latin America*, ed. R. E. Greenleaf (New York: Knopf, 1971), pp. 63–72.

[35] Outstanding among these efforts is the work of such men as Toribio de Benavente (Motolinía), Bernardino de Sahagún, Jerónimo de Mendieta, and Diego de Landa. By the same token, however, much was irretrievably lost by the destruction of native books and documents through the ravages of conquest and by overzealous missionaries.

centuries of settled colonial life. At the top of the institutional order stood the crown, sacrosanct symbol of unity, determined at all costs to maintain a centralized structure within which church, trade, and secular government would be strongly controlled and the affairs of the colonies in general tightly administered to the ultimate glory of the mother country. To this end masses of reports, legal briefs, invoices, and other documents were laboriously prepared in duplicate and triplicate and duly moved about by a veritable army of lawyers and bureaucrats who worked assiduously both in Spain and in the Indies to maintain the proper flow of legalities through the proper channels. At the bottom of the order was the Indian, the indispensable labor source without whose efforts the colonies literally could not continue, and whose soul was to be saved even if his body was frequently lost. Between crown and natives stood the colonists, lay and ecclesiastical, firmly battling crown and each other for control of Indian labor and lives and adroitly managing their affairs around and about and in spite of, yet with deep respect for, the flood of directives from above. Both crown and colonists found their tasks greatly complicated by the tremendous decline in Indian population, and we have seen some of its consequences in the preceding pages. The shape of colonial society and the relationships between land and people that evolved in New Spain during the next 100 years, and to which we shall turn next, reveal more of the effects of this demographic catastrophe and also indicate some solutions to the problem.

11

Land and Society

Spaniard and Indian

While basic economic, political, and religious institutions were crystallizing in New Spain, adjustments also were occurring on the level of social organization as conquering Spaniards, Negro slaves, and indigenous peoples created a new colonial society. This new society derived its structural and conceptual roots from the social systems of both late-medieval Castile and preconquest Mesoamerica. Its dynamics lay in the biological and cultural interactions among Indian, Spaniard, and Negro.

The social behavior and attitudes of the "white" or Spanish component of Spanish America were patterned after the principles underlying the position of the nobility in Spain. Superior social quality in both cases was predicated on lineage and traditional family status and on the criterion of "purity of blood," essentially a religious concept purporting a background of proper Christian orthodoxy untainted by Jewish or Muslim affiliation. In Spain purity of blood was essential for membership in religious and military orders, artisans' guilds, and municipal bodies, and for receipt of university degrees. Similarly in Spanish America, where "purity" was extended to also include freedom from Indian or Negro blood, this criterion was a legal prerequisite for high positions in ecclesiastical and university posts and in the merchants' and miners' guilds.

In both Spain and Spanish America monetary wealth traditionally did not influence social position and, in fact, many members of the lesser Spanish nobility, the knights or *hidalgos*, were often in serious financial straits. Although in the later colonial centuries a favorable economic position often aided substantially in the attainment and maintenance of high social position, social status was not regarded in economic terms. It was, instead, a matter of family position and religious orthodoxy and of individual pride and self-perception.[1]

These attitudes were automatically assumed by any and all Spaniards who reached the Indies regardless of their original social standing. To be sure, many of the early conquistadors and later settlers represented families of nobility, particularly of the lesser, hidalgo, rank, but many colonists also derived from more common origins as craftsmen and peasants. In the Indies, however, as members of the conquering society, even the humblest emigrant automatically regarded himself as a superior member, a "noble," of colonial society. As such he also felt entitled to an "honorable" life free from demeaning manual labor or technical crafts, which would be performed instead by those of darker skin who had been conquered.

Just as the Spanish element of Spanish American society assumed, and was legally confirmed in, the favored status of a kind of colonial nobility regardless of original station, so the Indian component, as we have seen, was assigned the lower category of conquered laborer. For the vast majority of the native population this position did not differ greatly from their status within the preconquest social systems. Although much remains to be learned concerning the sociopolitical structures of preconquest Mesoamerica, it is clear that in both the Mexican-Guatemalan highlands and the Maya lowlands society included an upper strata of nobility who controlled political and religious institutions and were supported with produce and labor by a lower class of commoners, most of whom were agriculturalists, and by serfs and slaves, generally war prisoners, debtors, or criminals.

In central Mexico, where the social hierarchy contained additional complexities, the nobility was composed of *tlatoque* (sing. *tlatoani*) or hereditary rulers of small states (tributaries in turn to the highest tlatoani, the Mexica emperor), assisted by various lesser nobles or *pipiltin* who held numerous bureaucratic posts. The pipiltin were almost equaled in status by certain high-ranking commoners, including the pochteca, full-time skilled craftsmen, and especially professional warriors. In contrast, most commoners, the *macehualtin* (sing. *macehualli*) were rural farmers, organized into ranked and stratified kinship-based territorial groups called *calpultin* (sing. *calpulli*) which composed the fundamental unit of social structure. The calpulli functioned as the basic unit of land tenure, tax payment, and corvée labor, formed a military company with its own training institution, and conducted common religious ceremonies. Often the members of a calpulli constituted a rural settlement.[2]

The sociopolitical hierarchy of the lowland Maya was less complex and

---

[1] J. H. Elliott, *Imperial Spain, 1469–1716* (London: Edward Arnold, 1963), pp. 52–55 and 99–105; Lyle N. McAlister, "Social Structure and Social Change in New Spain," *Hisp. Amer. Hist. Rev.* 43 (1963):350–57.

[2] William T. Sanders and Barbara J. Price, *Mesoamerica* (New York: Random House, 1968), pp. 152–59; Jacques Soustelle, *The Daily Life of the Aztecs* (Stanford: Stanford Univ. Press, 1961), chap. 2.

seems to have been composed of large unilineal descent groups whose hereditary rulers governed political, military, religious, and long-distance trading activities. Many of the 16 small states in Yucatán at the time of the conquest were ruled by a hereditary ruler, the *halach uinic,* assisted by local town leaders or *batabs* who either inherited their position or were appointed by the halach uinic. The batabs, who were responsible for local judicial, military, and executive functions, were assisted in turn by various lesser officers.[3]

Within the colonial social system the position of commoner (macehualli) persisted, although, as a being new to European eyes, the Indian was also accorded a separate legal status as a perpetual minor and ward of the crown. As such he was entitled, at least theoretically, to special protection under the patronage of encomenderos, missionaries, and various civil officials. Special courts of law were established for Indian litigation, and natives were officially exempted from certain taxes. On the other hand, most Indians paid tribute (primarily money and maize), in itself a mark of subjugation, and were forbidden to conclude legal contracts, to purchase wine, to wear Spanish dress or ride saddled horses, or to bear arms; in other words, Indians were not to assume the cultural paraphernalia that defined the nobleness inherent in being Spanish.[4]

However, these stipulations did not apply with equal weight to all natives. Although the vast majority assumed the low social status assigned to them, an Indian nobility also continued to exist. This group was recognized as such by the crown, exempted from tribute payments, and granted special hereditary privileges including permission to own and travel in properly accoutered carriages with retinues of Indian servants, to carry swords, and to wear Spanish dress. The highest rank of the colonial native nobility was held by hereditary leaders termed by the Spaniards *caciques,* who probably represented at least in part a continuation of the preconquest tlatoque, batabs, and halach uinics. Lesser members of the colonial nobility or *principales* also may have had general connections with the preconquest pipiltin and their Maya counterparts (members of the caciques' families were also designated principales).[5] For many, however, a position within the native colonial nobility probably was a step upward socially. This mobility in turn derived from a process of

[3] Ralph L. Roys, *The Political Geography of the Yucatan Maya,* Carnegie Institution of Washington Publication no. 613 (Washington D.C., 1957), pp. 1–10; idem, *The Indian Background of Colonial Yucatán* (Norman: Univ. of Oklahoma Press, 1972).

[4] McAlister, "Social Structure and Social Change," p. 358; Charles Gibson, *Spain in America* (New York: Harper & Row, 1966), p. 114; Magnus Mörner, *Race Mixture in the History of Latin America* (Boston: Little, Brown, 1967), pp. 45–47; William L. Schurz, *This New World* (New York: Dutton, 1954), pp. 54–61.

[5] McAlister, "Social Structure and Social Change," pp. 358–59; Ronald Spores, *The Mixtec Kings and Their People* (Norman: Univ. of Oklahoma Press, 1967), chap. 5; Charles Gibson, "The Aztec Aristocracy in Colonial Mexico," *Comp. Studies in Soc. and Hist.* 2 (1960):169–96; William B. Taylor, *Landlord and Peasant in Colonial Oaxaca* (Stanford: Stanford Univ. Press, 1972), chap. 2.

political Hispanization that became particularly characteristic of Indian communities after the midsixteenth century.

During this time, in order to hasten Christianization and facilitate tribute collection, a concerted effort was made by the crown to resettle any scattered native families who did not reside in traditional native community centers or in the newly organized ecclesiastical congregaciones into similarly organized civil congregaciones.[6] In addition, a policy of separation was decreed which attempted to prevent moral corruption and physical abuse of native peoples by forbidding the settlement of "undesirable" non-Indians in any Indian community. (In Spanish towns Indians were to reside in their own sections or barrios.) Consequently the local government of native towns fell to the Christian Indian elite, although a Spanish corregidor held regional jurisdiction and linked Indian government with the Spanish hierarchy.

In spite of local leadership the organization of native town government, particularly on the upper levels, basically followed the form instituted in Spanish cities. A gobernador, a powerful community position often held by a cacique, presided over the municipal council or cabildo staffed by various notables. The cabildo differed from its Spanish counterpart primarily in the exceptional florescence of lesser posts which accompanied the usual roster of alcaldes and regidores. Indeed, the number of scribes, native police, judiciary members, and *mayordomos* or custodians of municipal lands, herds, and markets grew so numerous and the details of community government were handled with such rigorous exactitude for Hispanic forms that it has been suggested that native community government of the late sixteenth century served as a new channel to absorb the energies of the elite which in preconquest times had been directed toward the conduct of warfare and organized religious ritual, activities the conquest had effectively ended.[7]

This strongly Hispanicized community organization also served as an intermediary or buffer between the Spanish overlords and the lower class of native residents, for to some extent it protected the domestic life-styles of the indigenous population from direct Hispanic contact. At times, however, caciques and principales became oppressive agents themselves, demanding extensive personal services and acquiescing in their own self-interest with the aims and demands of corregidors, encomenderos, and other Spanish administrators. As a result, it was not uncommon for the ordinary residents of sixteenth-century native towns to find that their heaviest overseers were the elite of their own society.

[6] Howard F. Cline, "Civil Congregations of the Indians in New Spain, 1598–1606," *Hisp. Amer. Hist. Rev.* 29 (1949):349–69; L. B. Simpson, *Studies in the Administration of the Indians in New Spain,* Ibero-Americana no. 7 (Berkeley: Univ. of California Press, 1934), part 2.

[7] Charles Gibson, "Spanish-Indian Institutions and Colonial Urbanism in New Spain," in *37th International Congress of Americanists* (Buenos Aires, 1969), 1:233–34; idem, "The Transformation of the Indian Community in New Spain, 1500–1810," *J. of World Hist.* 2 (1955):581–607.

The Castas

Naturally, in a situation of conquest and colonization miscegenation was common. Many factors encouraged this intermingling, particularly during the early years of the colonial experience when few eligible Spanish women emigrated to the Indies. Yet the crown was seriously concerned that the colony be stabilized by married settlers. Since even married Spanish men headed for New Spain frequently neglected to take their wives with them, the crown in 1501 reluctantly permitted formal marriage between Spaniard and Indian. This intermixing was further encouraged when marriage was made a requirement for receipt of an encomienda and for various local government posts.[8]

The first generation of Spanish-Indian offspring (*mestizos*), who often were of legitimate birth or if illegitimate were frequently recognized by their fathers, generally found a cultural identity and social acceptance with one or the other of the parental groups. However, as the number of mestizos continued to increase, both absolutely and in relative terms as Indian population began its drastic decline, the social and legal status of the mestizo became increasingly marginal.

The primary stigma that those of Spanish and Indian parentage now came to suffer, and that removed them from acceptability as members of Spanish society, was the taint of illegitimacy unrelieved by recognition by the father. Though in the early decades of the sixteenth century intermarriage between Spaniard and Indian was not opposed, as a colonial Spanish elite began to evolve and as the number of Spanish women in the colony increased, the prestigeful criteria of family ancestry and purity of blood necessitated that marriages be contracted between families of proper pedigree. Few "honorable" Spaniards now took native wives, although concubinage with Indian women continued to be widespread. The offspring of these extramarital unions found it increasingly difficult to be received as "whites" and often did not wish to be classed as conquered Indian. Consequently, the latter half of the sixteenth century witnessed the growth of a sizable population of persons who had no legal place within the official system of "white" and Indian.[9]

The Negro had also entered the stream of miscegenation at an early date, and the mixed, increasingly "marginal" population included mulattoes of white-Negro ancestry and zamboes, or Indian-Negro offspring, plus those derived from further intermixing between mestizo, mulatto, and zambo. (All these peoples of mixed background are frequently discussed as a single category termed *castas*, but sometimes termed mestizos in a broad sense. However, it is useful to restrict the term mestizos to

---

[8] C. E. Marshall, "The Birth of the Mestizo in New Spain," *Hisp. Amer. Hist. Rev.* 19 (1930):161–84; Mörner, *Race Mixture,* pp. 21–29 and 35–40.

[9] Mörner, *Race Mixture,* pp. 42–43; Stanley J. Stein and Barbara H. Stein, *The Colonial Heritage of Latin America* (New York: Oxford Univ. Press, 1970), pp. 60–64.

Spanish-Indian offspring, and to distinguish them from those whose ancestry contained an element of Negro admixture.) In addition to illegitimacy, those with real or imputed Negro ancestry also carried the social disparagement, low legal status, and cultural prohibitions associated with slavery (even if they themselves were free) and with "impure" blood, for Africans were not generally associated with orthodox Christianity. Consequently those of African descent were considered fit only for unskilled labor, and along with Indians also paid tribute.

However, though they, too, were tribute payers, Negroes, zamboes, and mulattoes did not enjoy the protection and humanitarian efforts made on behalf of the Indian by the crown and church. On the contrary, the panacea for the troublesome problem of Indian labor, both in its moral aspects and in its failure through depopulation, was sought in the use of Negroes as slaves.

Considered physically repellent and morally and psychologically undesirable, Negroes, whether slaves or freedmen, were restricted in their movements and type of dress and were forbidden to carry arms, to participate in public or church offices, or to intermarry with either Spaniards or Indians. Alliances between Spaniard and Negro remained relatively infrequent, but in spite of legal restrictions miscegenation between Negroes and Indian women was soon quite common. Unhappily, although the offspring of these unions assumed the legal status of the mother and thus were considered technically free, they were never free of the social stigmas and legal constraints placed on their African ancestry.[10]

By the late sixteenth century the presence of a sizeable population of persons who were not accorded acceptable status within the formally recognized social hierarchy was creating problems. In spite of the crown's policy of separation it became increasingly difficult to prevent free Negroes, mestizos, and other mixed peoples from settling in or near Indian villages, particularly as native lands became available through depopulation. As Indian villages became in fact more and more open to other social segments, mestizos and other members of the castas gradually assumed positions of authority within the native community.

Simultaneously, the protective influence of the native cabildos began to wane. As the Indian population declined the plethora of municipal posts decreased significantly. Furthermore, the remaining community officials now were forced to assume a larger tribute burden, for the number of laborers or monetary tribute levied on the village usually reflected a rate obtained during more prosperous times with no adjustment for population loss. To be sure, after the midseventeenth century the Indian population slowly began to increase (its numbers perhaps augmented largely by mestizos who had adopted Indian life-styles), but the overall population level remained far below that of the early sixteenth century. The void in community life created by Indian depopulation (and other reasons for

[10] David H. Davidson, "Negro Slave Control and Resistance in Colonial Mexico, 1519–1650," *Hisp. Amer. Hist. Rev.* 46 (1966):235–53; Mörner, *Race Mixture*, pp. 16, 19, 30, 40–41, and 53–70; Schurz, *This New World*, chap. 5.

vacating that we shall note shortly) was filled to a large extent by castas. As a result, during the seventeenth century New Spain's rural society increasingly came to be dominated by members of the mixed population.[11]

Many mestizos and other castas did not settle in the countryside but instead sought economic support and social anonymity in the cities, especially in Mexico City. Here some found employment as domestic servants or as low-paid workers in various trades and industries. Yet many positions were prohibited to mixed and especially Negroid persons, so that castas were often forced to turn to peddling, begging, prostitution, and crime. To compound difficulties, as Spaniards and the mixed population increased the native agricultural laborers declined and basic foodstuffs and other goods frequently were in short supply in the city, especially for the disadvantaged. The severity of economic problems and the socioracial inequalities and tensions between the relatively few, inordinately wealthy, white upper class and the miserable masses of mixed and native poor erupted in frequent street brawls, rebellions, and violent riots that made life in Mexico City and other Spanish cities an often difficult affair, particularly for the ill-fed, poorly housed, and impoverished lower classes.[12]

Given this situation, those castas who were unable to find a suitable livelihood in the cities resorted to the frequently illegal hand-to-mouth existence of vagrants and vagabonds. From the sixteenth century on, colonial society contained thousands of these wanderers who, as bandits, beggers, gamblers, and thieves, traveled about from place to place living by their wits and by occasional employment. Their numbers were augmented by natives fleeing their increasingly disrupted communities and the growing tribute burdens and by unruly bands of escaped Negro slaves or *cimarrones* who roamed and settled the long stretches of otherwise uninhabited rough country between towns where they survived by tending small subsistence plots and robbing passing travelers and mule trains.[13]

In reaction to the growing numbers of mixed peoples, and especially to those who were poverty-stricken "rougher" elements, the white elite grew more and more defensive as the colonial centuries advanced. Yet at no time was social mobility completely frozen. Individuals frequently successfully "passed" from a lower social category to a more advantageous one, for in the increasingly biologically mixed colonial society phenotypic appearance soon became quite unreliable as an indicator of a man's

[11] Gibson, "Transformation of the Indian Community," p. 597; Mörner, *Race Mixture*, pp. 97–100.

[12] Poor transportation systems further aggravated effective distribution of the harvests, and speculators frequently worked to corner the market in order to raise prices. Chester L. Guthrie, "Riots in 17th Century Mexico City," in *Greater America, Essays in Honor of Herbert Eugene Bolton* (Berkeley: Univ. of California Press, 1945), pp. 243–58; Marshall, "Birth of the Mestizo," pp. 179–80; Charles C. Cumberland, *Mexico, The Struggle for Modernity* (London: Oxford Univ. Press, 1968), p. 57.

[13] Mörner, *Race Mixture*, pp. 75–78; Eric R. Wolf, *Sons of the Shaking Earth* (Chicago: Univ. of Chicago Press, 1959), chap. 11; Marshall, "Birth of the Mestizo," pp. 176 and 181–82; Gibson, "Transformation of the Indian Community," p. 597.

ancestry and thus of his social and legal status. Sociocultural characteristics such as language (native or Spanish), dress, community identification, occupation, wealth, education, and a person's self-identification became more important criteria for determining social and legal position. As a result, an individual of Indian biological ancestry might successfully claim legal status as a mestizo, and in so doing avoid tribute, while ambitious mestizos and light-skinned mulattoes could be absorbed into the social ranks of the whites, sometimes by purchasing a special license declaring them legally white. On the other hand, of course, social mobility could also lead in the other direction. As a result of economic hardships or other strokes of personal bad luck individuals of Spanish ancestry might become culturally affiliated with the mixed population, and mestizos could fall into the poverty that characterized the Indian masses.[14]

Officially passage to the Indies was open only to religiously "pure" citizens of the kingdoms of Castile and Aragon, and, in fact, the preponderance of conquistadors and colonists seem to have derived from southern Spain (Andalusia, Estremadura) and from the Castilian provinces in central Spain.[15] In order to maintain religious orthodoxy, colonial security, and economic monopoly the crown prohibited the free entry of non-Christians and foreigners into Spanish America. Nonetheless, non-Spanish Europeans were present. For example, crown restrictions did not apply as firmly to skilled artisans, engineers, and others with technical training considered useful for the colonies. Similarly, among the friars men of Italian, Flemish, French, German, and other nationalities could be found. The de facto opening of the trade monopoly brought additional non-Spaniards to the shores of the Indies. Mention can be found in the documents of the times of various other individuals—Protestants, Jews, Genoese, Englishmen, Irish, and Germans—who settled quietly and unobtrusively in the interior cities or hung about the seaports as deserters or abandoned seamen. In general, while foreigners always composed a small minority in the colonies, they were more numerous than has frequently been thought. Here again the prohibitory laws could, as usual, be successfully circumvented.[16]

Towns, Trades, and Transportation

Although the members of the castas suffered legal and social discrimination, colonial society was greatly dependent on their services, particularly in areas such as smuggling and bootlegging, which were technically illegal but necessary activities if basic economic needs were to be met in the face

[14] Mörner, *Race Mixture,* pp. 68–70.

[15] Irving Leonard, "Colonial Society," in *Colonial Hispanic America,* ed. A. C. Wilgus (New York: Russell & Russell, 1963), pp. 240–41; Elliott, *Imperial Spain,* p. 67; George M. Foster, *Culture and Conquest* (New York: Wenner-Gren Foundation for Anthropological Research, 1960), pp. 30–32.

[16] Leonard, "Colonial Society," pp. 244–46; Mörner, *Race Mixture,* pp. 12–13; Schurz, *This New World,* chap. 6.

of tight mercantilist restrictions. Many of the castas' economic contributions were more respectable, too. It was largely through their efforts that the numerous trades and crafts which sprang up in Spanish towns and cities to help meet the colonists' material wants were sustained. Those relatively few mestizos and mulattoes (and also urban Indians) who were so fortunate as to be gainfully employed frequently worked as glassmakers, carpenters and cabinetmakers, tailors, bakers, leatherworkers and shoemakers, and smelterers and ironsmiths. The craftsmen associated with these and similar trades were usually organized into licensed guilds or *gremios,* more or less closed mutual aid, religious, and economic organizations which, among other things, regulated production, controlled production quality, collected the necessary taxes, and maintained an exclusivist policy which assured control of the guilds by whites.

Guild members were categorized as apprentice, craftsman, or master-craftsman. Although most guilds admitted castas (and some, such as the saddlers and embroiderers, admitted natives) into the apprentice ranks, relatively few mixed bloods or natives succeeded in attaining the position of master craftsman with authority to open a shop of one's own. Gremio officials generally reserved this status for whites only. Some guilds, such as the potters, prohibited membership at any rank to those with Negro ancestry, while still more exclusive groups, for example, the painters, dyers, veterinarians, and gold and silversmiths, preferred white members in all categories. In contrast to many of the craft guilds, a form of mass production, used most notably in the manufacture of tobacco products and of textiles, depended entirely on non-Spanish labor. Working behind locked doors, under deplorable sweatshop conditions of exploitation and oppression which were notorious even then, mulattoes, Negroes, and many Indians, often prisoners from the local jails, were forced to labor in the noxious textile *obrajes* of Mexico City, Puebla, Tlaxcala, and other towns.[17]

The obrajes and gremios produced most of the crafted and manufactured products consumed locally (although well-to-do Spaniards frequently preferred the status and sometimes the quality accruing to imported European goods). For the most part they did not supply markets at any great distance from the town or city center. This localization of urban production was due to several factors. For one thing, the institutions which commanded most attention in the Spanish city tended not to be economic but rather religious and political, since these were the spheres of life which most strongly identified Hispanic pride, honor, and social superiority and which regulated the orderly, civilized, Christian life that urban living typified for the Spaniard.

The physical layout of Spanish American urban centers further illustrates this point. With few exceptions the focus of the cities was not in

[17] Leonard, "Colonial Society," pp. 252–54; Charles Gibson, *The Aztecs Under Spanish Rule: A History of the Indians of the Valley of Mexico, 1519–1810* (Stanford: Stanford Univ. Press, 1964), pp. 243–46 and 397–402; Gibson, *Spain in America,* pp. 127–28; Cumberland, *Mexico,* pp. 102–4.

terms of economic production.[18] Instead the heart of the Spanish community centered about a central plaza surrounded by municipal offices and the church or cathedral, together with important commercial (but not craft) buildings. The residences of the leading merchants, important government and church officials, and other members of the social elite also stood nearby. Beyond this central nucleus lay the homes and workshops of the socially (and economically) less well-to-do, including the streets where the various guild members lived and worked. At the very outskirts of the community sprawled the squalid wards or barrios of the native and castas poor.[19]

The hazardous and inefficient transportation system of the colonies also limited distribution of raw materials and locally produced goods and encouraged regional isolation rather than trade and travel. Most land routes were merely narrow trails along which (weather permitting) freight was moved by slow trains of mules and burros (muleteering was a common occupation for Negroes and castas) and, in the worst stretches, by human carrier. Even major cart roads were rough and difficult to travel, and passersby were subject to attack by numerous bandits and highwaymen in the long empty stretches between inhabited towns. Because of the attendant risks, goods transported any great distance over land (for example, from Mexico to the distant highlands of Central America) were generally much costlier than locally produced items. Therefore, although some raw materials and finished products were shipped considerable distances, most notably cacao, cochineal and indigo, hides, cotton, and textiles, towns tended toward craft self-sufficiency, and each produced essentially the same manufactured goods. This duplication, in turn, further obviated the need for wider exchange systems.[20]

In like manner the residents of towns and cities were largely fed by produce grown in the nearby countryside by Indians or, in the tropical lowlands, by Negroes. For the Indian and rural castas maize, beans, squash, maguey, and other indigenous foods grown in small subsistence plots continued to provide the bulk of the diet, although European vegetables such as onions and garlic were readily accepted and in the tropical lowlands bananas, plantains, and sugar cane also became staples. However, other European foods, most notably barley and wheat, were rarely consumed by Indians, though their labor provided vast quantities of this staff of life for the Spaniards and mestizos of the towns and cities.

By 1600 the cultivation of wheat had introduced the simple, ancient Mediterranean *ard* or wooden "scratch" plow, drawn by a team of oxen. The addition of plow agriculture and of more elaborate canal and reservoir irrigation practices to the various slash-and-burn techniques and simpler irrigation patterns of ancient Indian usage extended cultivation,

---

[18] Only the mining communities and the seaports had fundamental economic reasons for existing. Gibson, "Spanish-Indian Institutions," pp. 235–37 and 239; idem, *Spain in America*, pp. 122–26.

[19] Gibson, *Spain in America*, pp. 125–26; Foster, *Culture and Conquest*, chap. 4.

[20] Lesley Byrd Simpson, *Many Mexicos*, 4th ed. rev. (Berkeley: Univ. of California Press, 1967), chap. 14.

FIGURE 11.1 Plundering robbers were an all-too-common menace along the roads of New Spain. Additional color was added by the rough life of Indian, Negro, and *casta* muleteers engaged in freighting. From John Frost, *The History of Mexico and its Wars* (New Orleans: Armand Hawkins, 1887), p. 23.

especially of wheat and maize, into grass-covered areas which in pre-Hispanic times had had relatively less agricultural significance. The introduction of domestic animals also broadened the productivity of land areas beyond that which had been known before. The rural native population quickly added chickens, sheep, and pigs to their pattern of domestic production and used the burro as a beast of burden. Commercial raising of the larger class of livestock—horses, cattle, and mules—was primarily in the hands of whites and other non-Indians who also owned vast flocks of sheep since, unlike cultivation, livestock raising was not considered menial for whites. Large herds of these animals soon provided meat, beasts of burden, tallow, and especially hides for export.[21]

Unfortunately, the introduction of domesticated animals and plow agriculture also contained negative features. During the middle decades of the sixteenth century livestock expansion was virtually out of control.

[21] François Chevalier, *Land and Society in Colonial Mexico,* trans. A. Eustis, ed. L. B. Simpson (Berkeley: Univ. of California Press, 1970), pp. 50–114; Gibson, *Aztecs Under Spanish Rule,* pp. 300–327 and 344–47; Clarence Haring, *The Spanish Empire in America* (New York: Oxford Univ. Press, 1966), chap. 13; Bailey W. Diffie, *Latin-American Civilization, Colonial Period* (New York: Octagon Books, 1967), chap. 5.

FIGURE 11.2 The markets of Mexico have precedence in both western European and pre-Hispanic Mesoamerican practices. During the colonial period, as in later years, they generally were held daily for larger towns and cities, and weekly or biweekly for smaller settlements. From Carl Sartorius, *Mexico. Landscapes and Popular Sketches* (London: Trübner and Co., 1859), opposite p. 19.

In southern and central New Spain herds of cattle not only ravaged unoccupied pasture lands, but also raided the maize fields of Indian villages. Over-grazing of hillslopes, plowing of lower slopes (steep slopes of necessity remained under tlacolol cultivation), and deforestation through the heavy cutting of timber for colonial building and for the production of charcoal, which the Spaniards and then the Indians used for heating and cooking, resulted in sheet erosion and gullying which quickly turned extensive highland areas of central Mexico and Central America into agricultural wastelands which still exist today.[22]

The foodstuffs and other resources produced by the hinterland were exchanged for urban craft products in the urban marketplace. (Significant quantities of maize also were obtained as part of Indian tribute.) In order to better control and guarantee a supply of products for urban consumption public fairs or markets were held in the plaza on officially designated days under the watchful supervision of town officials who carefully regulated the price, weight, amount, and quality of the goods sold. In the larger markets money was the usual medium of exchange, but

[22] Chevalier, *Land and Society*, pp. 93–98; Gibson, *Spain in America*, pp. 152–53.

in smaller communities direct barter was common, with maize and cacao beans serving to facilitate exchange.[23]

Another practice which affected local production and distribution of resources outside the official marketplace was the technically illegal, but nonetheless common, *repartimiento de comercio.* In conjunction with manufacturers, livestock raisers, and the merchants of Mexico City, corregidors, caciques, and other local powerholders obtained supplies of such diverse items as farm animals, tools, wax candles, textiles, intoxicating beverages, and silk stockings which they resold at exorbitant prices to natives who were forced to accept them in exchange for cash or produce whether they wished the goods or not. The corregidor then pocketed the profits. In this manner a consumers' market was assured for any temporary surplus of livestock or manufactured goods which could not be disposed of otherwise.[24]

The Growth of the Landed Estate

Regional complexes, each composed of a consuming town or city surrounded by a producing hinterland, were united formally under the centralizing political and religious institutions of colonial rule. Economically, however, we have seen that they tended to form localized, self-sufficient isolates which looked inward rather than outward. This inward orientation was accelerated during the seventeenth century when a serious drop in silver production still further reduced both local and overseas trade and commerce and created a "century of depression." Concurrently, sociopolitical control of regional complexes also became considerably decentralized in fact, if not in theory, as a result of the growth of large landed estates.

The growth of landed estates and of a landed aristocracy was preconditioned and facilitated by a number of factors. The scattered colonial settlement pattern characteristic of central and southern New Spain, further emphasized by the additional empty space deriving from Indian depopulation, created large, uninhabited stretches which rapidly filled with herds of cattle and flocks of sheep. The expanses of semiarid country stretching over northern Mexico, again broken only occasionally by small mining communities, also held potential for large landholdings.[25]

In a different vein, the crown's perennial shortage of funds provided an impetus for the rise of influential persons who would maneuver to obtain property in these uninhabited territories. In its precarious financial state the crown, in spite of its concern for political centralization, encouraged wealthy private individuals to assume much of the cost of

[23] Gibson, *Aztecs Under Spanish Rule,* pp. 352–60; David Kaplan, "The Mexican Marketplace Then and Now," in *Essays in Economic Anthropology,* ed. June Helm (Seattle: Univ. of Washington Press, 1965), pp. 80–84.

[24] Gibson, *Spain in America,* p. 151; idem, *Aztecs Under Spanish Rule,* pp. 94–96.

[25] This discussion of landed estates rests heavily on Chevalier's *Land and Society in Colonial Mexico,* which should be consulted for further details.

military advance and colonization. Consequently, in return for various privileges well-to-do colonists developed private armies to subdue the territory and establish settlements.

These influential leaders drew much of their support and manpower from the large numbers of relatives and dependents who surrounded any man with income of some sort. Following the traditional practice of the Iberian Peninsula (and Mediterranean countries in general), a wide range of cousins, nephews, in-laws, and other relatives filled to overflowing the house of the socially and economically better off and played important roles in every type of family enterprise. Additional support was gained from various "hangers-on" of low social status who also enjoyed the hospitality of the more affluent in exchange for various small services. The ties created by the institution of *compadrazgo,* or godparenthood, created yet another field of contacts who could be tapped in support of the programs and connivances of the influential.[26]

These men of means frequently brought their retinue of clients and relatives to the service of even higher officials and ministers, including the king himself, for whom they provided services and confidential missions in return for privileges and rewards such as access to land, renumerative public office, and titles of nobility. Although the crown initially viewed the potential for personal power and influence that such arrangements created with considerable concern, through its financial plight it finally succumbed to a tradition which could provide private armies and wealth for colonization at no direct expense to the royal treasury, but which also encouraged the rise of a colonial aristocracy.

In addition to vast stretches of uninhabited land and pressures and traditions encouraging the rise of powerful individuals, preconditions favorable for the growth of landed estates also can be found in pre-Columbian Mesoamerican patterns of landholding. Generally three major systems of land tenure can be identified in preconquest Mexican society. Community lands, including fields for cultivation, untilled fields, and woodlands, were held in common by the calpulli with privileges of usufruct allotted to each married man. Each community also was responsible for the cultivation of additional "public lands" which provided support and tribute for the elite and the military. Finally, members of the aristocracy also held private estates which were cultivated by land-bound serfs and slaves.[27]

After the conquest the private estates of the nobility and the community lands of the calpulli were recognized and reserved as such by the crown. The "public lands," on the other hand, technically became crown property, and it was from this territory that modest land grants (*peonías* and *caballerías*) were made to soldiers of the conquest. The viceroy, who was responsible for grants, also issued deeds in an effort to encourage badly needed wheat cultivation and for production of sugar cane.

In spite of the official emphasis placed on agricultural development, by

---

[26] Chevalier, *Land and Society,* pp. 30–35 and 148–84.
[27] Ibid., pp. 16–23; Soustelle, *Daily Life of the Aztecs,* pp. 72–73 and 79–81.

the end of the sixteenth century the amount of cultivated land was very small in comparison with the vastness of the total territory. In addition, in spite of the press for grain, grantees frequently reserved large portions of their lands for sheep-raising or even abandoned agriculture entirely for livestock in bad harvest years and as declining Indian population made the repartimiento crews on which wheat farmers depended for labor increasingly difficult to obtain. Consequently, much of this territory readily joined that appropriated for the raising of animals by the growing number of cattle barons who were rapidly gaining control of the immense reaches of uncultivated and increasingly uninhabited land.

In contrast with agricultural pursuits, livestock raising was facilitated by the fact that even large herds of sheep and cattle required relatively few hands to oversee them; thus labor was less of a problem. Livestock raising, along with public office holding and mining, also was considered a proper occupation for prestige-conscious whites. Finally, again unlike agriculture where viceregal efforts were oriented toward expansion of insufficient production, the rapid natural increase in herds during the midsixteenth century provided a problem of overabundance.

The consequences of this surfeit were several. Since the oversupply of livestock drove meat prices low, large herds of animals were necessary in order to be reasonably profitable undertakings for stockmen. The growth of the herds also necessitated efforts to divert the stream of animals away from the more settled agricultural areas of central and southern Mexico, where depredations to communities could not be controlled, toward the vast, thinly populated grasslands which stretched north on either side of the central northern plateau in the same general zone as the great silver mines. The development of the mines further stimulated the rise of estates. Far from the main centers of supply in the south, the scattered mining communities depended on nearby pastoral and agricultural holdings to provide food for laborers and mules, horses, and hides for the operation of the mines.[28]

Concurrent with the growth of animal husbandry was the question of control over grazing land. In medieval Castile, pasture and untilled fields were held in common, open to all.[29] In early New Spain royal laws proclaimed a similar pattern. However, anticipating potential landed estates (the traditional means to establish a prestigious family name and lineage), stockmen during the sixteenth century acquired land via outright seizure of unoccupied territory, grants from the viceroy, who was faced with a fait accompli of land grabbing, and cheap purchase or usurpation from natives, whose communities invariably controlled the most fertile and well-watered valleys.

Encroachment onto native community land was particularly prevalent in central and southern New Spain, where native population was concentrated. To some extent community holdings were protected by the mis-

[28] Stein and Stein, *Colonial Heritage*, p. 38; Chevalier, *Land and Society*, pp. 40–41 and 166–69.

[29] Cf. Charles J. Bishko, "The Peninsular Background of Latin American Cattle Ranching," *Hisp. Amer. Hist. Rev.* 32 (1952):491–515.

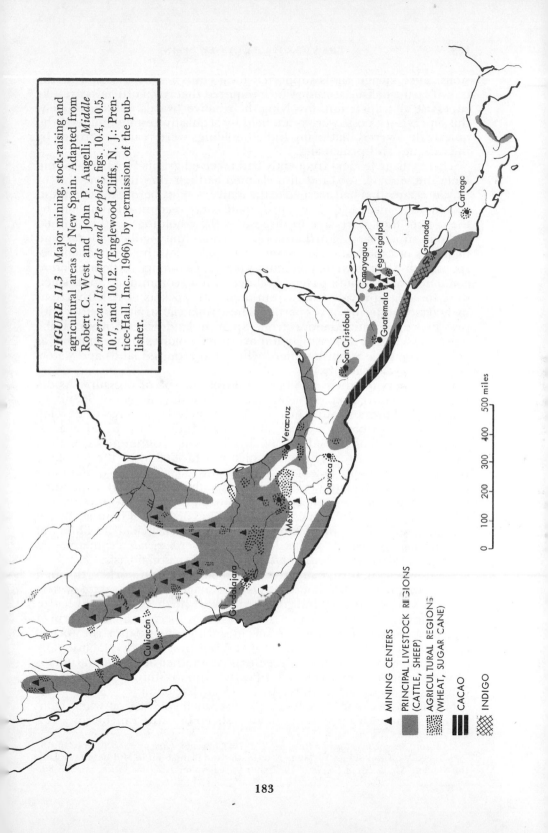

FIGURE 11.3 Major mining, stock-raising and agricultural areas of New Spain. Adapted from Robert C. West and John P. Augelli, *Middle America: Its Lands and Peoples*, figs. 10.4, 10.5, 10.7, and 10.12. (Englewood Cliffs, N. J.: Prentice-Hall, Inc., 1966), by permission of the publisher.

Cartago

Granada

Tegucigalpa

Comayagua

Guatemala

San Cristóbal

Veracruz

Oaxaca

México

Guadalajara

Culiacán

▲ MINING CENTERS

PRINCIPAL LIVESTOCK REGIONS (CATTLE, SHEEP)

AGRICULTURAL REGIONS (WHEAT, SUGAR CANE)

CACAO

INDIGO

0   100   200   300   400   500 miles

sions, since village lands supported local church activities, and by the crown's paternalistic attitude which required that royal officials carefully supervise all transactions involving their native "wards." Unfortunately, the supervisory posts were often held by acquisitive estate builders who quickly discovered that many Indian holdings were really controlled by the caciques and principales.

These village leaders frequently had received grants for sheep-raising from the viceroy, too, and also claimed as their due the same sort of private estates that had accrued to the native nobility before the conquest. In addition, since caciques and principales were recognized as nobility by the crown, they were free to dispose of their holdings as they wished without supervision. Furthermore, as community gobernadores and members of cabildos, caciques and principales were held personally responsible by the crown for community tribute payments. As depopulation continued and tribute-payers declined, these community spokesmen were forced to provide funds from their own pockets or risk imprisonment or sequestering of properties. These financial straits, together with pressures and intimidations from Spanish landowners, marked the hard-pressed and increasingly impoverished colonial native nobility as prime targets for Spanish settlers, who often acquired lands and waters from them very cheaply.[30]

Landowners for their part faced a different type of pressure. As depopulation reduced repartimiento crews and as the number of Spaniards requiring laborers steadily increased, it became imperative to develop new avenues to obtain workers. Depriving Indians of the means for adequate independent subsistence by depriving communities of their fields proved an effective device which was facilitated by the problems facing the community notables. Consequently, many native communities came to be completely hemmed in or totally absorbed by expanding estates. When native population began to increase in the seventeenth century what lands still remained to the villages proved far from sufficient for the needs of the inhabitants. Faced with insufficient livelihood at home, villagers turned to labor on the estates or *haciendas,* sometimes as permanent workers, often on a temporary or seasonal basis.

Landowners, in turn, maneuvered to retain access to workers through sharecropping and debt bondage. Debt peonage, whereby estate owners advanced sums of money and goods to natives who then technically had to repay the debt through labor on the lord's estate, became a major form of native labor control during the seventeenth century (after the formal abolishment of labor repartimiento) and was thoroughly established by the beginning of the eighteenth century. As another inducement Indians were frequently given small plots of estate land to cultivate for their own subsistence needs in return for labor on the hacienda.[31]

Similar tactics were employed against small mestizo or white communities where citizens owned modest sheep or cattle ranches or a few

[30] Gibson, *Aztecs Under Spanish Rule,* pp. 274–76; Chevalier, *Land and Society,* pp. 210–18.
[31] Eric R. Wolf and Sidney W. Mintz, "Haciendas and Plantations in Middle America and the Antilles," *Soc. and Econ. Studies* 6 (1957):390–93; Chevalier, *Land and Society,* pp. 277–88.

caballerías of cultivated land, while the community itself claimed common fields and pastures for grazing work and meat animals. The judicial functions of a Spanish town generally offered some recourse against encroachment by large landowners. In many cases, however, by fair means or foul, large estate owners again sought to obtain laborers, especially badly needed *vaqueros* (herdsmen), stewards, and overseers, by seizing community lands and thereby forcing community inhabitants to work on the estate.[32]

Many of these ambitious landholders were self-made men: encomenderos who, with the decline of the encomienda, expanded their private landholdings; miners who accumulated lands as investments and to supply their mines; merchants of Mexico City who aimed to safeguard their commercial fortunes and to join the socially prestigeful rural aristocracy by investing their wealth in land. Many also sought government positions in order to bolster their control and networks of authority.[33] Whenever possible, however, these men of growing influence continued to enjoy the benefits of urban life by establishing a town house in Mexico City where the cream of society congregated and leaving the immediate affairs of their country estates to poor white, Negro, mulatto, and mestizo overseers and vaqueros.

Although cattle barons and other estate owners worked assiduously to increase their holdings during the sixteenth and seventeenth centuries, they did not develop and exploit their resources with the same zeal. To be sure, development was hindered by a lack of ready capital, the use of traditional technologies, and a very limited urban market for hacienda products which would quickly have been flooded had all available land been put into production. These restraints were accentuated further when the mining boom collapsed in the midseventeenth century, creating economic depression and contraction in New Spain. Trade now slowed to a standstill, overseas exports dropped, and there no longer was a market at the mines. Hacienda production was reduced almost entirely to meeting only its own needs and those of the relatively few regional towns and cities which, on the other hand, grew increasingly dependent on the hacienda for essential foodstuffs as Indian communities lost their lands.[34]

Yet in addition to these restrictions other factors made profits and economically efficient operations less important to the hacendado than ownership of land per se. To a great extent the goal which the aspiring aristocrat pursued emphasized achievement of the power, social prestige, and influence that derived from ownership of a large estate and protection of this position by competition with like-minded rivals who also sought land and labor. To this end the hacendado maneuvered by all means possible to attain a monopoly of control over all the lands and

[32] Chevalier, *Land and Society*, pp. 139–41 and 222–26.

[33] The ever-useful dependents and relatives were frequently settled in smaller regional posts, while the head of the estate maneuvered for a more rewarding position in the capital or an audiencia center.

[34] Wolf and Mintz, "Haciendas and Plantations," p. 393; Chevalier, *Land and Society*, pp. 176–78.

FIGURE 11.4   View of the Hacienda de Chapingo, in the Valley of Mexico. The estate produced crops for nearby Mexico City. From H. G. Ward, *Mexico,* 2d ed., enlarged, vol. II (London: Henry Colburn, 1829), between pp. 94–95.

resources of his region, without regard to his ability to fully utilize them productively.[35]

The landed aristocracy was considerably strengthened in its position in midcentury when the crown, which heretofore had issued its grants free of charge as rewards for service, offered formal recognition of all titles and landholdings for a fee. As usual the crown's main motive was to obtain cash. To the landowner title confirmation and settlement meant that the many irregularities deriving from illegal transactions and unauthorized purchases would be removed and clear, legally valid, and unassailable title would be had to land.[36]

As a result of these diverse developments rural estates became virtually autonomous social, political, and economic systems. This is seen most clearly and in most exaggerated form in the vast reaches of northern Mexico where immense estates emerged during the seventeenth century.[37] Because of the distances separating the northern mines and grasslands from the centers of royal authority in central Mexico, lords of the north not only maintained their own armed retainers, often numbering hundreds of men, but also established virtually complete control over

---

[35] Chevalier, *Land and Society,* pp. 176–78 and 299–307.
[36] Ibid., pp. 265–77.
[37] See Taylor, *Landlord and Peasant,* chap. 4, for comparative discussion of hacienda conditions in the Valley of Oaxaca.

FIGURE 11.5 Rancheros. Although the great haciendas have received most scholarly attention, smaller privately owned landholdings or *ranchos* were also part of the colonial landscape. These small holdings were worked by the owner (ranchero) himself, with the help of his immediate family or with a few hired hands, all of whom depended on the produced crops for subsistence. From Brantz Mayer, *Mexico; Aztec, Spanish and Republican,* vol. II (Hartford: S. Drake and Company, 1852), opposite p. 23.

the political offices of the region. On their own vast holdings these rich and powerful men also held unquestioned and absolute authority.

The hacienda itself comprised varied resources including thousands of horses, tens of thousands of head of cattle and sheep, orchards, perhaps vineyards and a winery, streams, dams and irrigated croplands, mines, crushers and smelters, scrub woodlands for charcoal, flour mills, and workshops. Estate laborers either lived off the hacienda in nearby communities (a common pattern in the more populous regions of central and southern Mexico) or comprised population centers on the estate itself (a frequent practice in the sparsely settled north) near the chapel and fortified magnificence of the manor house. Work on the estate was directed by mulatto, mestizo, and free Negro overseers who, as social misfits, frequently found the empty stretches and encapsulated life of the hacienda much to their liking. Many more of the restless, roaming vagabond castas were temporarily employed on the estates when they weren't cattle rustling. On very large estates small farms or *ranchos* on the outskirts of the property were often leased to mestizo ranchers whose rents provided income to the estate and who also provided services when needed.

Much of the actual labor, of course, was furnished by families of peons who often were associated with haciendas throughout their entire lives. Yet, given conditions of the times, life dependent on a hacienda probably provided benefits which were unavailable or at best uncertain outside the boundaries of the estate, and there is reason to think that peons not infrequently found their position quite acceptable. As laborers they received advances of money, were usually provided with small plots on which to raise subsistence crops, were clothed and sheltered, had access to estate commissary stores, were given medical treatment of sorts, were assured of defense, had their tribute paid, and were able to hold their positions even if they failed in meeting their credit payments. Given the alternatives of this time of depression, peonage, even though exploitative, provided greater security and material benefits than could be found as an independent agriculturalist, as a rootless vagabond, or in the poorer wards or barrios of the urban centers.[38]

In their drive to control territory and sources of wealth, private estate owners encountered considerable competition from the church which acquired immense landholdings of its own and, in its capacity as moneylender, obtained numerous liens on other private holdings.[39] Although the church was legally forbidden to own land, it was allowed to accept gifts, legacies, and charitable donations of all sorts from Spaniards who considered it highly prestigeful to endow a convent, college, or hospital and who arranged for generous gifts and endowed masses in their wills. The church then invested this capital in farm land, flour mills, sugar refineries, and cattle droves, financed the construction of innumerable ecclesiastical buildings, and supported educational and charitable services.

Foremost among the Orders and secular clergy in the acquisition and management of huge estates was the Society of Jesus, which eventually owned the largest flocks of sheep, finest sugar plantations, and best-managed estates of New Spain. The secret of Jesuit success lay largely in a superior understanding of business and agronomy and in more efficient operations. In return, the Order's economic independence, social influence, and political power were constantly strengthened.

The church in general also obtained income to operate its varied educational and charitable activities and to support the hundreds of men and women seeking a livelihood within its charge through the interest derived from loans and mortgages secured on the rural properties of private hacendados. By the second half of the seventeenth century many landowners were heavily mortgaging their unproductive holdings to provide for endowed masses, a daughter's dowry, an annuity for a younger son, or general coverage of the expected life-style in a year of bad harvest or drought. Although such loans were originally short-term, they commonly came to be extended almost indefinitely. Many hacendados soon became little more than managers for clerical creditors, and by the end of the colonial period most haciendas were heavily burdened with debt.

---

[38] Gibson, *Spain in America*, p. 156; Chevalier, *Land and Society*, pp. 292–99.
[39] Chevalier, *Land and Society*, chap. 7.

Thus ownership of land did not by any means automatically signify wealth, and individual hacienda families frequently became impoverished within three generations.[40]

Yet a hacendado elite continued to exist, even though its composition varied, because land offered the safest investment for the fortunes made in the two areas of the colonial economy which were profitable—international trade and, when conditions warranted, mining. We have already noted briefly the stimulus which early mining provided for landed estates and the value of the latter as a source of supplies for extractive industry. The relationship between land and mercantile wealth requires a brief discussion now.

By dint of hard work, thrift, and careful building of business confidence urban merchants, specifically those of Mexico City who were associated with the monopolistic trade with Spain, frequently amassed sizable fortunes which, however, had to be invested if they were to be kept intact. In the absence of a banking system, the purchase of land and development of entailed estates seemed to provide the best immediate opportunities for safeguarding a fortune which otherwise would be distributed and dissolved among future heirs. Another road to the same end was achieved through marriage between socially prestigeful but financially hard-pressed landed aristocrats and socially less distinguished but rich merchants' families, and these alliances became increasingly frequent as the colonial period progressed. However, as we have seen, because of the low productivity of the hacienda the wealth that flowed from merchant enterprises (or from mining) into land was usually either spent or transferred to the coffers of the church within a few generations.[41]

These economic facts of colonial life also render more comprehensible the bitter rivalry which developed in colonial society between those Spaniards born in Spain, known as peninsulars (*peninsulares*), and those born in Spanish America, termed creoles (*criollos*). Business and commercial activities were often in the hands of peninsulars, many of whom were originally of humble European origins. Upon arriving in the Indies these immigrants found posts in the businesses established by their relatives, perhaps as young shop assistants in enterprises operated by an already established uncle. Marriage with the uncle's daughter together with years of hard work eventually could bring financial success as well as social prestige.

To such industrious social-climbing newcomers the activities of the established creoles often seemed unenterprising and unproductive and, in fact, there seems to have been some basis for this attitude. The scions of established colonial families generally obtained their livelihood without much personal effort from landed estates, augmented sometimes by a

---

[40] Ibid., pp. 253–57; D. A. Brading, *Miners and Merchants in Bourbon Mexico* (Cambridge: Cambridge Univ. Press, 1971), pp. 208–19.

[41] Chevalier, *Land and Society*, pp. 144–45; Gibson, *Spain in America*, p. 129, Brading, *Miners and Merchants*, pp. 115–17; McAlister, "Social Structure and Social Change," pp. 366–68.

profession such as law or medicine or, most commonly, by a position within the church. However, these sources provided little economic remuneration. Much to creole disgruntlement, more rewarding posts in the upper echelons of the political and ecclesiastical realm were usually unavailable since the crown reserved these for royal favorites from Spain (who also were thought to be potentially more loyal to the crown). Similarly, positions within the rewarding world of mercantilism were generally unobtainable since the semihereditary, heavily endogamous merchant families reserved their openings for immigrant relatives. Thus the creole, as a member of the landed aristocracy, stood high in social prestige yet was frequently in economic difficulties. In these straits he thoroughly resented the airs assumed by the peninsular who, though often considered socially inferior, stood on much better ground financially. In return even the lowest peninsular considered the creole not only inherently unenterprising, unreliable, and somewhat provincial, but also possibly "stained" by the closer affiliation with Negroes and Indians that life in Spanish America necessitated.[42]

The Seventeenth Century

By the death of Philip II in 1598, the Indies had begun to come of age. The succeeding seventeenth century in New Spain was an era of crystallization, of consolidation, of settling in. It was also a period of continued readjustment to the decline in native population and to the collapse of the mining industry. In place of wealth derived from native tribute and from silver, ownership of land now became a foremost measure of social position and influence.

Like the encomienda, the landed estate or hacienda also provided a means of control by a relatively small urban-oriented social elite over much larger numbers of rural castas and natives, together with the means for a properly prestigeful elitist style of living. However, where the encomienda was oriented toward and dependent upon the survival and continued operation of indigenous social and economic community patterns, the hacienda evolved as a means of coping with a declining Indian population and a disintegrating native social and economic pattern. The hacienda also acted further as an acculturative mechanism, particularly for those native laborers who lived and worked permanently on the estate and who thus were removed from their traditional social and economic systems.[43]

The hacienda is further viewed as an integral part of the pattern of isolationism and provincialism that attended the economic depression of

[42] Gibson, *Spain in America*, pp. 130–31; Stein and Stein, *Colonial Heritage*, pp. 66–67; Brading, *Miners and Merchants*, pp. 108–12 and 208–15.

[43] James Lockhart, "Encomienda and Hacienda: The Evolution of the Great Estate in the Spanish Indies," *Hisp. Amer. Hist. Rev.* 49 (1969):411–29; Robert Keith, "Encomienda, Hacienda and Corregimiento in Spanish America: A Structural Analysis," *Hisp. Amer. Hist. Rev.* 51 (1971):431–46.

the seventeenth century and heightened greatly the tendency for cities and their hinterlands to turn inward to their own resources and to champion their own local interests to the exclusion of wider integration or orientations. Under the all-pervasive paternalistic authority of the hacendado the hacienda also provided a haven of sorts for the restless, rootless mixed peoples who originated through the inevitable miscegenation among Indian, Negro, and Spaniard, yet were legally and often socially rejected. The power of the hacienda master also competed successfully with the centralized authority of the state, which often seemed to dissolve in the vast, distant reaches of rural New Spain. Here power came to be fragmented among a number of rich and powerful men each of whom, bolstered and supported by large retinues of relatives and dependents, competed with the others for ever greater influence and authority. Many of these rural landowners had strong family ties with the urban aristocracy of rich merchants, and the affairs of the colony in general were largely decided by these interlocking aristocratic family units. This is not to say, however, that white society formed an integrated whole. On the contrary, one of the most bitter splits in a society rent from top to bottom with social differentiations fell between creoles and peninsulars.

This rivalry was but one of the many intrasocietal fissions that characterized seventeenth-century New Spain. The privileged few, generally whites, were offset by the underprivileged many, primarily the castas, Negroes, and Indians. Each category of castas was also a separate group with its own legal and social directives. Hacienda, Indian community, and Spanish town similarly were oriented toward their own affairs and their own problems, as were merchants, craftsmen, priests, lawyers, and corregidors. In short, the social fabric of New Spain was highly cellular, just as economically cities and towns formed local isolates with their regional hinterlands. Much of this separateness had legal foundations and in this context was considered by the crown as a means of promoting social stability. Thus each socioeconomic group—hacienda, Indian community, Spanish town, gremio, merchant guild, and ecclesiastical organization—was recognized and licensed or titled separately by the crown and given autonomous charge of its own affairs and range of activities. All corporate organizations and regions, of course, were tied to Spain, which was caught up in her own problems under the ineffectual rule of the seventeenth-century Hapsburgs. But the contacts with the mother country were becoming more remote and less persuasive, although respect for the crown and the hierarchical system was still a major force holding together the disparate classes and corporations which composed New Spain.

12

Late
Eighteenth-Century
Adjustments

Bourbon Reorganizations

In 1700 the Spanish Hapsburg monarch Charles II died without an heir. Two claimants stepped forward to contest the throne of the far-flung Spanish empire: Archduke Charles of Austria, a Hapsburg, and Philip of Anjou, grandson of Louis XIV and member of the Bourbon house which ruled France. The resulting War of the Spanish Succession was finally settled in 1713 in favor of the Bourbon ruler, now Philip V, and a new dynasty assumed the throne of this impoverished country.

Imposition of Bourbon rule was advantageous in many ways for Spain and the colonies, for readjustments now were made in European affairs so that attention could be concentrated on the serious economic and fiscal problems of the mother country and the empire.

In undertaking a reexamination of the organization and operation of the Spanish state the Bourbon rulers were reflecting the current "climate of the times." In Spain, as in western Europe in general, the eighteenth century, the Age of Enlightenment, saw growing skepticism toward traditional beliefs and widespread interest in improving material conditions and promoting useful knowledge in commerce, industry, and agriculture. New concerns with practicality and empiricism and efficiency and rational organization were widely expressed. As "enlightened despots," monarchs of the day and their ministers considered social, economic, and humanitarian reforms and readjustments, while at the same time they strove defensively to attain new heights of absolute royal power and national authority.

Philip acted quickly to introduce such changes in Spain. He worked to reduce traditional regional and class separatism and privileges and to rejuvenate political, economic, and fiscal affairs on a more nationwide basis. To facilitate these adjustments a new system of administration, derived from the French and based on territorial units called "intendancies," was instituted at the district level of government. By the second half of the eighteenth century, under the effective and enlightened reign of one of Spain's more capable monarchs, Philip's second son, Charles III (1759–88), improvements began to be felt.[1]

Spanish administrators were well aware, too, that developments in Spain, particularly economic growth, depended greatly on economic conditions in the colonies and on the nature of the ties linking them with Spain. They also fully realized that a number of economic and political problems had developed in Spanish America over the past century that limited its value to Spain as a source of revenues and as a consumers' market for Spanish goods. They further knew that England, along with France and other European nations, was taking new advantage of colonial weaknesses to channel away a good share of Spanish American trade and commerce. Consequently there was a general reexamination and partial reorganization of the administrative and economic bonds of empire during the second half of the century.

Stated in broad terms, the crown sought to reemphasize centralized crown policy and authority, to reassert the primacy of the mother country toward the increasingly self-oriented and self-regulated regions and peoples of Spanish America, and to increase the flow of revenues and precious metals to Spain. Colonial government, which had become notoriously sluggish, inefficient, and corrupt, was reorganized and hopefully tightened by a reduction in the number of officials and by efforts to control graft and plug fiscal loopholes. Most of these changes were instituted at the district level of administration where corregidors and their associates had long regarded their positions as private monopolies allowing self-enrichment at crown expense. During the 1780s their posts were abolished and local administration reorganized under the intendancy system.

New Spain was now divided into provinces (intendancies) with local capitals—forerunners in Mexico of the modern states of the Republic—under the direction of intendants who, in turn, supervised a limited number of district officers or subdelegates. Under the direction of king and viceroy intendants were responsible for financial, judicial, military, and administrative functions, implemented all royal and viceregal decrees, and exercised the ecclesiastical patronato. They also were expected to encourage local commerce, industry, and agriculture and to build local improvements such as bridges, roads, and street lights. In an effort to avoid corruption better salaries were provided, too.

[1] Richard Herr, *The Eighteenth-Century Revolution in Spain* (Princeton: Princeton Univ. Press, 1958); Stanley J. Stein and Barbara H. Stein, *The Colonial Heritage of Latin America* (New York: Oxford Univ. Press, 1970), pp. 86–96.

For awhile many abuses were checked, functions and responsibilities were clarified, the crown's receipt of revenues increased, and new life was infused into colonial administration.

On the other hand, although the post of intendant was to be granted to peninsulars rather than to creoles in order to assure a greater degree of cooperation and, presumably, greater loyalty to the crown, in actuality many of the same creoles who had held positions as corregidors under the former system returned as intendants and subdelegates. In addition, official reimbursement at the subdelegate level was still inadequate, and it was difficult to effectively implement the new controls and limitations on local administrative offices. Consequently, by the end of the century many of the old abuses had reappeared and district government was again highly personalized and corrupt.[2]

The crown's efforts to reimpose regalism also extended to the rich and powerful ecclesiastical domain, where a number of special immunities and powers were revoked or reduced. The most dramatic move struck at the Society of Jesus, by now the wealthiest, most influential, and most controversial of the Orders, which was also suspected of encouraging undue populism and of maintaining loyalty and obedience to the papacy rather than to the crown. These and other difficulties between Rome and the Jesuits and the Spanish Crown eventually culminated in 1767 in the expulsion of the Jesuits from all the Spanish dominions. In New Spain the extensive and valuable properties of the Order were confiscated by the state and then came to enhance still further the holdings of prominent creole landowners. Their excellent educational institutions were allowed to decay, too, and Indian affairs in the mission regions fell into disarray.[3]

Economic and fiscal revival in Spain and Spanish America also necessitated readjustments in commercial ties between mother country and colonies. Therefore trade restrictions were loosened and liberalized. The special privileges and restrictive control of trade enjoyed by the handful of wealthy and powerful merchant-monopolists associated with the monopoly ports of both Spain and the Indies came under strongest attack. To break the hold of the merchant-monopolists the numerous import and export duties were reduced in both Spain and America; the slow, expensive, and inefficient flota system gradually was abandoned and finally terminated (1778) to permit more flexible individual sailings, and all major ports in both Spain and America were opened to direct overseas trade. In addition, the financing of overseas shipping was readjusted so many more traders, satisfied to work on a more modest scale, could enter the commercial picture and compete with some success with

[2] Charles Gibson, *Spain in America* (New York: Harper & Row, 1966), pp. 167–73; Howard F. Cline, "Viceroyalty to Republics, 1786–1952: Historical Notes on the Evolution of Middle American Political Units," in *Handbook of Middle American Indians*, ed. Robert Wauchope (Austin: Univ. of Texas Press, 1972), 12:138–45; D. A. Brading, *Miners and Merchants in Bourbon Mexico* (Cambridge: Cambridge Univ. Press, 1971).

[3] Magnus Mörner, ed., *The Expulsion of the Jesuits from Latin America* (New York: Knopf, 1965).

the former monopolists. As a result of these measures, mercantile competition expanded considerably, and both prices and profits began to fall.[4]

To stem their losses many rich merchants quickly invested their remaining capital in agriculture and mining. These sudden and substantial capital investments contributed in turn to a dramatic expansion of the mining industry. The interplay of complex factors behind this revival, particularly the boom of the 1770s and after when Mexican silver mines became the greatest producers of silver in the world, is by no means clearly understood. Renewed capital investment, which provided the means to renovate old mines and open new ones, was certainly one aspect. Reduced production costs were another. Applications of the newest advances in technology played a part, too, as did various tax exemptions. Special privileges or *fueros* were also granted to make mining a more desirable occupation both socially and legally. The net effect was a renewed realization of revenues from mining for the crown and a general revival of trade and commerce.[5]

Reassertion of crown authority involved not only economic and administrative realignments, but also strengthening of colonial defense. Heretofore defense had been divided among a few thousand regular forces located almost entirely in garrisons on the northern frontier and in the principal ports and supplemented by a colonial militia which was generally disorganized, lacking in equipment, and only rarely mobilized. The larger cities and coastal towns generally saw to their own protection with units of cavalry and infantry sponsored by the cabildos and craft guilds and intended for use only in extreme emergency. Then the Seven Years War against England (1756–63) revealed the vulnerability of Spanish defenses in the Caribbean. Consequently the colonial army was thoroughly overhauled and reorganized.

As traditionally had been the case with other corporate interest groups such as merchants, the church, craft guilds, and, more recently, mining, the new Army of New Spain also received special rights and privileges or *fueros* which granted various exemptions and immunities to military personnel and allowed independent military jurisdiction outside the royal or ordinary court system for officers and men and their families.[6] On the other hand, since it recruited its members from all social categories except Indians, the militia also cross-cut traditional social and economic classifications. The army resolved the complexities of colonial social identification into two main categories and organized white or Spanish companies composed of light-skinned mestizos and "whites" and companies of dark-skinned persons who were known as *pardos* in military terms. The rejuvenated military also accorded fresh avenues of prestige and honor to

---

[4] Stein and Stein, *Colonial Heritage,* pp. 100–104; Brading, *Miners and Merchants,* pp. 27–29 and 95–128.

[5] D. A. Brading, "Mexican Silver Mining in the 18th Century: The Revival of Zacatecas," *Hisp. Amer. Hist. Rev.* 50 (1970):665–81; Brading, *Miners and Merchants.*

[6] Discussion of the growth of a colonial army is based on Lyle McAlister, *The fuero militar in New Spain, 1764–1800* (Gainesville: Univ. of Florida Press, 1957).

FIGURE 12.1 Patio or amalgamation court of the Hacienda de Salgado in Guanajuato. After ores of nearby mines were crushed to a fine mud, the mix was spread in the patio to be amalgamated with mercury. Mules were repeatedly driven through the amalgam to promote the mixing of silver with mercury. From H. G. Ward, *Mexico,* 2d ed., enlarged, vol. II (London: Henry Colburn, 1829), between pp. 198–99.

the younger sons of the creole aristocracy who sought commissions as officers, while at the same time it offered a respectable calling with protection from civil authorities for the hard-pressed lower classes who filled the ranks.

Thus during the latter half of the eighteenth century the colonial army became a unique and potentially very powerful organization by virtue of the opportunities it offered persons from all walks of life and by virtue of the special privileges and protections of the *fuero militar* which placed its personnel beyond the reach of civil authority. Not surprisingly many officers and men chose a military career precisely for the opportunities it offered for protected personal gain and advancement. As long as the crown retained the political loyalty of the colony the army's full potential for independent and virtually uncontrollable power was held in check. But as crown control gradually diminished under Charles III's less capable successors, the army stood ready to fill the gap.

Although the reforms of Charles III were not continued by his successors and contraband trade and political corruption and exploitation continued to thrive, in general the late eighteenth century saw a new vitality in colonial life. By means of adjustments in governmental and economic policies implemented by several highly competent viceroys, the economy had revived significantly. The renewed purchasing power generated by the mining boom revived interregional exchange between the mining and livestock-rich north and the agricultural and craft-manufacturing central and southern provinces of Mexico so that manufactured cloth, ceramics, silverware, and sugar from the south moved north in exchange for leather, wool, mules, horses, and silver. Regions situated between this renewed exchange flourished most of all. In the Bajío, for example, a unique combination of mining, agriculture and animal husbandry, manufacturing (particularly of textiles), and highly profitable trade offered renewed employment for large numbers of Indians, Negroes, and castas, and exceptional prosperity for provincial creole aristocrats.[7]

On the other hand, the Bourbon adjustments still failed to remedy many of the grievances of Spanish America and Spain. The empire's basic economic problems, though somewhat ameliorated, remained. Spanish industrial production remained insufficient to meet American needs. American industry, still based on craft manufacturing, was unable to fill the gap. Thus a considerable market remained for goods from other European countries, and Spain continued to see much of the wealth of America flow to England, France, and the Netherlands.[8]

In Spanish America wealth and privilege, ownership of land and mines, and access to high political office were still restricted to a small proportion of the population. Although improved trade, commerce, and craft manufacturing and the army provided additional jobs for some, overall economic opportunity remained limited, and large numbers of poor and unemployed continued to crowd the unsanitary slums of the urban centers and to roam the countryside, all the more so since the eighteenth century was also a time of sustained population growth.

The Corporate Indian Community

Bourbon readjustments also had little effect on the Indian community, which had evolved its own mechanisms of community self-protection and solidarity during the centuries of the colonial experience. To be sure, population loss had precipitated the disintegration of many traditional native communities, while civil and ecclesiastical congregaciones had relocated and reorganized others. Hard-pressed and unscrupulous caciques and principales and corrupt corregidors and labor-hunting hacendados had taken further toll of community resources, draining people,

---

[7] Eric R. Wolf, "The Mexican Bajío in the 18th Century," in *Synoptic Studies in Mexican Culture*, M. S. Edmonson et al. (New Orleans: Middle American Research Institute, Tulane Univ. 1957); Brading, *Miners and Merchants,* chap. 6.

[8] Royal receipts of revenues from various taxes, tribute, and crown monopolies as well as precious metals increased greatly, but expenditures more than kept pace so that for the Spanish government the eighteenth century was one long fiscal crisis.

wealth, and land from village control. In another sense, however, con-gregaciones and haciendas contributed to the organization of a defensive solidarity which effectively protected the colonial native community from total dissolution and assimilation into the wider colonial society. The con-gregaciones provided a corporateness and a religious focal point for community affairs, while the mere existence of the rapacious hacienda, where many villagers labored to augment their traditional subsistence base, unified the community against this common threat.

By the eighteenth century the solidarity of the native community was expressed primarily through religious forms. Because of the growing pressures and responsibilities on gobernadores and cabildo members to meet Spanish demands for tribute and labor, the once-prestigeful posts in civil community government had become a burden to be avoided if at all possible. Enthusiastic political activity had waned after the sixteenth cen-tury and was replaced by active interest and participation in church affairs and organizations, although informal but highly influential groups of elders maintained a special authority and guardianship over community traditions and heritage.[9]

The sense of personal security and collective identity provided by religious activities was expressed by community fiestas, by the cult of the patron saint, and by membership in religious brotherhoods known as cofradías. The Indian cofradías of the seventeenth and eighteenth cen-turies derived from church-affiliated mutual aid and worship associations which originated in the European Middle Ages and were quite common in Spain. Transferred to Spanish America, and in the form developed in Indian communities, cofradías provided mutual aid associations of vary-ing sizes and complexity. In most cases, in return for monthly payments by the members, the cofradías assured a specified number of annual masses for the community and for the souls of deceased members and guaranteed to members in good standing the necessary materials and preparation for the largest single expense an Indian was likely to incur in his lifetime, a Christian funeral.[10]

The cofradías also helped finance community holy day celebrations which were otherwise paid for by community funds. Indeed, candles, flowers, fireworks, and other expenses associated with the elaborate pro-cessions, feasts, dances, and decorations that accompanied the celebra-tions of Indian Christianity were the major community expense in late colonial times.[11] In turn, the regular observance of fiestas and holy day ceremonies provided avenues for cohesion and the preservation of native community traditions and solidarity through public demonstrations of community existence and through the propitiation of supernatural be-ings entrusted with the care of the community on a higher, spiritual level.

[9] Charles Gibson, *The Aztecs Under Spanish Rule: A History of the Indians of the Valley of Mexico, 1519–1810* (Stanford: Stanford Univ. Press, 1964), p. 193.

[10] Gibson, *Aztecs Under Spanish Rule,* pp. 127–35; George Foster, "Cofradia and Compa-drazgo in Spain and Spanish America," *Southwestern J. of Anthro.* 9 (1953):1–28.

[11] Charles Gibson, "The Transformation of the Indian Community in New Spain, 1500–1810," *J. of World Hist.* 2 (1955):600.

Most important of these deities was the patron saint of the community, and the cult surrounding the worship and veneration of the saint provided another expression of communal identity and significance.

The native community was also protected to some extent by an outside earthly power, the hacendado. Like the native colonial nobility of the sixteenth century, the hacendado of the seventeenth and eighteenth centuries formed a protective buffer between the village and the wider world, guarding and protecting "his" Indian laborers against undue harassment from outsiders. In addition, the small amounts of cash and goods earned by villagers through hacienda labor provided income to support community religious activities. The native community, in turn, became a dependent or client of the hacendado, ready to serve the powerful patron as he should require.

Another church-affiliated mechanism which provided a measure of personal security was the institution of *compadrazgo* or coparenthood. This practice, which also emerged from medieval European society, had its primary expression in the rite of Catholic baptism in which godparents promised to guide the newly received member of the church in the proper religious training. At first compadrazgo, which was introduced to native populations of the Indies in the earliest days of the conquest (although a form of ritual godparenthood may have existed in preconquest societies, too), seems to have been mainly a formality, but as the sixteenth century progressed the institution became widespread among Indians, who apparently found the ties of ritual kinship to be of wider social and economic value.

There is still much to be learned concerning the usages of compadrazgo during the colonial period, but in general a network of coparents (*comadres* and *compadres*) and of godparents (*padrinos* and *madrinas*) undoubtedly provided channels of mutual aid and support within and between all segments of colonial society. For example, ritual kinship ties facilitated relationships between powerful encomenderos and hacendados and their clients. With respect to native society, it has been suggested that one factor behind the widespread acceptance of ritual coparenthood was the growing number of children orphaned as a result of epidemics and the consequent need for (and thus value accorded to) godparents, who might be called upon to fill the role of natural parents should the nuclear family be broken by death.[12]

Although in actuality individual members of the native community and the community as a whole could not be completely divorced from the outside world, time and effort spent in community religious celebrations and sodalities oriented members toward activities that provided a shield of defensive solidarity for the community and for its inhabitants. The considerable expenses entailed by these activities, in addition to tribute requirements, created additional pressures toward social and economic

---

[12] Gibson, *Aztecs Under Spanish Rule,* p. 152; Foster, "Cofradia and Compadrazgo," pp. 1–28; Sidney W. Mintz and Eric R. Wolf, "An Analysis of Ritual Co-Parenthood (Compadrazgo)," *Southwestern J. of Anthro.* 6 (1950):341–68.

unity. To further this solidarity, all personal resources were to be consumed within the community for community functions. There was little tolerance for individual accumulation of wealth or for the use of income to purchase goods produced outside the native sector. This discouragement of active participation in the wider colonial economy, together with a high degree of agricultural self-sufficiency and defensive residential separation, combined with maintenance of native languages, distinctive dress styles, and traditional preferences in diet to effect the continued separation of the Indian community and the life-style it protected from Hispanic society.[13]

In contrast with the corporate native community, members of the marginal castas were moving closer to eventual admission into the wider society. By the end of the colonial period the increase in castas population and the gradual breakdown of barriers to integration with white society made exclusion increasingly difficult. The growing numbers of castas eventually had to be socially recognized simply because there was no firm basis for permanently excluding them. Unlike corporate Indians, mestizos, mulattoes, zamboes, and also Negroes were not economically self-sufficient but were involved in numerous legal and extralegal dealings with the colonial economy. They spoke Spanish, dressed according to Spanish dictates, preferred Hispanic foods, and lived in Spanish communities where they were subject to essentially the same system of civil and ecclesiastical laws, although to be sure differing degrees of privilege altered the application of these regulations. As the eighteenth century advanced castas obtained positions in the military and in lesser bureaucratic and ecclesiastical offices and entered the guilds of artisans in growing numbers or established their own craft shops and stores. Consequently, by the end of the colonial period the system of castas was rapidly crumbling. "Whites" and members of the castas increasingly interacted in the same social structure although still separated by extreme degrees of variation in wealth, social position, and privilege.[14] As the castas entered Hispanic society, only the corporate Indian community was left to stand defensively outside the larger social whole.

[13] Eric R. Wolf, "Closed Corporate Peasant Communities in Mesoamerica and Central Java," *Southwestern J. of Anthro.* 13 (1957):1–18.

[14] Magnus Mörner, *Race Mixture in the History of Latin America* (Boston: Little, Brown, 1967), pp. 68–70 and 102; Gonzalo Aguirre Beltran, "The Integration of the Negro into the National Society of Mexico," in *Race and Class in Latin America,* ed. Magnus Mörner (New York: Columbia Univ. Press, 1970), pp. 11–27.

13

Outposts of Empire

Padres and Presidios
on the Northern Frontier

The center, the heartland, of New Spain, where population and resources were concentrated and where Hispanic-American society assumed its basic characteristics, encompassed a relatively small portion of the total territory included within the formal boundaries of the viceroyalty. Throughout the colonial period conquistador-explorers, soldiers and missionaries, and miners and ranchers continued to push north, away from the core, into new lands. At the turn of the seventeenth century, the expanding frontier extended approximately from the mouth of the Río Grande through Cerralvo and Santa Barbara to San Felipe y Santiago on the Sinaloa River, with the far-flung outpost of New Mexico newly established a leap ahead on the verdant upper Río Grande. During the seventeenth and eighteenth centuries the frontier advanced along coastal plains and mountain foothills to encompass most of Sonora and parts of Chihuahua, Coahuila, Nuevo Leon, and northern Tamaulipas. Indeed, New Spain's formal territorial claims stretched even into California and east through Texas to the territory of Louisiana and the wilds of La Florida, borderlands held primarily to contain French, English, and Russian rivals on the North American continent.[1]

Although all these vast and far-off reaches were technically subject to

[1] Herbert E. Bolton, *The Spanish Borderlands* (New Haven: Yale Univ. Press, 1921); Charles Gibson, *Spain in America* (New York: Harper & Row, 1966), chap. 9; Silvio Zavala, "The Frontiers of Hispanic America," in *The Frontier in Perspective*, ed. W. D. Wyman and C. B. Kroeber (Madison: Univ. of Wisconsin Press, 1965), pp. 36–58.

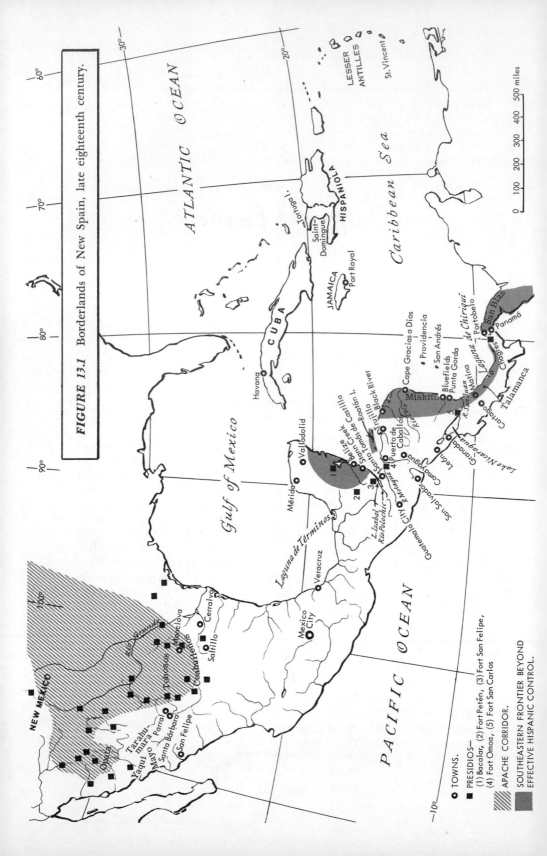

FIGURE 13.1 Borderlands of New Spain, late eighteenth century.

○ TOWNS.
■ PRESIDIOS—
(1) Bacalar, (2) Fort Petén, (3) Fort San Felipe,
(4) Fort Omoa, (5) Fort San Carlos

APACHE CORRIDOR.

SOUTHEASTERN FRONTIER BEYOND
EFFECTIVE HISPANIC CONTROL.

the same administrative program that guided the colonial heartland, the frontiers evoked a distinctive style of conquest and colonization. Part of this contrast was due to sheer geographical distance from the major centers of population and resources; this isolation was compounded by poor transportation and communication which made it difficult to obtain materials and to be closely integrated with the heartland. However, much of the distinctive configuration of frontier culture reflected the nature of the indigenous culture patterns encountered in these regions, particularly as these life-styles affected the issue of Indian control.

In the central heartland of New Spain, which to a large extent coincided territorially with the densely settled, highly organized, largely agrarian region of native Mesoamerica, effective control of the large native populace was rather easily and (after an initial period of conquest) peacefully achieved. At the state level of command Spanish domination was attained by removing the indigenous ruling elite from their high positions of political-religious authority and replacing them with Hispanic institutions and administrators. Locally the members of Indian communities continued to serve their new masters with tribute in goods and services much as they had served native rulers before them. As a result the Spaniards were able to obtain control over sufficient native labor to create a stable, settled, Hispanic-American colony.

As they moved beyond the indigenous high culture area of Mesoamerica into northern Mexico the Spaniards no longer encountered densely populated native states with sedentary tribute-payers preadapted to support new lords. The few agriculturalists situated along the Pacific coast and foothills of the Sierra Madre Occidental could offer little tribute. In the vast central plateau of north Mexico and in the northeast even these small villages were missing, and the Spaniards faced a militant and mobile population loosely organized into elusive bands. The traditional seminomadic ways of these hunter-gatherers were further enhanced by their rapid adoption of horses. Although many natives were captured to provide labor in mines and on haciendas, absolute control of the indigenous population was thwarted by their propensity to retreat into the unconquered vastness of the northern plateau or the security of rugged sierras. Bands of mounted warriors would then periodically emerge from these refuge areas to attack pack trains and raid the precarious Spanish frontier settlements.

If the territory were to be made safe for Hispanic colonization and if such elusive and disruptive savages were to be civilized and effectively incorporated into the structure of colonial society as tribute-paying Christian laborers, they would have to be permanently pacified, that is, settled into villages and instructed in those arts and crafts that the Spaniard associated with stable community life. The crown entrusted this formidable task to certain of the Mendicant Orders, particularly the Franciscans and, until their expulsion, the Jesuits.

In addition to a sincere interest to extend the sacred and secular benefits of Hispanic culture to those still in pagan darkness, the missions

FIGURE 13.2 The mission of San Ignacio, Sonora, built in 1776. At the start of a new mission the chapel was usually a small, rough shelter. As the mission prospered, ornately painted and furnished stone and adobe edifices, such as this, were built. Courtesy of Thomas Hinton.

and their directors assisted wider imperial purposes, too. The hardy and undaunted friars served well as explorers and diplomatic agents for the crown in these borderlands. Since churchmen were among the best educated and intellectually disciplined persons of the day, they were admirably suited to observe, report, and advise on the resources and situations in new regions. Furthermore, as men of peace they were frequently received in troubled areas with less suspicion and hostility than were military personnel.[2]

Although he played important roles in matters of secular politics, the missionary still considered religious training to be the primary goal of mission life. Consequently the chapel formed the focal point of the new community where the friar hoped to settle and educate roaming frontier natives. Nearby were built a home for the padre and a school to offer instruction in doctrine, music, reading, and writing. The homes of the

[2] For its part, the crown, operating as usual with limited funds, supported the mission program primarily where it would extend and hold frontier areas threatened with intrusion by other European powers. Herbert E. Bolton, "The Mission as a Frontier Institution in the Spanish American Colonies," *Amer. Hist. Rev.* 23 (1917):42–61; Edward Spicer, *Cycles of Conquest* (Tucson: Univ. of Arizona Press, 1962), chap. 11.

Indians stood beyond the main church and other mission buildings which in hostile country were protected by a thick wall and fortified gate-tower to guard padres, mission Indians, and nearby Spanish settlers against militant raiders.[3]

Secular skills relating to agriculture, stock-raising, and crafts received considerable attention, too, for one of the goals of frontier mission life was to teach the converts the discipline of Christian work through routinized daily labor, as well as to prepare them to be economically self-supporting within the framework of Hispanic society. Thus the missions provided spinning and weaving rooms and maintained carpenter shops, blacksmith shops, and tanneries. The lands surrounding the community were turned into irrigated vineyards, orchards, and fields of maize, grain, and other foods. Thousands of head of cattle, horses, sheep, and goats roamed mission ranch lands some distance away. In fact, much to the chagrin of the friars, many of the Indians who accepted mission life apparently did so more for material than for spiritual benefits.[4]

The mission community was also formally organized and granted official recognition within the administrative structure of civil government common to frontier and heartland alike. A native gobernador, alcaldes, and other officers who constituted the cabildo were appointed by regional Spanish authorities. Additional native officials were appointed by the friar to direct and oversee various church and community activities. This chain of command made it possible for one or two missionaries to maintain a semblance of productive order among hundreds of often newly settled natives who frequently represented diverse and sometimes mutually hostile bands and tribes. However, the missionaries also accepted military assistance in their relations with Indians and fully endorsed the application of Spanish law and its penalties in their communities. In more difficult areas a few soldiers from the nearest presidio were posted at the mission and administered whatever corporal punishment, usually whipping, that was deemed necessary to enforce compliance with mission regulations and activities. Such chastisements were readily applied, and not infrequently mission whippings were "last straws" sparking Indian revolts, at which point military garrisons were again called upon to assert the primacy of the Spanish state.

The presidios stretched across the frontier created a long and slender line of small fortifications garrisoned with a few dozen poorly equipped, low-paid defenders. These military men were expected to patrol the immense distances between posts, to recapture mission runaways, and to protect the missions and other settlements against marauding natives. Although missions and presidios often cooperated, at times considerable friction arose between padres and soldiers when missionaries objected to

[3] At the start of a new mission it was also customary to resettle several acculturated Indian families from older missions at the new post as teachers and examples to the new community. Tlaxcalans from central Mexico and Tarascans from Michoacan were among the most notable of these native instructors in the north.

[4] Bolton, "The Mission as a Frontier Institution," pp. 42–61; Spicer, *Cycles of Conquest*, pp. 285–306.

the immorality or insubordination of the presidial guard. These complaints frequently were well founded, for the soldiery was a rough lot composed of regular troops and local militiamen augmented by castas who had run afoul of the law and had been assigned to the frontier garrisons in lieu of prison sentences.[5]

Unruly soldiers were not the only secular evil against which missionaries labored to protect their charges. Natives by the hundreds were lured to work in the mines and at general labor or to serve as household servants for well-to-do Spaniards living in the towns that dotted the frontier. On the outskirts of these trade, mining, or administrative centers a floating population of poverty-stricken castas, detribalized vagabond Indians, and other drifters offered ready introduction to worldly sin and decadance. The friars often felt more kindly toward the exposure to Spanish culture which their neophytes received as permanent or temporary laborers on the widely scattered haciendas, yet here, too, conflicts arose when hacendados appropriated Indian lands and when their herds disturbed native settlements and water supplies. In short the missionary ideal of the self-sufficient native agricultural community as a civilizing institution standing apart physically and culturally from the Spanish town and hacienda was not always well received by Spanish administrators and frontier settlers, for the latter wanted immediate access to Indian labor and land and encountered serious economic competition from the better-protected and more efficiently operated agricultural and pastoral holdings of the mission communities.

In a similar vein, not all of the indigenous tribes of the north received the friars and presidial guards with the same alacrity, and many successfully resisted mission efforts. The varied reactions to the mission program encountered among native peoples of northwest and north-central Mexico illustrate this well. A brief examination of conditions among the Tarahumara, Mayo and Yaqui, Opata, Tobosos, and Apache provides a further glimpse into some of the problems of frontier life faced by natives, friars, and civil settlers alike.

Most of the seasonally mobile Tarahumara, who traditionally resided in scattered settlements in the rugged highlands and along the eastern foothills of the Sierra Madre Occidental, reacted to the demands and disruptions of mining settlements, haciendas, and missions by retreating from their lowland territory into the more inaccessible reaches of the highlands. Here they continued traditional culture patterns and successfully defended their territory with armed resistance. Actually some items of Hispanic culture were accepted, but in a form restyled to fit the framework of Tarahumara practices rather than vice versa. Thus the few missions which, in spite of revolt and warfare, were established in upland areas by determined friars became primarily ceremonial and social rather than residential centers for the local populace, who continued to live in

[5] Cf. Rex Gerald, *Spanish Presidios of the Late Eighteenth Century in Northern New Spain*, Museum of New Mexico, Research Records no. 7 (Santa Fe: Museum of New Mexico Press, 1968).

nonnucleated, isolated homesteads. Similarly, the introduction of cattle and sheep, which furnished meat to supplement traditional agriculture and wool for clothes and blankets, also facilitated economic independence and isolation from wider Hispanic society. Consequently, although a few lowland communities were eventually overwhelmed by miners and missions, the majority of Tarahumara were able to remain defensively autonomous within their mountain fastnesses.[6]

Missions were much more successful among the Mayos and Yaquis who lived across the mountains from the Tarahumara along rivers of the Pacific coastal plain. As sedentary agriculturalists these tribesmen already inhabited fairly compact, well-organized settlements, and the missions simply intensified this trend. The friars' agricultural interests also coincided with similar native concerns and met with resounding success. New crops and agricultural techniques fared well on the fertile river bottomlands, significantly raising the traditional standard of living. The Yaquis and Mayos readily accepted the new religious beliefs and practices, too, and native community officials and missionaries cooperated well in overseeing village life.

For a century the missions flourished in peace. Then, in the late seventeenth century, silver was discovered at the edge of nearby mountains. With mining came Spanish frontiersmen and settlers who viewed the Mayos and Yaquis as potential mine and hacienda labor and coveted the lush farm and pasture lands developed by the missions. The ensuing tensions and discords culminated in a bloody Indian revolt. Almost every mine and hacienda in the area ultimately was abandoned, and thousands of natives and Spaniards died or fled the area. The former economic prosperity and peaceful mission life of the Mayo and Yaqui valleys was irrevocably shattered.[7]

A third pattern of Indian-Spanish relations developed among the Opatas of central Sonora, whose villages were located in widely separated intermontane basins. There was relatively little communication between these small settlements, isolated as they were by rugged mountainous terrain, and missionization proceeded at varying speeds among the diverse communities. Before missions were established, however, mines and haciendas had spread throughout Opata territory, and many Indians already had been drawn to mining camps and towns. Spanish frontiersmen and Opata warriors also allied in mutual defense against raids by hostile, nomadic Apache from the northeast who menaced both Spanish settlements and Opata communities in the late seventeenth century. This association in a common danger may explain the relative lack of land encroachment or forced labor in Spanish-Opata relations. The absence of these usual grounds for frontier friction greatly furthered amiable contacts. Ties of compadrazgo bound Opata and Spanish families together, and Opata women and castas even intermarried. Spaniards praised

[6] Spicer, *Cycles of Conquest*, pp. 25–39.
[7] Ibid., pp. 46–60.

Opatas as industrious, brave, and even somewhat "civilized." Consequently the Opata moved much closer to eventual assimilation into the
lower echelons of Spanish colonial society than did either the Tarahumara or the Mayos-Yaquis.[8]

Interactions of quite a different sort developed between Spaniards and
the hunting-gathering bands of north-central Mexico. Because of the
inhospitality of both geography and natives, Spanish advance into the
northern plateau was halted approximately at the lake region of southern
Coahuila. In the unsettled territory between the outposts of Saltillo and
Monclova on the east and the Parral mining district on the west roamed
small groups of Tobosos, Coahuileños, and other desert bands. These
hunter-gatherers had readily learned to ride horses and were attracted to
the material goods available at Spanish settlements. In order to obtain
blankets, clothing, Spanish weapons, livestock, and other booty, small
bands of mounted warriors periodically swept out of the desert for sudden dashes into Spanish towns and haciendas or to waylay mule trains.[9]

Neither missionaries nor presidial guards were very effective in this
constantly troubled area. Settled, agrarian mission life was not compatible
with traditional native practices, and runaways were frequent, while many
other mission neophytes died from a variety of illnesses. The meager ring
of poorly equipped presidios established around the edges of this refuge
area were similarly ineffectual in maintaining a permanent peace. Instead, a vicious cycle of raiding, peacemaking, and rebellion was set into
motion. With increasing efficiency, wave after wave of northern
bandsmen moved south to raid Spanish settlements, suffer Spanish re-
prisals, agree to a tentative peace settlement and be settled at a mission,
and later escape to their desert territory and resume the raiding pattern.
In this process death from warfare and disease and scattered resettlement
among Spanish missions, haciendas, and mines gradually reduced the
aboriginal population to virtual extinction.[10]

Into the vacuum created by the disappearance of the indigenous bands
of north-central Mexico stepped the Apache, last and most successful of
the northern fighters. During the late seventeenth and throughout the
eighteenth centuries these fearsome and highly effective raiders gained
control of a vast corridor of rugged terrain hundreds of kilometers wide
which stretched across the north from the New Mexico settlements into
Sonora, Chihuahua, and Coahuila (Figure 13.1). Setting out from base
camps in this isolated region bands of mobile warriors raided, stole, and
burned Spanish settlements and those of their native allies, such as the
Opatas, on a grand scale.

Like other "professional raiders" before them, the primary goal of
Apache attacks was not to kill, but to plunder the weapons, food, and

---

[8] Ibid., pp. 91–101.

[9] Similar depredations also were conducted by frontier bandits, bands of restless hacienda
laborers and drifting native, casta, and Negro vagabonds.

[10] W. B. Griffen, *Culture Change and Shifting Populations in Central Northern Mexico* (Tucson:
Univ. of Arizona Press, 1969).

horses which had become economic necessities. Thus they refused to meet the Spanish forces in any lengthy battle, but moved in small groups, striking into Spanish territory whenever a good opportunity arose. Toward the end of the eighteenth century Spanish authorities attempted to entice the Apache to settle near presidios by offering food rations, liquor, and Hispanic trade goods at these military posts. (Apaches apparently were deemed too hopeless a case to be "civilized" by missions.) This tactic was somewhat successful, and bands of Apaches began to settle down in the vicinity of the presidios to an idle life of economic dependency. Mines and ranches reappeared in some of the devastated areas, and the once-fierce raiders seemed under control. It would be a short-lived peace, however, for the Apache would soon revert to their raiding patterns with no diminution of ferocity.[11]

The mission program in northern Mexico was expected to acculturate the diverse indigenous peoples of this vast region to "civilized" Hispanic life-styles and to prepare them for eventual incorporation into the hierarchical organization of the Spanish state. These attempts fell considerably short of total success. Efforts to institute Hispanic forms of community life generally proved ineffectual among the seminomadic peoples of the north. Where mission communities were established among more settled tribes the new forms of Hispanic town organization were frequently incorporated within traditional political systems or simply added to traditional forms as a new department of government for dealing with foreigners. The expulsion of the Jesuits and the disruptions of Apache raids finally destroyed effective Spanish control over the missions by the end of the colonial period, and local native communities became politically autonomous by default. Since Spanish frontiersmen and settlers found native labor difficult to control in the north (although hundreds of Indians did work in mines and on haciendas), Spanish efforts in this hinterland gradually became oriented less to exploitation of native labor and more to acquisition of the better Indian lands for haciendas. This usurpation, which left the native community with only the less-productive territories, again encouraged separateness and isolation.

Consequently, by the end of the colonial period that portion of the indigenous population of northern Mexico still resident in native communities stood significantly outside the wider social, economic, and also political framework of Hispanic frontier life. Outside the communities there were, of course, detribalized Indians who, as individuals, had broken their traditional kinship and community ties and had merged with the heterogeneous, footloose, poverty-stricken lower class of the Hispanic world. Many more would join these ranks in the years following independence from Spain.[12]

---

[11] Spicer, *Cycles of Conquest,* pp. 229–40; Jack D. Forbes, *Apache, Navaho and Spaniard* (Norman: Univ. of Oklahoma Press, 1960).

[12] Spicer, *Cycles of Conquest,* part 3. Illustrative of the loss of Spanish controls is the fact that Spanish governors ceased to collect tribute in many regions of the north.

Privateers and Buccaneers
in Central America

South and east of the central heartland, from the Isthmus of Tehuantepec to Panama, the colonists of New Spain faced another frontier in Yucatán and Caribbean Central America. Let us begin with Yucatán. Spanish colonial settlement in the peninsula centered on the administrative capital, Merida, located in the dry northwestern corner of Yucatán. Here resided encomenderos and hacendados who supported their lifestyle by raising livestock on rural holdings worked by Maya laborers from nearby native villages. South and east of Merida effective Spanish control of land and native labor grew progressively weaker. Isolated Valladolid marked the edge of the frontier beyond which independent Maya villages existed free of labor and tribute obligations. In this unconquered territory a sparse population of native agriculturalists pursued an economically self-sufficient and politically independent existence in small scattered settlements located in the tall rain forest and swamp regions of eastern and southern Yucatán and the Petén.[13]

The major Spanish settlements in Central America were situated in the temperate uplands on the Pacific side of the central mountains where sedentary natives, fertile agricultural lands, mines, grasslands for livestock, pine forests for shipbuilding, and warm coastal plains for growing indigo were found. Nonetheless, in many respects the citizens of Guatemala City, San Salvador, Comayagua, Leon and Granada, Cartago, and other colonial towns lived apart from the mainstream of colonial life in Mexico. Transportation and communication were slow and difficult, and after the initial years of conquest and colonization relatively few new settlers came to these outposts of New Spain. The pattern of colonial life that evolved in the quiet provincial towns focused instead on Guatemala City, capital of the most heavily populated and prosperous Central American region, seat of the audiencia and the archbishop, and commercial headquarters for a clique of wealthy and influencial merchants who controlled the import-export business (centered mainly on cacao and indigo) and directed the livestock market for Guatemala, Salvador, Honduras, and Nicaragua. This north and westward orientation toward Guatemala City also contributed to the failure to effectively colonize the Caribbean coast of Central America to the south and east, where hostile natives roamed at will in mountains and tropical lowlands (Figure 13.1).[14]

Although these unsettled regions contained little to directly recommend them in Spanish eyes, they were of interest in at least one important

[13] Arnold Strickon, "Hacienda and Plantation in Yucatán," *América Indígena* 25 (1965):35–63.

[14] Troy S. Floyd, "The Guatemalan Merchants, the Government and the *Provincianos*," *Hisp. Amer. Hist. Rev.* 41 (1961):90–110; Ralph L. Woodward, Jr., "Economic and Social Origins of the Guatemalan Political Parties (1773–1823)," *Hisp. Amer. Hist. Rev.* 45 (1965):544–66.

respect. The isolation of the Spanish colonists of Central America from the central Mexican heartland and the existence of a long, unsettled Caribbean frontier with many rivers leading to the interior created ideal conditions for "illegal" trade and commerce. Throughout the duration of the colonial period the Central American colonists augmented their legitimate business interests with smuggling and dealing in contraband goods. Their major collaborators were the British, who, together with the French and Dutch, worked assiduously to obtain a share of the wealth of Spanish America by raid, trade, and colonization along the Caribbean frontier.

The earliest smugglers and raiders in the Caribbean were the French, who, among other things, seized treasure ships, raided the Honduranean coast, and captured Chagres in Panama. During the Elizabethan period (the latter half of the sixteenth century) the French were joined by numerous English raiders and traders, and official Spanish-English animosities were expressed by open attack on Spanish ships and ravages against Spanish settlements by daring privateers such as Sir Francis Drake.[15]

In order to strengthen their position in the Caribbean France, England, and the Netherlands then turned to colonization of islands and mainland frontiers that were not effectively occupied by Spain. The small islands of the Lesser Antilles were settled in this way, as were portions of the larger islands when France obtained the western third of Española, known as Saint-Dominque, and England acquired control of Jamaica. Small, primarily English settlements also sprang up on the Caribbean coast of Central America at Belize in eastern Yucatán and at Cape Gracias a Dios and Bluefields on the eastern coast (Miskito coast) of Nicaragua. Although some settlers concentrated on agricultural pursuits, many sought a more adventurous livelihood in commercial-military dealings with the Spanish colonies, and during the latter half of the seventeenth century the Caribbean again was increasingly upset by attacks on shipping and Spanish settlements.

In contrast to the Elizabethan era, however, most depredations now were conducted by free-lance pirates and buccaneers who generally worked for their own gain independent of official sanctions. Many of these gentlemen-of-fortune were based at Port Royal, Jamaica; others had headquarters on the island of Tortuga and the adjacent coast of Saint-Dominque. Other pirate lairs were hidden among the many small islands of the Caribbean and at the isolated settlements of Belize and the Miskito Coast on the Central American shore. From these vantage points hundreds of buccaneers and adventurers such as William Dampier and the infamous Henry Morgan sallied forth to raid ships of any nation. At one time or another, virtually every accessible Spanish settlement from Veracruz to Venezuela was burned and plundered. Even more distant

[15] B. B. Solnick, *The West Indies and Central America to 1898* (New York: Knopf, 1970), pp. 47–64; J. H. Parry, *The Establishment of the European Hegemony, 1415–1715* (New York: Harper, 1961).

FIGURE 13.3 Francis Drake taking aboard loot and prisoners at Guatulco (from an eighteenth-century engraving). Pirates and buccaneers were by no means restricted to the Caribbean shores of New Spain, but operated along western coasts, too. Reprinted by permission of the publishers, The Arthur H. Clark Company, from *Pirates on the West Coast of New Spain, 1572–1742,* by Peter Gerhard.

Pacific coast towns such as Granada and Leon proved vulnerable because of ready access from the Caribbean via the San Juan River and Lake Nicaragua. By the end of the seventeenth century the depredations of these daring outlaws had become so disruptive that England and France joined with Spain to put an end to their filibustering activities. Those pirates who still survived their hazardous enterprises gradually settled down to a more peaceful existence as island settlers or as logwood cutters and traders at various points along the mainland frontier.[16]

Yet the Caribbean did not remain peaceful for long. Throughout much of the eighteenth century formal wars raging between the major European colonial powers were felt in the West Indies. Belize, now the foremost non-Spanish colony on the Central American frontier, was the scene of a number of attacks and counterattacks between England and Spain, and smaller British settlements at Roatan in the Bay Islands, Black River in northeast Honduras, Cape Gracias a Dios, and Bluefields were also upset.

Spanish American colonists did not sit idly by throughout these years while their towns were raided and foreign settlements established on the frontiers. To be sure Spain's retaliation was not effective in the long run. Most of the Caribbean islands and mainland rim became part of the

[16] Solnick, *The West Indies,* pp. 65–74; C. H. Haring, *The Buccaneers in the West Indies in the XVII Century* (London: Methuen, 1910); A. P. Newton, *The European Nations in the West Indies, 1493–1688* (London: Black, 1933).

colonial holdings of other countries, either officially or by de facto occupation and control. Nonetheless efforts were made to limit and repulse these advances. Let us note the nature of this retaliation along the Central American frontier where Spanish Americans faced two major opponents: the British and the militant native inhabitants of the Caribbean shore.

The crown's initial reaction to the presence of foreign corsairs in Caribbean waters was to fortify the most important ports, including Havana, Veracruz, and Portobello. There was also a general tightening of the trade route between Guatemala City and Caribbean coastal points in the late sixteenth century. Trade with distant Trujillo, which had been frequently raided, was sharply reduced, and a new deepwater port, Santo Tomás de Castilla, was established on the Gulf of Honduras in order to reduce the vulnerable coastal voyage between Golfo Dulce (Lake Izabal), the entryway via the Motagua Valley to Guatemala City, and the former port, Puerto de Caballos, which also had been frequently attacked (Figure 13.1).[17]

It was shortly thereafter, in the early decades of the seventeenth century, that the first foreign settlers appeared at the mouth of the Belize River. By the 1630s a small colony was established to facilitate smuggling and to exploit the abundant stands of logwood that grew in the river backswamps. English lumbermen, planters, and traders were also organizing small settlements on the islands of Roatan, San Andres, and Providencia, and at Cape Gracias and Bluefields on the adjacent Miskito Coast.[18]

As we have seen, it was not long before these isolated settlements were transformed into pirate lairs and jump-off points for raids at sea and against the Central American provinces of New Spain. The buccaneers were considerably aided in their excursions by indigenous allies from the eastern Nicaraguan coast, the so-called Miskito Indians. The Miskito were a small but growing mixed population whose biological origins derived from miscegenation between indigenous coastal natives living in the vicinity of Cape Gracias and Negro slaves and refugees, some of whom had been brought to the coast by the British as plantation laborers, while others had sought asylum on the isolated shore from servitude in the West Indies or in the Honduranean mines. Their zambo offspring readily served as guides and provisioners for the buccaneers, receiving in return cloth, beads, machetes, and especially guns and ammunition which they themselves then used to intimidate and raid more timid indigenous tribes of the interior.[19]

Against the combined threat of buccaneers and militant Miskito Indians the Hispanic colonists of Central America applied the standard

[17] Troy S. Floyd, *The Anglo-Spanish Struggle for Mosquitia* (Albuquerque: Univ. of New Mexico Press, 1967).

[18] Alan K. Craig, "Logwood as a Factor in the Settlement of British Honduras," *Caribbean Studies* 9 (1969):53–62; J. J. Parsons, *English-Speaking Settlements of the Western Caribbean*, Yearbook of the Association of Pacific Coast Geographers (Cheney, Washington, 1954), 16:3–16.

[19] Mary W. Helms, "The Cultural Ecology of a Colonial Tribe," *Ethnology* 8 (1969):76–84.

frontier formula of presidios and missions. One fort was established on the Río Dulce to protect the Bay of Honduras, while another was constructed on the Río San Juan near the entrance to Lake Nicaragua. At the end of the seventeenth century a third presidio was established in the wilds of the Petén to protect Chiapas and Guatemala against possible incursions from Belize; shortly thereafter Fort Bacalar was built in eastern Yucatán for similar reasons. None of these military installations was very formidable, however, and no offensive action was taken.[20]

The missionaries, Dominicans and Franciscans, were equally unsuccessful in their efforts to pacify the unconquered natives roaming the heart of the Petén and the interior mountains and Caribbean slopes of Honduras, Nicaragua, and Costa Rica. The missions were intended to break the relationships between these natives and the Miskito, who intimidated the interior tribes but also brought them English trade goods. The most promising mission prospects appeared to lie among the Talamancan tribes in southeast Costa Rica, and by the beginning of the eighteenth century 16 mission communities had been established along the highland frontier. But the restless natives did not find mission life agreeable and so fled to the protection of the mountains. In Nicaragua and Honduras missions were additionally handicapped by Miskito attacks, and little headway was gained among the scattered interior tribes who preferred the tools and cloth obtained through trade with Miskito and English to the sedentary agrarian life demanded by Spanish padres.[21]

In the early eighteenth century the ties between Miskito and English were strengthened when England fortified the Miskito Coast and claimed it as a protectorate. Miskito raids now became more fearsome, too, and Spanish frontier settlements in Honduras, Nicaragua, and Costa Rica were attacked and looted in a manner comparable to Apache depredations on the northern frontier. Although some of these raids were instigated by the English, the hostilities frequently were not condoned by the coastal settlers who much preferred peaceful relations with the Spanish frontier so as to augment their sugar plantations and dyewood cutting with contraband trade.

The opportunities for such trade were numerous. The Matina coast, a rich cacao-producing area of Costa Rica, was a favorite rendezvous for Englishmen from Punta Gorda (also Dutch from the Antilles) and Hispanic Costa Ricans from the highland centers who journeyed to the coast twice a year ostensibly to direct cacao harvests, but also to exchange local resources for English manufactured goods. In Nicaragua cacao, cattle, gold, and tobacco moved down the Río San Juan, the Bluefields River, and the Río Coco to be exchanged for foreign manufactures. An even more active trade thrived along the Honduranean frontier. Cattle, horses, and mules from the interior savannahs, indigo from upland valleys, and precious metals from the Spanish mines were conveyed along the many rivers leading to the coast to the English settlement at Black

[20] Floyd, *Anglo-Spanish Struggle*.
[21] Ibid.

River. In Guatemala the most frequently used contraband route was the Río Polochic, which flowed from the Verapaz hinterland into the Gulfo Dulce.[22]

Once again Spanish authorities made sporadic efforts to end Miskito raids, reduce contraband trade, and counterbalance English fortifications with presidios and rejuvenated missions, but still without success. A more definite step toward resolution of the problem of the English in Central America seemed to appear on the diplomatic front when, in 1786, as part of a wider package of Anglo-Spanish negotiations, England agreed to abandon all her coastal settlements except Belize and to recognize Spanish sovereignty over this settlement in exchange for continued logwood and mahogany cutting privileges. In spite of formal treaties, however, the diverse residents of Belize refused to acknowledge Spanish authority and stubbornly considered themselves independent of Spanish control. Similarly, although the Caribbean coast of Nicaragua and Honduras now lay open to Spanish occupation, little was done to establish effective claim to this territory. The long history of Miskito hostility did not encourage Hispanic settlement in eastern Nicaragua, and in Honduras colonization was successful only at Trujillo. Gradually small settlements of English reappeared, and contraband trade was renewed and flourished.

Consequently, by the end of the eighteenth century settlements along the eastern frontier of Central America still contained primarily English-speaking logwood and mahogany cutters, traders of European and Jamaican background, and even a few Yankees from the newly independent United States, as well as a considerable number of Negroes and mulattoes, both slaves and freemen. This ethnic and cultural diversity was augmented by the arrival of the Black Carib, a mixed population of Negro and Island Carib origins, who in 1797 were deported by the British from the island of St. Vincent in the Lesser Antilles (where they had emerged as a fugitive Negro-Indian society) to Roatan in the Bay Islands. From here many Black Carib moved to the mainland where, in succeeding decades, they settled along the coast of the Gulf of Honduras from Black River to Stann Creek in Belize.[23] East of the Black Carib, in eastern Honduras and Nicaragua, the seacoast and lower reaches of the rivers continued to be populated by small villages of Miskito, while farther inland a variety of small bands and tribes were slowly becoming extinct. In eastern Costa Rica Negroes, mulattoes, and zamboes from the Matina Valley cacao plantations shared the lowlands with the Talamancans, who sought refuge in the isolated mountains and plains of southern and southeastern Costa Rica.

Much of what we have outlined concerning the Caribbean frontier of New Spain was also characteristic of large portions of colonial Panama.

[22] Ibid.; M. D. Olien, *The Negro in Costa Rica*, Developing Nations Monograph Series, no. 3 (Winston-Salem: Wake Forest University, 1970), part 2; Woodward, Jr., "Economic and Social Origins," pp. 554–56.

[23] D. M. Taylor, *The Black Carib of British Honduras* (New York: Wenner-Gren Foundation for Anthropological Research, 1951).

Except for the trans-isthmian route, the environs of Panama City, and a narrow strip of Pacific coastal plain to the west, this mountainous territory remained outside effective Hispanic control. Therefore English, French, and Dutch privateers and buccaneers, drawn by the wealth of the Hispanic trade route, once again found an isolated Caribbean coast ideally suited for rest, resupply, and rendezvous. They again met native allies, too, in the Cueva-Cuna who inhabited the banks of streams and rivers in eastern Panama. Missionary pressures and forced labor in the Spanish towns of the Pacific coast had imbued the Cuna with a strong antipathy toward the Spanish. Like the Miskito, the Cuna also went to sea with the pirates and served as guides and supplementary warriors for buccaneers wishing to cross the isthmus to attack Hispanic settlements. Counterattacks and general unrest continued until late in the eighteenth century when, after piracy had waned, eastern Panama and the Cuna fell into peaceful isolation.[24]

Most of the Guaymí Indians in the rugged interior of western Panama also remained apart from Spanish influence. Early military efforts to penetrate their mountain hinterland had failed, and mission centers fared little better since many of their neophytes fled from the communities to the protection of the central highlands. In contrast to the Miskito and Cuna, however, the Guaymí allowed relatively little contact with privateers and pirates, although portions of their territory including Almirante Bay and Chiriqui Lagoon were favorite rendezvous for buccaneer fleets. To be sure, trade with these foreigners had initially yielded metal tools, beads, and similar desirable items, but pirate depredations among the natives shortly replaced friendship and commerce with hostility and avoidance.[25]

In summary, except for Portobello, the Matina Valley, and western portions of the north shore of Honduras, the Caribbean lowlands of Central America remained outside effective Spanish control during the colonial period. Instead, indigenous natives, Negroes, mixed populations of mulattoes and zamboes, and various non-Hispanic Europeans, especially English-speakers, endowed this frontier with a distinctly non-Hispanic flavor. Spanish efforts to divert and limit this foreign penetration and to extend the political-religious authority of the crown into these frontier regions met with very little success. The financial outlays for missions and military defense had only diverted badly needed resources from the Central American colonies themselves, thereby helping to maintain the provincialism and underdevelopment that marked these Hispanic centers as targets for foreign traders and smugglers. The poverty of the Central American republics also would make them vulnerable to foreign interference after political independence from Spain.

[24] D. B. Stout, *San Blas Cuna Acculturation: An Introduction* (New York: Wenner-Gren Foundation for Anthropological Research, 1947).
[25] Philip D. Young, *Ngawbe* (Urbana: Univ. of Illinois Press, 1971), chap. 2.

part three

THE CHALLENGE

OF

NATION-BUILDING

14

The Age of Caudillos

Independence from Spain

At the close of the eighteenth century the European powers stood on the brink of a new era of competition, change, and expansion. Technological improvements heralded the advent of the Industrial Revolution, most notably in Great Britain. On the continent the French Revolution unleashed social and political forces that would transform the shape of European society and give rise to the growth of nation-states. Industrialization and nation-building together would underwrite a dynamic expansion of European energies and influence in the nineteenth century. As the new order began to take form, even the foremost supporters of the traditional seignorial pattern gradually gave way before it. So it was that under the press of a new Europe the Spanish empire reached its final collapse in the initial decades of the nineteenth century.

The immediate pressures engendering this break centered on the conflict between Spain and Napoleonic France. In 1807 the forces of Napoleon Bonaparte overran Spain, forcing the abdication of the Spanish Bourbon ruler, Charles IV. The Spanish citizenry responded to this conquest with bitter guerrilla warfare, and by 1814, with British assistance, they had forced the French army back over the Pyrenees and returned Charles's son, Ferdinand VII, to the throne. Ferdinand attempted to restore strict and absolute monarchical rule, but was forced to submit to a liberal constitution more in tune with the revolutionary times which advocated reductions in crown authority and traditional class privileges.[1]

[1] Cf. R. A. Humphreys and John Lynch, eds., *The Origins of the Latin American Revolutions, 1808–1826* (New York: Knopf, 1965).

These events sparked concern and confusion in the Spanish American colonies, particularly among the elite, who were destined to play the leading roles in the coming storm.[2] When the Spanish monarchy fell to the French invaders the viceroy, audiencia officials, and other royal colonial agents suddenly found their source of authority gone. Creole-dominated cabildos in the capitals and the provinces quickly took advantage of this opportunity to challenge the peninsular administrators for governmental control. However, they did not demand immediate political independence. Instead all contestants asserted their claims to power in the name of the deposed king as a holding action until he should be restored to the Spanish throne. In the interim of uncertainty defense of the colonies fell to the refurbished colonial army which stood ready in case France or England might attempt to replace Spain in the Americas.

These external threats did not develop seriously, but another and in some ways greater fear haunted the elite: that of rebellion by the masses of castas, Negroes, and Indians in the absence of royal control.[3] Their worst fears seemed about to be realized in 1810 when a popular rebellion erupted in north-central Mexico among the prosperous laborers and entrepreneurs of the Bajío who had become increasingly impatient with Indian tribute requirements, guild restrictions, sales taxes, slavery, and other limitations of the traditional colonial order that hindered full realization of their growing economic potential.

The initial uprising was originally plotted by a group of creoles who intended to gain control of the peninsular power center at Mexico City in the name of Ferdinand. Aroused to action by the premature discovery of the plot by royal officials, a rural creole priest, Father Miguel Hidalgo y Costilla, issued the call to arms to his parishioners. Soon, however, the movement grew out of control, and tens of thousands of armed raiders—mestizos and Indians, peons, miners, and cowboys—looted stores and marketplaces, murdered and massacred, and burned the homes and estates of the socially privileged, peninsular and creole alike, reducing the provinces west and north of Mexico City to a state of anarchy. They were finally subdued with fearful loss of numbers by a peninsular army.[4] But then a second and better-organized uprising appeared to the south, in Guerrero and southern Michoacan. This movement was ably directed by one of Hidalgo's followers, another parish priest, José María Morelos y Pavón, who preached a revolutionary program of independent rule and social and economic reform that de-

---

[2] The masses of Indians, Negroes, and castas had no direct hand in the break with Spain.

[3] Although the creole elite had agitated for greater economic and political participation and readily seized the opportunity for political prominence when royal authority collapsed, nonetheless they remained staunch supporters of the traditional social hierarchy which defined and validated their aristocratic status.

[4] Charles C. Cumberland, *Mexico, The Struggle for Modernity* (London: Oxford Univ. Press, 1968), pp. 113–22; Hugh Hamill, *The Hidalgo Revolt* (Gainesville: Univ. of Florida Press, 1966); Lesley Byrd Simpson, *Many Mexicos,* 4th ed. rev. (Berkeley: Univ. of California Press, 1967), chap. 19.

manded the dissolution of the large landed estates and the restoration of land to Indian villages. But Morelos's vision was premature, and all branches of the elite rallied to put down this intolerable challenge to the traditional social order.[5]

The Spanish American elite then encountered another threat to their high position, this time from the crown itself as Ferdinand conceded to the liberal constitution in Spain. Although political independence had not been a primary question during this troubled decade, official separation from the mother country now appeared to be the only alternative if the privileges of the elite, creoles and peninsulars alike, were to be safeguarded from the ominous threat of change sounding in Spain. To protect their favored status quo against the possibility of liberal legislation from abroad, the conservative elite of New Spain declared their formal independence from Spain in 1821 and initiated self-rule as a monarchy under Colonel Agustín Iturbide. However, Iturbide's reign was short-lived, and the new Empire of Mexico soon fragmented into smaller political units officially oriented toward constitutional and republican governmental structures. Thus the provinces of Central America (except for Chiapas) broke away from Mexican control in 1823 to form the United Provinces of Central America, and then fissioned further into five separate republics, Guatemala, El Salvador, Honduras, Nicaragua, and Costa Rica. (Panama remained part of New Granada or Colombia.)

This fragmentation of the former viceroyalty into six independent polities was indicative on a higher level of the regionalism, localism, and self-interest groups which confronted each of the new republics on a more limited scale and greatly hindered the establishment of effective centralized national governments. Regionalism and protection of special group privileges and interests were, of course, characteristic of colonial society where corporations and interest groups were purposely encouraged and balanced against each other as a means of maintaining royal control. Legislative ties linking all units to the royal bureaucracy and common loyalty to the symbol of the crown often masked this basic divisiveness. However, when the cohesion provided by the Spanish crown and bureaucracy was removed, regionalism and social, economic, and political interest groups emerged unchecked.

The most dramatic representation of the supremacy of regional forces (next to the dissolution of New Spain into six separate political entities) is seen in the rise of the *caudillo* to political prominence. Although central governments technically were organized and self-styled as republics, de facto political control fell to aggressive, regional military chieftains and political bosses or caudillos. The continuous clashes between caudillos and their bands of rough followers as they competed vigorously for the personal prestige and material rewards that could be derived from control of local and sometimes national power positions filled the decades

[5] Cumberland, *Mexico*, pp. 123–26; Wilbert H. Timmons, *Morelos: Priest, Soldier, Statesman of Mexico* (El Paso: Texas Western College Press, 1963); Simpson, *Many Mexicos*, chap. 19.

immediately following independence with violence and seeming anarchy.[6]

The military had acquired new prestige and influence during the struggles prior to independence. Now its leaders took advantage of the political reorganization and confusion necessitated by independence to assert this power and to seek wealth and social prestige in their own behalf. In like fashion military control provided opportunities for society's dispossessed to move into and benefit from the public power arena. After independence administrative use of colonial socioracial terms and the accompanying legal restrictions which had underlaid the colonial system of castas were officially terminated in all the new republics (though their social expression still remained), and slavery was abolished. All persons were declared free and equal citizens under the law and remained separated only by economic distinctions of rich and poor. Now former slaves, mestizos, mulattoes, and Indians who had fled their communities used military service to seek their social and material fortunes. These brash soldiers formed support units for ambitious military officers, younger sons of elite families or mestizos risen through the ranks, who vied fiercely with each other for the public offices, privileges, and material spoils that in turn would yield the ultimate goals of power and social prestige.

The age of caudillos was marked by violence and destruction, yet caudillo politics was not haphazard. On the contrary it formed an organized political system with a predictable set of rules for its successful exercise. The caudillo or chieftain rose to prominence by attracting a group of armed followers bound to him by personal ties of loyalty (a practice with colonial precedent in the private armies and bands of retainers that surrounded rich and powerful men). He demonstrated his dominance and worthiness for such support by personal bravado, charisma, and deeds of valor.

In addition to charisma, courage, and the ability to deal skillfully in interpersonal relations, the caudillo was obliged to keep his band of supporters adequately rewarded for their loyalty with material goods and benefits. Since caudillos rarely held personal fortunes it was imperative to seek resources wherever they could be found and to obtain them by extortion, manipulation, or force of arms, if necessary. Unfortunately, it was virtually impossible for most caudillos to maintain a constant flow of spoils sufficient to satisfy their followers and sustain their own elite-oriented life-styles. Yet failing this return supporters would readily abandon their erstwhile chief (often at critical moments on the field of battle or by assassination) and join the (temporarily) more remunerative ranks of

---

[6] The rise to power of caudillos was also predicated on the failure of the civilian creole elite to develop effective national governments after independence. Although locally powerful, the landowners were unable to form a permanent alliance among themselves as a political unit. Most opposed such centralizing efforts since an effective central government would undercut their local family powers.

another. Consequently most caudillos' rise to power was short-lived and their demise frequently violent.[7]

The most successful of these military-political leaders were able to survive long enough and to attract bands of supporters, often groupings of lesser caudillos and their retinues, on a scale large enough to achieve national recognition, even to become heads of state. While they held this high office lieutenants and other clients could expect lucrative military promotions and politically useful and profitable positions in legislative bodies and other government offices, and the proceeds of the national treasury and the receipts of the customs houses would maintain the socially prestigeful life-styles sought by power-conscious backers. In the ceaseless quest for funds desperate dictators even turned abroad, particularly to England, for loans negotiated at disastrous interest rates. Sooner or later, however, support would shift in favor of another, and a palace revolt would oust the president, whose successor, often one of his closest associates, would eventually suffer a similar fate.

Although military officers composed the dominant force in politics during these decades, the political scene was further complicated by heated controversies between "federalists" and "centralists" and between "liberals" and "conservatives" (all of whom were of the elite or hopeful of rising into its ranks). These positions differed over proper distribution of power and authority and the degree of sociopolitical readjustment needed to effect this distribution. Federalists usually favored a greater degree of regional autonomy in economic and political affairs and local benefit from regional resources, while centralists backed unified centralization of resources and authority. Liberals professed to wish to ease some of the traditional barriers to sociopolitical advance and particularly opposed the privileged ecclesiastical courts and the great wealth and power of the church, although they were by no means antireligion. Conservatives were intent on preserving the status quo in social and economic structures and upheld ecclesiastical privileges. In general the wealthier and more established members of the elite—landowners, upper clergy, higher bureaucrats, and established army officers—held conservative views in the interests of their favored positions. Less affluent but ambitious younger army officers, merchants, miners, professionals (doctors and lawyers), lesser bureaucrats, and intellectuals supported the liberal approach in the interests of their own elitist aspirations. To some extent "liberalism" included "federalism" while "conservatism" allied with "centralism," but these associations were far from standard. In actuality all groups were directed by army officers who readily assumed the banner of a convenient cause and formed alliances with others regardless of dogma in order to benefit personal rivalries, schemes, and ambitions.[8]

[7] Eric R. Wolf and E. C. Hansen, "*Caudillo* Politics: A Structural Analysis," *Comp. Studies in Soc. and Hist.* 9 (1967):168–79; Charles Chapman, "The Age of the Caudillos," *Hisp. Amer. Hist. Rev.* 12 (1932):281–300.

[8] Stanley J. Stein and Barbara H. Stein, *The Colonial Heritage of Latin America* (New York: Oxford Univ. Press, 1970), pp. 158–73.

Mexico's First Fifty Years

The era of caudillism in Mexico is frequently identified by the name of the most successful of this breed of politician in that country, Antonio López de Santa Anna. Although Santa Anna was the most illustrious of his day, dozens of provincial caudillos emerged in every region of Mexico. Some remained local figures of power and authority, while others entered the chaotic theatre of central government where, over a period of some 50 turbulent years (approximately 1820–70), more than 30 different individuals took frequent turns at the presidency, heading more than 50 governments. Needless to say, effective national rule was hardly possible under these conditions.

Santa Anna's Mexico was also in bad shape economically. The rebellions prior to independence had destroyed some of the richest mines and had significantly interfered with the operations of many more. As abandoned shafts filled with water, once-prosperous mining communities were reduced to poverty. Agriculture and animal husbandry likewise had suffered as rebels and retaliatory troops burned haciendas and villages, looted towns, and destroyed crops and livestock. A ravaged countryside spelled misery for the urban centers which were dependent on their hinterlands for food and raw materials. Commerce and craft production collapsed, plunging thousands of urban labors into destitution.[9]

The troubled decades following independence did little to improve this picture. To be sure mining very slowly began to improve as gallerys were drained and reshored and newer machinery introduced. This postindependence mining revival was underwritten by foreign investers from northern Europe and the United States. The British were particularly eager to organize companies, provide new, expensive machinery, and send skilled experts to direct operations on the premise that new technology and an influx of capital would stimulate renewed exploitation of the rich natural resources still hidden in the Mexican earth. Although many of these ventures failed, some succeeded, and the influx of foreign capital and technology definitely rejuvenated Mexican mining.[10]

Urban textile manufacturing also gradually improved. New machinery was imported and a series of mechanized spinning and weaving mills were established. Yet because it was an infant industry the goods it produced were expensive and fell short of meeting total demand. Cheaper wearing apparel continued to be imported from Great Britain and the United States, and there was a thriving business in contraband textiles. Other products—oils, soaps, pottery, and shoes—were locally manufactured in many regions but generally on a craft rather than industrial basis.

[9] Cumberland, *Mexico*, pp. 130–40.

[10] Cumberland, *Mexico*, pp. 148–55 and 163–73; Matías Romero, "British Investors and the Real del Monte Mine: Mexico, 1824–1848," in *Foreign Investment in Latin America*, ed. M. D. Bernstein (New York: Knopf, 1966), pp. 71–75.

In the countryside agriculture provided basic subsistence, but little more. Actually there was little incentive to produce for any but local markets, for transportation was even worse than in colonial days, and the rough cart roads and pack animal paths were usually in terrible condition. Cargo-carrying mules and carts averaged only a few kilometers a day, and while stagecoaches managed 14 or 16 km (9 or 10 miles) per hour, passengers would be well jostled and bounced. Travelers could also be assured of meeting numerous highwaymen and bandits, who had been plentiful before but whose numbers became legion in the chaotic years following independence. Under these conditions the cost of transporting agricultural produce and craft and industrial products for any considerable distance was simply prohibitive. Consequently the economy remained highly regionalized and essentially subsistence-oriented.[11]

Poor and dangerous transportation was one major hindrance to economic recovery, and the deplorable fiscal affairs of the central government was another. In spite of a plethora of taxes, income from domestic sources was far too small to meet government expenses. Most government monies were derived from exorbitant import-export duties, which ran as high as 50 to 60 percent of the declared value of the goods, and from a series of foreign loans issued mainly by Great Britain at exorbitant interest rates which, in turn, consumed a large share of the customs duties. A few million dollars were also obtained from the United States in exchange for California, New Mexico, and Texas.[12]

Over 90 percent of these diverse monies flowed to the upper echelons of the burgeoning military and had little impact on the wider economy. While generals grew rich and their wives conspicuously over-jeweled, the cities, towns, and countryside were beset with begging, thieving, hungry, and poorly clothed vagabonds and *léperos*. Even those who were able to find honest employment were hard-pressed to support a wife and family on the meager wages paid to a farm or mine laborer or a textile worker.

Much of the economic chaos and political turbulence of these decades was reflected in and further complicated by rivalries expressed in a clerical context since the church, by virtue of its involvement at various social levels, readily mirrored and symbolized the social, economic, and political inconsistencies, opportunisms, and inequalities characteristic of society at large. To those of the established elite who favored the church the ecclesiastical hierarchy as represented by the bishops and other upper clergy typified the rightful order of society. Like themselves, the church was wealthy, privileged, and protected, and if the church should prove vulnerable to certain liberalizing pressures that threatened these bastions of the traditional order, then what security could there be for others in high station? Opposing this conservative view were those "liberals" who saw in the life of the church all that was unsavory and reactionary in society; who viewed the church as a greedy, grasping body that sucked up land and property, charged outrageous fees for its ministrations, and

[11] Cumberland, *Mexico*, pp. 155–62.
[12] Ibid., pp. 144–47.

FIGURE 14.1 The Zapotec village of Santiago Guevea in the nineteenth century. After independence from Spain the inhabitants of Indian communities such as this were no longer protected wards of the Spanish state and therefore were unable to resort to special legal protection against loss of their holdings by measures such as Juarez's reforms. From Frederick Starr, *Indians of Southern Mexico* (published by the author, Chicago, 1899), pl. CI.

generally resisted changes that liberals considered necessary to ameliorate contemporary conditions. Underlying this anticlericalism was the fact that with the government and general economy in poor fiscal condition the church's wealth was a major source of potential revenue for the financially hard-pressed liberals seeking power.

Until midcentury proclerical conservative elements generally maintained control of government, and attacks on the church and the established order were minimal. However, in 1854 the "liberals," under Benito Juárez, took over the national government and set about to remedy the country's ills. The main thrust of their reforming efforts was directed against corporate landholding bodies, particularly the church, whose wealth was needed by the new government and whose concentration of land the liberals considered a major factor hindering agricultural productivity and the general standard of living. Consequently, a series of decrees required the church to sell all its real property not used strictly for religious purposes, reduced ecclesiastical fueros, provided for civil registration of births, deaths, marriages, and religious vows, secularized cemeteries, and required clergy to perform sacraments even if the applicant could not pay the fees. Not surprisingly clergy-supported revolts soon erupted in various parts of the country, and the bloody and destructive War of the Reform raged from 1857 to 1861. The war, which saw the defeat of the clerical forces, generated even harsher anticlerical legislation including outright confiscation of church property and the abolition of tithes.[13]

Thus the liberals under Juárez significantly secularized Mexico and damaged the wealth and privileged position of the church. But the formal eradication of privileged corporate landholding bodies also gravely affected another special enclave, the corporate Indian community. The stipulations of the reform legislation applied to these landholding units, too. Convinced that corporate native communities were incapable of efficient land utilization and that private rather than corporate ownership of land would be more conducive to agricultural development, Juárez's government stipulated that communal lands be divided among heads of families as private holdings. Unfortunately many Indians did not know how to safeguard their new property and soon lost their land to hacendados or other land grabbers. Others, particularly those who received title to the better lands, operated their now private holdings to produce income for their own personal ends rather than for community benefit.[14]

To stem this tide of liberalism the conservative elite in desperation looked for support abroad. After hearing their plea, France, for reasons of her own, agreed to challenge the liberal government by reestablishing a monarchy in Mexico under Archduke Maximilian of Austria.[15] From 1862–67, in the face of fierce liberal resistance, the unfortunate Emperor Maximilian sought to establish a royal government in Mexico until France, faced with other problems at home, withdrew her troops and abandoned him to his fate. Juárez and his liberals then returned to power in a Mexico that had now added foreign invasion to its list of woes, and resumed the task of rebuilding a war-torn country until the death of Juárez in 1872.

Unity and Separatism in Central America

Regionalism heightened by mountainous terrain, poor transportation, political chaos, general economic stagnation, and clerical conflicts also characterized the age of caudillos in Central America. Indeed, because of Central America's greater poverty and long de facto localism and isolation from the major colonial centers during the centuries under Spanish rule, these problems emerge with even greater clarity and force among the provinces of the former audiencia of Guatemala. They were heightened

[13] Ibid., pp. 173–87; Simpson, *Many Mexicos,* chap. 22.

[14] George M. McBride, *The Land Systems of Mexico* (New York: American Geographical Society, 1923).

[15] Periodically over the previous 40 years various European countries had tried without great success to have their Mexican loans repaid and property damage claims resulting from civil upsets honored. When diplomatic requests failed, expeditionary forces were landed to back demands for payment of debts. It was in this context that France was interested in the elite's proposals.

further by long-standing resentment of Guatemalan control, which was another primary factor behind the dissolution of Central America into the five small republics of Guatemala, El Salvador, Honduras, Nicaragua, and Costa Rica.

Political separation from Spain was achieved with Mexico's declaration of independence in 1821. In 1823, after the collapse of Iturbide's "empire," the Central American provinces (with the exception of Chiapas) proclaimed their independence from Mexico and formed an independent government as the United Provinces of Central America. From its inception, however, this federation was torn by strife among political and regional factions led by power-seeking governors and military officers, and weakened by a lack of effective central leadership. The mutually competitive towns, which in aggregate composed the federation, were generally uncooperative, having united mainly out of a common concern for protection in these troubled times. The central administration was also severely handicapped by an empty treasury and by disagreements regarding the structure and powers of the new government.[16]

The landowners, churchmen, and merchants of Guatemala saw their interests best served by a strong centralized government located in Guatemala City. In contrast, many of the leading citizens of towns in El Salvador, Honduras, Nicaragua, and Costa Rica considered the prospect of Guatemalan control intolerable and pressed for a less centralized, federated form of government. This conflict was complicated further by disagreements between the "conservative" element of landholders and churchmen throughout the provinces, who shared a common interest in preserving the traditional sociopolitical status quo, and those of "liberal" persuasions who, again under an anticlerical banner, wished to shake loose some of the economic power and wealth of the conservative elite, particularly that of the church, for their own social and political improvement. In spite of these various ideologies, in Central America as in Mexico political activities during the first 50 years of independence emphasized acquisition of personalized power and wealth through force of arms, and except for strikes against the church, political party labels and slogans held relatively little real significance.

Attacks against the property and privileges of the church (most significant in Guatemala where the church was strongest), and through it against the conservative element in general, were very common during the years of the federation when "liberals" and "federalists" under the direction of Francisco Morazán controlled the central government. Morazán and his associates had real need of ecclesiastical wealth because the financial situation of the federation was tenuous. What income was derived from forced domestic loans from the well-to-do, from tobacco and gunpowder monopolies, from customs duties, and from loans from

[16] Thomas L. Karnes, *The Failure of Union: Central America, 1824–1960* (Chapel Hill: Univ. of North Carolina Press, 1961); Dana G. Munro, *The Five Republics of Central America* (New York: Russell and Russell, 1967), pp. 24–31, 164–67, and chap. 9; Chester L. Jones, *Guatemala, Past and Present* (Minneapolis: Univ. of Minnesota Press, 1940); F. M. Stanger, "National Origins in Central America," *Hisp. Amer. Hist. Rev.* 12 (1932):18–45.

British banking houses did little to establish a financial base for the new government. As might be expected, these monies were used primarily for officials' salaries and to support military forces which were engaged in almost constant internecine strife. Economic development also fared poorly, for in Central America as in Mexico the economy virtually came to a halt during these troubled years.[17]

Political support for the federation was just as shaky. The location of the federation assembly in Guatemala City and the fact that such levies and taxes as actually were collected derived almost entirely from Guatemalans fueled fears among the other provinces that Guatemala would assume de facto control. In turn, the Guatemalan conservatives opposed having to carry a disproportionate share of the financial burden of the federation and deplored the liberal attitudes of those in power. Finally, in 1838, the federation began to collapse and the five tiny provinces went their individual ways.

As they began their separate yet constantly intermeshed histories as independent polities, the Central American republics revealed notable variations in the outcome of their approaches to more or less common economic problems and political goals. Three major orientations can be discerned: that of Guatemala; that of the three middle states—Nicaragua, Honduras, and El Salvador; and that of Costa Rica. To a great extent these differences were rooted in the regional administrative patterns developed during the colonial period. In this context it is important to remember that Guatemala City, as the seat of colonial authority for Central America, had developed the necessary institutional and governmental apparatus for the formal administration of this territory during the colonial centuries. In contrast, the colonial towns of Nicaragua, Honduras, El Salvador and, to a more limited extent, Costa Rica were the recipients of directives from the Guatemalan capital and had neither opportunity nor necessity to develop highly centralized governmental machinery of their own.

We must take partial exception to this statement in the case of Costa Rica. Although formally part of the Guatemalan sphere, Costa Rica lacked sufficient colonial wealth to be of much interest to Spain and was located too far from Guatemala City for effective administration from this capital. Furthermore, the province's isolation was preferred and encouraged by the residents of the meseta central towns who wished to handle their own affairs without interference. Consequently, the Costa Rican communities had developed and relied on their own administrative organization to a great extent and cherished an attitude of neutralism and de facto political separateness from the rest of Central America during the centuries under Spain.

Variations in the composition of colonial Central American society and

[17] R. S. Smith, "Financing the Central American Federation, 1821–1838," *Hisp. Amer. Hist. Rev.* 43 (1963):483–510; Mary Holleran, *Church and State in Guatemala*, Columbia University Studies in History, Economics, and Public Law, no. 549 (New York: Columbia Univ. Press, 1949); Mary W. Williams, "The Ecclesiastical Policy of Francisco Morazán," *Hisp. Amer. Hist. Rev.* 3 (1920):119–43.

in the availability and distribution of prestige-conferring wealth were also significant factors influencing the economic and political diversity of the nineteenth-century republics. Guatemalan society was divided between a small but wealthy and powerful Hispanic urban elite and a large, poor, and politically inactive rural Indian work force, although castas (or *Ladinos* as they are known in Guatemala) were present in limited numbers.

In Nicaragua, Honduras, and (to a lesser degree) El Salvador, where conquest and colonization had upset native society to a much greater extent than in Guatemala, the ratio of conqueror to conquered had been less extreme. Therefore control of native labor yielded less wealth to the elite. Miscegenation was more common, too, not only between Spaniard and Indian, but also with Negroes imported as mine laborers in Honduras or as workers in Nicaraguan shipyards. Thus the Hispanic centers of Nicaragua, Honduras, and El Salvador came to be composed predominantly of mestizos and other castas, although a small but influential Spanish elite maintained the highest levels of society, particularly in El Salvador.

In Costa Rica warfare and European diseases had effectively removed many of the indigenous inhabitants of the meseta central even before firm colonization had begun. Little Indian labor and few Indian women remained available for Spanish use. Therefore, in contrast to the usual colonial situation, Costa Rican society was constituted primarily of self-sufficient Hispanic small farmers who quietly tilled the soil to meet basic subsistence needs.[18]

As a result of these social, economic, and administrative contrasts, the new republics revealed varying degrees of susceptibility to caudillism after independence and the dissolution of the federation. In Guatemala, where an administrative structure stood intact, federation government was replaced by a stable military dictatorship under Rafael Carrera (1844–65). Although Carrera was a mestizo, he was supported and maintained in his position by the wealthy conservative elite of landowners, merchants, and high clergy who cooperated effectively to maintain peace and their privileged status quo.

Nicaragua, El Salvador, and Honduras, in contrast, were plagued by regionalism and political instability. Governments rose and fell rapidly as ambitious military officers plotted their personal advancements without much restraint.[19] The frequent political turnover and accompanying turmoil in the middle states can be attributed to a number of factors. Unlike Guatemala, there was neither a well-entrenched rich and powerful elite nor significant colonial administrative machinery that could be adapted to the needs of new republics. Consequently, numerous ambitious mestizos knew few checks on their search for the wealth that gave power and social prestige. However, the poverty of these regions, combined with the considerable number of caudillos, made it extremely

[18] Munro, *Five Republics,* pp. 50–59 and 167–68; Jones, *Guatemala;* Stanger, "National Origins in Central America," pp. 18–45; Karnes, *Failure of Union,* chap. 1.

[19] Rivalries were frequently voiced in terms of civil war between leading towns. In Nicaragua, for example, the major clashes occurred between Leon, stronghold of liberal professionals and intellectuals, and Granada and its conservative elite.

difficult for an ambitious chief to find adequate sources of wealth for his supporters for any extended period of time, so that his day in the sun was usually brief, and political turnover rapid. In addition, the closeness of international border zones and the hospitality extended by neighboring governments, including Guatemala, to erstwhile caudillos allowed defeated chieftains to flee to a temporary exile when they fell from power. There they would plan a new coup while awaiting more favorable conditions for a return which not infrequently was effected with the direct assistance of their hosts.[20] This interference also considerably enhanced political tensions, especially for Honduras, which shared borders with three of the other four Central American countries. On the other hand interstate interference also seems indicative of mutual recognition of basic similarities and common problems. It is noteworthy in this context that during the nineteenth century Nicaragua, Honduras, and El Salvador made a number of diplomatic efforts, albeit unsuccessful, to confederate politically again.[21]

Costa Rica, as usual, preferred to remain aloof from the difficulties besetting her neighbors, and after the dissolution of the original federation she took little interest in new confederation efforts. Bolstered by an already existing administrative apparatus, government generally was conducted with less upset and with longer periods of stability than in the three middle states, although internal political conflicts were not entirely avoided. Political stability was also greatly favored by a growing economy and by wider and more equitable distribution of income and wealth among the members of society. Costa Rica's farmers sought the means for a prestigeful life-style in the production of coffee as an export crop rather than in caudillism and revolution. Coffee had been introduced in the late eighteenth century, and plantings had been encouraged by the government both before and after independence from Spain. Commercial shipments of high-value and high-quality beans to Great Britain were initiated in the 1830s, and not long thereafter production began to boom. As the national income improved cart roads were constructed to link major cities and hinterland coffee *fincas* (estates) of the meseta central and to connect them with the port of Puntarenas on the Pacific coast.[22]

Guatemala also profited from commercial dealings with Great Britain during these years, exporting cochineal via Belize (which now had become a major Central American trade center) for England's textile manufacturers. The middle states, particularly Nicaragua, were affected less

[20] From the point of view of the assisting regime, this meddling in the political affairs of a neighboring country was an alternate means of achieving a temporary posture of power and prestige when other sources, such as wealth and property, were hard to come by.

[21] Munro, *Five Republics,* pp. 72–126 passim; William S. Stokes, *Honduras, An Area Study in Government* (Madison: Univ. of Wisconsin Press, 1950); Stanger, "National Origins in Central America," pp. 18–45; Karnes, *Failure of Union.*

[22] James L. Busey, "Foundations of Political Contrast: Costa Rica and Nicaragua," *West. Polit. Quart.* 11 (1958):627–59; R. J. Houk, "Development of Foreign Trade and Commerce in Costa Rica to the Construction of the First Railway," *The Americas* 10 (1953)·197–209; Munro, *Five Republics,* pp. 138–45; Stanger, "National Origins in Central America," pp. 18–45.

by British trade than by growing international rivalry between Great Britain and the United States regarding control of a trans-isthmian route across Central America.

The value of such a crossing had been appreciated from the earliest years of Spanish conquest when trails and waterways connected the narrow stretch of land between Nombre de Dios and Panama City. Another route, also used to some extent in colonial times, lay to the north, where goods and passengers could move by boat along the Río San Juan and across Lake Nicaragua and then had only to cross a narrow neck of land to reach the Pacific Ocean. The United States' acquisition of California in 1846, and especially the discovery of gold, awakened new interest in this interoceanic passageway. In 1848 Cornelius Vanderbilt secured permission from Nicaragua to transport Yankee passengers through the country by the Río San Juan route. (The United States also obtained rights of transit across Panama by a treaty with Colombia and many travelers used this route. A railway was soon constructed to facilitate travel and Washington began to consider the prospects of building a canal across the narrow Panamanian Isthmus.)

Concurrently Great Britain, viewing the United States' interests in an ocean-to-ocean passageway with considerable alarm, sought to dominate the San Juan waterway by reestablishing her earlier claims to the Miskito Coast. Control of this strategic route became a major issue between the two countries, and their diplomatic maneuverings, sometimes with a show of military strength, added fuel to the turmoil of Nicaraguan politics at midcentury. The issue was eventually quieted by a treaty which provided for joint Anglo-American control of any canal which might be built. The two nations also agreed not to occupy, fortify, colonize, or otherwise assume dominion over any part of Central America, including the Miskito Coast. Thereupon Great Britain finally ceded the Miskito Coast and the Bay Islands to Nicaragua and Honduras in 1859 and 1860. However, Belize, strategically located for Central American and Caribbean commerce, remained part of the British empire and was officially recognized as the colony of British Honduras in 1862, although Guatemala continued to claim sovereignty.[23]

The formal transfer of the Miskito Coast to Nicaragua and Honduras had little effect on this Caribbean frontier. The republics did not extend effective control over these regions, and they continued to lie beyond the range of Hispanic influence. Similarly, in Guatemala and Costa Rica large tracts of "national" territory, particularly in the lowlands, still remained beyond effective national direction. For that matter, the subsistence-oriented daily lives of the many lower-sector families in Hispanic towns and countryside were not greatly affected by the fluctuating political fortunes of the social elite and those aspiring to join their ranks.

---

[23] Robert Naylor, "The British Role in Central America Prior to the Clayton-Bulwer Treaty of 1850," *Hisp. Amer. Hist. Rev.* 40 (1960):361–82; D. R. Radell, "Exploration and Commerce on Lake Nicaragua and the Río San Juan—1524–1800," *J. of Inter-American Studies and World Affairs* 12 (1970):107–25; Karnes, *Failure of Union*.

15

Railroads
and Revolution

Prelude to the Storm

During the last decades of the nineteenth century caudillism in its more violent forms subsided in Middle America, particularly in the larger republic, Mexico. Although military-backed competition for wealth and power continued, the techniques for acquiring these ends became more subtle and more institutionalized. They also grew more centralized in focus, for the decline in rough regional caudillism was directly related to the rise of capital cities as centers of business and government and the emergence of strong national presidents with firm control of the military and the means to pacify competitors' search for wealth.

The growing power of the capital cities and of the presidencies rested in turn on expanding economic ties with industrializing nations of western Europe and with the United States, ties which would bring in their wake new forms of "colonial" control. These nations, motivated by their own expansionary interests, provided the central governments with wealth of various sorts. Some of this foreign investment involved railroads and telegraph networks, which reduced regional isolation and autonomy to some extent and expanded the influence of capital centers farther into the hinterlands. Regional caudillos then redirected their interests toward the central governing organizations since the major sources of wealth now were available through these channels (allied, in turn, with foreign interests). As they did so, peace and a measure of political stability gradually returned.

In Mexico this welcomed respite from discord was achieved under the rule of Porfirio Díaz, a most astute and very capable caudillo of the new order, who in 1876 began an efficient dictatorship destined to last for 34 peaceful years. The peace of the Díaz period was achieved and maintained by heavy-handed police action against the plague of rural bandits and against indiscreet opponents of the regime. Military officers, possible rivals, were either exiled or mollified by generous salaries and lucrative opportunities for self-enrichment. In addition Díaz frequently shifted command-post personnel to reduce ties of personal loyalty between officers and men of the ranks. The focus of the army shifted accordingly from caudillo-controlled regional factions and militias to a more "nationalized" and disciplined standing army with loyalties, admittedly rather fragile, inclined more to the central authority.[1]

Díaz's success in controlling the military was due not only to his own courage and political sophistication, but also to expansion in certain sectors of the Mexican economy which greatly increased the wealth available for distribution to the higher strata of military and civilian elite. Díaz and his very able body of advisors and supporters were strongly aware of the contrast between the rapidly industrializing nations of western Europe and the United States and the economic backwardness and lethargy of Mexico. In line with the prevailing theories of economic and social development, Porfirian rule aimed to overcome this deficiency and obtain visible economic "progress" in Mexico by maintaining political order through governmental controls in order to encourage laissez-faire economic activities. More specifically, economic "success" would be achieved by increasing production of agricultural products and extraction of raw materials primarily for export. Necessary financial assistance would be provided by private foreign investment.[2]

The United States, England, Germany, and France, in turn, were seeking raw materials and markets for manufactured goods to spur their industrial growth. They found cheap labor, political stability, and many opportunities for investment and trade in Díaz's Mexico. With the aid of foreign capital, machinery, and technological expertise a network of railway lines was thrown across the most productive regions of the country; agricultural estates increased their production of export crops; bituminous coal and petroleum reserves were explored; mining was further stimulated; and paper mills, cement plants, and even a steel mill were developed. Yet industrialization was more apparent than real. Only a small proportion of the population was employed in manufacturing, and internal demands were still far from satisfied. Virtually all the finer grades of manufactured goods continued to be imported.

The money, machinery, and technological ability of foreigners were

---

[1] Discussion of the Díaz period has leaned heavily on Charles C. Cumberland, *Mexico, The Struggle for Modernity* (London: Oxford Univ. Press, 1968), chap. 8.

[2] Stanley J. Stein and Barbara H. Stein, *The Colonial Heritage of Latin America* (New York: Oxford Univ. Press, 1970), pp. 190–91; Leopoldo Zea, "Positivism and Porfirism in Latin America," in *Ideological Differences and World Order*, ed. F. S. C. Northrup (New Haven: Yale Univ. Press, 1949), pp. 166–91.

generally welcomed by the Mexican elite. At the same time there were serious misgivings concerning the influx of United States interests, for the aggressive northern neighbor was fast becoming a hemispheric power. Its motives in encouraging Mexican development were considered suspect, and the possible outcome was viewed with alarm. Nonetheless, the Yankees' influence grew. For example, in spite of strong Mexican preference for east-west rail lines to connect Pacific and Caribbean regions and ports with the central capital (and to avoid rail ties with the United States), three of the major Mexican railway lines built by United States companies also ran north-south to connect Mexico City and the mines and refining centers of the north with the rapidly expanding United States railway system.[3]

The need for "progress" was particularly apparent in the agrarian world, by far the dominant economic sphere. Here the vast majority of the Mexican population still made its living with digging stick, hoe, and ox-drawn plow. As part of a broad program of agrarian review, the government requisitioned extensive land surveys in order to ascertain the extent of "public" or "vacant" land falling under government control. Members of any organization wishing to survey were granted one-third of the land they measured as payment. The other two-thirds remained with the government for sale to other private individuals and companies. Close to 100 million acres were surveyed, distributed, and sold in this fashion.[4]

Unfortunately, in the feverish process of land grabbing it was very simple to claim as "vacant" lands territory belonging to poor and powerless private individuals and corporate groups, particularly Indians. As we noted previously, the holdings of the corporate Indian community had already been seriously challenged by Juárez's reform laws, which required division of land into private holdings. Now both private Indian landholders and villages with corporate land still remaining frequently lost their fields to unscrupulous surveyors and land grabbers, while hacendados took advantage of the tenor of the times to quietly encroach on neighboring Indian lands. It has been estimated that by the end of Díaz's rule as many as 90 percent of the heads of rural households may have been left landless. Only a small percentage of the remaining native communities still managed to protect their landholdings. Even fewer were able to continue communal land tenure.[5]

Most surviving Indian communities were located in the more inaccessible southern highlands of Mexico, in Chiapas, or in the states surrounding the Basin of Mexico. In these regions villagers reacted to the fragmen-

[3] Cumberland, *Mexico*, pp. 211–24 and 227–31; Marvin D. Bernstein, "Introduction," in *Foreign Investment in Latin America*, ed. Marvin D. Bernstein (New York: Knopf, 1966), pp. 3–26.

[4] Cumberland, *Mexico*, pp. 198–202; Nathan Whetten, *Rural Mexico* (Chicago: Univ. of Chicago Press, 1948), pp. 86–89.

[5] Whetten, *Rural Mexico*, p. 89; Manning Nash, "The Impact of Mid-Nineteenth Century Economic Change Upon the Indians of Middle America," in *Race and Class in Latin America*, ed. Magnus Mörner (New York: Columbia Univ. Press, 1970), pp. 170–83.

FIGURE 15.1 Village lands, the lifeline of the native community for almost 4,000 years. Maguey plants form boundaries between these fields of the Otomi village of Huixquilucan, state of Mexico. From Frederick Starr, *Indians of Southern Mexico* (published by the author, Chicago, 1899), pl. I.

tation and depletion of their lands by strengthening community social solidarity. New emphasis and significance was accorded the civil and religious orientations that had developed during the colonial centuries in response to earlier pressures on Indian life-styles. The corporate Indian community now appears structured primarily about a hierarchically ranked series of interlocking and increasingly prestigeful civil and religious offices. Household heads held positions within this structure on a rotating basis, usually serving terms of one year for each office with several years respite between tours of duty. Beginning on the lower levels as young men, over the years the men of the community moved upward through the series until the most dutiful and successful attained an honored and prestigeful old age as respected and highly influential elders or *principales* (see Figure 15.2).

Since civil-religious offices also imposed heavy economic burdens on the incumbents, a substantial share of household resources was channeled and consumed within the village for community purposes. In this fashion the economic defensiveness that we noted before in the colonial Indian community, where comparable civil and religious offices and obligations also existed, was maintained. Persons holding office, which is to say most, if not all, household heads at one time or another, were expected to provide sufficient quantities of food and liquor, incense, candles, and fireworks for the rituals associated with their positions. This intracommunity expenditure then limited the funds available to purchase other outside goods and consumed the individual wealth that might otherwise prove disruptive to community solidarity. In return, the social prestige

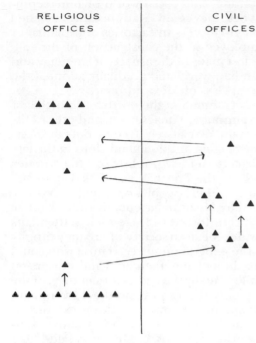

RELIGIOUS
OFFICES

CIVIL
OFFICES

FIGURE 15.2 Simplified version of the traditional hierarchy of civil-religious offices found in the Tzeltal municipio of Oxchujk', Chiapas. Note the pattern of climbing alternately from religious offices to civil offices. Adapted, by permission of the author and the publisher, from Henning Siverts, "Political Organization in a Tzeltal Community in Chiapas, Mexico," *The Alpha Kappa Deltan* (now *Sociological Inquiry*), vol. 30, no. 1 (1960) diagram 2, p. 20.

and honor accorded by the community to those who obeyed its dictates provided reward for conformity, while envious gossip and accusations of witchcraft pressured those who strayed from the proper performance of their civil-religious responsibilities.[6]

In this manner the nineteenth-century corporate Indian community in Mexico, faced with new threats to its existence from the outside world, developed new heights of defensiveness which protected it from the wider economy and society. To be sure the increasingly "closed" corporate community could not avoid the wider world entirely. As lands were lost individual members became increasingly dependent on wider economic participation, generally as hacienda laborers or as sellers of craft items in the marketplace, to obtain the wherewithal for basic subsistence and for community expenditures. Yet wherever possible the community as a whole endeavored more than ever to keep its members' individual contacts with the outside at a minimum. It channeled those village affairs that required outside affiliations through the few trusted community representatives who had attained the higher, most responsible community offices.

The closed corporate community provided a haven for some of the Indian population, but, as they lost their lands, many more were perma-

[6] Frank Cancian, "Political and Religious Organizations," in *Handbook of Middle American Indians*, ed. Robert Wauchope (Austin: Univ. of Texas Press, 1967), 6:283–98; Pedro Carrasco, "The Civil-Religious Hierarchy in Mesoamerican Communities," *American Anthropologist* 63 (1961):483–97.

nently forced into the wider economic and social world of nineteenth-century Mexico to earn a living as best they could. Many became hacienda laborers, other worked as unskilled laborers in factories and plants, or joined the tens of thousands employed in the construction of the railroads. In the process they rapidly lost many of the aspects of language and dress that had tied them to the Indian world and gradually adopted the speech and life-style of the general class of Mexican poor.

This procedure was particularly common in the north and northwest where the Mayo and Yaquis, Tarahumara, Pima, Opata, and other Hispanicized native peoples had remained relatively free of outside pressures for several decades after the decline of colonial missions in the late eighteenth century. Now, as railroads and telegraphs drew the frontier closer to the Mexican heartland on the one hand and tied it to the expanding United States on the other, these peoples once more saw their lands and water resources usurped by Mexican hacendados and frontier developers. Consequently, many were forced to leave their settlements and find a livelihood within the wider Mexican society where they rapidly moved toward assimilation with the general populace. Those who could actively resisted this steady encroachment onto their land and subversion of their life-styles, at least for awhile.[7] But by the end of the century, of the groups we have been considering only the Yaquis and the Tarahumara retained their ethnic and cultural identity to any significant extent.[8]

Some of the surveyed "public" lands and the lands lost by native communities became smaller family-worked ranchos, but much was added to the already sizable haciendas, which had previously benefited from the dismantling of church properties during Juárez's reform. Hacendados also had increasing numbers of impoverished laborers at their command. Thus large rural estates and the landed aristocracy reached new heights of land and labor control during the Díaz period. At the same time, in line with Díaz's program for economic development, many hacendados were changing the production emphasis of their estates from local subsistence products to a more single-minded concern with cash crops primarily for foreign export to the United States, Britain, France, and Germany. This shift in emphasis was effected by the greater availability of capital for estate development (thanks to foreign investments), which facilitated the introduction of more modern machinery, and by the growth of railroads linking the heretofore isolated and inward-looking hinterlands with seaports and the United States rail system and permitting transport of bulkier goods of lower value. Unfortunately this reorientation also caused increasing hardship for the landless laborer since, among other things, serious food shortages resulted.[9]

To recapitulate, the years of peace, order, and political stability under

---

[7] Most aggressive were the Mayo and especially the Yaquis, who waged destructive guerrilla warfare for much of the latter half of the nineteenth century.

[8] Edward Spicer, *Cycles of Conquest* (Tucson: Univ. of Arizona Press, 1962), pp. 39–41, 60–83, 102–4, 112–14, and 334–41.

[9] Cumberland, *Mexico*, pp. 203–10; Whetten, *Rural Mexico*, pp. 98–107.

Díaz permitted the development of sorely needed communication and transportation networks and encouraged general national economic growth. Nonetheless, in spite of economic "progress" the economy remained essentially colonial in orientation. It was still geared to importing staples and manufactured goods and exporting raw materials and foodstuffs (precious metals and other ores and unprocessed agricultural and pastoral products) which benefited the continuing industrialization of Europe and North America but linked Mexico to foreign controls and the ups and downs of foreign markets over which she had no control.[10]

Furthermore, only a very limited portion of the population benefited from these improvements. The elite guarded its privileges jealously. Military officers, politician-lawyers, and financiers and businessmen (often representatives or business partners of foreign firms operating in Mexico) prospered through the power and social prestige that traditionally accrued to estate owners, for with the income from their various activities they all had acquired large landholdings too.

At the same time, however, the gap between the comforts and benefits of elite life-styles and the destitution and poverty of the lower sector of society, who constituted 90 percent of the total population, was more acute than ever before. The vast majority of the population were illiterate, landless hacienda peons whose life expectancy averaged little more than 30 years in 1910 and who lived on a day-to-day basis in a culture of poverty. Earnings were sparse, food was expensive and scarce, the diet poor, housing and sanitation intolerable, medical care rudimentary, and infant mortality appallingly high. The relatively few employed in urban industry—in factories or in textile mills—fared no better, for they received only a few *pesos* in wages for long hours of work. Yet labor organizations were forbidden and strikes and protests were fiercely put down by the army.[11]

In the opinion of the elite, the poor were poor not because they were underpaid, uneducated, and restricted from access to resources and opportunities, but because they wished to be poor and because they had neither the intelligence nor the ambition to improve their lot. The elite themselves did all they could to avoid involvement with what they considered an incompetent and worthless segment of society. They enjoyed the pleasant life of the modernized capital where electric lights, streetcars, and marble palaces symbolized their prosperity. They delighted in imported luxury foods and Parisian fashions. They relaxed with European literature and music and educated their children abroad, closing their eyes as much as possible to the ominous signs that portended the seriousness of the coming upheaval.

[10] Stein and Stein, *Colonial Heritage*, pp. 135–44, 152–55, and 172–73; Sanford Mosk, "Latin America and the World Economy, 1850–1914," *Inter-Amer. Econ. Affairs* 2 (1948):53–82.

[11] Cumberland, *Mexico*, pp. 190–93, 224–27, and 233–36; Stein and Stein, *Colonial Heritage*, pp. 183–85.

The Storm

The chaos of blood and rebellion that broke forth in Mexico in 1910 was many-faceted. No single leader or program emerged as a central focus, as a rallying point. Mexico's problems were many, and the revolution reflected multiple grievances. Nonetheless, out of the confused welter of armies and issues general patterns may be discerned. In its broadest terms the Mexican Revolution is revealed as the clash of long-standing discontents allied with and given renewed focus by demands of a new economic and technological system—the dynamic industrialism of the United States and northern Europe—against the conservative bulwarks of an older, seignorial order. In closer focus the revolution can be viewed as a double movement in which social reforms for the landless poor and elitist ambitions of an economically hard-pressed "middle sector" of struggling professional men, ranchers, merchants, and small businessmen, many of whom were liberals and mestizos, were combined in somewhat uneasy partnership against the high and wealthy conservative elite.

After independence the mestizo and other formerly dispossessed "mixed" persons had tried to achieve a measure of economic advantage and social and political power through caudillo politics and through alliance with the more "liberal" elements of the upper class, who also sought to improve their positions. Their ambitions had fallen short, however, as the conservative landholding elite secured its hold over resources and power under Díaz. Now aspiring mestizos pursued their goals by enlisting support from the opposite direction and joining with the exploited hacienda peon and Indian villager in common cause against the status quo that denied one group land and mobility and the other social prestige, political leverage, and economic opportunity. This time they would be more successful; the day of reckoning had come at last for those who would still deny the dreams of Father Morelos and the demands of the Bajío dissidents.[12]

The initial stage of the revolution involved two rural movements, one located to the south of the Basin of Mexico and one to the north, both for different reasons opposing the reactionary national government. In one sense this upsurge of regionalism is a familiar theme, for regional interests often claimed equal weight, frequently even priority, over the concerns of the Mexico City government during the colonial period and

---

[12] This discussion of the Mexican Revolution is based on Eric R. Wolf, *Peasant Wars of the Twentieth Century* (New York: Harper & Row, 1969), chap. 1. See also Cumberland, *Mexico*, chap. 9; J. W. Wilkie and Albert Michaels, eds., *Revolution in Mexico: Years of Upheaval, 1910–1940* (New York: Knopf, 1969); R. A. White, "The Zapata Movement and the Revolution," in *Latin American Peasant Movements*, ed. H. A. Landsberger (Ithaca: Cornell Univ. Press, 1969), pp. 101–69.

in the nineteenth century.[13] But now the discontents reflected in rebellion in north and south also bore the mark of the divergent paths of colonial and nineteenth-century development experienced in the northern frontier and southern sections of the heartland, respectively.

The southern movement centered in Morelos, a densely populated region with prosperous sugar haciendas in the valleys and Indian communities in the nearby hills. After about 1880, however, as the expanding haciendas increasingly commercialized and mechanized, they pushed hard against the native villages, absorbing lands and water sources. A long-nurtured antagonism to the encroachment of the hacendados broke forth. Under the leadership of a local rancher, Emiliano Zapata, the native villagers, allied with smaller landholders, small merchants, and similar economically "middle-range" persons, engaged in open revolt. The movement, which was aimed primarily at the breakup of the hacienda and land reform, quickly spread throughout the villages of the southern provinces. Arms were crude and homemade and supplies often uncertain, but under Zapata's skillful leadership tens of thousands of men and women, organized into small, village-based guerrilla bands, succeeded for years in holding off government troops under Victoriano Huerta, a conservative who was attempting to reimpose a Díaz-type regime.[14]

Quite a different rebellion developed in the far north, in Chihuahua. This was a land of growing towns, commercial development, and industrial potential. However, much of this economic growth was strongly linked via Díaz's elite to United States business firms, which siphoned off important raw materials, and was further hindered by the limits of Mexican domestic needs which were kept low by the pattern of hacienda life. Ambitious businessmen, independent merchants, professionals, incipient industrialists, and various other socially ambitious middle-sector groups strongly opposed the usurpation of natural resources and general heavy investments in Mexican business by United States and European interests. They also resented the favoritism shown toward things foreign by the conservative elite of the central government and the personal fortunes realized therefrom.

The militant forces who converted these discontents into revolution were recruited from the distinctive labor force of the north, which included the highly mobile and adventuresome mestizo vaqueros who worked on vast cattle and cotton haciendas and who not infrequently were linked with bandits, smugglers, and cattle rustlers. Out of this medley emerged a heterogeneous cavalry of cowboys, ranchers, bandits, and other laborers under the general direction of a former hacienda peon turned bandit, Doroteo Arango, better known as Pancho Villa.

[13] Nonetheless, it was always recognized that Mexico City, with its access to the sea and the customs duties at Veracruz, was the pivotal power center for those who would control the country.

[14] Díaz resigned from the presidency under pressure in 1911.

FIGURE 15.3 Railways played an important logistic role in the Mexican Revolution. Here a Villista force has blown up a locomotive. Courtesy of the El Paso Public Library.

There was little in common between the rebellions of north and south. Land reform, the major goal of Zapata's villagers, was not a goal of the northern forces. In fact, as Villistas seized haciendas the holdings frequently passed into the hands of Villa's generals, who thus became a landed elite in their own right, directly opposed to land reform. In further contrast to Zapata's rural agriculturalists, Villa's armies were able to obtain ample supplies of armaments via the United States in exchange for stolen cattle and cotton and thus waged a much more offensive campaign.

The armies of these valiant revolutionary leaders destroyed much of the power of the conservative central government. But neither Villa nor Zapata was oriented toward or sufficiently experienced in the political machinations necessary to create a new national government. This problem was taken up instead by a third, smaller revolutionary group, the Constitutionalists. The Constitutionalists, however, were split into two factions. The "liberals" under Venustiano Carranza, a landowner and former senator under Díaz, generally favored political reform somewhat in the order of the nineteenth-century liberal position. Carranza's supporters were largely educated lawyers and other professional men, some of whom had had some governmental experience, who were anxious to remove the aged incumbents of the old regime in order to have a chance for power themselves and preferred that change come about more slowly and without overt governmental force. The "radical" wing of the Constitutionalists, under Alvaro Obregón, was of a different persuasion. This group favored social and economic reforms by direct governmental action on a scale that the more moderate liberals considered as undesirable as the Díaz machine. The radicals' social views were not as extreme, however, as the more anarchistic demands of the Zapatistas and Villistas, for whom, ideologically speaking, centralized governmental powers of any sort were anathema.

The final struggle for power was fought now between the various revolutionary contenders. After Villa suffered a major defeat in 1915, and as Zapata became increasingly isolated in the southern mountains, the prize fell to the moderate Carranza. However, since Carranza had made statements in favor of social reforms in order to hold the two wings of the Constitutionalists together against the strength of Villa and Zapata, when a constitutional assembly was convened in 1916 many of the demands of the radical wing were written into the new constitution. Thus the blueprint for a new Mexico technically included, among other things, the dissolution of large estates, land redistribution and the reinstitution of communal holdings, abolition of debt peonage, labor legislation guidelines, and the assertion of national rights over resources within the country.[15]

By 1920 revolutionary militarism had reached its peak and peace and stability slowly returned. It remained now to institutionalize the new order, an immense job complicated by the destruction of transportation and communication lines, huge foreign and domestic debts, a generally wrecked economy, and an immense loss of life suffered during more than a decade of turmoil. The task of reconstruction proceeded, but slowly, in fits and starts.

[15] Whetten, *Rural Mexico*, pp. 114–23; Lyle C. Brown, "Mexico's Constitution of 1917," in *Revolution in Mexico*, ed. J. W. Wilkie and A. L. Michaels (New York: Knopf, 1969), pp. 112–15.

16

The Banana-and Coffee-Republics

Haciendas and Plantations

Many of the features characteristic of Mexico during the Díaz period were also found in the Central American republics during the late nineteenth and early twentieth centuries. Here, too, the elite were concerned with maintaining political order and stability in order to encourage economic "progress" through production of cash crops for foreign export, and foreign industrializing powers, particularly the United States, became increasingly involved in the republics' economic and political affairs. On the other hand, cash cropping produced monocrop economies to a far greater extent in Central America than in Mexico, where a greater range of economic alternatives was available, and foreign intervention in Central American affairs frequently was much more blatant than in Mexico. Nor were the inequalities, hardships, and discontents of the general populace expressed in social revolution in Central America during these decades. Political upsets, when they occurred, were oriented toward maintaining rather than changing the established sociopolitical order.

Before we consider these points further we must describe the concept of the "plantation" form of estate agriculture and contrast this mode of estate operation with the general characteristics of the hacienda system.[1] As we have seen, the typical hacienda of the colonial period was operated on a rather low-pressure basis. Little capital was required, and manual labor and traditional tools and techniques were relied on as much as

[1] This discussion is derived from Eric R. Wolf and Sidney W. Mintz, "Haciendas and Plantations in Middle America and the Antilles," *Soc. and Econ. Studies* 6 (1957):380–411. Cf. George L. Beckford, *Persistent Poverty* (New York: Oxford Univ. Press, 1972).

possible. In addition to a main crop, a diversified range of products was produced for local or regional market demands and as basic subsistence for estate laborers and the hacendado's family.

Furthermore, the value of the hacienda lay not only in the subsistence and income it produced, but also in the life-style this income made possible. Quite apart from its productivity, ownership of a hacienda was an important criterion underwriting the position of a landowner and his family as prestigeful members of the social elite. The hacendado as a social superior, in turn, interacted with his estate laborers on a strongly personal and long-term basis. In keeping with the low level of capital involved in estate operations, hacienda laborers were paid for their efforts mainly with the personal assurance that they would receive basic subsistence for their lifetimes through usufructuary rights to small plots of hacienda land and through personalized loans and services provided from birth to death by the patron.

The plantation form of agricultural estate, in contrast, organizes and exploits labor and resources in a distinctly different fashion. The plantation is strictly a business operation. It is oriented first and foremost to realizing a profit from the sale of (usually) a single cash crop produced in bulk for export to a foreign market generally located in an industrializing country that imports raw materials or certain foodstuffs for its own economic interests. In order to increase efficiency and profits, machinery is used wherever possible in the production and preparation of plantation export crops. The need for elaborate and expensive equipment also means that plantations require a heavy input of capital, usually more than a single individual can provide. Consequently, ownership is frequently corporate. But the businessmen who finance the operation often reside in a foreign country and leave local affairs to managers.

Efficiency and profits require that relationships between local managers and plantation laborers be structured as impersonal business arrangements as much as possible. Therefore laborers are hired on a wage basis. On these terms, however, they also face the insecurity of being fired or at least laid off if market conditions fluctuate or for other reasons. There is little leeway for personalized relationships and little manager interest in workers' personal well-being. Furthermore, as wage earners laborers are expected to provide for their needs and those of their family through their own efforts, without the cushion of patronage, though possibly with the support of labor unions which, however, are usually strongly opposed by the plantation ownership. With cash at hand subsistence needs are met primarily by purchases at stores and plantation commissaries rather than by subsistence cultivation. In this manner the laborer is brought into participation with a wider commercial network. However, this growing dependence on cash purchases for subsistence needs carries with it the further consequence that changes and fluctuations in the wider cash economy will now have a direct impact on the standard of living of the rural worker.

These comparisons between hacienda and plantation systems contrast them as ideal types or conceptual models. In reality, during the nineteenth century when many haciendas were transformed toward the plantation form of organization, agrarian estates in Middle America frequently included features of both types.[2] Estate operations at this time also reveal the tensions inherent in this transformation. Much of the discontent and hardship suffered by the rural population of late nineteenth-century Mexico reflected dislocations and readjustments generated by a gradual yet pervasive change from personalized hacienda toward impersonal plantation modes of operation.[3]

Another notable example of the transition from the hacienda to the plantation system is found in nineteenth-century Yucatán.[4] In the decades following independence from Spain the self-sufficient cattle and maize hacienda economy of north and northwest Yucatán was superseded by a growing emphasis on sugar production, both for local needs and for export. However, sugar cane grows best in the wetter central and eastern frontier sections of the peninsula, where independent Maya maize cultivators had remained outside effective Hispanic control throughout the colonial period. Now, in the 1830s, expanding sugar estates quickly usurped the better subsistence lands and crucial water sources of the frontier communities. The estates also placed a heavy labor burden on the local Maya. Unfortunately intensive plantation labor was required during the same months when the slash-and-burn maize plots on which the Maya depended for basic subsistence had to be tended.

After some years of desperation over land usurpation, forced labor, and the interference with traditional subsistence patterns, the Yucatecan Maya erupted in rebellion in 1847.[5] A year later four-fifths of the peninsula was held by rebels, but Yucatecan forces gradually regained control of their former territory. Those Maya still unconquered retreated into the isolated forests of Quintana Roo (see Figure 19.3) where they developed a highly defensive military and religious organization for their scattered villages.[6]

The so-called Caste War of Yucatán failed in its rather utopian dream to drive the Spanish-Mexican elite from the peninsula. But its destructiveness did effectively end sugar production in Yucatán. Nonetheless, the plantation economy was soon revived in the north and northwest, this time emphasizing large-scale production of henequen for export to the United States (see Figure 19.3) where the recent introduction of the

[2] Some plantationlike characteristics also can be found in estate organization during the preceding colonial period.

[3] Conversely, the impersonal nature of relationships between owner-managers and laborers on plantations often were somewhat ameliorated by concessions to the human needs of workers and their dependents.

[4] Arnold Strickon, "Hacienda and Plantation in Yucatán," *América Indígena* 25 (1965):35–63.

[5] The factors underlying the outbreak of hostilities were varied and complex. Indian land and labor problems became open issues only when joined with mestizo dissatisfactions with impediments to social mobility and with political disagreements between Mexico and Yucatán.

[6] Nelson Reed, *The Caste War of Yucatán* (Stanford: Stanford Univ. Press, 1964).

McCormick reaper was creating a rapidly expanding market for the rot-resistant, insect-repelling baling twine. The operation came to be heavily financed by North American capital, particularly after expensive steam-powered raspers were introduced, and the market was controlled by International Harvester, to which company many Yucatecan planters soon owed sizable debts. Once again demands of weeding, harvesting, and processing on a large scale required an extensive labor force. One hundred thousand or more Maya (more than one-third of the Maya population of the peninsula) were pressed into service via debt peonage, gradually to be transformed from self-sufficient agriculturalists into a rural proletariat.[7] Even the turmoil of the Mexican Revolution, from which isolated Yucatán was largely spared, failed to disrupt henequen production. Indeed, income from the Yucatecan estates, which prospered from an increased demand for fibers during World War I, helped greatly to shore up the new revolutionary government.

Coffee and Bananas

Hacienda-plantation systems also dominated Central American economies after 1860, bringing an era of prosperity to the estate-owning "principal families" as long as world markets were high. Two major crops, coffee and bananas, formed the basis for estate agriculture, and either singly or together they provided the bulk of the national exports of Guatemala, El Salvador, Honduras, Nicaragua, and Costa Rica (Table 16.1).

TABLE 16.1
COFFEE AND BANANA EXPORTS OF CENTRAL AMERICA IN 1913
As a Percentage of Total Exports

	Guatemala	El Salvador	Honduras	Nicaragua	Costa Rica
Coffee	85	80	3	64	35
Bananas	6	—	51	6	51

SOURCE: Compiled from estimates of export values in Dana G. Munro, *The Five Republics of Central America* (New York: Russell and Russell, 1967), p. 266.

Coffee was raised in the western, Hispanic sections of Central America, generally on the Pacific slopes of volcanoes where rich soil and temperate climate provided ideal growing conditions (see Figure 19.3). Following the lead set by Costa Rica well before midcentury, Guatemala, El Salvador, and to a lesser extent Nicaragua turned to large-scale coffee production in the 1860s and soon produced high-quality beans that

[7] Strickon, "Hacienda and Plantation," p. 57; Victor Dahl, "Alien Labor in the Gulf of Mexico 1880–1900," *The Americas* 17 (1960/61):21–35.

FIGURE 16.1 Picking coffee berries in Costa Rica. Woodcut, 1880, from the Bettmann Archive, Inc.

found a ready market in Europe and the United States. Although the majority of the coffee estates or *fincas* were owned by a handful of wealthy Central Americans, many of the largest, best-equipped, and most productive belonged to foreigners, mainly Germans but also Britishers and North Americans. Even the estates held by Central American nationals usually were heavily mortgaged to European banks and firms, which advanced the necessary capital for their operation and then assumed a large measure of control over sale of the crop. Consequently, one way or another coffee production and marketing came to be controlled largely by foreigners.[8]

The growing emphasis on coffee production had a number of ramifications in techniques of land and labor control. In order to encourage coffee growing Central American governments distributed blocks of "public" lands free of charge or sold them at low prices to persons willing to cultivate. In Costa Rica, where coffee was confined mainly to the crowded meseta central, this measure encouraged land concentration and resulted in the rise of a handful of large landholding families, although the greater part of the meseta central continued to be divided into small farms where

[8] Dana G. Munro, *The Five Republics of Central America* (New York: Russell and Russell, 1967), pp. 17–23 passim, 93–95, 112, 142, 162–63, and 265–68; R. J. Houk, "Development of Foreign Trade and Commerce in Costa Rica to the Construction of the First Railway," *The Americas* 10 (1953):197–209.

FIGURE 16.2   A small *finca* family in the Costa Rican coffee district. From *The Romance and Rise of the American Tropics* by Samuel Crowther, p. 210. Copyright 1929 by Doubleday & Company, Inc. Reproduced by permission of the copyright owner.

coffee cultivation supplemented staple crops. In Nicaragua the distribution and sale of "public" lands meant loss of communal land for natives of the north-central province of Matagalpa; these natives then were frequently coerced into serving as estate laborers.

A far more severe program of land loss and labor coercion occurred in Guatemala, where coffee was grown on the southern slopes of Pacific piedmont volcanoes and in the Alta Verapaz. In order to assure a large and regular supply of native labor for coffee growers (especially since the huge reservoir of highland Indian labor, protected by closed corporate communities, refused to work voluntarily), communal ownership of land was formally abolished in an effort to undermine the economic self-sufficiency of the native community and thereby force the inhabitants to work outside the village. In the more isolated highland regions, where it was difficult to enforce the law, community holdings were not greatly affected by this legislation. But in areas more accessible to ambitious coffee producers, control over community lands was frequently lost to estate owners.[9]

Additional legislation legalized several forms of debt peonage. One

[9] Estate owners did not necessarily utilize the former Indian lands for coffee growing. They turned their land acquisitions into labor pools, allowing Indians to continue to cultivate the land for subsistence, but on condition that the agriculturalist would perform whatever labor functions the estate owner wished elsewhere on his coffee holdings. Munro, *Five Republics,* pp. 66–70; A. Dessaint, "Effects of the Hacienda and Plantation Systems on Guatemala's Indians," *América Indígena* 22 (1962):323–54.

category of agricultural laborer (*colonos*) contracted to live and work for periods of four years on an estate. Once there the laborers were encouraged to incur debts that then tied them permanently. Other workers (*jornaleros*) were bound solely by debts, for their agreement rested entirely on the obligation to work until continuously advanced loans of money or goods were repaid. Potential laborers who were not bound to an employer by debt were subject to forced labor under an arrangement known as the *mandamiento* system. Under mandamiento, in a manner strongly reminiscent of earlier colonial practices, native communities were compelled to furnish groups of laborers to coffee fincas for periods of a week to a month per year as planters needed them.[10]

The rapid growth of coffee plantations, together with additional pressures generated by population increase in the highlands, forced thousands of Guatemalan highland Indians out of their defensive regional and community self-sufficiency and into at least partial involvement in a wider export economy. In comparable fashion, large-scale coffee production itself was made possible and further stimulated by improvements in the transportation and communications networks of the Central American republics. Railway lines, frequently financed with North American capital, and occasional carriage and automobile roads were built to link major cities to each other and to Pacific seaports. (Rural regions continued to be served by slow oxcart and pack mule.) Guatemala and Costa Rica also established connections to the Caribbean with rail lines from Guatemala City to Puerto Barrios and from San José to Puerto Limón, respectively.

Construction of the San José–Puerto Limón railroad line ushered in the second Central American plantation emphasis, one based on commercial production of bananas. However, there were significant contrasts between coffee fincas and banana plantations. Large-scale coffee estates involved wealthy Central American nationals as estate owners at least to some extent, employed native labor exclusively, were located in settled Hispanic regions, and to a considerable degree continued hacienda forms of owner-laborer relations and traditional elite prestige rewards. In contrast, banana cultivation was directly and entirely controlled by foreign corporations, generally employed foreign laborers under distinctly plantation forms of manager-laborer relations, and involved heretofore isolated and undeveloped sections of lowland Central America (see Figure 19.3). Further ramifications of these contrasts made banana production the center of considerable controversy.

The construction of the San José–Puerto Limón railway (1871–90) was engineered by a North American, Minor C. Keith, who agreed to undertake the awesome task of building a rail line through the hot Caribbean lowlands of Costa Rica in return for certain concessions granted by the

[10] Munro, *Five Republics*, pp. 59–66; Chester L. Jones, *Guatemala, Past and Present* (Minneapolis: Univ. of Minnesota Press, 1940), pp. 150–61; Nathan L. Whetten, *Guatemala, The Land and the People* (New Haven: Yale Univ. Press, 1961), pp. 118–20.

Costa Rican government.[11] In the so-called Soto-Keith contract, the prototype for many later concessions, Keith received rights to the railroad for 99 years, 800,000 acres of undeveloped national domain along the rail line for his own use, and sweeping exemptions from internal taxes and customs duties for the next 20 years. In return, the government received one-third of the railroad company shares and rights to one-half of the net proceeds to be realized from any rental or sale of the land given to Keith.[12]

In order to finance the construction of the railroad and to provide freight in the regions it traversed outside the meseta central, Keith planted his lands with bananas, and as early as 1880 he was shipping small loads to New Orleans. The eastern lowlands proved so well adapted to banana cultivation that the fruit farms soon became more valuable than the railroad. As a market for the exotic tropical fruit developed in the United States and Great Britain, numerous small planters, frequently North Americans, began to grow limited quantities of fruit in the Caribbean lowlands of Costa Rica, Nicaragua, Honduras, Guatemala, and also Panama.[13] Meanwhile, in 1899 Keith's interests merged with another banana operation to form a new company, United Fruit. By 1930 the United Fruit Company had become the leading producer of bananas in Central America, gradually absorbing most of the small planters or forcing them out of business. The Standard Fruit and Steamship Company, which also grew out of the merging of smaller companies in 1924, remained its most significant competitor.[14]

As United Fruit expanded it came to control hundreds of acres of isolated Caribbean lowlands along the Guatemala–Puerto Barrios rail line in the lower Motagua valley, along the northern coastal plains of Honduras, in the area of Limón in Costa Rica, and around Bocas del Toro in western Panama. (Standard Fruit's holdings were located primarily in eastern Nicaragua and northern Honduras.) Large areas of tropical bush and forest were cleared and planted in bananas. Self-sufficient company towns with North American hospital clinics, schools, churches, houses, commissaries, and social clubs sprang up on the coast to provide for the needs of foreign administrators and thousands of laborers. Railroad networks linked plantations with company-built and company-controlled port facilities at Puerto Barrios, Tela, Puerto Cortés, Puerto Limón, and Almirante. United Fruit's "Great White Fleet" of over 100 fast, refrigerated ships rushed literally millions of stems of the perishable fruit to foreign markets each year, particularly during the "banana boom" from

[11] A concession, legally speaking, is a contractual agreement between a government and a corporation or individual granting specific assurances, rights, and privileges from the government in return for particular investments, building, or services from the investor.

[12] C. D. Kepner and J. H. Soothill, *The Banana Empire* (New York: Vanguard Press, 1935), pp. 44–48.

[13] As well as in the West Indies and northern South America.

[14] Kepner and Soothill, *Banana Empire;* C. D. Kepner, *Social Aspects of the Banana Industry* (New York: Columbia Univ. Press, 1936); C. M. Wilson, *Empire in Green and Gold* (New York: Holt, 1947); S. May and G. Plaza, *The United Fruit Company in Latin America* (Washington, D.C.: National Planning Association, 1958).

FIGURE 16.3 Bananas were harvested by a "gang" of three men. A "cutter" cut the banana stalk beneath the bunch, a "backer," shown here, carried the stem either to freight cars or to the "muleman" who loaded it onto mules. From *The Romance and Rise of the American Tropics* by Samuel Crowther, p. 287. Copyright 1929 by Doubleday & Company, Inc. Reproduced by permission of the copyright owner.

1900 to 1930. A once-quiet hinterland of Central America now hummed with activity as United Fruit (and to a lesser extent Standard Fruit) established firm social, economic, and political control.

From the point of view of United Fruit's directors this merciless drive toward acquisition of large landholdings and near monopoly of Central American banana production was sound business procedure. Commercial production of bananas was a high-risk operation, for the valuable fruit was susceptible to a number of natural hazards. Bad weather, including frequent floods and hurricanes, could seriously affect production. Soil depletion was a common problem, and newly cleared land could become exhausted in 5 to 20 years. Bananas also proved susceptible to a number of devastating diseases. If commercial banana production was to be profitable these risks had to be counteracted as much as possible.

Acquisition of large amounts of land was the initial approach taken to balance potential loss, for when disease or hurricanes or soil exhaustion forced the abandonment of acreage in one area, other lands and plantings remained profitable elsewhere. Efforts were also made in the early decades of the twentieth century to experiment with other commercial crops in order to develop alternatives to bananas and diversify production.

Large-scale plantings of cacao, coconuts, abacá (Manilla hemp), and pineapples were tried, but for various reasons none proved to be as financially rewarding as bananas.

By 1930 United Fruit adopted another approach to the problem of risks in response to widespread banana disease and soil exhaustion. The company encouraged small private planters, often former employees, to lease or buy company land and plant their own holdings of bananas which would be sold to United Fruit. With this technique the company was able to avoid the financial losses involved in handling poorer-quality fruit and could concentrate solely on purchasing better-grade stems. It was also better able to regulate the supply of bananas to meet market demands, for if necessary even good fruit brought to the docks for sale by the planters could be rejected on grounds that the bunches were bruised or too ripe or otherwise unfit. Thus the private planter, rather than the company, would have to absorb the loss. United Fruit finally withdrew from large sections of the Caribbean lowlands to smaller Pacific coast holdings in the late 1930s as a result of continued plant disease. As a result of these risk-reducing techniques it was able to accomplish this transition without sustaining crippling financial loss even though Pacific operations necessitated higher production costs.[15]

United Fruit's success in manipulating its business environment was due in large measure to its relations with Central American governments and its contribution to national economies. In the early decades of its growth United Fruit and Central American governments seemed to have mutual interests. The Central American republics contained large sections of unused lowland savannah, swamp, and tropical forest and were badly in need of railroads and national income. In return for cheap acreage, exemptions from taxation, and a generally free hand in the areas it acquired, United Fruit agreed to develop the regions with railroad lines and port facilities and to extend the railroads to the national capitals and population centers so as to unite the interior with the Caribbean coast. Payments by United Fruit on its fruit exports also contributed as much as 40 to 70 percent of the total export revenue received by the various Central American countries.

Unfortunately there were less desirable aspects to this "partnership" too. In order to assure political conditions favorable for its operations United Fruit (like other foreign corporations with Central American investments) frequently became involved in national politics in the various countries where it had commercial interests, lobbying, manipulating, and supporting with money and arms if necessary those political groups and governments willing to grant generous concessions, while working to defeat less friendly factions. It soon became apparent, too, that railway lines which served the distant banana plantations were quickly built, but extensions of these services to the political capitals and population centers

[15] This material is derived from the analysis by Michael D. Olien, "Cultural Ecology and the Study of Complex Socio-Economic Systems: The Case of the United Fruit Company in Costa Rica" (unpublished manuscript, 1971).

of the country were often slow in coming. The company also closely associated its interests with those of other North American enterprises in Central America, including mines and electrical plants.[16]

In addition United Fruit received growing censure from increasingly disenchanted Central American nationalists over its handling of its Caribbean empire. Critics pointed out that managerial posts invariably were held by North Americans rather than by nationals of the country where operations were located. Attention also was drawn to the plight of company workers, who frequently were forced to accept part of their wages in the form of commissary coupons. These coupons could only be spent at company-owned stores where imported and local foods were sold at company-determined prices, much to the dismay of local merchants who were often unable to compete with United's commissary organization. Work was often temporary, too, in any one district, for soil exhaustion and plant disease forced the abandonment of many farms. Laborers then either returned to their homes, were relocated in another banana division, or became subsistence agriculturalists, drifters, or migrants along the coast.

Hispanic Central Americans also protested the "Africanization" of the Caribbean lowlands by English-speaking, Protestant West Indian Negroes, thousands of whom were imported by the fruit companies as laborers on the railroads and plantations. To be sure, Central American nationals were not entirely excluded, but both Standard Fruit and United Fruit preferred to hire large numbers of West Indians. This practice was instituted partly because Nicaraguan, Costa Rican, and Honduran workers frequently were reluctant to leave the temperate uplands for the hot lowlands; partly because West Indians spoke a dialect of English and thus were able to communicate more readily with North American managers; and partly because, as strangers to the region, West Indians had little recourse but to rely on the companies' accommodations for them regardless of how satisfactory these living and working conditions might be. (Some local natives, such as the Miskito, also readily cooperated with the fruit companies as small independent planters, while others, such as the Talamancans of eastern Costa Rica, still preferred to avoid contact with foreigners.)

For many years the companies resisted workers' efforts to unionize. However, when labor organization did arise after World War I United Fruit faced a series of strikes protesting wages, unemployment, and commissary credits. Many of these strikes gained national sympathy in Central America. They brought a renewed flood of anti–United Fruit and anti–North American protests charging that United Fruit was using the territory and resources of the republics of Central America primarily for its own interests and profits and that Central America was little more than a pawn in the hands of United States big business. Big business included the United States government, whose political interests in Central America increased as its citizens' economic interests expanded. The

[16] Kepner and Soothill, *Banana Empire*, pp. 342–45.

northern neighbor also reserved the right, as expressed in the Monroe Doctrine, to concern itself with the activities of other nations of the Western Hemisphere as an integral part of its own national defense.

The United States in Central America

United States involvement was a powerful factor in both the internal and external affairs of the Central American republics at the turn of the twentieth century and thereafter. This interest was predicated on the desire of the United States to obtain and maintain peace and political stability in Central America, both to provide a favorable climate for the millions of dollars of United States business invested there and to guard the national security of the United States. To achieve these ends the United States took steps to suppress political upheavals, to support governments friendly to United States interests, and to keep alert for any international complications (such as might arise, for example, from efforts to collect outstanding Central American foreign debts) which could affect the military or political status of countries close to the Caribbean Sea and the Panama Canal.

The United States' initial efforts to become influential in Central American affairs were diplomatic in tone. Central American governments on the whole were more stable after 1870, with smoother changes of office and fewer revolts by internal political dissidents. Nonetheless, as foreign economic interests had grown, the political life of the republics repeatedly had been upset by the machinations of foreign corporations seeking concessions. There also were numerous instances of political interventions across national borders resulting from the schemes of two ambitious Central American presidents, Justo Rufino Barrios, president of Guatemala from 1873 to 1885, and José Santos Zelaya, president of Nicaragua from 1893 to 1909. Each of these men held the elusive but still tantalizing vision of a politically unified Central America which would be united through his personal power and under his personal direction, and each worked accordingly, during his respective time in office, to place political allies in the presidencies of the other Central American countries. In an effort to ameliorate the resulting turmoils and to protect the lives and property of its citizens and other foreigners, the United States proposed various conciliatory meetings and conventions with the parties involved.[17]

The most notable of these assemblies was the 1907 Washington Conference, convened to defuse a threatened war among Nicaragua, El Salvador, Honduras, and Guatemala. Delegates to the conference finally pledged their governments not to interfere in each other's internal af-

---

[17] Munro, *Five Republics*, pp. 88–91; Thomas L. Karnes, *The Failure of Union: Central America, 1824–1960* (Chapel Hill: Univ. of North Carolina Press, 1961); Wayne Clegern, "Change and Development in Central America, 1840–1900," *Caribbean Studies* 5 (1966):28–34.

fairs, not to allow use of national territory as a base of operations for those opposing neighboring governments, and to cooperate in furthering mutual interests and welfare. Unfortunately implementation of decisions reached at the conference was more difficult. Zelaya particularly ignored its resolutions (at least so it seemed to the United States government), refusing to recognize the "right" of the United States to intervene in Central American affairs. Moreover, he discussed the question of a trans-isthmian Nicaraguan canal with various foreign powers and conceded to a British firm the right to construct and operate an interoceanic railroad across Nicaragua. This posed an intolerable situation from the perspective of the United States which considered it essential for its security that Nicaragua's potential canal route be kept from European hands. Consequently, when Zelaya's presidency was threatened by a revolt in 1909, his opponents were assured of success by open financial and military support from the United States.[18]

This foreign backing was intensified a few years later, in 1912, when United States Marines openly quelled a retaliatory revolt against the new regime and then remained in Nicaragua to protect the incumbent government. The regime in turn accepted United States offers of loans to refund pressing foreign and domestic debts and, to secure these loans, ceded control of the customs houses, the currency system, the national railway, and even internal revenues to North American banking firms and allied corporations. The Nicaraguan government also signed a treaty granting the United States rights in perpetuity to build a trans-isthmian canal through Nicaragua and to establish a naval base on the Gulf of Fonseca.

Such blatant intervention seriously alarmed the other Central American republics, which expressed strong disapproval of the heavy-handed United States policy. Nonetheless, the Central American political arena quieted considerably. If political upset and serious financial problems had brought the United States Marines and foreign economic controls to Nicaragua, might they not be sent elsewhere with the same consequences if the United States felt conditions warranted it? Indeed, signs of trouble anywhere in Central America now frequently brought a North American warship to the nearest port. The United States was already attempting to reorganize Honduran finances and had approached Guatemala and Costa Rica with similar intentions. In view of Nicaragua's new status as a virtual United States protectorate, Central American leaders were extremely apprehensive that the end result for all might well be political absorption by the expansionist-minded Yankees.

Moreover, the United States by now had acquired another strong reason for maintaining a firm hand in Central American political affairs. Political stability in the Central American republics was essential to the security of the newly constructed Panama Canal. At the same time United States control of the Canal Zone and free-wheeling political intervention

[18] Munro, *Five Republics,* chaps. 9 and 10; J. O. Baylen, "American Intervention in Nicaragua, 1909–33: An Appraisal of Objectives and Results," *Southwestern Soc. Sci. Quarterly* 35 (1954):128–54.

in Panamanian politics provided another glaring example of United States activity in Central America. Indeed the Republic of Panama owed its very existence as an independent polity in part to United States interest in constructing a canal across the isthmus. With this goal in mind the United States in 1903 had pressured Colombia, which heretofore had included Panama as part of its national territory, into granting the independence sought by Panamanian separatists. The United States then immediately signed a treaty with the new government that granted the United States possession, again in perpetuity, of a 16-km strip across the isthmus over which the United States would have full use, occupation, and control, with rights to appropriate whatever other land or waterways were considered necessary for the construction, operation, and maintenance of the canal. The United States also received authorization to assure the protection of the canal and to maintain sanitation and order in the terminal cities of Colón and Panama City.[19]

By 1914 the canal was completed and became the controversial economic lifeline for the Republic of Panama, whose political life was similarly guided by military and diplomatic intervention by the United States. Just as Panama's significance during the Hispanic colonial period had rested on its near monopoly of trans-isthmian trade, so the fortunes of Panama as an independent republic would be heavily dependent upon the canal.

Meanwhile, to the west, the bitter antagonism toward continued United States supervision of Nicaraguan affairs had sparked an armed confrontation between the United States military and Nicaraguan guerrilla forces directed by General Augusto Sandino. Sandino opposed both the North American occupation and the government it supported. Defying United States Marines and the American-trained Nicaraguan national guard, Sandino and a few hundred men successfully rallied the support of disenchanted nationals and won much sympathy in Latin America. From bases deep in the isolated, heavily forested mountains of north-central Nicaragua, the guerrilla chief launched a bitter and destructive campaign from 1927 until the Marines were finally withdrawn in 1933. However, the Nicaraguan government continued to cooperate with United States policies, while Sandino, treacherously assassinated by members of the increasingly powerful national guard, joined Zelaya as one of Central America's great heroes.[20]

Overview

As the republics of Central America moved into the twentieth century internal political power was still firmly controlled by military officers and by wealthy landowners. In spite of constitutional trappings, strong presi-

[19] Sheldon B. Liss, *The Canal: Aspects of U.S.-Panamanian Relations* (Notre Dame: Univ. of Notre Dame Press, 1967).

[20] Neill Macaulay, *The Sandino Affair* (Chicago: Quadrangle Books, 1967); J. O. Baylen, "Sandino: Patriot or Bandit," *Hisp. Amer. Hist. Rev.* 31 (1951):394–419; Baylen, "American Intervention in Nicaragua," pp. 128–54.

dents backed by military support ruled with firm, personalized control, further guaranteeing their positions by distributing political offices and other forms of largesse to friends and relatives. In the international political arena, the strategic importance of the entire isthmian region to the United States was primary. This position, in turn, generated political intervention and contributed to the growth of a strong anti–United States ideology in Central America.

The Central American national economies rested heavily on the large-scale production of two major export crops, with little development of manufacturing and industry. Home crafts and regional production of small items such as candles, shoes, soap, and cigarettes provided a few essentials, but most manufactured goods, including textiles, furniture, agricultural machinery, and railway materials, continued to be imported from the United States and Europe. Economic development and stability were almost entirely dependent on the fluctuations of the world market for coffee and bananas, fluctuations over which Central American producers had little, if any, control. Furthermore, even when prices were high the income realized from plantation products and from customs duties on imports and exports was not effectively reinvested toward further economic diversification and development. It was diverted, instead, into the coffers of United States and European bankers and businessmen, into servicing foreign debts, and into support of the socially prestigeful life-style of the Central American elite.

Meanwhile the vast majority of the population continued to exist as subsistence farmers and poorly paid agricultural laborers. They, too, were directly affected by world market fluctuations. When prices fell (as at the turn of the century, before World War I, and especially during the great depression) already meager wages were cut and workers were laid off. Growing unemployment then placed new demands on a subsistence economy already strained by increased rates of population growth. Yet except for Costa Rica, where the laborers' plight and the first stirrings of labor organization generated a limited amount of welfare legislation, little effort was made by Central American governments to alleviate the hardships faced by the majority of the populace. Central American society remained divided between the relatively few families of the elite who controlled the wealth and directed the affairs of the republics, and the masses of poor, uneducated, politically insignificant wage laborers and rural subsistence agriculturalists whose major concern was simply to survive.[21]

[21] Munro, *Five Republics;* Sanford Mosk, "Latin America and the World Economy, 1850–1914," *Inter-Amer. Econ. Affairs* 2 (1948):53–82.

17

The Two Faces
of Mexico

Nation-Building

The states of Middle America entered the midtwentieth century as "developing" nations challenged to nationalize and industrialize their colonial economies and societies so as to attain the structure and organization of "nations" or "nation-states." There are many features characteristic of a nation-state, but the most definitive aspect lies in the realm of government and political control. A state becomes a nation when the central or national political organization becomes the dominant controlling authority of the country—when all other power groups (such as regional political bosses and large landowners) no longer are able to act as independent political elements, but are controlled by the national organization.

The procedures of nation-building are complex and complicated, and no two countries proceed in exactly the same fashion. Nonetheless some problems and requirements are common to all. For example, on the most basic level nationalizing requires definite delineation of national boundaries, use of a common language by all the populace, and development of effective, technologically modernized systems of transportation (roads, railroads, airplanes) and communication (radio, television, movies) that can link the populations of geographically remote regions with the national centers and thereby facilitate their eventual economic, social, and political integration into a single nation-state.

However, the integration facilitated by common language and by transportation and communication systems must be activated by a truly national leadership. Nation-building requires a nationwide government able to effectively and directly extend its authority to every individual. This expansion of governmental supervision is accomplished by legislation and by control of the means to enforce the laws. It also requires organization and support of new interest groups (political parties, labor unions, agrarian associations) among the heretofore politically unrecognized and ineffective lower sectors of the population. These new groups play a crucial role in nation-building for several reasons. First, they offer direct contact between the people at large and the central government. Second, they provide the populace with alternate paths for activity and solutions of grievances; these paths weaken traditional monopolies of control over people and resources by special-interest elite groups that otherwise would stand between the central government and the general population as power-blocs themselves. In other words, when labor unions or political parties function the laborer can turn to channels other than the landowner for solution of problems, thus weakening the monopoly of control desired by the landowner and strengthening and extending the influence of the central government with which the unions or parties connect.

To support the independence of the national government, both with respect to possible internal power-seeking competitors and in external relationships with other nations, a more or less self-sustaining, mechanized agricultural and industrial economy also must be built. This economic "modernization" requires the introduction of industrial technologies in place of more primitive technological methods and a geographically mobile labor force freed from bondage to local agrarian holdings and able to move wherever workers are needed. For this reason agrarian reform is frequently an important aspect of nation-building. But agrarian reform itself is not enough. Changes in land tenure must be coordinated with wider systems of resource distribution so that the benefits of increased wealth are not monopolized by a small group of elite but are distributed among the general population. This distribution must be effected in such a way that most of the populace can achieve a level of income that allows for a standard of living above the basic subsistence level.

These diverse aspects of nation-building and "modernizing" can be ordered into a succession of developmental phases: first, the rise to power of a leadership oriented toward the growth of national government; second, transformation of the economy and society from a predominantly rural, agrarian pattern to a predominantly industrial and increasingly urban way of life; finally, extension of the effects of urban-industrial life throughout the entire society. This sequence of restructurings and reorganizations has yet to be realized in its totality by any nation, although some, including most of the major world powers, are well along.[1]

By virtue of close to 500 years as political and/or economic colonies of western Europe and then the United States, the countries of Middle

---

[1] C. E. Black, *The Dynamics of Modernization* (New York: Harper & Row, 1966).

America nave much farther to go. Their immense task is made even more difficult by runaway population growth and because other powerful nations already have attained more advanced economic and political stages of nation-building. With respect to the first point, rapid population increase during the twentieth century has frequently required that resources for economic development be diverted instead to meeting little more than basic subsistence needs for the growing populace.[2] Second, the less developed nations of Middle America cannot solve their nation-building problems in a vacuum, but also must contend with international pressures generated by more powerful industrial nations.[3]

The only organization within any Middle American country that is sufficiently powerful, or at least potentially so, to carry out the social, economic, and political restructurings of nation-building in the face of rapid population increase and international complications is the central government. We have seen how, after a period of political diffuseness and decentralization following independence from Spain, centralized governments began to emerge in the republics of Middle America during the last half of the nineteenth century. However, these governments were not national in scope, for they depended on the elite for much of their strength and thereby remained oriented toward support of elite activities with little concern for the lower sector. The economic and political interests of the elite focused primarily on continued development of a colonial export economy geared to large-scale production of foodstuffs and raw materials for the industrial powers of western Europe and the United States. Concurrently the upper sector grew further and further removed from those less fortunate, especially the poverty-stricken rural laborers and subsistence agriculturalists who had no voice in the corridors of government.

In a desperate effort to have their grievances heard and rectified, Mexico's townsmen and rural villagers finally rose in revolt, and the colonial elite of the largest of the Middle American states went down to defeat along with the government it supported. Then began the struggle in the name of the Revolution to fashion an effective national government, an industrial economy, and a new society.

Implementing the Revolution

There is little question that in many ways revolutionary Mexico has been among the more successful Middle American countries (and notable among the countries of Latin America in general) in resolving problems of nation-building to date. However, as we shall see, social justice and the

---

[2] Population increase has accelerated from about 1 to 2 percent per annum during the eighteenth and nineteenth centuries to between 3 and 4 percent at the present time.
[3] Richard N. Adams, *The Second Sowing* (San Francisco: Chandler, 1967), chap. 1.

economic goals sought by revolutionary leaders have not proceeded at an even rate. To some observers the direction of this unevenness and its consequences threaten to cancel the successes of the revolution.

The first aim of the revolutionary leaders was to establish a strong, centralized, and truly national government able to keep the peace and direct the course of social and economic change. The new government faced its initial challenge from the many local political bosses and independent-minded revolutionary generals still at large. The political power of the hacendados was not broken until the Cárdenas administration (1934–40) when the large landed estates were dissolved. As the revolutionary government worked to consolidate its control, foreign investors also felt its growing power. Foreign managers were removed from the railroad system and rich and exceedingly valuable oil fields on Mexico's east coast, developed by United States and British companies in the late Díaz years, were expropriated by the Mexican government.

As old power blocs weakened the national government encouraged the formation of new political groups. Agricultural and industrial workers were organized into associations and unions, and, along with the new national army and growing national bureaucracy, they became significant political bases for the national government. Overtures were extended to the Mexican business community and also to the church to bring them, too, more fully into public affairs via the central government. By 1940, even though many were still hungry, poorly clothed, and illiterate, an economic and political base had been laid for the new nation.[4]

In the years following these initial decades of organization the goals of nation-building have been pursued through a national administrative structure centered on a firm presidential office and supported by the major political party, the *Partido Revolucionario Institucional* or PRI. The basic function of the PRI is twofold: to distribute political power throughout the national territory and among diverse interest groups while continuing to concentrate, contain, and control this power base within the structure of a single organization. Therefore on the one hand the PRI extends the arm of the federal government across the states of the Republic so as to facilitate communication and mobility between local communities and interest groups and the central administration. On the other, it checks the rise of potential power competitors, maintains the general peace, and assures the supremacy of both the party and the central government by incorporating the major occupational, economic, and political interest groups of the revolution within the party organization.

For this reason the PRI contains three main divisions: agrarian organizations deriving from land reform programs (The National Peasant Confederation); industrial labor unions (the Confederation of Mexican

---

[4] R. Vernon, *The Dilemma of Mexico's Development* (Cambridge: Harvard Univ. Press, 1963), pp. 70–87; A. L. Michaels, "A Summary of the Cárdenas Epoch," in *Revolution in Mexico: Years of Upheaval, 1910–1940,* ed. J. W. Wilkie and A. L. Michaels (New York: Knopf, 1969), pp. 273–78; Charles C. Cumberland, *Mexico, The Struggle for Modernity* (London: Oxford Univ. Press, 1968), pp. 307–20.

Workers); and a catchall "popular" sector which includes professionals, civil service unions, and smaller agricultural and urban workers' associations. At the present time the interest groups with more conservative leanings—the military, the church, and businessmen—are not included within the formal party organization, although military officers can and do pursue individual political careers as candidates for political office and business interests are a primary concern of the government. (It should be clearly understood that the PRI and the government are not identical, even though there is close structuring between them).[5]

The activities of these diverse interest groups are closely monitored by the central administration, which (in a manner not unlike the Spanish Crown's organization of colonial government) maintains a balance among them by administrative techniques or by checking and balancing the programs of almost every organization and territorial unit against those of other associations. Particularly significant is the manner in which the government counters the interests and demands of business and industry with those of the labor unions and vice versa. In so doing, of course, it prevents the leaders of these powerful organizations from becoming independent challengers to the central government.

Another set of basic revolutionary goals sought by the government and the PRI involves agrarian reform. Here again the Cárdenas administration is noteworthy, for Cárdenas, yielding to mounting political pressure from reform groups, was the first president to vastly expand the program of agrarian reform. By 1941 almost one-half of Mexico's arable cropland had been granted to nearly one-fourth of the total population in the form of communal holdings of cultivable land, pasture, and woodland known as *ejidos*. Tools and seed were provided and credit facilities extended through special Ejidal Banks which also acted as agents for the sale of produce.[6]

In spite of similarities of form, it is important to realize that there are significant points of contrast between ejidos and the communal landholdings so strongly attacked by Juárez's Reform Laws. Ejidal lands are not owned directly by the villages receiving title to them, but remain the property of the national government. Consequently, although ejidal lands are redistributed by a village ejido representative to community household heads for private family cultivation, they cannot be legally sold or mortgaged. Obviously, too, government ownership of ejidal lands and extension of credit for development provide a prime mechanism tying the rural community (or at least those families receiving ejidos) to the larger national arena. Indeed, this nationalizing aspect of ejidos was a prime factor behind Cárdenas's vigorous implementation of land reform. He pursued this program over the protests of private landholders who ar-

[5] Martin C. Needler, *Politics and Society in Mexico* (Albuquerque: Univ. of New Mexico Press, 1971); Richard M. Morse, "The Heritage of Latin America," in *The Founding of New Societies*, ed. L. Hartz (New York: Harcourt, Brace, & World, 1964), pp. 169–71.

[6] Cumberland, *Mexico*, p. 299; Nathan Whetten, *Rural Mexico* (Chicago: Univ. of Chicago Press, 1948), pp. 124–28; James W. Wilkie, *The Mexican Revolution: Federal Expenditure and Social Change since 1910*, 2nd ed. rev. (Berkeley: Univ. of California Press, 1970), pp. 189–91.

gued, with some justification, that the small plots of ejidal land would be less productive economically than larger privately owned lands.[7]

In spite of this encouraging start, after 1940 the agrarian reform program gradually was relegated to secondary significance as preference was given to business and industrial developments.[8] The role of the central government has been of major significance here, too, necessarily so since large amounts of capital have been needed to develop and operate expropriated oil fields, fertilizer plants, railroads, and electrical power plants, all of which are now under national control. A new generation of rich merchants, bankers, industrialists, and agrarian capitalists also has risen to prominence. In judicious and carefully controlled (again by the government) association with foreign (United States) investors, this business-agricultural-industrial elite has stimulated commerce and industry and developed a diversity of new industries and manufactures, creating steady growth and expansion of the national economy. Close to one-third of the total population is now employed in business and industry, and during the last decade or so incomes for skilled and semiskilled workers have increased more rapidly than the cost of living.[9]

In spite of this growth manufacturing and industry remain concentrated in only a few centers, primarily in northeast Mexico and the central basin (Figure 17.1). The heart of the industrial complex lies in bustling Mexico City and surrounding towns in the Basin of Mexico where smog and air pollution attest to thousands of automobiles and a wide range of industrial and manufacturing plants. Other notable manufacturing areas are located in the Puebla basin, the Guadalajara area, and the region around Saltillo and Monterrey in northern Mexico, which is the focus of the iron and steel industry. These industrial enterprises rely heavily on extensive petroleum, sulphur, and natural gas deposits that stretch along the Gulf Coast from the Río Grande to Tabasco and the Yucatán Peninsula. Drilling rigs, pipelines, storage tanks, and modern towns have transformed this region. Coal reserves in Coahuila and modern hydroelectric plants located on the escarpment of the central highlands provide additional power resources.[10]

The former frontier of northern Mexico also has become the major region where modern scientific knowledge and technology have been applied to agriculture. Mechanized commercial agriculture in this arid territory has been realized largely through large-scale, government-sponsored irrigation projects. Once again, however, only certain sections of the northern plateau and of the lower courses and deltas of the rivers of northwest Mexico can be feasibly irrigated in this way. Yet in these now

[7] Cumberland, *Mexico,* pp. 294–307; Whetten, *Rural Mexico,* pp. 129–151, 182–214, and 240–81.

[8] Business and industry received a further boost during World War II by the increased foreign demand for Mexican manufactured goods and the necessity to manufacture substitutes for imports no longer available because of the war.

[9] Cumberland, *Mexico,* pp. 320–21; Wilkie, *Mexican Revolution,* pp. 201–3.

[10] Cumberland, *Mexico,* pp. 304–5; R. C. West and J. P. Augelli, *Middle America: Its Lands and Peoples* (Englewood Cliffs, N.J.: Prentice-Hall, 1966), pp. 323–50.

FIGURE 17.1 Major industrial and mechanized regions of Mexico. Together with large-scale stock raising and commercial production of sugar, coffee, and other crops, these areas contribute most of the gross national product. Adapted from Robert C. West and John P. Augelli, *Middle America: Its Lands and Peoples* (Englewood Cliffs, N.J.: Prentice-Hall, Inc., 1966), figs. 11.15, 11.23, 11.24, and 11.28, with additions from Charles C. Cumberland, *Mexico, The Struggle for Modernity* (Oxford University Press, 1968), pp. 300–301, by permission of the publishers.

well-watered regions hundreds of thousands of acres farmed with modern agricultural methods produce a range of agricultural products. Some of these farms are large, privately owned holdings. Other large farms of a size suitable for modern technology are organized as a variant of the ejido. These "collective" ejidos (which account for less than 10 percent of total ejido lands) are not broken into individual household plots, but are collectively worked as a unit by the members of the community who then receive shares of the harvest according to the type and amount of labor performed.[11]

[11] Raymond Wilkie, *San Miguel: A Mexican Collective Ejido* (Stanford: Stanford Univ. Press, 1970); Whetten, *Rural Mexico*, pp. 215–39.

FIGURE 17.2 A family rests at the market place in the town of Pátzcuaro, Michoacan, where a major regional market is held on Fridays. Photograph by Carol Bales/VAN CLEVE.

The impressive expansion of hydroelectric plants, oil refineries, modern textile plants, irrigated farming, and the like is reflected in the gains shown on government economists' charts in such indicators of national economic health as gross national product and national per capita income. Yet the fact remains that this economic growth has been unevenly distributed among the total population. It has been extended only slightly to that 50 percent of the populace who live in the crowded countryside of the densely populated central basins and in the distant upland valleys of southern Mexico and Chiapas. In sharp contrast with the prosperous farmers and businessmen of the increasingly urban north and with the cities of the Basin of Mexico where the products of manufacturing and industry find their major markets, many of the rural villagers of the center and south continue to follow largely preindustrial agrarian lifestyles and remain significantly unintegrated with the national economy and society.

Herein lies the fundamental problem facing contemporary Mexico. Over three million persons (1960 census) still speak Nahuatl, Maya, Zapotec, Mixtec, or another of the more than 30 native languages still represented in Mexico as a primary or only language, and these people frequently reside in protective corporate Indian communities.[12] Even

[12] Anselmo Marino Flores, "Indian Population and its Identification," in *Handbook of Middle American Indians*, ed. Robert Wauchope (Austin: Univ. of Texas Press, 1967), 6:20–24; Wilkie, *Mexican Revolution*, pp. 212–13.

more significant is the fact that although this figure now represents less than 10 percent of the total population, due to the rate of general population growth (3–4 percent per annum) the number of native language speakers is steadily increasing in absolute figures. The majority of *campesinos* (rural dwellers) today, however, are Spanish-speaking wage laborers, agriculturalists, and craftsmen resident in more or less "open" mestizo communities where there is no strong defensive community organization and where few, if any, community strictures are placed on individual and household interaction with the wider society. Nonetheless, for a variety of reasons this involvement often remains marginal.[13]

In both "closed" corporate Indian villages and "open" mestizo communities household and community continue to depend on centuries-old patterns of subsistence agriculture based on maize cultivation. Variants of slash-and-burn horticulture with digging sticks, hoes, and machetes predominate on often heavily eroded hillsides; oxen and wooden plows are used where land is sufficiently level. In order to pay debts and acquire small amounts of cash and various material goods and foodstuffs not produced within the village workers may seek seasonal jobs on commercial farms outside the village and, again following an old pattern, agricultural and craft items may be produced for sale or exchange at a regional marketplace.[14]

In a few areas the regional market system is organized into a so-called "solar system" in which literally thousands of villagers from surrounding communities congregate at regular, often weekly, intervals at a large, centrally located market and administrative town. Smaller "satellite" marketplaces are operative in surrounding villages on specified days within the weekly cycle. The Valley of Oaxaca offers one of the best examples of the "solar system" market organization. The hub of this regional economy is the city of Oaxaca where a large market is held every Saturday. On Sunday the market is at Tlacolula, on Monday at Miahuatlán, on Tuesday at Ayoquesco, on Wednesday at Etla and Zimatlán, on Thursday at Zaachila and Ejutla, and on Friday at Ocotlán. A similar cycle is found among the villages around Lake Pátzcuaro in Michoacan where a large number of Tarascan and mestizo agricultural communities specialize in the production of different products (pottery, basketry, textiles, woodcarving, etc.) for the market.[15]

[13] Eric R. Wolf, "Types of Latin American Peasantry: A Preliminary Discussion," *American Anthropologist* 57 (1955):452–70; Eric R. Wolf and Edward C. Hansen, *The Human Condition in Latin America* (London: Oxford Univ. Press, 1972), pp. 71–99.

[14] Adams, *Second Sowing*, pp. 73–89; Angel Palerm, "Agricultural Systems and Food Patterns," in *Handbook of Middle American Indians*, ed. Robert Wauchope (Austin: Univ. of Texas Press, 1967), 6:26–52.

[15] Village specialization is a feature of regional economies in general, including the Oaxaca system. R. Waterbury, "Urbanization and a Traditional Market System," in *The Social Anthropology of Latin America*, ed. W. Goldschmidt and H. Hoijer (Los Angeles: Univ. of California Press, 1970), pp. 126–53; David Kaplan, "The Mexican Marketplace Then and Now," in *Essays in Economic Anthropology*, ed. June Helm (Seattle: Univ. of Washington Press, 1965), pp. 86–89; M. Nash, *Primitive and Peasant Economic Systems* (San Francisco: Chandler, 1966), pp. 58–83.

It is important to realize that in spite of the busy exchange these regional market systems remain quite limited in terms of further economic development. Each system exists independently of the others, that is, the regional markets do not connect to form an overall market system with a single set of operatives. Although each of the regional economies is tied to the national economic network by traveling merchants and by outside buyers and sellers, they form the weakest link in the national market economy. Furthermore, unlike business firms and commercial agriculture that are heavily capitalized and organized specifically to achieve greater capital accumulation for reinvestment and economic growth, campesino households relying on subsistence agriculture are small producers whose little available capital is generally spent for immediate consumption. The marketplace economy is limited accordingly in its potential for growth and for restructuring into forms that could mesh better with the business-industrial world.[16]

Many campesinos supplement their subsistence agriculture with poorly paid wage labor on plantations. Some, especially campesinos of economically "open" villages, may produce small amounts of a cash crop—coffee, vanilla, sugar cane, or rice—which is then sold to outside buyers who handle processing, marketing, and profit-making. However, since wages are low and since only limited quantities of a cash crop are produced, the amount of cash received is small, restricting immediate purchasing ability. As a result, the campesino frequently becomes caught in a web of credit relationships with rural storekeepers. Because of his limited amount of cash, the wage laborer or cash-cropper is obligated to seek goods on credit to help support his family during the periods before the harvest is ready to give him work in the fields or to provide him with a crop for sale. The relationship that then develops between storekeeper and client is rather delicate, for the storekeeper, preferring to deal in hard cash, wishes to keep his credit extensions as minimal as possible without losing his customer, while the customer tries to obtain as much on credit as he can without losing his reputation for repaying. Here again, although these ties of credit form an important point of contact between the countryman and the wider national economy, they do not provide a means by which the campesino can move into greater participation with the national economy.[17]

Nor has the creation of individual (as opposed to collective) ejidos, which are particularly common in central and southern Mexico, greatly improved the campesinos' economic marginality. On the contrary, for corporate Indian communities the renewed emphasis on subsistence agriculture made possible by ejido lands has actually encouraged continuation of social and economic separateness. Ejido plots are too small for modern forms of agricultural technology or for production of significant surpluses, and *ejidatarios* remain hindered by lack of sufficient credit.

In order to raise their level of productivity individual ejidos sometimes

---

[16] Kaplan, "Mexican Marketplace," pp. 84–94.
[17] Wolf and Hansen, *Human Condition*, pp. 120–23 and 130–35.

are combined into larger units. For example, blocks of contiguous ejidos have been reconsolidated through renting and sharecropping into corporately managed farm units where the tenant (an entrepreneurial farmer) provides financing for seeds, water, fertilizers, and modern equipment, while the ejidatario provides the land. Although renting and sharecropping are technically illegal, these regulations are openly violated without difficulty, and the larger farm units that result, like the collective ejidos, can be effectively plowed and harvested with modern machinery.[18]

In spite of its economic failings, land redistribution received new impetus during the administration of López Mateos (1958–64), who distributed more land during his years in office than any other president since Cárdenas. Notable inroads also have been made in related areas of rural development such as transportation, health, education, sanitation, and general community development. Indeed, since 1960 the government has cited with renewed vigor the elimination of poverty and illiteracy as one of its major goals.[19] Since there are still many campesinos who do not own enough land for even a minimal level of subsistence and millions more who remain illiterate, without adequate housing or running water or hygienic sewage disposal or even shoes, there is much still to be done. Unfortunately rural development programs frequently face disheartening difficulties. Part of the problem has been due to simple lack of funds as federal expenditures have tended to favor industry, trade, and commercialized private agriculture more than rural development.[20] But larger barriers are erected by the conservative nature of the social structure of contemporary Mexico.

Although the revolution removed the colonial landholding elite from its position of dominance and power, the two-part colonial social structure of elites and masses still remains. The growth of business, industry, and central government has replaced the hacendado oligarchy with a new group of urban elite—engineers, architects, scientifically trained farmers, economists, bankers, and financiers—identified by a particular complex of manners, dress, general social behavior, and attitudes. While the source of wealth for the contemporary upper sector is no longer based on ownership of large landed estates, the pattern of elite life continues very much as before.[21]

Now, as then, the highest affairs of business, industry, and government are conducted by rich and powerful men each working through highly personal networks of contacts afforded by a large circle of close kinsmen, compadres, friends, and acquaintances of political groups and sports clubs. Many of the professions, the numerous lesser positions in business and industrial firms, and the large number of civil service posts that a growing government has created are filled by salaried white-collar employees of more modest economic means who usually have personal

---

[18] Charles J. Erasmus, "Upper Limits of Peasantry and Agrarian Reform: Bolivia, Venezuela, and Mexico Compared," *Ethnology* 6 (1967):349–80.

[19] Wilkie, *Mexican Revolution*, pp. 89–96.

[20] Ibid.

[21] Adams, *Second Sowing*, chap. 3.

and political connections with persons of higher position and who strive as best they can on the salary at hand to emulate the life-style of the high elite.[22]

This occupationally diverse and economically middle-range segment of the upper sector includes the rural elite of the many regional towns scattered about the Mexican countryside. These towns form important points of contact between the national-industrial economy, polity, and society and that of the agrarian order. The most important serve as *cabeceras* or administrative and political centers (like county seats) for the hamlets and villages in the immediate hinterland.[23] The town also contains a regional marketplace and a number of permanent commercial establishments, as well as electricity, modern water systems, schools, and doctors. It serves further as a center of communications, and maintains telegraph, telephone, and postal service. From here transportation can be arranged to the city or, in the other direction, to the outlying villages.

Town life is the focus of potentially mobile campesinos who may be trying to move closer to the national economy and political structure. It is also the preferred place of residence for the local mestizo elite, whose interests, attitudes, and activities as expressed in such criteria as wealth, clothing style, education, occupation, facility in Spanish, and family background are quite distinct from that of the Indian or campesino resident in the countryside or recently moved into the lower levels of town society. The town elite, who make their living by a combination of commercial agriculture and ranching, storekeeping, and government bureaucratic posts and as commercial middlemen, look to the city for their goals and behavioral guidelines. They use their income to maintain a prestigeful standard of living for themselves (cars, telephones, television, farm equipment) and especially for their children, for whom they hope to provide a better life through good education and a position in one of the professions. Consequently, the younger generation of town elite usually moves outside the town to higher educational facilities and permanent jobs in the cities. This drain, in turn, opens positions in the town to aspiring campesinos who may have acquired sufficient education and capital to open a small store or invest in commercial agriculture. As small-scale farmers and artisans, these ambitious countrymen will likely take up residence in town, to begin their own slow move into town society.[24]

[22] Because this economically middle-range sector of society continues the interests and values of the higher elite, it is not considered from the point of view adopted here to constitute a distinct socioeconomic "middle class" with distinct interests and orientations of its own, although many observers have taken this position. Compare Adams, *Second Sowing*, pp. 47–69 and 131–32; J. J. Johnson, *Political Change in Latin America: The Emergence of the Middle Sectors* (Stanford: Stanford Univ. Press, 1958); Wolf and Hansen, *Human Condition*, pp. 191–200.

[23] This entire complex of cabecera and subordinate communities forms a *municipio*, the lowest territorial unit of the national governmental structure.

[24] Louise Margolies, "The Rural Elite in a Mexican Municipality," *Anthropological Quarterly* 42 (1969):343–53; Norman Humphrey, "Social Stratification in a Mexican Town," *Southwestern J. of Anthro.* 5 (1949):138–46.

Although the town offers possibilities for social mobility from countryside to town and from town to city, the town can only exist by virtue of the production, consumption, and labor of the campesinos still dwelling in the countryside. Their surplus agricultural products feed the town, their need for household goods and village ceremonial items provides business at the stores, and they serve as domestics in elite households and as cheap seasonal and part-time labor for commercial agriculture. Yet, in spite of the fact that economically the town depends on the countryside, in order to verify and solidify their social positions and social mobility the mestizos of the town are careful to maintain traditional colonial patterns of social distance with the countryside, especially with those campesinos living "Indian" life-styles.

As we have seen, colonial society, while heavily dependent on Indian labor, worked assiduously to keep the Indian socially, politically, residentially, and juridically separated and subordinate. With independence the Indian received legal equality; 100 years later, after the dissolution of the large estates and debt bondage, he became legally free to move about in pursuit of economic opportunities. Yet in actuality, by the efforts of the rural elite the economic and sociopolitical status of the Indian has frequently remained separate and subordinate to this day. The town mestizo elite is able to effect the continuation of this colonial pattern of superior-inferior social relationships through their activities as "power brokers," that is, by serving as power-holding mediators or points of contact between the inhabitants of the Indian community and the mestizo world.[25] For example, in many instances the central marketplace is controlled by town mestizos who collect market taxes and act as price controllers and middlemen, buying wood and food from Indian villagers at a low price for resale later at a profit, and supplying them in turn with manufactured clothing, tools, fireworks, and other paraphernalia needed for village ceremonies. Mestizos also operate as creditors and as moneylenders, an important function and position of power since cash is scarce. They then control the offices that channel workers to local wage-labor openings. Mestizo landholders, who in turn are also hindered by lack of capital, continue to depend on cheap workers and Indians who must labor to repay their debts. Town mestizos also maintain charge of all bureaucratic offices and positions of authority within the municipal or regional administration.

The town mestizos are able to maintain a monopoly of local administration and of economic transactions because of their literacy and command of the Spanish language and their greater knowledge of the methods of Mexican commerce and administration. The Indians' continued use of a native tongue and only partial command of Spanish, together with a high rate of illiteracy and lack of understanding of mestizo political affairs, hinder their abilities in the marketplace and in matters of administration

[25] It is important to stress, however, that maintenance of this position by town mestizos reflects the fact that they, too, are affected by the low capital, low productivity, and limited market opportunities that characterize the agrarian regions of Mexico.

FIGURE 17.3 View of San Cristobal Las Casas, Chiapas. Such regional towns and their surrounding hinterland must be more closely integrated with the national economy and society if nation-building is to succeed in Mexico. Courtesy of Michael D. Olien.

and provide obvious markers of cultural difference and thus of "inferiority." Even the prevalent ties of compadrazgo between Indians and town mestizos, while personalizing relationships and interactions, actually accentuate social and economic differences and the inferiority and dependence of the Indian. The corporate Indian community itself also facilitates the continuation of this duality by encouraging and rewarding maintenance of colonial Indian culture patterns. While individual Indians are sometimes able to break away from the bounds of their community, the conservative colonial social, political, and economic dichotomy between Indian and mestizo continues to curb integration into a single national socioeconomic system.[26]

Even the efforts of government agencies to advance the Indian's standard of living and reduce his dependency are hindered by these attitudes. Rural educational programs and the role of the rural schoolteacher are a good case in point. The rural schoolteacher is another example of a go-between or "broker" standing at a critical juncture between the institutions of the rural community, particularly the Indian village, and the institutions of the wider system. Like the rural elite "power brokers" whom we mentioned above, schoolteachers and others like them (agricul-

[26] Rodolfo Stavenhagen, "Classes, Colonialism, and Acculturation," in *Masses in Latin America,* ed. I. Horowitz (New York: Oxford Univ. Press, 1970), pp. 235–83; Benjamin N. Colby and Pierre L. Van den Berghe, "Ethnic Relations in Southeastern Mexico," *American Anthropologist* 63 (1961):772–92; Henning Siverts, "Ethnic Stability and Boundary Dynamics in Southern Mexico," in *Ethnic Groups and Boundaries,* ed. Frederick Barth (Boston: Little, Brown, 1969), pp. 101–16.

tural agents, public health officials) frequently operate to keep the Mexican world and the Indian community separate by maintaining a social distance between them even while officially encouraging interaction.[27]

Again the raison d'être for this approach can be found in the social system. Many rural teachers are ambitious, socially mobile but still low-status mestizos or acculturated Indians just moving into the lower ranks of the upper sector of society and anxious to advance their careers and social position within the mestizo world. Therefore they are eager to satisfy the teaching requirements set by their superiors in the national educational bureaucracy. But in order to emphasize their mestizo social position, teachers also work to keep a clear distance and distinction between themselves and their Indian students. Their position requires them to explain the rudiments of the Spanish language, the history, geography, national holidays, and general culture of Mexico, arithmetic, and modern farming methods. At the same time, however, teachers frequently communicate an attitude of distinct dislike and rejection of their young charges, whom they typically regard as poor, uncivilized, stupid, and incapable of learning. The children, in turn, consider the subject matter boring and irrelevant to their lives and find interactions with these representatives of the mestizo Mexican world (among the first they consistently meet) distinctly unpleasant and degrading. As a result they are reinforced in their own traditions all the more. In short, instead of drawing the Indian closer to Mexican culture and society, government educational efforts frequently serve to encourage his continued separation.[28]

Another example of the problems and processes involved in interactions between national agencies and peoples of the town and countryside is afforded by the activities of the regional courts of law. Investigations have shown that town-dwelling mestizos frequently use the town or regional courts for a wide variety of public and private business, especially disputes over family problems and property contests. In contrast, Indians living in smaller rural villages and hamlets prefer to handle their problems in their own court under the direction of local officials who are elected to the office by the community. In general Indians are extremely reluctant to deal with the regional court where higher court costs are charged and where, they feel with some justification, they will be treated more harshly. Therefore, even if a case is not satisfactorily settled at the local level, it probably will not be taken higher. This is particularly true of family disputes, for the local Indian customary laws concerning such topics as common-law marriage, village endogamy, and witchcraft frequently are not recognized by national law.[29] The mestizo officials of the higher regional court, in turn, find dealing with Indians a frustrating matter. Even though they may be fairly knowledgeable about Indian

[27] Richard N. Adams, "Brokers and Career Mobility Systems in the Structure of Complex Societies," *Southwestern J. of Anthro.* 26 (1970):315–27.

[28] Robert Hunt and Eva Hunt, "Education as an Interface Institution in Rural Mexico and the American Inner City," *Midway Magazine* 8 (1967):99–109.

[29] The major exception concerns homicides, which villagers prefer to send outside the community for adjudication in order to rid the village of a dangerous deviant.

customary law, as representatives of the national laws judges cannot (or refuse to) yield to customary Indian procedures. This approach, of course, only encourages Indians to maintain their separatism.[30]

In spite of the distinctions encouraged by rural schools and rural courts, there are other areas of contact which have led to significant changes in the organization of the protective corporate Indian community. The presence of various government agents and the imposition of local (municipal) government staffed in all key positions with mestizo officials have reduced and transformed the traditional civil offices of the Indian community and challenged the authority of traditional political-religious leaders (principales). Civil offices are now filled by election or by appointment by the governor of the state rather than by passage through the traditional civil-religious hierarchy, and requirements for posts rest on such skills as literacy or ability to speak Spanish rather than on years of demonstrated service to the native community. Consequently, in many Indian communities the civil-religious hierarchy has lost virtually all its traditional civil offices, leaving only the religious positions functioning. In some instances the number of religious offices has increased, apparently to offset the loss of civil offices. In other cases the traditional religious offices also have gradually weakened and attenuated. They too may be expected to disappear eventually. As the traditional civil-religious hierarchy declines, of course, the corporate Indian community loses its defensive structure and its control over its population and becomes increasingly "open" to outside influences.[31]

Where they are still maintained, however, the religious offices and accompanying ceremonial activities continue to play important functions, not only in "closed" communities but also in communities that may have become considerably "open." Broadly speaking, the system appears to function best where the rural Indian population continues to exist in social isolation or deprivation with respect to Mexican society. Where this situation is found and if communal, private, and/or ejidal landholdings are sufficient to provide a fairly self-sufficient subsistence base for the community so that supplementary outside labor is kept low, ceremonial activities may continue as a major focus of community solidarity and "Indian" identity.[32]

However, wherever individuals have been forced or enabled to become involved in wage labor or small-scale trading outside the village, requiring them to learn more Spanish and exposing them directly to mestizo culture, the traditional ceremonial system has become increasingly limited and voluntary in terms of personnel and finances. Broader outside contacts bring greater awareness of the range of available consumer items. Personal income may be used to begin cash cropping, pursue a craft for commercial purposes, buy a truck, or open a small store. Consequently,

[30] Eva Hunt and Robert Hunt, "The Role of Courts in Rural Mexico," in *Peasants in the Modern World,* ed. P. K. Bock (Albuquerque: Univ. of New Mexico Press, 1969), pp. 109–39.
[31] Billie R. DeWalt, "Changes in the Cargo Systems of Meso-America," *América Indígena* (in press).
[32] Erasmus, "Upper Limits of Peasantry and Agrarian Reform," pp. 374–78.

the cash once spent largely for community fiestas is now likely to be invested elsewhere. The traditional religious ceremonies then are supported mainly by the poorer families of the community who, aware that they are failing to do as well as others in the cash economy, defensively look to the traditional system for a sense of status and personal prestige. Yet because they are poor, the number of ceremonies may decline and the costs of sponsorship may be reduced as much as possible. Frequently under these circumstances costs are met by house-to-house collections which serve to spread the expense among a group of persons. This adjustment to economic realities stands in sharp contrast to the traditional pattern of individual sponsorship with heavy personal expenditure.[33]

Not surprisingly persons wishing to keep resources directed towards support of the traditional religious hierarchy and those desiring to utilize resources for greater involvement with the mestizo world also come to differ with respect to sociopolitical loyalties and general world view. The "traditionalists' " loyalties remain with their community; they have little, if any, identification with the nation. They are "sons of the village" rather than of Mexico, and they continue to seek security, protection, and aid in the produce of the soil, in the greater degree of social equality and cooperation that characterizes Indian society, and in the patron saint of the community, rather than from outside secular agencies. Those with greater experience in the mestizo world, on the other hand, are more likely to consider themselves not only village members but also Mexican citizens. They may associate with the PRI or another political party. They view the community as part of the political structure of the republic and look to the government for policies and programs to aid the village. They work to advance their own interests via personal wheelings and dealings within the highly competitive networks of social ties characteristic of mestizo society.[34]

As these contrary interest groups and orientations emerge, the Indian community as a whole becomes vulnerable to internal conflicts and outside pressures and frequently breaks into opposing parties and factions. The competing factions are commonly directed by particular individuals who, by whatever wider experiences they have acquired, are able to operate within both community behavior patterns and national or mestizo behavior patterns. These individuals become another type of power broker at the juncture between community and nation.

The role played by these power brokers can be viewed as a contemporary version of the control by political boss that has been a distinctive feature of local, regional, and sometimes even national political activity during much of the colonial and postcolonial periods. Backed by relatives, dependents, and members of his faction, the local boss or "cacique" exercises informal but very effective control over many community activities and handles contacts with outside agents. He may coordinate distribution of Indian labor among mestizos needing workers for their

[33] Ibid., pp. 374–78.
[34] Stan Wilk, "Terminal Loyalties in a Mexican Community" (unpublished manuscript, 1971).

cash crops; he may interpret and regulate the local application of the agrarian code; he aids in community decisions and mediates local problems, protecting villagers against brushes with state and federal law. He is an influential person who can "get things done" both inside and outside the community in a manner that is often personalistic, arbitrary, and technically illegal—but effective. The cacique's ability to assist people through his contacts and influence strengthens his body of personal supporters which, if he wishes, he can pledge to regional or national political figures. If he becomes linked with a national political party his position can furnish another channel by which the central government may reach into the community.[35]

Nonetheless, like all power brokers the cacique is in a position that is by definition a delicate one. If he is to be successful he must balance his community activities with the demands of outside agents without unduly offending either side. If he fails in either direction, if his community followers turn to another political boss, or if the agents of the national government and other outside contacts bypass him to deal with the villagers through other means, his position will be lost.

The changes occurring in corporate Indian community organization are due in large measure to increasing population. The growing press of people on land and other resources due to an expanding birth rate, drastic reduction in the infant mortality rate, and a longer life expectancy cannot be satisfactorily accommodated by the limited productivity of small plots of land cultivated with traditional technology. Insufficient land and inability to provide for basic needs present the corporate community with two alternatives: either extreme poverty or, what is more likely, greater involvement with the outside cash economy via wage labor and production of cash crops.

Nor, of course, is population pressure restricted to Indian communities. The countryside in general is faced with the problem of producing enough to keep pace with the growing number of people. Various solutions have been tried. In addition to augmenting subsistence agriculture with cash crops or with wage labor, from 1942 to 1964 hundreds of thousands of countrymen living in the central and northern states sought seasonal work in the United States under contract as field hands or *braceros*. Many others entered illegally as "wetbacks," and still others have emigrated permanently. Migrations of landless farmers from the heavily populated central highlands into less densely populated frontiers is another approach. Some of these colonists have moved to the northern irrigated districts, while other settlements have been established with modest success in river-basin developments along the Pacific and Gulf coastal lowlands of Michoacan, Chiapas, Veracruz, and Tabasco.[36]

[35] Paul Friedrich, "The Legitimacy of a Cacique," in *Local-level Politics*, ed. M. J. Schwartz (Chicago: Aldine, 1968), pp. 241–69; Paul W. Drake, "Mexican Regionalism Reconsidered," *J. of Inter-Amer. Studies and World Affairs* 12 (1970):406–7.

[36] Richard B. Craig, *The Bracero Program* (Austin: Univ. of Texas Press, 1971); Matthew Edel, "Determinants of Land Settlement Success in Lowland Mexico: An Inter-Communal Comparison" (mimeographed, 1971).

Additional thousands of persons, one-third to one-half of those who move, are turning not to the frontiers but to the cities, especially Mexico City, in an onrush of rural-urban migration that has become a major characteristic of twentieth-century Latin America in general.[37] The transition to urban life is usually accomplished with a minimum of stress and upset. The initial adjustments are eased by maintaining close ties of kinship and mutual aid with rural relatives. Relatives who preceded the new migrant to the city also will likely help, often by providing living space in their own cramped rooms. Many urban migrants eventually build a home of sorts in one of the squatter settlements or shantytowns (called *colonias proletarias* in Mexico) that spring up literally overnight on vacant lands on the city's outskirts. Colonias have been mushrooming at a tremendous rate, particularly during the past two decades. It has been estimated that in the mid-1960s over half of the population of Mexico City lived in this type of settlement.[38]

Employment, a primary goal of migrants to the city, may be a greater problem because, in spite of a rapidly growing business-industrial sector, the city cannot absorb all the potential labor coming to it. Accurate statistics are lacking, but it appears that while a large percentage do find jobs, in the sense that few people who want work actually do nothing, many are really underemployed, working only a few days a week at low pay. Some will work as artisans, small tradesmen, and skilled workers, but many will be employed in some type of service job—as waiters, domestics in the homes of the upper sector, at unskilled jobs in factories, construction, and transportation, as newspaper and market vendors, as shoeshiners, etc.

Even though the income from such jobs is extremely low and the economic conditions of life for urban migrants often appear appalling, the new urban dwellers are generally pleased with the opportunities for improvement that the city offers, and few return to the countryside where incomes and living standards are even lower. They are willing to endure substandard housing and living conditions, at least for awhile, in return for the realization of such goals as acquiring property in a colonia or finding (hopefully) steady work or improving education opportunities for the children.

Since they generally find their urban life-styles more satisfactory than not, urban migrants do not constitute a threat to political stability in Mexico, even though in the urban centers, especially Mexico City, the extremes of wealth and poverty have become more accentuated than anywhere else in the country. On the other hand, this rapid urbanization, with the attendant overcrowding and the increased need for schools,

[37] By 1960 50 percent of Mexico's population was classified as urban. Mexico City is now the third largest city in the hemisphere; only New York City and Buenos Aires are larger.

[38] Oscar Lewis, "Urbanization without Breakdown: A Case Study," *The Scientific Monthly* 75 (1952):31–41; Wayne A. Cornelius, Jr., "Urbanization as an Agent in Latin American Political Stability: The Case of Mexico," *Amer. Polit. Sci. Rev.* 63 (1969):833–57; D. S. Butterworth, "A Study of the Urbanization Process among Mixtec Migrants," in *Peasants in Cities*, ed. William Mangin (Boston: Houghton Mifflin, 1970), pp. 98–113.

FIGURE 17.4 In the Oaxaca Valley Doña Rosa continues an ancient craft. Photograph by Carol Bales/VAN CLEVE.

transportation, decent housing, medical services, streets, sewers, and water, is straining the public services of the government, thus limiting even more the efforts that can be put toward the countryside.[39]

Speaking of the nation as a whole, regardless of whether members of the lower social sector seek a livelihood through small private landholdings or ejidos, struggle to make ends meet with supplementary wage labor or cash crops, take a job in city services, or move to the frontiers, none of these alternatives brings the lower sector of society significantly into the business-industrial economy of the urban elite and white-collar workers who constitute the upper sector. A strong nation-oriented government has evolved, but its ties to the masses are still incompletely operative. In addition, there has been an overall attenuation (rural elite notwithstanding) of the traditional forms of interrelationship that directed interactions

[39] Cornelius, "Urbanization as an Agent," pp. 833–57.

between the lower sector and the elite during the colonial period when the labor of the lower class directly supported the elite and the elite in return provided for personal security and needs beyond the immediate reach of the lower sector. During the latter half of the nineteenth century, as the haciendas were transformed into capitalistic, mechanized estates and as centralized government subverted regional caudillos, the interrelationships between elite and lower sector became increasingly impersonal and monetized. Then as landed wealth was replaced by commercial agriculture, urban-based business and industry, and high finance in the twentieth century, the gap between elite and lower sector widened further because rural labor was no longer essential to the operation of the business-industrial economy; with their low level of income the lower sector also could not provide much of an internal market for the products of manufacturing and industry.[40]

The problem is most acute in the underdeveloped rural regions of central and southern Mexico. Here the campesino and especially the Indian is beset with the limitations of insufficient arable land and traditional technology, limited availability of cash, and inadequate credit, often compounded by mechanisms maintaining social boundaries between mestizo and Indian and thus limiting economic opportunities for the latter. To be sure, government agencies are seriously trying to improve living conditions and to bring the campesino into greater involvement with the national economy, but these efforts not infrequently fall considerably short of total success.

Therefore, although Mexico has made great strides in alleviating the problems of its underdeveloped agrarian regions and by all measures has made notable improvements, a high level of poverty still persists. Furthermore, in spite of migrations to the cities, the population of the countryside is increasing in absolute terms even if statistically it is decreasing relative to the total population. In 1910 70 percent of the total population, 10.8 million persons, were rural dwellers. In 1970 only 41 percent of the population still lived in villages under 2,500 persons,[41] but in absolute figures this statistic included about 20 million persons. (This is also a conservative estimate of Mexico's current rural population, for many persons following essentially rural life-styles live in villages larger than 2,500.)[42]

The Mexican Revolution: Success or Failure?

The persistence of low standards of living and of social and economic marginality among a growing number of persons raises the question whether the Mexican Revolution is or is not succeeding. We have taken a

[40] Wolf and Hansen, *Human Condition*, chap. 7; Adams, *Second Sowing*, pp. 268–72.

[41] This is the official definition of rural community in the Mexican census.

[42] K. Ruddle and D. Odermann, eds., *Statistical Abstracts of Latin America*, 1971, Latin American Center (Los Angeles: University of California, 1972), p. 69; Wilkie, *Mexican Revolution*, pp. 218 and 221.

somewhat pessimistic approach by emphasizing the persistence of marginal regions with a marginal rural population. But it is also true that Mexico has achieved a great deal since 1910, including a stable political structure and organization that is actively extending the benefits of science, modern technology, and a growing national economy to millions. Most of the population now speak the national language, at least to some extent. An extensive network of roads and railroads fans out from the center of the nation. Although 24 percent of the population 10 years old or older remained illiterate in 1970, 76 percent were able to read and write. Similar figures could be cited for matters of housing, sanitation, and medical care. The problem remains, however, in the absolute figures: the fact that although increasing millions benefit, the number of persons who continue to share incompletely in the achievements of the revolution, who still stand outside the national economy and society, continues to grow; the fact that, for example, in spite of tremendous reduction in illiteracy in relative terms, by 1960 there were more people unable to read and write in Mexico than there were in 1910.[43]

This situation has generated renewed concern among those who are working to implement the goals of the revolution. In this spirit President López Mateos in 1960 propounded a program of "balanced" revolution which called for an equal expenditure of federal funds among administrative, economic, and social activities. Since the federal budget contains more money than ever before, more funds should be available for the elimination of poverty. Yet simple expenditure of money may not be the entire answer. There remains a question as to whether the revolutionary program is still feasible as it now stands. Land reallocation remains a major tenet, but there is not enough arable land left for the 2 million or so still landless campesinos who qualify for ejidos, and we have noted the economic failure of existing ejidos. The futility of working to improve living conditions at the community level when the region as a whole remains economically underdeveloped and socially conservative is another problem.[44]

Nonetheless, in spite of these difficulties, if the political, social, and economic achievements of the revolution to date are viewed against the situation as it existed just prior to 1910 the accomplishments are unquestionably impressive. Unfortunately the continued press of present-day problems remains, and there can be no resting on past laurels except for encouragement for continued and greater efforts in the future. Yet this sense of encouragement may be one of the most significant contributions of the revolution. As long as the people of Mexico continue to believe, as many do, that with work, education, and good fortune there is a chance for individual improvement and mobility within the existing system, as

[43] Wilkie, *Mexican Revolution*, pp. 208–9 and 214; cf. Cumberland, *Mexico*, pp. 285–94 for a general review of education since 1920.
[44] Stanley R. Ross, ed., *Is the Mexican Revolution Dead* (New York: Knopf, 1966); Wolf and Hansen, *Human Condition*, pp. 294–307; Juan de Onis, "Mexican Revolution after 60 Years," *The New York Times*, December 2, 1970, sec. 1, p. 12.

indeed there has been for millions, the possibility of more violent extremist reactions to the numerous shortcomings and incompleteness of the revolution to date is considerably defused. The task that remains, then, is to continue to meet these aspirations sufficiently to keep the hopes—and the peace—alive.

18

Reform and Reaction

in

Central America

The Setting in Brief

In contrast with Mexico, the republics of Central America stand at the threshold of development into modern nation-states. In terms of the threefold process of nation-building briefly outlined at the beginning of Chapter 17, most of the Central American states are still in the initial phase of consolidating nation-oriented leadership and developing truly national governmental structures.

Strong centralized governments, a fundamental prerequisite for nationalization, were not firmly achieved in most of the republics until the 1930s when they appeared in response to the depression. At this time the export-oriented monocrop economies on which the Central American states depended were badly shaken. As the economic condition worsened, unemployment and social unrest hit the countryside; the situation was complicated and accelerated by population growth. The nervous elite sought reassurance against the possibility of rural uprisings by supporting strong presidents. Thus Guatemala, Honduras, Nicaragua, and El Salvador all fell under the rule of heavy-handed "depression dictators" (Ubico in Guatemala, Carías in Honduras, Hernández Martínez in El Salvador, Somoza García in Nicaragua) who, by legislation, control of the military, and harsh suppression of any opposition established both peace and order in turbulent times and the primacy of the central government, especially the presidency, over political competitors.

Other prerequisites for nation-building also have been slow in coming. Industrialization remains in its infancy; export economies based on large-scale production of coffee, bananas, and, since World War II, cotton continue to support a conservative aristocracy of landholders (Table 18.1). To be sure, national wealth and income have increased, particularly from stimulation of industry and agricultural diversification as a result of World War II. Yet this increased wealth continues to benefit the elite most of all. The majority of the population still endure a low standard of living as unskilled urban workers, subsistence agriculturalists, and seasonal or permanent workers on commercial agricultural estates and cattle haciendas. On the other hand, the growth of national wealth has brought to the forefront of the contemporary sociopolitical scene the members of the middle sector who, though still small in numbers in Central America, are vociferously calling for reform in the distribution of this wealth.

TABLE 18.1

COFFEE, BANANA, AND COTTON EXPORTS OF CENTRAL AMERICA
in 1957, 1967, and 1971
as a Percentage of Total National Exports

	Coffee			Bananas			Cotton		
	1957	*1967*	*1971*	*1957*	*1967*	*1971*	*1957*	*1967*	*1971*
Guatemala	79.01	34.2	33.8	7.98	—	6.2	4.22	15.9	9.0
Honduras	19.01	13.6	12.3[a]	61.08	49.8	51.0[a]	—	—	—
El Salvador	78.15[b]	47.6	40.6	—	—	—	15.61[b]	8.1	12.7
Nicaragua	40.03	14.4	29.3	—	—	—	30.60	38.2	22.5
Costa Rica	48.63	38.2	26.3	38.66	21.7	28.4	—	—	—
Panama	—	—	—	63.97	53.5	56.4	—	—	—

[a] 1970 data.
[b] 1956 data.
SOURCES: 1957 data from *Statistical Abstracts of Latin America, 1957*, Committee on Latin American Studies (Latin American Center, University of California, Los Angeles, 1959), p. 39; 1967 data from *Statistical Abstracts of Latin America, 1967*, ed. C. P. Roberts (Latin American Center, UCLA, 1968), p. 204; 1971 data from *Statistical Abstracts of Latin America, 1971*, ed. K. Ruddle and D. Odermann (Latin American Center, UCLA, 1972), p. 363. By permission of the publisher.

Although the processes of nation-building have barely begun, Central America has been thoroughly involved in major international events of the post–World War II era, particularly the competition between the United States and forces of the communist sphere in the Caribbean. In this international arena Central American governments generally continue to be dominated by the United States. Several of the isthmian republics were directly involved in United States military action vis-à-vis Cuba, where the social revolution of 1959 once again alerted the United States and Latin America to the potential of the lower sectors as fuel for explosive change and reform. All the Central American countries have received considerable military and technological assistance from the United States, which hopes to avoid other social revolutions by providing funds and personnel for gradual and peaceful development. However, the current association between the United States and Central America is not smooth by any means. From the point of view of many (though by no means all) Central Americans the economic and military assistance offered by the United States as part of its program to maintain political stability in these republics is neither meaningful nor useful. They frequently find greater significance in the approach to foreign aid and development favored by socialist and communist powers, which are less concerned with economic and technological development per se and place more emphasis on reform programs that will redistribute the national wealth and income among a larger proportion of the population.[1]

Receptivity to reform programs of this sort by sizable segments of the Central American population reflects the fact that there are growing pressures for sociopolitical and economic change in Central America. Here we must note again the growing restlessness of the nationalistic, ambitious, liberal "middle sector" of Central Americans—professionals, intellectuals, lesser army officers, office workers, businessmen, teachers, and skilled workers—who are demanding a larger political voice and a greater share of the benefits accruing from postwar economic prosperity. We also must note the burgeoning population growth (between 3 and 4 percent annually for all countries) and increasing population pressure on traditional subsistence resources. This press, in turn, has generated increased poverty in overpopulated rural heartlands and stimulated both rural-urban migrations to the capital cities and colonization of still relatively empty frontier areas. We must remember, too, that low levels of income and thus of purchasing power continue to prevent approximately two-thirds of this growing population from significant participation in the national economy. As a result internal market potentials and overall growth of national economies are severely limited.

Both the United States and the Soviet bloc have been concerned with the implications of these and related problems and have approached Central America from the general foreign policy orientation characteristic of each. Unfortunately this interest frequently has resulted in escalation rather than diminution of problems. Nowhere is this seen better than in Guatemala.

A Revolution Fails

From 1931 to 1944 the Republic of Guatemala was firmly directed by a strong presidential figure, General Jorge Ubico. In a manner not unlike Mexico's Díaz, Ubico controlled the military, brooked little opposition, and supported the benefits accruing to foreign investors and the small Guatemalan elite from banana and coffee estates served by the cheap labor of Guatemala's Indian masses. At the same time, however, the Ubico

[1] Richard N. Adams, "Social Change in Guatemala and U.S. Policy," in *Social Change in Latin America Today*, R. N. Adams et al. (New York: Vintage, 1960), pp. 231–84.

regime also undertook a basic step in nation-building by bringing the elite under closer governmental control. This was accomplished by making adjustments in local and regional political structures and by replacing debt peonage, over which landowners had control, with a rigidly enforced vagrancy law which gave the central government control over the all-important labor supply. Since the regulations of the vagrancy law applied almost exclusively to Indians, the elite continued to be assured of labor for their estates. However, replacement of debt peonage by vagrancy laws transferred an important element of power from the landowners to the central government.[2]

Then came World War II, stimulating national economic growth and bringing to the forefront of the national political arena the socially mobile middle sector who demanded an increasing political voice and a greater share of the national income. Ubico's conservative regime now was confronted with a small but growing opposition coalition composed of students, lawyers, teachers, skilled workers, and smaller businessmen. With the aid of ambitious younger military officers this predominantly urban group succeeded in replacing Ubico in 1944–45 with a reform candidate, Juan José Arévalo.[3]

Arévalo and his supporters used the now strongly centralized national government to implement serious social, political, and economic reforms. Many of these changes were oriented toward establishing direct governmental contact with Guatemala's campesinos in order to integrate this large number of heretofore politically inert peoples into the nation at large, for if the campesinos could emerge as a significant political force they could break the power of the traditional elite and thereby strengthen the reform government.

To this end important legislation, including a labor code and the so-called Law of Forced Rentals, was enacted. Under these regulations estate laborers and urban workers were encouraged to unionize and directed on how to obtain wage increases, indemnities, and improved labor conditions from their employers. Landless individuals, particularly colonos and other plantation workers, were entitled to rent small parcels of unused land at low cost from private landlords and from government-controlled territory.

Local branches of national political parties were also organized, and suffrage previously restricted to literate males over the age of 18 (thus effectively removing virtually the entire Indian population from the vote) now was extended to all literate persons and illiterate males.

Arévalo's program soon encountered difficulties, partly due to the lack

[2] Chester L. Jones, *Guatemala, Past and Present* (Minneapolis: Univ. of Minnesota Press, 1940), pp. 160–66; Nathan L. Whetten, *Guatemala, The Land and the People* (New Haven: Yale Univ. Press, 1961), pp. 120–22.

[3] Richard N. Adams, ed., *Crucifixion by Power* (Austin: Univ. of Texas Press, 1970), pp. 174–205; Franklin D. Parker, *The Central American Republics* (London: Oxford Univ. Press, 1964), chap. 5; Richard N. Adams, *The Second Sowing* (San Francisco: Chandler, 1967), pp. 237–47; John D. Martz, *Central America: The Crisis and the Challenge* (Chapel Hill: Univ. of North Carolina Press, 1959), chap. 2.

of funds and trained administrators to implement it and partly due to opposition from the privileged conservative elite, including the landowning Guatemalan aristocracy and the major foreign concern, United Fruit. In 1948–49 United Fruit sustained a broad strike among its workers, who avidly took to unionization and demanded higher wages, better living conditions, and other fringe benefits. The company appealed to the United States Congress, which was sympathetic both to its plight and to that of the Guatemalan elite. As this opposition "right" developed, a militant, strongly nationalistic "left" also emerged; the latter urged Arévalo's government to take even firmer stands against the traditional elite and foreign interests. Although he was in considerable sympathy with the left's demands, the moderate Arévalo tried to avoid overt association with this segment because of the presence of labor organizers with communist and socialist connections in its ranks.

In 1951 Arévalo was replaced in office by Colonel Jacobo Arbenz Guzman, an avid nationalist. Arbenz did not oppose Communist support if it would help defeat the foreign corporations and hasten internal reforms. Consequently during his years as president the Guatemalan Communist party became highly influential in the national congress and in the administration of agrarian committees, labor unions, and an organization commonly known as the *Union Campesina* which was also oriented toward aiding and politicizing the rural population. In addition, under Arbenz the reform program was given another bold and critical direction which attacked the power of the large landowners, both nationals and foreigners, through the system of land tenure. To the dismay of the Guatemalan elite and United Fruit, large estates and unused lands, including fruit-company acreage, were expropriated by the government and leased to former estate laborers.

Needless to say the opposition of the conservative elite and the foreign corporations increased while the Arbenz government encouraged continuing labor challenges to United Fruit and to the North American–controlled railroad and utilities companies. Tension mounted as Arbenz, responding to growing pressure from the opposition, sought to tighten his position by seeking military aid from the Soviet Union, while the United States, declaring a staunch "anti-Communist" position, provided arms and money for a Guatemalan opposition group under Carlos Castillo Armas.

In June, 1954 Arbenz was removed from office by the Guatemalan military who feared that he and the Communists intended to arm the campesinos and undercut the regular army. With the approval of the military and the support of the United States, Castillo Armas now assumed the presidency.

Castillo Armas quickly instituted a tightly controlled regime which considerably slowed the reforms of his predecessors. He worked to regain the support of the traditional upper sector power groups who had so swiftly reacted against Arbenz's agrarian reforms and his threats to the established military. Therefore, those aspects of the revolution that were

most threatening to the power and position of the traditional aristocracy
were removed. Arbenz's agrarian law was revoked and land returned to
the large landowners and United Fruit, although unused lands could still
be expropriated under favorable terms of payment and credit facilities
were made available. The Communist party was outlawed and labor
unions and other political parties and organizations were shorn of many
of their leaders and their powers. They still remain few in number and
heavily controlled today.

Although agrarian and labor reforms were curtailed, the national
economy prospered, supported by high coffee prices on the world market
and by large amounts of renewed United States aid which (in direct
contrast to the nationalistic aims of the original revolutionary leaders) the
new government sought and welcomed. United States capital and companies now entered Guatemala in unprecedented numbers, and United
States technical, military, and economic aid was rapidly increased. United
States diplomatic influence strengthened, too, and in the early 1960s the
incumbent regime actively assisted the abortive efforts of the United
States to halt the Cuban revolution.[4]

In response to this renewed intervention by the United States,
Guatemalan liberals once more clamored for reform. So far they have
been held in check by the conservative elite and forbidden significant
legal political activity. Consequently many would-be reformers have remained inactive. Others, however, have turned to clandestine operations,
and hard-pressed *guerrilleros* operating in cities and frontier areas have
become the principal expression of active opposition to the present government. With the assistance of the United States this opposition has been
kept sharply curtailed, but the open interest, support, and encouragement of their activities by sympathetic socialist governments, especially
Cuba, makes the entire Guatemalan situation more complicated and
potentially more dangerous.[5]

Meanwhile, the national wealth remains in the hands of the upper
sector, whose social and political prerogatives continue to be protected.
Indeed, under postrevolutionary governments upper sector interest
groups have organized and proliferated and noticeably grown in power,
to the point where the central government has begun to show concern lest
the military, the church, wealthy businessmen, and large estate owners
become a significant independent challenge to the national authority.
This florescence of the upper sector has been facilitated and reinforced
by economic growth in all areas of the economy, including industry,
commerce, utilities, banking, and export (but not subsistence) agriculture. Meanwhile, the small-scale agriculturalists and laborers of the lower
sector (some 70 percent of the total population) have experienced a slight
drop in the proportion of national wealth they have received over the last

[4] Charles W. Anderson, "Politics and Development Policy in Central America," *Midwest J.
of Polit. Sci.* 5 (1961):332–50; Adams, *Crucifixion,* pp. 139–41.
[5] Adams, *Crucifixion,* pp. 214–17 and 267–77; Luis Mercier Vega, *Guerrillas in Latin
America,* trans. D. Weissbort (New York: Praeger, 1969).

20 years and remain hard-pressed for resources of land and income adequate to make ends meet.[6]

The majority of the Guatemalan population, and especially the Indian sector, continue to live in the interior valleys, plateaus, and Pacific piedmont of the temperate highlands. The highlands can be conveniently divided into an eastern region of lower, gentler mountains and more open country and an extremely broken, rugged west and northwest region (which topographically continues into Chiapas). Because of the difficulties of transportation and communication and the limitations placed on European plow agriculture by steep slopes and narrow valleys, the west and northwest have remained predominantly Indian (as has highland Chiapas, which really forms a single cultural unit with Indian Guatemala). The less forbidding eastern highlands and southeast piedmont, together with the Motagua Valley, are heavily Ladino with fewer Indians. Guatemala City, by far the largest urban complex or "primate city," lies on the border between the eastern and western highlands.[7] (The term *Ladino*, commonly used in Guatemala and adjacent parts of Central America and Mexico, is applied primarily to lower and middle sector persons who culturally and linguistically are non-Indian.)[8]

In many respects the current position of Guatemala's Indians is comparable to that of the Mexican Indian population. An "Indian problem" exists in both countries in the sense that those persons who continue to speak an indigenous language as mother tongue, follow pre-Hispanic and colonial forms of agriculture, and abide by a distinct set of more or less corporate community customs still stand outside the national economy and society to a great extent. In Mexico this segment of the population now forms only a small proportion, relatively speaking, of the rural population and of the total national population. However, in Guatemala Indians living in communities of varying degrees of corporateness constitute over 43 percent of the total population of 4.2 million (1964 census). Their integration or lack of integration into the national economy and society is therefore of major importance for those concerned with the country's future.

Today, as during the long centuries of the colonial and postindependence eras, the Guatemalan highland Indian continues to be subject to social, economic, and political orientations and demands emanating both from within his community and from the wider Hispanic world. However, as in Mexico, the quickened pace and general nature of the events of the late nineteenth and twentieth centuries, combined with rapid population growth, have generated new pressures which have notably affected

[6] Adams, *Crucifixion*, chap. 6.

[7] Ibid., pp. 155–62; Richard N. Adams, *Cultural Surveys of Panama-Nicaragua-Guatemala-El Salvador-Honduras*, Pan American Sanitary Bureau, Scientific Publication no. 33, pt. 4 (Washington, D.C., 1957); papers by M. Nash, C. Wagley, S. Tax and R. Hinshaw, and R. Reina in *Handbook of Middle American Indians*, ed. Robert Wauchope (Austin: Univ. of Texas Press, 1969), 7:30–132.

[8] Adams, *Cultural Surveys*, pp. 267–70; Sol Tax et al., *Heritage of Conquest* (Glencoe: Free Press, 1952), pp. 76–96.

FIGURE 18.1 The market at Antigua, Guatemala, established in the ruins of a Jesuit convent. The picturesque colonial city was formerly the site of the capital of Guatemala until seriously damaged by earthquake in 1773. Courtesy of Michael D. Olien.

Indian economic activities, the sociopolitical structure and functioning of the corporate Indian community, and, to a lesser extent, the general structuring of Indian-Ladino relations.

Although the west and northwest mountains are difficult to traverse, the Indian population travels about a good deal. Much of this activity concerns economic matters supplemental to subsistence maize agriculture such as regional marketing and labor on more distant Ladino plantations. Regional markets and individual and community specialization in production of crafts (pottery, furniture, blankets, grinding stones, etc.) and agricultural produce (maize, wheat, vegetables, and also sheep) for market exchange are well developed within the extensive ecological diversity of the highlands and between highlands and Pacific lowlands. The "solar system" form of market exchange described in Chapter 17 also is found; indeed, the interactions among the 14 communities on the shores of Lake Atitlan provide one of the best examples of this type of regional exchange in Middle America.[9]

In addition, regional economies and individual families have been slowly yet significantly affected by national (even international) economic networks during the last several decades. Local craft items, including hand-spun cotton thread, pottery, and loom-woven cotton textiles, have been replaced by commercial yarns, manufactured textiles and clothing,

[9] Sol Tax, "The Municipios of the Midwestern Highlands of Guatemala," *American Anthropologist* 39 (1937):423–44; idem, "Economy and Technology," in *Heritage of Conquest*, Sol Tax et al. (Glencoe: Free Press, 1952), pp. 43–75.

and metal pots and pans. Other manufactured goods including hoes and machetes, matches, liquor, and some nonlocal food specialties such as coffee and sugar also have become necessities, although at the same time there has been an upswing in local production of craft items for the tourist trade.[10]

Highland Indians contact the national and international economies most directly through the experiences and cash income obtained as laborers on coffee fincas of the Pacific piedmont and on the more recently established cotton estates of the Pacific coastal lowlands. Although forced labor laws no longer are operative, hundreds of thousands of highland Indians, propelled by growing population pressure on highland land resources, continue to seek work on the estates in order to augment subsistence agriculture and craft production with small amounts of cash that will purchase manufactured goods. Some workers become permanently attached to the estate as resident colonos and gradually lose their Indian language, dress, customs, and identity as they become increasingly "ladinoized." Many others, however, undertake the trek to the finca on a seasonal basis during the coffee or cotton harvest and then return to the highlands and the corporate Indian communities.

The limited wages earned by these seasonal estate laborers not only provide for household necessities but also facilitate the continued observance of the rituals and fiestas required by the civil-religious hierarchy characteristic of the traditional Indian community. However, the civil aspects of the traditional hierarchy have been drastically altered by political changes instituted during the decade of the revolution (1944–54). The same period of national reform introduced changes in the formal municipal organization controlled by the local Ladino elite which, together with the Indian civil-religious hierarchy, had provided local government prior to the revolution.

One of the reform movement's aims was to "open" corporate Indian communities and extend political decision-making to the population at large by removing the monopoly of village and municipal political control from the hands of both the traditional Indian elders and the local caciques and Ladino elite. To this end various new measures were enacted, including suffrage for Indian men and competitive elections whereby local municipal officials, supported by a plethora of new political parties, would no longer achieve their posts by appointment by Indian principales and local Ladino political chiefs as was done under Ubico. The civil-religious hierarchy of the traditional Indian community and the traditional role of the community elders or principales were directly affected by these measures along lines comparable to what we have already seen in Mexico. The civil offices of the hierarchy became separate from the religious and frequently declined. The authority of both the Indian elders and the traditional Ladino elite was seriously undercut by the influence of new "power brokers" such as political party representatives and Union

[10] Sanford Mosk, "Indigenous Economy in Latin America," *Inter-Amer. Econ. Affairs* 8 (1954):3–25.

Campesina agents, who now opened opportunities for younger men to become politically active through the electoral process and by participation in local branches of the national political parties and mass organizations.[11]

One consequence of this reorientation was the emergence or heightening of local factionalism. Factional splits occurred in a variety of contexts, sometimes forming along formal political party lines and in other cases developing between Indians and Ladinos or within the Indian population itself as new government supporters and nation-oriented groups opposed traditional conservatives on various issues. The factions sometimes took religious guise as change-oriented Protestants and reform-minded Catholic catechists opposed traditional status-quo Catholics. Regardless of the specific issues and the lines along which fissioning occurred, in all cases the major question was the same: who shall dominate the life of the community—those groups representing social and political change or the forces supporting the traditional way of life? In each instance the outcome depended largely on conditions specific to each community, but the very fact that alternatives now existed resulted in many cases in a weakening of defensive community solidarity and the opening of community organization to new influences and alternatives emanating from the national political arena and wider economic sphere.[12]

Competitive elections lost their efficacy and many of the new younger leaders were summarily disposed of during the Castillo Armas counter-revolution. Nonetheless the unity and protective security of many communities had been irretrievably modified from traditional (i.e., what is considered "most" Indian today) standards and practices. Inhabitants of modified communities became bilingual (but with the Indian language still as mother tongue), and men began to dress in Western-style clothing although women continued to wear Indian costumes. It is probably only a matter of time before such modified Indian communities become even more ladinoized, with both men and women wearing Ladino dress and speaking Spanish as sole or primary language, thereby becoming very similar to the lower class Ladino farmer or rural laborer.[13]

However, this process of ladinoization is long and slow, and cultural pluralism probably will continue for a long time in highland Guatemala. For one thing, although the Guatemalan Indian population is slowly declining relative to the Ladino,[14] it continues to grow in absolute terms (about 312,000 Indians in 1778 but 1.8 million in 1964). In addition,

---

[11] Roland H. Ebel, "Political Change in Guatemalan Indian Communities," *J. of Inter-Amer. Studies* 6 (1964):91–109; Richard N. Adams, ed., *Political Changes in Guatemalan Indian Communities, A Symposium,* Middle American Research Institute Publication no. 24 (New Orleans: Tulane University, 1957).

[12] Ebel, "Political Change in Guatemalan Indian Communities," pp. 91–109.

[13] Adams, *Cultural Surveys,* pp. 271–74; Whetten, *Guatemala,* chap. 4.

[14] From approximately 78 percent Indian in 1778 to 65 percent in 1900 to 43 percent in 1964. Adams, *Cultural Surveys,* p. 279; Anselmo Marino Flores, "Indian Population and Its Identification," in *Handbook of Middle American Indians,* ed. Robert Wauchope (Austin: Univ. of Texas Press, 1967), 6:20–24.

within most areas of the highlands inhabitants of many communities, both Indian and Ladino, retain pride in and desire to continue traditional practices. Nor, as we shall see below, do the highlands hold much potential for future national growth and development.[15]

In much of the west and northwest highlands Indians and Ladinos emphasize and maintain sharp group distinctions based on clearcut cultural contrasts. The Indians living in the rural villages and hamlets of each municipio traditionally have considered themselves a distinct unit. Although they interact continuously with Indians of other municipios, each municipal Indian population maintains distinctive dress and housing type, speaks a common Maya dialect as primary language, recognizes particular saints, engages in a distinctive craft or agricultural specialization in addition to subsistence agriculture, and maintains a unique set of customs, beliefs, and rituals for ceremonies of birth, marriage, and death. The Spanish-speaking Ladinos of the municipio usually live in the central municipal town and seek a livelihood in storekeeping, local landowning (much land is rented out to Indians), and cash crops. Although few in number compared to the Indian population, Ladinos compose the local elite and to some extent continue to control local political processes.[16]

In the eastern highlands Ladinos predominate numerically in both town and countryside, while Indians are considerably fewer in number and much more "modified" and "ladinoized" than in the west. Nonetheless social positions are still sharply delineated and crystallized. As the inhabitants of the Indian community have acculturated to Ladino beliefs, dress, language, and economic and political activities, so that ethnic differences are less apparent and less useful as a means of social identification, Ladinos, particularly the acutely status-conscious local and regional elite, have sharpened and tightened social distinctions. Consequently, in spite of growing cultural similarity, an Indian-Ladino dichotomy is still maintained.[17]

The colonos resident on agricultural estates have developed a particular subculture of their own. As finca laborers Indians from many municipios, with a hodgepodge of languages and customs, are thrown together in a new setting. Gradually common dress and language emerge, specific Indian practices are abandoned, and contact with the highland communities ultimately is lost. But this does not mean that colonos become Ladinos. Instead they tend to enter a cultural limbo in the sense that although they no longer fit into Indian society and in fact live among Ladinos as Ladinolike individuals, they are not considered Ladinos because of personal habits such as speaking dialectical Spanish. This loss of traditional behavioral guidelines without significant integration into

[15] Rodolfo Stavenhagen, "Classes, Colonialism, and Acculturation," in *Masses in Latin America*, ed. I. Horowitz (New York: Oxford Univ. Press, 1970), pp. 235–83; Benjamin N. Colby and Pierre L. Van den Berghe, "Ethnic Relations in Southeastern Mexico," *American Anthropologist* 63 (1961):772–92.

[16] Tax, "Municipios of the Midwestern Highlands," pp. 423–44.

[17] Cf. Norman B. Schwartz, "Assimilation and Acculturation: Aspects of Ethnicity in a Guatemalan Town," *Ethnology* 10 (1971):291–310.

Ladino culture, together with the general restrictions and impersonality of finca life, often leads the colono to a rather dissolute and personally disturbing life.[18]

Even greater deculturation and disorganization occur among the growing numbers of mobile rural laborers, generally "new" Ladinos (i.e., Ladinos only one or two generations removed from Indian forebears), who seek jobs on corporate (e.g., banana) plantations. In spite of material gratifications and improvements in the way of acceptable housing, better sanitation, schooling, hospitals, electricity, etc., the absence of traditional kinship ties and village life creates social "rootlessness" among individuals and families who are personal strangers to each other though they live and work on the same plantations. Under these circumstances it is understandable why both finca laborers and mobile rural laborers such as banana workers are particularly amenable to organization by outside political agencies, as evidenced by the colonos' gradual receptivity to labor unions and the mobile laborers' vigorous support of Communist activities during the revolution.[19]

As we indicated above, one of the major factors sending Indians to the fincas and rural laborers to the plantations is continued population growth in the highlands which places increasing pressure on limited highland resources and necessitates the search for economic supplements and alternatives to subsistence agriculture and small farming. This search for economic alternatives has also brought about a continuing migration of Ladinos from the eastern highlands to Guatemala City and its immediate environs and to the smaller cities and the countryside of the heretofore underpopulated Pacific coastal plain.[20] Highland Indian subsistence agriculturalists (mainly Kekchi from Alta Verapaz) and Ladino laborers from the eastern highlands have also moved into the Lake Izabal region and the southern Petén where land is readily available.[21]

These new foci of migration—Guatemala City, the Pacific coastal plain, the northeast (Izabal), and the north (the Petén)—contrast with the traditional highlands in a number of ways which, when considered together, provide some indications of the future pattern of regional growth in Guatemala. All the new areas are peopled predominantly by non-Indians, while the Indian population continues to center in the west and northwest highlands. Because most capital and land for development are available in Guatemala City and the lowlands, the new regions tend to be linked economically and politically with national interests of the upper sector,

[18] Adams, *Cultural Surveys,* p. 287; Newbold Stokes, "Receptivity to Communist Fomented Agitation in Rural Guatemala," *Econ. Dev. & Cult. Change* 5 (1957):338–61.

[19] Richard F. Behrendt, "The Uprooted: A Guatemalan Sketch," *New Mexico Quarterly Review* 19 (1949):25–31; Stokes, "Receptivity to Communist Fomented Agitation," pp. 338–61.

[20] This coastal region is developing into a major agrarian zone due to the introduction of cotton as a large-scale export crop. Adams, *Crucifixion,* pp. 353–79.

[21] William E. Carter, *New Lands and Old Traditions: Kekchi Cultivators in the Guatemalan Lowlands,* Latin American Monographs, 2nd series, no. 6 (Gainesville: Univ. of Florida Press, 1969).

FIGURE 18.2 Women of the Guatemalan highland town of Patzun at the village well. The characteristic dress of blouse, long skirt, and broad sash, the lack of footgear, and the habit of carrying burdens on the head are some of the features defining the "Indian" status of these villagers, who still speak Cakchiquel. Courtesy of Phil Clark and of the Field Museum of Natural History.

while the highlands, lacking land and capital, remain heavily regional and local in orientation. Similarly, most of the urban and industrial growth is concentrated in certain of the migration areas, particularly in the department of Guatemala, leaving the highlands still predominantly rural. In short, the lowlands and the Guatemala City metropolitan areas are becoming increasingly significant as the national structure grows, while the highlands, though still the most heavily populated area and the traditional seat of Guatemalan life and culture, fall behind.[22]

As is the case in the lowlands, the majority of the migrants to Guatemala City and its environs are Ladinos (although some are very recently "ladinoized" from an Indian background) who have turned their backs on low-paying plantation jobs or plots of land in the countryside too small to be economically feasible in search of better opportunities in the city. Their numbers have greatly increased the population of Guatemala City, making it by far the largest urban center in the country.[23]

Guatemala City also continues as the focus of economic, social, and political power and the preferred place of residence for wealthy

[22] Adams, *Crucifixion,* pp. 125–36 and 155–73.

[23] The population of Guatemala City was about 600,000 persons in 1964 as compared with 285,000 in 1950. The next largest city, Quezaltenango, had a population of about 45,000 in 1964.

businessmen, high government officials, large estate owners, doctors, lawyers, and engineers, who enjoy the privileged life of cars, servants, and large mansions in prestigeful suburbs or fashionable center-city districts. This cosmopolitan and sophisticated urban elite frequently knows little or nothing about the life-styles of the majority of the city-dwellers, especially those who live in the poverty of the *colonias* that have sprung up on the fringes of the city, particularly since World War II.

The migrants and general lower sector residents who live in the abject conditions of the crowded slum and squatter settlements face a rather precarious livelihood. There is very little large-scale industry in Guatemala City and little formal bureaucratization, so that most labor is absorbed in small-scale craft, service, and trading activities. Many persons work in small commercial enterprises, as watchmen in private homes or businesses, as odd-job men in shops and restaurants, or in personal services, while even more remain self-employed (if they are not unemployed) as peddlers, small-scale traders, independent craftsmen, or tailors. Some, though relatively few, are workers in large-scale construction companies, in factories, or in transportation companies. Nonetheless almost all types of employment are rather uncertain in terms of job stability and do not produce much income. Only a modicum of city welfare services exist, and no unemployment or sickness benefits are provided. Housing, lighting, sewage disposal, water, and police protection are all in short supply for low-income areas.[24]

Following the time-honored pattern, lower sector individuals and families counter these insecurities and obtain what opportunities are available in the city for the poor and uneducated by establishing individual networks of personalized contacts with persons in higher economic and social positions who may be able to offer assistance. The tradesman, shoemaker, or domestic servant approaches his employer, or a well-to-do merchant or government official, or perhaps a high-placed relative for advice, small loans, and trading permits; he reciprocates with the assurance of continued service, perhaps at a rate of pay lower than average, or of a steady supply of craft products for a wholesaler.

On the other hand, while formation of diverse personal networks between those lower and those higher on the socioeconomic and political scale involves individuals from the urban lower sector in a range of urban activities, these networks nevertheless limit formal organization and group solidarity within the lower sector as a whole. As a result, persons of the lower sector, for all the poverty and hardship they endure, are not in and of themselves an effective political force either for maintaining or changing conditions of power and wealth.[25]

Among urban workers self-awareness of group social cohesion and of potential political influence is only likely to occur in the few businesses

[24] Bryan Roberts, "Politics in a Neighbourhood of Guatemala City," *Sociology* 2 (1968):185–202.

[25] It was in just these situations that urban labor unions arose during the Arévalo-Arbenz regimes.

with large-scale employment where the size of the operation makes personal ties between owner-managers and workers rare and where workers can oppose management over low pay and poor working conditions. However, such conditions are common in rural settings, particularly between laborers and managers on estates and plantations and among independent small farmers without enough land. As a result, in spite of the rapid influx of poor and dissatisfied persons to the increasingly crowded city, among the lower sectors conditions structured for potential change are still more frequent in the countryside than in the urban centers.[26]

Patterns of Change
in the Middle States

To date the conservative economic and political elite of El Salvador, Nicaragua, and Honduras have maintained their power with relatively little effective opposition from more liberal proponents of nation-building. Would-be reformers, in turn, have been careful to avoid those "excesses" of reform policy, such as land redistribution, which proved the undoing of significant reform actions in Guatemala. Nonetheless pressures for change are rising close to the political surface.

In the tiny country of El Salvador control of economic and political life is divided between a relatively small clique of very wealthy and very powerful elite families, who reap the economic benefits of large coffee and cotton estates, and younger, middle-range military officers, many of whom are of middle sector backgrounds, who advocate a measure of reform. Together with other members of the middle sector this element of the military was responsible for the sequence of events that wrested control of the government in 1944 from the dictatorial hands of El Salvador's depression dictator, General Hernández Martínez, and then in 1948 from his ineffectual successor. In their stead a carefully orchestrated politics of accommodation or "controlled revolution" was instituted. Under this program the younger officers of the military who direct the government have undertaken to maintain political stability, suppress "radical" ideologies and organizations, and placate the traditional elite on the one hand while, on the other, extending moderate social and economic reforms to reduce agitation for change among other elements of the middle sector. So far this approach has yielded discernible improvements, most notably in the field of public works (highway construction, housing projects, and large hydroelectric plants on the Lempa River) where particular emphasis has been placed on developing potential for industrial growth.[27]

[26] Roberts, "Politics in a Neighbourhood of Guatemala City," pp. 185–202; idem, "The Social Organization of Low-Income Urban Families," in *Crucifixion by Power*, ed. Richard N. Adams (Austin: Univ. of Texas Press, 1970), pp. 479–514.

[27] Parker, *Central American Republics*, chap. 6; Charles W. Anderson, "El Salvador," in *Political Systems of Latin America*, 2d. ed., ed. Martin C. Needler (New York: Van Nostrand Reinhold, 1970), pp. 71–91.

To remain reconciled with the agrarian-oriented conservative elite, whose economic and political support they need to stay in power, the government has had to move very slowly with respect to labor and agrarian reform. There have been no serious attempts at land reform, and labor unions, agrarian leagues, and similar organizations are limited, although since 1960, largely as a result of the successful Cuban revolution, efforts have been made to improve the working conditions of rural laborers. The landowning members of the elite have vigorously opposed many of these measures, however, and implementation of moderating legislation has been slow and difficult. Nonetheless, while the traditional elite view development programs somewhat askance, so far they have agreed with government leaders that orderly attempts at change that also purport to protect the position and privileges of the elite as much as possible are preferable to the possibility of rural uprisings organized by radical "communist" elements.[28]

Land redistribution in particular remains a delicate issue, yet the need for land reform and for a wider distribution of wealth is especially pressing because of El Salvador's serious population problem. The tiny republic is experiencing population growth at the tremendous rate of 3.6 to 3.8 percent per year. However, with extensive acres of the best lands devoted to export crops of coffee and cotton or to cattle haciendas, there simply is not enough land to provide subsistence crops for the lower sector. Most campesinos either supplement subsistence agriculture with sale of handicrafts and seasonal labor on coffee fincas or become permanent resident colonos on cotton estates where they depend on the estate owner to provide essential food, housing, and a small amount of cash. Furthermore, unlike the other countries of Middle America, El Salvador does not have undeveloped frontier lands to provide an outlet for its burgeoning population. Consequently, tens of thousands of Salvadorans have migrated to the capital city and to adjacent areas of neighboring Central American countries, particularly Guatemala and Honduras, where population pressures are not as great. Unfortunately the presence of Salvadoran squatters on Honduran land has frequently sparked border incidents between these two countries and remains a point of contention between the respective governments.[29]

The situation in Honduras is not as potentially explosive as in El Salvador. Honduras is not faced with serious population pressure, for there is ample land for expansion (though much is mountainous). Nor is there an "Indian problem" complicating the task of development as in Guatemala. As with Nicaragua and El Salvador, the contemporary population of Honduras is primarily Ladino or ladinoized Indian. Instead, the limitations on nation-building in Honduras are those produced by overall poverty and geographical isolation, complicated by the particular difficulties generated by sharp regional imbalances in development and orientation.

The prosperous north coast is currently the country's most important

[28] Anderson, "Politics and Development Policy," pp. 332–50.
[29] Cf. David Browning, *El Salvador, Landscape and Society* (Oxford: Clarendon Press, 1971).

economic region. Thriving commercial centers and production of bananas and various subsidiary crops under the auspices of the United Fruit and Standard Fruit companies continue to attract a growing proportion of the Honduran population, both permanently and seasonally. However, this region, which is also quite mixed racially due to the immigration of Antillean Negroes seeking plantation work, remains heavily oriented toward the Caribbean rather than toward the rest of Honduras. In contrast, the traditional areas of Hispanic settlement in the interior mountains and basins of the central and southwest sectors of the country look to the capital city, Tegucigalpa. These regions generally remain under small- and medium-scale subsistence and cash crop cultivation by independent agriculturalists farming scattered, often remote holdings, although in some areas large cattle haciendas and lumber tracts predominate. Finally, a large portion of the extensive coastal plain to the northeast and east remains a thinly populated (by Miskito and other Indian groups), undeveloped frontier still awaiting significant orientation in any direction. Effective integration of these diverse regions into a national whole remains far from accomplished.[30]

To be sure, notable steps have been taken toward the eventual realization of this goal. The postwar years have seen increasing agricultural diversification and development of light industries in the few major cities. During the term of office of the energetic Juan Gálvez (1949–54, succeeding the dictatorial Carías), and especially during the administration of Ramón Villeda Morales (1957–63), official recognition of labor unions and a new labor code were granted in response to a general strike. With the exception of the banana region, however, labor unions have not been effectively extended to most of the population. Similarly, Villeda Morales's efforts to activate various agrarian reform laws have not resulted in significant change. This is partly due to lack of support by political and military leaders at the local level and partly because outside of the banana region there is relatively little large-scale agriculture and less of an "agrarian problem" since land for any who want it generally is available.[31] More recent administrations have slowed the official course of social and economic reforms, but in terms of nation-building this more conservative trend is not too significant. Until such basic prerequisites as transportation and communication are improved, Honduras will remain at a low level of development regardless of the official position of the government.[32]

It is significant to note, however, that since the majority of the population are independent agriculturalists and since large landholdings are few compared to other Central American countries, the cosmopolitan elite that holds grimly to its prerogatives elsewhere in Central America is quite

[30] Adams, *Cultural Surveys,* part 6.

[31] Even coffee is grown by small and medium landholders since the rugged terrain precludes large contiguous areas suitable for coffee production.

[32] Parker, *Central American Republics,* chap. 7; Charles W. Anderson, "Honduras," in *Political Systems of Latin America,* 2d. ed., ed. Martin C. Needler (New York: Van Nostrand Reinhold, 1970), pp. 93–107.

small in number in Honduras, less wealthy, and relatively less significant politically. Instead the rural elite (the local or regional upper sector of locally respected "old" families) traditionally has assumed a greater role in the operation of the national government. Similarly, given the availability of land and the slow growth of industrial development (and therefore jobs) in the cities, Honduras has not experienced as much of a rural-urban migration as have other Middle American countries; only the north coast shows movements along this line. The urban middle sector, often highly politicized elsewhere in Middle America, also remains very small. In short, Honduras's general poverty and low level of economic development at least have obviated many of the contrasts between extreme rich and poor that exist elsewhere in Middle America, and thereby they have reduced the actual or potential conflicts that have emerged as a result of this contrast in most of the other republics.[33]

Defenders of the aristocratic status quo in Central America have had consistently strong support in Nicaragua ever since Anastasio Somoza, commander of the American-trained national guard that emerged to power after the Sandino affair, assumed the presidency in 1936. Unlike his contemporaries—Ubico in Guatemala, Hernández Martínez in El Salvador, and Carías in Honduras—who were forced from office by pressures for reform in the 1940s, "Tacho" Somoza continued to control Nicaragua until he was assassinated in 1956. He has been succeeded in office by his two sons, Luis and Anastasio, Jr., who have continued the family regime with only minor interruptions to the present.

With the support of the national guard, enormous family wealth, a far-reaching political machine, the continued friendship and generous aid of the United States, and the awe and respect generated by sheer power, the Somoza regimes have maintained a firm hand on the political controls of the country for over 35 years. To be sure, the regimes of the sons have showed somewhat more flexibility than that of the father. Roads, ports, schools, and social security legislation have been provided on a moderate scale. Sufficient changes have been introduced in the labor code (again since the Cuban crisis) to avoid serious strikes, and agricultural diversity, mechanization of estate agriculture, and industrialization have been encouraged. In fact, under the Somozas economic development has proceeded at a particularly rapid and flourishing pace. However, the benefits of growing industry and mechanized commercial agriculture have flowed almost entirely to the friends of the Somozas and to the family itself, whose ownership or control of the national airline, the merchant fleet, the largest textile factory, the cement plant, sugar mills, cotton gins, and a number of other light industries as well as large cattle, cotton, sugar cane, and rice estates has made them one of the wealthiest families in the world.[34]

---

[33] Anderson, "Honduras," p. 96; Martz, *Central America*, chap. 4.

[34] Parker, *Central American Republics*, chap. 8, Charles W. Anderson, "Nicaragua," in *Political Systems of Latin America*, 2d. ed., ed. Martin C. Needler (New York: Van Nostrand Reinhold, 1970), pp. 109–31.

FIGURE 18.3 The new Managua Inter-Continental Hotel, built to encourage the tourist trade, was constructed in pyramid form to reflect the theme of Maya ruins. In December 1972 a major earthquake reduced downtown Managua to ruins itself. Courtesy of Alan B. Emmering.

Yet it is undeniable that the Somozas' personal interest and large capital investments in industry and agricultural development and diversification have spurred much necessary growth in the national economy. Nonetheless, while economic development proceeds apace with the active support of the governing elite, little has been done to improve the general standard of living for the Nicaraguan campesino. The national guard further assures that those anti-Somoza elements who would champion the cause of the lower sector remain within specified limits of ineffectual dissent.

To gain a fuller understanding of the Somoza regimes we must consider some additional features of Nicaraguan politics. Since the beginning of the colonial era Nicaragua has been extremely prone to rivalries and dissensions that have divided the general population, particularly the elite and the residents of the major towns, on various issues. The country has had a difficult time developing common grounds for unity even among population sectors with seemingly common interests. Given this background of upper sector factionalism, it is understandable that political stability has been most readily achieved only when a foreign power steps in, as the United States did earlier in the century, or when dictatorial presidential figures, such as the Somozas, appear. Therefore it is not entirely unreasonable to suggest that in spite of its firm control of power and its propensity for acquiring immense family wealth from national resources, the long Somoza regime has facilitated national economic development not only by providing investment capital and encouragement but also by assuring political stability. To be sure the lower sector has benefited little, but Nicaragua is not much worse than most of the other Central American countries in this respect.[35]

Nicaragua, like Honduras and Guatemala, also continues to be a country of strong regional contrasts. The eastern or Caribbean lowland (Miskito Coast), which comprises over 50 percent of the national territory, remains a thinly populated, generally non-Hispanic hinterland (see Chapter 19). Within Hispanic Nicaragua over half the population continue to live in the Pacific coastal region, the preferred area for settlement in colonial times and the nineteenth century, too. The largest cities, including the capital, Managua, are located here, while the countryside is divided among large coffee, cotton, and sugar cane estates operated by landless laborers. The interior central highlands, in contrast, are predominantly rural. Most highlanders are independent subsistence agriculturalists who cultivate small or medium-sized holdings with ox-drawn wooden plows and digging sticks. Some also supplement their farming with seasonal labor on cattle haciendas or smaller coffee fincas.

Many of the larger estates on the Pacific coastal plain are becoming considerably mechanized, more so than in most of the other Central American countries. This trend in agricultural modernization has tended to displace the estate laborers and has added to their difficulties. As human labor is replaced with machines, the worker has the choice of returning to the limited productivity and low standard of living provided by subsistence agriculture or of seeking such work as may be found in the still largely unindustrialized cities. In either case, the lower sector of campesinos and urban workers continues to be separated from the affluent world of the wealthy upper sector of landowners and businessmen-politicians.[36]

Serious economic inequalities and sociopolitical distance between the few and the many hold considerable potential for political upheaval when the Somoza regime finally weakens. In addition, the upset, when and if it occurs, could well be further complicated indirectly, if not directly, by the United States, which has continued its interest in Nicaragua and has steadfastly supported the Somoza governments. There is equally fertile ground for more radical socialist and communist ideas among the lower sector and its sympathizers and would-be organizers from certain of the middle and upper sector Somoza opposition groups, who not only have the success of the Cuban revolution for encouragement but also well remember the example set by their own compatriot, Sandino.

Costa Rican Reforms

During the great depression the lower sector of the Costa Rican population, like its counterparts elsewhere in Central America, was restless under the hardships of the lean depression years. Their dissatisfaction

[35] Anderson, "Nicaragua," pp. 118–19 and 127–30.
[36] Adams, *Cultural Surveys,* part 3.

was manifested in an outbreak of strikes, particularly in the banana regions where Communist labor organizers were at work. Unlike their counterparts in other Central American countries, however, the Costa Rican upper sector did not respond to this unrest by supporting harsh, repressive, depression dictators. Instead the Costa Rican governments of the 1930s (controlled by the wealthy as elsewhere in Central America) responded in more flexible fashion, legislating moderate economic reforms that in no way intended major economic reorganization but did recognize the need to improve conditions for labor.

This orientation toward public welfare continued during the 1940s under two controversial presidents, Rafael Calderón Guardia (1940–44) and Teodoro Picado Michalski (1944–48). However, the welfare and social security programs, labor code, income tax measures, and similar reforms proposed by Calderón and continued by Picado proved too radical for the rich landowners of the conservative upper sector, and their original acceptance of Calderón and Picado cooled. As this segment of support fell away, the Calderón and Picado administrations turned to the Costa Rican Communist party which, during World War II when the states of Central America were allied with the United States, Russia, and Great Britain against the axis powers, had been joined by various other workers' groups to form a respected and accepted political party, the Popular Vanguard.[37]

In cooperation with the Popular Vanguard, the governments of Calderón and Picado continued social and labor programs, only to encounter growing opposition from a new direction. The agricultural diversity and beginnings of industrialization generated by World War II appealed to various middle sector groups, which were frequently of rather liberal political persuasions, and to a new group of ambitious though generally more conservative businessmen who championed nationalization and reform as a road to power for themselves and opposed the monopolization of wealth and power by the traditional elite. These new voices, represented by Otilio Ulate Blanco and José Figueres Ferrer, opposed the Calderón-Picado administrations on several counts. Ulate and his associates, who favored economic prosperity and appealed to the business community, felt Calderón-Picado were moving too fast in the area of social reforms and opposed the influence of the Popular Vanguard. Figueres, who was supported by liberal middle sector groups, not only supported economic growth and prosperity for the businessman but also championed social change and a wider distribution of wealth among the general populace. He, too, as an avid nationalist, strongly opposed the alliance of Calderón-Picado with the foreign interests of communism.

In 1948 (the year Arévalo assumed the presidency of Guatemala) Ulate and Figueres and their supporters forced the ouster of Picado after a

---

[37] Parker, *Central American Republics*, pp. 256–301; James L. Busey, "Costa Rica," in *Political Systems of Latin America*, 2d. ed., ed. Martin C. Needler (New York: Van Nostrand Reinhold, 1970), pp. 133–49; Mario Rodríguez, *Central America* (Englewood Cliffs, N.J.: Prentice-Hall, 1965), pp. 20–26; Martz, *Central America*, chap. 6.

brief, two-month civil war; they then began a sequence of governments that have continued to favor social and economic reforms, although at varying speeds. Among other developments, the Communist party was banned and heavy capital taxes levied (affecting rich landowners most severely). A civil service was initiated, women were given the right to vote, and educational and social welfare programs including housing, social security, and roads were advanced. Banks, insurance companies, and utilities, heretofore largely under foreign control, were nationalized, although foreign investors continue to be assured of a welcome if they share the wealth and follow the business procedures recommended by the Costa Rican government.

The government has continued to extend social and economic benefits in many areas. Its success is due in no small measure to deliberate efforts to provide a program that will appeal to a wide range of interest groups. Thus stress is laid on policies that will improve the standard of living for rural and urban workers, expand middle sector managerial and white-collar openings, and assure the upper sector leaders of business, agriculture, and industry that their social positions will be enhanced by new economic opportunities. On the other hand, the difficulties of coordinating the often conflicting demands of such a wide spectrum of the citizenry have necessitated care and moderation in development, and it is noteworthy that one particularly touchy problem, land reform, has yet to be dealt with effectively.[38]

If we compare the course of events in Costa Rica over the last 40 years with the various situations we have seen elsewhere in Central America, we find here still another approach to contemporary problems of nation-building. The Costa Rican governments of the 1930s, although supported by the wealthy elite, assumed an ameliorative rather than repressive approach to pressures for change. The administrations of Calderón and Picado in the 1940s continued a path of reform that eventually alienated the conservative elite, thereby clearing the way for a continuation of the reform process by the post-1948 business and middle sector governments. In brief, we see in Costa Rica a growing recognition and acceptance of the need for reform by those in power and the gradual, peaceful implementation of changes through the administrative offices of successive governments. Given conditions elsewhere in Central America, where pressures for social and economic change frequently have met much more opposition, it is worth considering further how Costa Rica has been able to proceed with less disruption.

Here, as elsewhere in Central America, many of the factors underlying the contemporary situation are rooted in the structure of society as it evolved during the colonial period and the nineteenth century. First of all, Costa Rica's relatively smooth handling of the problems of the twentieth century derives from the country's history as a poor, isolated colonial province. Few in number, living close together on the meseta central, and lacking an exploitable Indian labor force, the colonial population of

[38] Anderson, "Politics and Development Policy," pp. 332–50.

Costa Rica retained a high degree of social and cultural homogeneity. Isolated from effective administration by Guatemala, the colony maintained its own administrative apparatus, an apparatus geared not to the exploitation and control of indigenous natives by Spanish masters but to the needs of the colonists as self-sufficient subsistence agriculturalists.

During the first half of the nineteenth century, as the middle states struggled to form viable governments of their own and Guatemala continued to control its Indian laborers, Costa Rica's farmers began to exploit a lucrative cash crop (coffee) and held firmly to their well-established position of self-government, isolation, and uninvolvement in isthmian political turmoils. As the nineteenth century progressed, the economic benefits of coffee production were realized by large landowners of El Salvador, Nicaragua, and Guatemala, too. In these republics this wealth remained almost entirely in the hands of a small elite group (and their foreign associates), and governments continued to be structured about and oriented toward preserving the dichotomy between rich and poor, landowner and laborer. In Costa Rica, however, income from coffee production was somewhat more widely distributed, since a larger proportion of the population was involved in coffee growing as independent farmers. There continued to be greater contact between those in power and the general populace and an on-going pattern of general interest in government activities among much of the population.

This is not to say that Costa Rica lacked a wealthy elite, for large landholdings were common, or that poverty-stricken campesinos were unknown, for there was considerable poverty among the smaller subsistence and cash crop agriculturalists, or that political equality was achieved, for Costa Rica had her share of strong presidential figures. Nonetheless, there was somewhat less economic disparity between the well-to-do and the rest of society than was the case elsewhere, and there was generally greater governmental receptivity to the opinions and problems of the citizenry at large.[39]

Today political parties are active, political opposition is freely spoken, election campaigns are vigorous, and newspapers are widely read. The appeal to a wide political base and the social and economic reforms of Figueres-Ulate and those succeeding them can be viewed not only as efforts to remain in power but also as attempts by the national government to further extend benefits of national wealth to the populace at large. As a result of their efforts, the citizens of Costa Rica on the whole enjoy greater material benefits than do those of other Central American states.

However, Costa Rica's greater degree of nation-building and of economic prosperity is a relative matter and must be kept in the proper context. The country remains primarily agricultural and industry is still limited. While approximately half the agricultural labor force are independent farmers owning and farming their own land or that of relatives (frequently with supplemental wage labor), large landed estates operated

---

[39] James L. Busey, "Foundations of Political Contrast: Costa Rica and Nicaragua," *West. Polit. Quart.* 11 (1958):627–59.

by seasonal workers or permanent colonos flourish. Nor have political activity and economic benefits been extended to all by any means, in spite of the relatively broad political spectrum. Residents of the metropolitan area of San José, the capital city, and of smaller towns and villages of the meseta central are the better-educated and politically more active segment of the population. Hence they share the benefits of national development to a far greater extent than the agriculturalists living in the still relatively unimproved rural districts. For these latter Costa Ricans (about two-thirds of the total population in 1963), educational opportunities remain limited and political influence and integration into national society remain insignificant. Here as elsewhere in Central America, rural standards of living range from the reasonably comfortable life-style of the successful agriculturalist with enough land for his family's needs to the landless laborer's struggle for bare subsistence.[40]

Nor is Costa Rica exempt from problems generated by rapid population growth. Although the overall population remains relatively low, the rate of increase has ranged from 3.5 to 3 percent during the decade of the sixties. Three-fourths of this population continue to live in the increasingly overcrowded meseta central where the press of people on limited land resources has generated considerable migration to the capital city and major towns.

However, there has been an unusual degree of spontaneous colonization of heretofore sparsely populated frontiers. In these regions squatter families have simply begun to clear the land for subsistence crops, coffee, and pasture for cattle. Migrations have moved rapidly to the east toward Puerto Limón and the Caribbean lowlands, to the west toward the Pacific coast via Puntarenas, to the north along the foothills of mountains and along the tributary rivers to the Río San Juan, and to the south, especially along the southeast Pacific coast where the United Fruit Company shifted banana operations from the Caribbean coast. Another major southern frontier development in the interior General Valley was greatly stimulated by construction of the Inter-American Highway through the northern half of the valley en route to Panama. As a result of all these population movements the rugged jumble of the Talamancan Range and the isolated plains of the Talamancan Valley (Sixaola Valley) remain the largest area still unoccupied by Costa Ricans.[41]

Problems in Panama

The Republic of Panama confronts many of the same problems found in the other five Central American countries, but with additional complications deriving from the presence of the United States via the Panama

[40] Victor Goldkind, "Sociocultural Contrasts in Rural and Urban Settlement Types in Costa Rica," *Rural Sociology* 26 (1961):365–80; Charles P. Loomis et al., *Turrialba* (Glencoe: Free Press, 1953).

[41] Robert E. Nunley, *The Distribution of Population in Costa Rica,* National Academy of Sciences—National Research Council Publication no. 743 (Washington, D.C., 1960).

Canal. In common with the republics to the west, the majority of the Panamanian population exist as poor subsistence agriculturalists, rural laborers, urban workers, or unemployed slum dwellers. In spite of sporadic middle sector pressures for reform the conservative elite powerholders—wealthy landowners and businessmen—have yet to implement effective social welfare programs and agrarian reform.

To some extent the elite has been able to avoid these issues through skillful manipulation of strong nationalistic sentiments generated among the population since the opening of the Panama Canal by the powerful presence of the United States. Let us note a few of the most inflammatory issues. The racial attitudes of North Americans living and working in the Canal Zone have aroused strong reactions from Panamanians who object to segregation practices and discriminatory labor policies that give higher pay to white United States employees than to Panamanian nationals. The obviously higher standard of living enjoyed by United States Canal Zone personnel has become a point of contention too, especially when Canal Zone conditions are compared with the life-style of the working sector of Panama City and Colón. There also has been intense competition between Canal Zone commercial companies and commissaries and Panamanian businesses. The controversy regarding Panamanian versus United States sovereignty over the territory occupied by the Canal Zone is probably the most heated dispute of all. By keeping attention drawn to such issues, the Panamanian elite has been able to redefine and redirect popular dissatisfactions and pressures for internal sociopolitical and economic reform into vehement opposition of the foreign power.[42]

To be sure there have been occasional efforts on the part of a few presidents to seek amelioration of grievances against the United States and to actively work toward a degree of social and economic reform. The administration of José Antonio Remón, president from 1952 until his assassination in 1955, was most outstanding in this respect. In spite of opposition from the traditional elite, Remón made serious efforts to modify the tax structure and to develop industry and agriculture. In a treaty with the United States he also attempted to establish a greater degree of Panamanian authority over public services in Panama City and Colón and to deal with a number of problems related to the Canal Zone. In later years, however, there has been considerable hesitancy on the part of the United States to significantly implement some of the provisions of the Treaty of 1955.[43] Similarly, it has proven extremely difficult to obtain the necessary organized support to continue programs of internal reform in Panama. The middle sector, which typically has found positions in commerce, teaching, and government jobs, is not well organized and has

[42] Lester D. Langley, "U.S.-Panamanian Relations since 1941," *J. of Inter-Amer. Studies and World Affairs* 12 (1970):339–66; John Biesanz and Luke Smith, "Race Relations in Panama and the Canal Zone," *Amer. J. Soc.* 57 (1951):7–14; Sheldon B. Liss, *The Canal: Aspects of U.S.-Panamanian Relations* (Notre Dame: Univ. of Notre Dame Press, 1967). The Pentagon's use of the zone as a military training center is also strongly controversial.

[43] Particularly in light of Egypt's nationalization of the Suez Canal in 1956.

had relatively little political influence, while the lower sector remains almost completely unorganized and insignificant as a political force.[44]

Dissatisfactions between Panama and the United States concerning the canal are also keenly watched and sometimes abetted by the Communist bloc, for the question of who is to control and operate this important waterway is one of strategic international significance. This situation, of course, places the government of Panama in a tempting power position in its own right, for it can, and occasionally has, used the canal issue as a bargaining point to manipulate both the United States and Communist powers in order to achieve concessions useful for its own ends. Since World War II, and especially after the Cuban Revolution, the Communist countries' interest in isthmian affairs has also taken the form of support for internal reforms. To date Communist sympathizers and members of the Communist party are few in number, but the continuing potential for conflicts over the complicated and explosive issues of the canal and over the need for internal economic and political reforms may make Panama a serious trouble spot in the near future.[45]

Of course, it may be possible to correct or defuse problem areas before they reach such levels of intensity. For example, steadily growing Panamanian nationalism has finally led the United States to agree to Panama's long-standing request to reconsider the delicate questions of Canal Zone sovereignty, canal management, and distribution of income from its operation. After a serious riot between Zone Americans and Panamanians in 1964 (the worst such incident in the by-no-means quiet history of United States–Panamanian relations), representatives of both countries sat down to renegotiate the existing canal treaty and also to consider the question of a new canal, for the present waterway is now too small to accommodate larger ships. To date preliminary proposals agreeing to eventually confer Panamanian sovereignty over the Canal Zone have been tentatively concluded. But United States opposition is still strong, and the situation remains highly explosive.[46]

In spite of these tensions and difficulties the fact remains that rents, revenues, and commercial activities deriving from the canal provide a sizable share of Panama's growing national income. Nonetheless, little of this income passes beyond the elite and certain of the middle sector. In spite of efforts to increase jobs in the Zone, the urban laborer still confronts problems of unemployment and poverty in the slum tenements and crowded squatter settlements of Panama City and Colón. His rural counterparts struggle to make ends meet via slash-and-burn agriculture and hacienda labor in the countryside.[47]

[44] Daniel Goldrich, "Panama," in *Political Systems of Latin America*, 2d. ed., ed. Martin C. Needler (New York: Van Nostrand Reinhold, 1970), pp. 151–66; Martz, *Central America*, chap. 7.

[45] Liss, *The Canal;* Martz, *Central America*, chap. 8.

[46] David Binder, "U.S. Agrees to Yield Sovereignty of Canal to Panama," *The New York Times,* February 8, 1974, sec. 1, p. 2.

[47] Cf. John Biesanz and Mavis Biesanz, *The People of Panama* (New York: Columbia Univ. Press, 1955).

Like most of the other Central American republics, much of the territory of Panama remains unsettled by Panamanian campesinos and unintegrated with Hispanic Panama. East of the Canal Zone most of the province of Colón has yet to be colonized by Spanish-speaking Panamanians. The same is true of hot, forested Darién, also a sparsely settled hinterland inhabited mainly by small populations of Choco Indians and Negroes from Colombia. Similarly, west of the Canal Zone the isolated, mountainous province of Bocas del Toro and northern portions of Chiriqui remain peopled primarily by Chibchan-speaking Guaymí.

The Panamanian campesino, in turn, has settled on both sides of the Canal Zone, in the Azuero peninsula, and along the Pacific coast and interior savannahs west of the peninsula to the Costa Rican border. Most of these countrymen cultivate small slash-and-burn plantings of rice, beans, maize, manioc, and plantains with digging stick and machete. Large cattle and sugar haciendas offer labor opportunities for some. Many campesinos, however, remain more or less self-sufficient as agriculturalists, existing on the produce of their fields and selling small agricultural surpluses and handicrafts to acquire pots and pans, manufactured cloth and clothing, salt, sugar, soap, and similar necessities from local country stores. Given the serious transportation limitations of the countryside (in spite of recent road-building programs), there is little opportunity for these isolated agriculturalists to participate in the national economy. Thus rural Panama continues to be a world apart from the cosmopolitan atmosphere of Panama City and the Canal Zone.[48]

On the other hand, lured by hope of jobs in the Zone, increasing numbers of campesinos are moving to the metropolitan area of Panama City which now includes over one-fourth of the national population. Unfortunately there has been a growing problem of unemployment in the cities due to population increase and fluctuations in Canal Zone employment since World War II. Yet even if Canal Zone jobs are not available, the migrants remain in the city, exchanging rural poverty for the problems of the urban poor.

In Summary

Looking back over the various patterns of reform and reaction that have taken place in the republics of Central America over the last four decades, we can discern certain general trends. During the difficult years of the depression and World War II the position of the central government was notably strengthened in all of these countries. Strong dictatorships frequently emerged, supported by the traditional elite (and the United States), which acted to maintain political stability and to strengthen the position of the presidency in reaction to growing unrest among estate colonos and poverty-stricken campesinos. At the same time, however, the traditional elite came under increasing attack from middle sectors anx-

[48] Adams, *Cultural Surveys*, part 2.

ious to obtain a share of the economic prosperity that followed World War II's stimulation of light industry and the agricultural export economy. Combining these interests with calls for reform for the lower sector, the middle sector challenged the traditional power holders during the decade of 1944–54, and most of the "depression dictators" (with the exception of Nicaragua's Somoza) fell from power. With greater or lesser success, efforts were now made to develop a permanent political base for the new middle sector governments by implementing social and economic reforms among the poor.

However, in order to survive in the power arena the reform governments could not entirely ignore the established elite, who were still dominant and powerful. If they were to remain politically significant the reform movements had to tailor their programs so that the privileged position of the elite would still receive support. Consequently, during the later years of the 1950s the traditional elite by one means or another was able to assert various countermoves that significantly modified the reform governments' programs, most notably with respect to agrarian reform. To be sure, the elite has worked carefully, especially after the Cuban Revolution of 1959 showed anew the explosive potential of the middle and lower sectors. It is no coincidence that in the first years of the 1960s the governments of Central America once again actively legislated various reform laws, especially programs for agrarian change. However, many aspects of these programs have yet to be effectively implemented, and social and economic change remains largely unrealized. In spite of a growing middle sector, Central America in general remains polarized between the few very rich and the many very poor.

It also becomes apparent that Guatemala and El Salvador, the states that during the earlier colonial period were economically the most prosperous and most tightly structured about a strong Spanish elite, are the states where reform movements have been most strongly modified by elite pressures today. The continued social and economic conservatism of Nicaragua and Panama also reflects their colonial heritage, for Nicaragua remains beset by the consequences of factionalism and Panama's national life continues to be dominated by the trans-isthmian passageway. On the other hand Honduras and Costa Rica, the poorest colonial provinces, appear to present the most promise for effective adjustment to contemporary pressures for change. Honduras, of all the republics the one most hindered by general poverty, has yet to realize sufficient economic means to approach problems of reform meaningfully. Yet overall poverty has also produced a relatively weak traditional elite, which may well facilitate eventual reform of the traditional system. Costa Rica, its faltering colonial economy bolstered by improved national income in the nineteenth and twentieth centuries, now contains a stronger elite sector. However, elite interests have been more successfully and peacefully countered by a history of significant popular political activity and an increasingly effective legislature. Costa Rica's reform governments, though moving carefully, have achieved noteworthy progress.

Nonetheless, all the states of Central America remain in early stages of nation-building. To be sure the central governments have all been greatly strengthened and expanded and have obtained firm control of the political structure and processes in their respective republics. Yet industrialization is limited and national economies still remain heavily agrarian and export-oriented with only a few major agricultural products underlying national income. Integration of peoples and regions into national wholes also has proceeded unevenly. Although many have been brought into contact with national economic and political structures, increasing numbers of the rapidly growing populations of the cities and the countryside remain politically unorganized and, because of their poverty, unable to participate significantly within national economies. Similarly, large frontier areas within the official boundaries of the republics remain only sparsely populated and economically unproductive in terms of national development.

19

Cross-National Perspectives
of
Central America

Directions and Orientations

We have seen in the previous pages that contemporary Central America faces in several directions. To greater or lesser degree the governments of the Central American republics have been confronted by problems of nation-building in an international climate dominated by world super-powers. At the same time the predominant patterns of economic and social life continue to be those characteristic of past colonial centuries. We also have noted that regionalism, a basic feature of the colonial period, continues to be a prominent aspect of contemporary Central America. In this final chapter we shall consider two additional facets of Central America's multidirectional orientation. We shall round out our earlier discussion of national and subnational (or regional) units of Central America with consideration of select aspects of contemporary Central American cultures that cut across national boundaries and are supra- or extra-national in their orientation and extent.

To be sure, many of the issues and topics treated under the rubric of national and regional frameworks could also be considered from the cross-national perspective. For example, each of the major social sectors of which any single republic is composed has more in common with its respective counterparts in the several republics than with other social sectors of the same state. In other words, in terms of behavior patterns and values the elite of the separate states have their closest affiliations with the elite of the other Central American republics; the middle sectors of each state, although highly nationalistic, share common aspirations across national lines; the poverty-stricken campesino or urban migrant of any one republic shares a common life-style with his counterparts throughout Central America. Likewise, although regional variations have emerged, the similarities of the colonial and independence experience have stamped common characteristics of language and culture across the heartland of Hispanic Central America. Attempts at confederation among the isthmian republics bear further witness to this commonality.[1]

The Caribbean Frontier

When considering extranational aspects of Central American culture it is also well to remember that large portions of Central American territory still remain largely outside the Hispanic culture sphere and that distinctive culture patterns have continued to evolve within these non-Hispanic reaches. The cultural orientations characteristic of the Caribbean coast and tropical lowlands from Panama to Yucatán are the major case in point.

Although in the formal or jural sense this territory is now officially included within the national boundaries of the Central American republics, British Honduras, and Mexico, in actuality the republics (with the partial exception of Costa Rica) have yet to effectively incorporate most of this frontier into their national political and economic structures. Instead, this extensive, thinly populated hinterland continues to be oriented more toward the Caribbean and the Anglo-American international centers than toward the Hispanic heartland of Central America. Hispanic influences are slowly increasing, but in many ways the Caribbean lowlands remain a separate and distinct cultural sphere within Central America.

The lowlands today are inhabited by populations following two main culture patterns. The first major life-style is found among various "native" or "Indian" peoples who dwell in scattered hamlets and villages in the interior mountains, forests, and savannahs and along the waterways of the coast, who practice slash-and-burn agriculture, hunting, and fishing, and who continue to speak dialects of Maya or various Chibchan languages. The second major culture pattern is followed by English-speaking, frequently Protestant, West Indian Negroes who usually prefer to live and labor in the small port towns that dot the coast, although some are rural agriculturalists and others are employed in the Canal Zone. Let us briefly consider certain aspects of each of these life-ways.

The contemporary Indian cultures bear the imprint of varying degrees of active contact of native peoples with representatives of non-Indian cultures. These contacts are usually of an economic nature. The general isolation of the Caribbean hinterland has kept political and social interactions with outside agencies low-key and infrequent for most Indian

---

[1] Richard N. Adams, "The Problem of National Culture," in *Miscellanea Paul Rivet, octogenario dicata* (Mexico: Universidad Nacional Autónoma de México, 1958), pp. 341–59.

populations.[2] Economic involvements with the wider world are of considerable importance. Although a variety of subsistence crops are regularly grown on small slash-and-burn plots and, augmented by fish and wild game, provide a large share of the food supply, supplementary foods and many material necessities must be obtained elsewhere. In order to acquire such necessary items of foreign manufacture as salt, soap, kerosene, clothing, dishes, machetes, fish hooks, guns and ammunition, transistor radios, sewing machines, safety pins, etc. native families (not unlike the contemporary rural "Indian" population of Hispanic Central America) seek wage-labor opportunities or sell local forest resources, agricultural products, cattle, or handicrafts to outside agents.

The frontier "Indian" populations vary notably in the degree to which this outside economic involvement is pursued. For example, of the groups we are considering, the Guaymí of western Panama and the Talamancans of eastern Costa Rica are still only marginally involved in external economic exchanges. When cash or manufactured goods are needed small amounts of rice, maize, beans, coffee, forest products, cattle, or pigs are sold or traded at rural stores, or jobs are sought as temporary or seasonal unskilled laborers on coffee fincas, cattle ranches, and banana plantations. But water containers, ropes and tumplines, hammocks, fishing nets, bags and baskets, dugout canoes and rafts, mortars and pestles, and other items are still crafted from the natural resources of the forests.[3]

The Cuna of eastern Panama and the Miskito of eastern Nicaragua and Honduras have been considerably more active in their pursuit of the benefits of the cash economy, although they too craft many household items from local resources. We noted in Chapter 13 the cooperation afforded buccaneers and English settlers of the Spanish Main by both groups in the seventeenth and eighteenth centuries, and we also noted the eagerness of the Cuna and Miskito to trade or raid for guns and ammunition and a variety of European trade goods. This enthusiasm for outside experiences and manufactured goods continues.

During the latter half of the nineteenth century many of the Cuna moved from the Panamanian mainland onto some 30 islands of the San Blas Archipelago that lie a kilometer or two offshore the Caribbean coast of Panama. Their move was encouraged at least in part by an expanding market for coconuts which grow well on the islands where the Cuna planted numerous groves as a cash crop. Manufactured goods were then obtained from visiting traders in exchange for coconuts (and, for a time, tortoise shell). At the same time many young men continued to travel widely throughout the world as sailors. Since about 1930 several thousand have found jobs in Colón, Panama City, and the Canal Zone as laborers and as waiters and assistants in bars, restaurants, and United States

[2] Religious affiliations may provide more intensive contacts. Various Catholic and Protestant mission groups are active in some areas.

[3] Doris Stone, *The Talamancan Tribes of Costa Rica*, Papers, Peabody Museum of Archaeology and Ethnology (Cambridge: Harvard University, 1962), 43, no. 2; Philip D. Young, *Ngawbe* (Urbana: Univ. of Illinois Press, 1971).

military mess halls. Some young women have also found work in the cities as domestics.[4]

The Miskito Indians of eastern Nicaragua and Honduras have also sought a variety of economic outlets. During the latter half of the nineteenth century many obtained foreign goods from local merchants in exchange for cakes and bundles of wild rubber. When the export market for wild rubber fell, some Miskito men found jobs as pine and mahogany cutters for foreign lumber companies. Others sought work in gold and silver mines opened in the Nicaraguan interior in the early twentieth century by Canadian and North American firms. Many also raised bananas for export under the direction of the Standard Fruit Company. After the decline of the banana boom (about 1940) jobs could still be found in pine lumbering camps owned and operated by North American companies.

However, since 1960, when lumbering also declined, wage labor has been hard to find and cash has become scarce, although sale of sea turtle meat and of small amounts of rice and beans to port towns and to mining camps provides limited income. During these periods of economic depression, which have been recurrent throughout the nineteenth and twentieth centuries as the fortunes of foreign speculators and entrepreneurs waxed and waned, the Miskito return to traditional techniques of subsistence agriculture, hunting, fishing, and handicrafts.[5]

It is also important to note that the diverse economic opportunities utilized over the past decades by the Miskito, the Cuna, and, on a lesser scale, the Guaymí and Talamancans, primarily have involved the men of these societies in contacts with Anglo-Americans or Hispanic Central Americans. Native women have had far fewer outside experiences and remain more conservative in their beliefs and practices. In addition women usually speak only their native language, while men are frequently bilingual (native language plus English and/or Spanish) to at least some extent. The greater conservatism of the women, however, plays an important role in perpetuating the native tongue and in maintaining traditional forms of social behavior. It is largely their influence, together with the general lack of Hispanic Central Americans in much of this hinterland, that has perpetuated distinctive Indian languages and non-Hispanic culture patterns among the rural native population of the Caribbean lowlands.[6]

A dual dependence on subsistence practices and the cash economy in situations requiring men to become involved in more prolonged contact with other cultures while conservative women remain as focal points of native customs is also characteristic of the Black Carib, whose villages dot the coast from Iriona, Honduras to Stann Creek, British Honduras.

[4] D. B. Stout, *San Blas Cuna Acculturation: An Introduction* (New York: Wenner-Gren Foundation for Anthropological Research, 1947).

[5] Mary W. Helms, *Asang* (Gainesville: Univ. of Florida Press, 1971); Bernard Nietschmann, *Between Land and Water* (New York: Seminar Press, 1973).

[6] Helms, *Asang*, pp. 23–24 and 109.

FIGURE 19.1 Miskito women laboriously harvest rice grown on seasonally inundated land along the Río Coco. Rice is regarded primarily as a cash crop, but in actuality it is also an important food staple. Photograph by Mary W. Helms.

During the latter decades of the nineteenth century fishing and slash-and-burn agriculture were augmented by sale of small lots of bananas, coconuts, citrus fruits, and similar produce to visiting North American fruit buyers. This work generally did not require Carib men to be away from home very much, but did provide sufficient cash income to purchase items of foreign manufacture.

During the twentieth century as commercial banana production grew to major proportions, Carib men turned to wage jobs as dock workers with United Fruit and Standard Fruit Companies in the port towns of northern Honduras, Guatemala, and British Honduras. This work necessitated greater periods of absence from the Carib villages, however, and gradually forced mothers, sisters, and wives to assume the major share of subsistence agriculture and child rearing. After the banana operations declined in the 1930s jobs were harder to find, but money had become an important part of the Carib economy. Some Carib men have continued steady employment with the banana companies, but others have found it necessary to seek other, more seasonal jobs. Those who have been forced to rely on seasonal employment are able to return to their villages periodically, but other men have settled more permanently into the life of the port towns and gradually have become acculturated to non-Carib customs.[7]

It is also appropriate to include in this brief survey of native peoples of the Caribbean lowlands the isolated villagers of sparsely inhabited southeastern Quintana Roo. These tropical forest communities of Maya-speaking maize agriculturalists (some of whom are descendants of refu-

[7] Nancie L. Solien Gonzalez, *Black Carib Household Structure* (Seattle: Univ. of Washington Press, 1969).

gees of the War of the Castes) have generally remained apart from and unfriendly to the wider society and polity of the Yucatán Peninsula and the Mexican nation. Indeed, prior to 1958, when a road was completed from Mérida to Chetumal, contacts with the outside world were limited mainly to dealings with itinerant merchants who undertook the difficulties of travel in this remote region of Yucatán to sell various manufactured items to the villagers and to purchase chicle in return.

Chicle has been an important ingredient in the manufacture of chewing gum, particularly from 1920 until the availability of cheaper synthetics in the 1950s. During these years gummy blocks of sap collected from trees of the *sapodilla* family by Quintana Roo villagers (and by *chicleros* from outside the region) found their way to large United States chewing gum firms—The Wrigley Company was a major importer. Chicle collecting became the main cash crop for the villagers, providing sufficient income to supplement slash-and-burn cultivation with tantalizing products of the industrial world.[8]

Chicle also has been a major export from the Guatemalan Petén and adjacent regions of British Honduras and Mexico (Chiapas, Campeche). Here chicle collecting is usually conducted by rural villagers who are provisioned and outfitted by Ladino contractors, many operating from Flores City, the commercial center and departmental capital of the Petén. These entrepreneurs, in turn, have contacts via Belize and Guatemala City with large outside firms which provide initial capital to finance the operations.[9]

As we noted in Chapter 16, the interests of foreign business corporations in the commercial possibilities of the Central American Caribbean lowlands also have been largely responsible for the immigration of thousands of West Indian Negroes to this frontier region. This English-speaking population, which derives primarily from the islands of the British West Indies (particularly Jamaica), began to arrive in the last decades of the nineteenth century to work as railroad and field hands on United Fruit and Standard Fruit Companies' far-flung banana plantations. Additional numbers found employment in the construction of the Panama Canal.

Most laborers arrived on the coast anticipating a temporary opportunity to earn some money and then expected to return home. Some did go back to the Antilles when the banana boom ended. Others, however, remained to seek a living as best they could. Currently a small population of West Indian Negroes and their descendants resides in port towns on the north coast of Honduras where banana production continues and in comparable towns on the Miskito Coast where they engage in various

[8] Alfonzo Villa Rojas, *The Maya of East Central Quintana Roo,* Carnegie Institution of Washington Publication no. 559 (Washington, D.C.: Carnegie Institution, 1945).

[9] Ruben Reina, "The Urban World View of a Tropical Forest Community in the Absence of a City, Petén, Guatemala," *Human Organization* 24 (1964):265–77; Nathan L. Whetten, *Guatemala, The Land and the People* (New Haven: Yale Univ. Press, 1961), pp. 146–48; cf. Ruben Reina and Norman Schwartz, "The Structural Context of Religious Conversion in Petén, Guatemala," *American Ethnology* 1 (1974):157–91.

trades, odd jobs, dock work, and, when wage labor is scarce, fishing and subsistence agriculture.

In Costa Rica the West Indian–derived population continues to center on Puerto Limón, but it also extends into the hinterland north and south along the network of railway lines that once served United Fruit's extensive plantations. Since the company withdrew from the area many of its former laborers have become subsistence agriculturalists or raise small cash crops of cacao or abacá (Manila hemp). Some augment this small-scale cultivation with dock work in Limón or work on large cacao plantations owned by United Fruit.

Since 1942 Costa Rica has exerted a greater degree of control over portions of its eastern lowlands; thus the Costa Rican Negroes of Limón province have experienced direct Hispanic contact to a considerable extent. While United Fruit controlled the coast, West Indian employees were effectively protected from Hispanic influence by the intervening presence of United States company administrators. After United Fruit's protective influence was removed, and as Costa Ricans from the meseta central began to expand into frontier regions, including Limón, the Negro population has come under direct pressure to learn Spanish, to educate their children in public schools where Spanish is used and taught,

FIGURE 19.2 School children in Puerto Cabezas, Nicaragua, parade in honor of September 15, Independence Day in Central America. Celebration of national holidays is one means of extending a sense of national identity to hinterland regions. Photograph by Mary W. Helms.

and to adopt Catholicism. Consequently, while English remains the mother tongue for many and Protestant churches continue to hold their Negro congregations, bilingualism and association with Catholicism is growing, especially among the younger generation.[10]

The many thousands of West Indians in Panama who are employed in the Canal Zone also have encountered Hispanic society. Unfortunately these associations have given rise to serious ethnic conflicts which only recently have somewhat abated. The ill feeling between Hispanic Panamanians and Negroes of West Indian background generally has focused on linguistic and religious differences. But the conflict basically reflects the fact that the West Indian population competes with Hispanic Panamanians for work opportunities in the Canal Zone where, because they speak English, West Indian Negroes are frequently preferred for employment by United States agencies. Nonetheless, in spite of these tensions many younger Antillean Negroes in Panama are learning Spanish and adopting Hispanic customs. As they do so they are readily assimilated into Panamanian society, for to the Hispanic Panamanians, who come in a variety of shades of skin color themselves, dark skin alone is not a sufficient criterion for socioracial distinctions.[11] Many other West Indians, however, prefer to preserve their linguistic and cultural uniqueness and remain a distinct cultural entity within Panama.

Belize

The diverse economic adaptations and the ethnic and linguistic diversity that characterize the Central American Caribbean lowlands are also found in the now self-governing colony of British Honduras or Belize, as it is now more properly termed. Over half of the population of British Honduras (Belize) is composed of English-speaking, predominantly Protestant, Negro or mulatto "creoles," some of whose ancestors were eighteenth- and nineteenth-century slaves and freemen, while more recent generations have derived from Jamaica. Today creoles represent all reaches of society. A highly educated elite directs national government (along with British officials) and engages in trade and commerce, while others are professionals, teachers, clerks, and civil-service workers of the middle sector. Most of this population live either in district towns or, preferably, in the traditional capital, Belize City, which constitutes the central focus and population core of the country. Lower sector creoles work in Belize City and in rural areas as lumbermen, in construction industries, or as chicleros; some also find jobs as seasonal plantation laborers, although in general the creole laborer prefers forestry activities to agricultural work.

[10] Michael D. Olien, "The Adaptation of West Indians to North American and Hispanic Culture in Costa Rica" (unpublished manuscript, n.d.).

[11] Charles Wagley, "On the Concept of Social Race in the Americas," in *Contemporary Cultures and Societies in Latin America*, ed. D. B. Heath and R. N. Adams (New York: Random House, 1965), pp. 531–45.

Perhaps one-fourth of the contemporary population of the colony of Belize is composed of Spanish-speaking Ladinos or "Spanish," as they are called locally, deriving from Yucatán and the Guatemalan Petén. The "Spanish" generally live in the north and the western interior sections of the country near border areas. Today most Ladinos earn livelihoods as small farmers and cattle ranchers; they also manage small stores, run trucks, and operate as chicle gatherers and contractors. However, from the midnineteenth century to about 1935 Ladinos in the northern district of Corozal owned large sugar cane plantations where the local Maya population labored.[12] After 1935 foreign investors established a central sugar refinery in Corozal. As the market for sugar expanded the Ladino landowners were unable to meet the new demand. This provided an opening for Maya laborers to augment their plantation work with small-scale independent cane production. As the region became increasingly oriented toward production of cane as an export crop it became closely integrated with national political and economic institutions. The local Maya were drawn to farmers' associations and labor unions and participated in political meetings and elections, while Ladino control of the regional economy was markedly undercut.

In contrast with the active involvement of Corozal Maya in nation-oriented associations and activities, the Kekchi Indians inhabiting the far southwestern region of British Honduras are much less involved with national affairs. This Maya population, an offshoot of the Guatemalan highland Kekchi of Alta Verapaz, may first have entered the area about 1890 as contract laborers on German-owned cacao, coffee, and rubber estates. After 1914, when Germans were interned by the British, the estates fell into disrepair and the Kekchis spread into the surrounding rain forest to establish independent villages. Later migrations of Guatemalan Kekchis appeared in response to Guatemalan political upheavals. Today the Kekchis remain fairly isolated slash-and-burn cultivators who also raise hogs or collect chicle to obtain the small amounts of money they need to purchase tools, guns and ammunition, cloth, food, etc. at district town stores or from traveling merchants.[13]

We have already discussed the fourth major ethnic group found in Belize: the Black Carib who dwell along the coast south of Stann Creek and work as fishermen, subsistence agriculturalists, and laborers in lumber camps and sawmills. Although in previous years the Black Carib tended to remain apart from national activity, since midcentury an increasing number have become active in labor organizations and have filled various local administrative posts as nurses, clerks, teachers, and district commissioner in the southern districts.

The colony of British Honduras or Belize currently enjoys self-rule and is expected to receive full independence (and a new capital city, Belmopan) in the near future, particularly if a settlement can be reached with

[12] Grant D. Jones, "Political Brokers and Maya-Mestizo Identification in Northern British Honduras (Belize)," (mimeographed, 1970).

[13] A. Terry Rambo, "The Kekchi Indians of British Honduras," *Katunob* 3 (1962):40–48.

Guatemala which continues to claim sovereignty over the territory. One of the major challenges that will confront the new government concerns the integration of the very diverse regions and populations of the country into a single national framework. To this end small air strips, roads, and schools are being established, and new forms of local village councils with ties to the central government have been initiated. However, the country's ethnic diversity may be more difficult to integrate. Most notable here is the conflict felt between creoles and Ladinos. The creole population tends to regard itself as the only true national sector. The Ladinos, in turn, resent this position, make a concerted effort to speak for things Spanish, and resist merging with the creole community.[14]

It is essential that the country develop economically, too, both in terms of local standards of living and overall national economic growth. Manufacturing and industry are virtually nonexistent. To date most economic activities have been directed to subsistence agriculture and to exploitation of forest products, particularly mahogany, cedar, and pine. However, lumbering has been a major activity since the seventeenth century, and most of the marketable timber stands are now seriously depleted. Consequently, the forests must be rehabilitated, new exports must be found, and food production expanded if the national economy is to begin to become viable.[15]

Economic Development and the CACM

The Caribbean hinterland gradually will become more Hispanic in culture pattern as Spanish-speaking campesinos, pressured by continuing population growth, spill over into the still sparsely populated lowlands from the congested Hispanic west. In this context the Caribbean frontier can be considered a demographic safety-valve for Central America and possibly an area of future economic development. Yet it is very likely that rural settlers migrating into these largely undeveloped regions will continue to emphasize subsistence agriculture using traditional techniques of human and animal labor. In other words, while the frontiers may serve to ease population pressures in an immediate sense, they do not appear to be slated for future development within the context of more mechanized, more scientifically managed, and more productive agricultural operations or industrial programs. Most development programs have been directed instead toward heartland areas of Central America where labor, wealth, and resources are more immediately available.

Economic development is a topic of common concern for all the Central American republics, for agricultural and industrial development is of critical importance if Central America is to meet even the basic needs of

---

[14] D. A. G. Waddell, *British Honduras: A Historical and Contemporary Survey* (London: Oxford Univ. Press, 1961).

[15] Norman Ashcraft, *Colonialism and Underdevelopment: Processes of Political Economic Change in British Honduras* (New York: Teachers College Press, 1973).

the dense population that it is predicted will inhabit the isthmus by the last decade of the twentieth century.[16] As they have confronted the issues of development the respective national presidents have encountered more or less comparable economic and political problems and pressures. They have also sought more or less common solutions to these problems, including an approach to economic development that is extranational in scope, the Central American Common Market (CACM). Before considering the Common Market, however, let us briefly review the rather rocky course of economic development programs in Central America since World War II, for the failure of these programs finally led to the Common Market effort.[17]

During the postwar years of the more liberal "reform" governments development programs appeared to be rather well received. But by the late 1950s, as reform efforts were modified and slowed by more conservative upper sector power groups, development programs were allowed to lapse. This slackening also reflected a general retrenching of Central American national economies as a result of a serious decline in the export markets on which the economies rested. As national incomes fell, development projects became increasingly dependent on foreign assistance, particularly the World Bank and the United States government, for financial support. Then as particular foreign aid programs expired, little effort was made by the Central American governments to try to carry on.

Hesitation to support economic development projects also reflected pressures brought to bear on national leaders by the elites. The upper sector feared that their interests and influence in government decision-making would be seriously undercut if the engineers, economists, and international development agency representatives who planned and expected to direct economic development programs were encouraged and supported. Presidents definitely needed the support of the traditional elite. Therefore, when faced with a choice between continuing economic development or staying in power, it is understandable that any success-minded president preferred to support his supporters.

In the early 1960s it appeared that the Central American governments had at last found a perfect solution to the dilemma. A decade earlier the United Nations Economic Commission for Latin America (ECLA) had suggested various approaches to Latin America's serious development problems. ECLA's major proposals called for strong support of development projects by national presidents on the one hand, and, on the other, creation of "regional" (i.e., supra- or extra-national) economic integration programs whereby several countries would cooperate jointly to form a common economic organization oriented particularly toward industrial growth.

For reasons we have just reviewed ECLA's first proposal was rather

[16] Wilbur Zelinsky, "Population Growth in Central America and the West Indies; Prospects and Problems," *Mineral Industries* 35 (1966):1–7.

[17] This discussion of economic development is derived from Gary W. Wynia, *Politics and Planners* (Madison: Univ. of Wisconsin Press, 1972).

90°

84°

21°

Mérida

YUCATÁN

QUINTANA ROO

CAMPECHE

M E X I C O

Chetumal

COROZAL

Belize

Stann Creek

PETÉN

BRITISH HONDURAS

BAY ISLANDS

Flores

Puerto Barrios

Puerto Cortés

Tela

La Ceiba

Iriona

CHIAPAS

NORTHWESTERN
HIGHLANDS

San Pedro Sula

L.
Izabal

ALTA VERAPAZ

H O N D U R A S

G U A T E M A L A

WESTERN
HIGHLANDS

R. Motagua

EASTERN
HIGHLANDS

Tegucigalpa

L. Atitlán

Guatemala City

EL SALVADOR

N I C A R A

XXXX

XXX

San Salvador

XXX

XXXXXX

León

XXXX

XX

Gulf of Fonseca

Managua

Granad

Lak

P A C I F I C

O C E A N

87°

XXXX   COTTON

HENEQUEN

COFFEE

(producing)
BANANAS
(abandoned)

INTER-AMERICAN HIGHWAY

0   50   100   200   300 miles

322

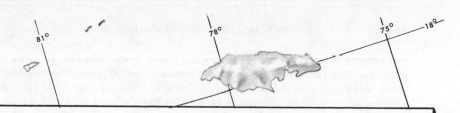

FIGURE 19.3 Central America and Yucatán: major commercial agricultural regions. Adapted from Robert C. West and John P. Augelli, *Middle America: Its Lands and Peoples* (Englewood Cliffs, N.J.: Prentice-Hall, Inc., 1966), figs. 13.4, 13.12, 13.23, 14.11, and 14.25, by permission of the publisher.

unpopular among Central American presidents. But the second major proposal was explored, and a supranational or "regional" economic network was formulated for Central America. This concept held promise of ameliorating such problems as lack of industrialization, unemployment, and general poverty without threatening national political or economic structures or traditional power groups. Furthermore, as we have noted in previous chapters, since independence the Central American republics have periodically attempted to cooperate in seeking solutions to common problems. Thus this contemporary move toward establishment of a regional economic framework was also based on well-established historical precedent.

In 1961 the Central American Common Market came into existence when the economic ministers of Guatemala, El Salvador, Honduras, and Nicaragua signed a general treaty agreeing to work toward common trade and industrial goals; in 1963 Costa Rica also joined. (The governing elite of Panama preferred to complete negotiations with the United States vis-à-vis the Canal issue before considering further a position within the Common Market.)[18] In broad terms the CACM aimed to stimulate economic development in Central America by creating a larger, Central America–wide consumers market for manufactured goods and by shifting emphasis from almost complete dependence on export agriculture to greater industrialization. More specifically the goals of the Common Market have been directed toward supplying jobs for Central America's lower sector and freeing the economies of the several countries from the constraints and uncertainties inherent in the export-oriented colonial economy that has typified the region as a whole for so long. To these ends the Common Market has worked to achieve greater diversification of industrial production within Central America, with particular emphasis on producing those manufactured goods that now are imported in exchange for export income from the sale of cotton, coffee, and bananas abroad.[19]

In addition to the political considerations, these goals have been approached from a Common Market standpoint because the Central American republics are too small individually to effectively industrialize on a separate basis. Given the very limited size of the consumer market to be supplied in each country, manufacturing and industrial plants, whose modern technology operates more efficiently as longer production runs are possible, would not be able to operate on a financially viable basis within any single country. However, if the five small national economies can be linked into a larger economic network, industrial plants that could not be effectively operated within any single isolated country can produce successfully in terms of the whole. Hence the Common Market has worked to achieve completely free trade between the Central American

[18] Charles F. Denton, "Interest Groups in Panama and the Central American Common Market," *Inter-Amer. Econ. Affairs* 21 (1967):49–60.

[19] Frank L. Keller, "ODECA: Common Market Experiment in an Under-Developed Area," *J. of Inter-Amer. Studies* 5 (1963):267–76; John R. Hildebrand, "The Central American Common Market," *J. of Inter-Amer. Studies* 9 (1967):383–95.

FIGURE 19.4 A sugar mill near Turrialba, Costa Rica. Small mills like this produce largely for local consumption. Courtesy of Michael D. Olien.

countries themselves and a common outside tariff wall to protect new local industries from foreign competition. It has also encouraged foreign light industry and manufacturing companies to establish plants and facilities in Central America and has favored joint ventures between foreign investors and Central American businessmen, too. In addition it introduced the concept of "integration" industries whereby, ideally, each country would be assigned one type of specialized industry that would not be established elsewhere in the area and would produce goods for the Central American region as a whole. Such a program would help distribute industrial plants equally throughout the Central American region and would encourage balanced growth rates among the several countries.[20]

During the decade of the 1960s, the CACM scored notable successes in a number of areas. Trade among the Central American countries was greatly stimulated. Impressive progress was achieved in moving toward common external tariffs for the member countries. Foreign capital and companies moved into Central America in response to the climate of investment stability and security generated by Common Market regulations. As the activities of the Common Market increased the viability of local industrial prospects and reduced the risks of investment, an increasing number of Central American businessmen began to invest some of their own wealth at home instead of directing it abroad as usual. The need for transportation and communication stimulated road building, particularly networks of roads connecting more distant sections with the

[20] Roger D. Hansen, *Central America: Regional Integration and Economic Development*, National Planning Association, Studies in Development Progress no. 1 (Washington, D.C., 1967).

Inter-American Highway. This highway, built by the United States in the postwar years as part of the Pan American Highway project, now passes through all the republics and has become the major Central American transportation artery (Figure 19.3). Many Common Market factories were located along this busy thoroughfare.

Unfortunately the CACM also faced a number of formidable problems. The concept of integration industries ran into difficulties at least in part because the United States, which has provided a good share of the CACM funding, has refused to allow its contributed funds to be used for what is in many ways a monopolistic program. Another difficulty has involved the matter of regional balance. Ideally, it would be highly advisable from the point of view of Common Market operations if the economic development of each state could be maintained at a level comparable to that of the others, since equal rates of growth would greatly enhance prospects for continued common cooperation and mutual benefit. Conversely, if one country pulls too far ahead of the rest it is more likely to protect its own interests at the expense of common goals, while if another falls too far behind it may see little benefit in continuing the association.

At its inception one of the strengths of the CACM lay in the fact that the level of economic development of all the states stood more or less at a common point. Nevertheless, in spite of various mechanisms (such as integration industries) that were proposed to maintain this commonality, significant imbalances have emerged and have seriously threatened the viability of the Common Market. El Salvador, with its particularly serious population problems, has worked vigorously to become the industrial and commercial center of Central America and to that end has tried to provide privileges that will encourage greater investment within its borders. A far more serious problem has arisen with respect to Honduras, which, as a result of its poverty, decided in 1971 that it could no longer continue its membership in the CACM. The low level of basic development in such fundamental preconditions for industrialization as roads and power plants had significantly reduced the number of new investments in Honduras.[21] To be sure, special preference was given to road building in Honduras and priority was assigned to Honduran products in an effort to ameliorate the country's problems and to make the area more attractive to industry. Yet Honduras continued to lag behind the other member countries and finally decided that she could no longer afford to continue the association. In 1972 the CACM crumpled further when Costa Rica, true to form, decided to pursue its economic interests independently and also withdrew from the organization.[22]

Even if Honduras and Costa Rica should decide to rejoin the Common Market additional problems fundamental to the organization's success

[21] A related factor is the fact that only a short span of the Inter-American Highway crosses the country at a far remote corner quite distant from Honduras's capital and other urban centers.

[22] "Trade Bloc Suffers Setback," The New York Times, January 25, 1971, p. 52; Dwight Heath, "Central America: Un-Common Market," Current History 65 (1973):72–76.

will still remain. For example, the underdevelopment of the Central American consumer's market remains a major concern. As we have seen in the previous chapter, most national income remains in the hands of very small elite groups while slightly less than half the population remains too poor to participate significantly within the money economy. Heretofore the lower sector's lack of involvement in the cash economy has not been of much significance to businessmen and to the landholding elite, for the market for plantation export crops lies abroad, outside Central America, and the lower sector's value within this economic context has rested solely in its labor. However, successful industrial development demands an internal consumers market, and as more Central American businessmen and agrarian capitalists have invested in the Common Market the low purchasing power of the majority of Central Americans has become an important concern. On the other hand, significant redistribution of national wealth, which would greatly help to increase the purchasing power of the lower sector, is strongly opposed by upper sector businessmen and estate owners.

Another problem involves balancing the Common Market's concern with industrial development with the agricultural export trade that still provides a large share of the income for Central America's national economies. To be sure, the CACM has not intended to entirely replace agricultural export, but has hoped instead to significantly augment and diversify the economy with a degree of industrialization. Yet as workers are drawn into industry it becomes necessary to produce a greater surplus of food for home consumption. It is difficult to stimulate increased food production as long as population continues to rapidly expand and the patterns of plantation labor and small-scale subsistence agriculture continue to predominate. Since the CACM cannot afford to alienate the landed elite, it has not made any serious efforts to develop agrarian programs that might help to resolve these problems.

During the decade of the 1960s enthusiastic observers of Common Market efforts also hoped that the CACM could play a significant role in encouraging and facilitating sociopolitical reforms for the Central American lower sector. It was anticipated that if members of the elite continued to invest in the fledgling Central American industrial world, and in so doing developed a positive stake in developing a growing internal consumer's market and in stimulating further economic growth, it would become easier for development agencies to press for additional changes at the national level. In fact, during the early years of the 1960s engineers and economists seemed to enjoy a greater measure of cooperation from national presidents. At this time the national leaders were under considerable pressure both from the CACM and from international aid agencies to accept new national planning agencies and/or revitalize earlier ones so that some degree of order could be attained in development programs. Since the national leaders were anxious to receive foreign aid and hoped that the Common Market would succeed, they agreed that national planning agencies could be established. However, the development planners soon found that while they were allowed to propose various reforms and development projects, their agencies received little financial support and their programs stood very little chance of actually being implemented. Under pressure once again from powerful conservative elite interest groups and handicapped by limited financial resources, national leaders generally avoided or ignored the planners' recommendations, preferring to protect the traditional political and economic system that supported them in office.[23]

Consequently, while some development projects were initiated and roads and public-housing projects and the like constructed, by the end of the decade national development programs in general remained very limited and generally ineffectual. The colonial social and economic structure of Central American society thus holds firm. Although nation-building has begun, conservative political interest groups continue to seek ways to avoid significant implementation of basic reforms that would spread the increasing national wealth more widely throughout society. As a result the lives of the majority of Central Americans today remain blighted by poverty. If population continues to burgeon and if the pace of reform continues to be slow and halting, the lives of their children will be burdened to an even greater extent tomorrow.

[23] Wynia, *Politics and Planners,* chap. 7.

Suggested Readings

General

WAUCHOPE, ROBERT, ed.
 1964– *Handbook of Middle American Indians.* Austin: Univ. of Texas Press. A multivolume series containing basic material on natural environment, prehistory, linguistics, physical anthropology, ethnohistorical sources, and ethnography and ethnology of Indian tribes and communities of Middle America, past and present.

WEST, ROBERT C., and JOHN P. AUGELLI
 1966 *Middle America: Its Lands and Peoples.* Englewood Cliffs, N.J.: Prentice-Hall. A cultural geography of the West Indies, Mexico, and Central America emphasizing settlement patterns and economy from pre-Columbian times to the present day. Numerous maps and illustrations.

WOLF, ERIC R.
 1959 *Sons of the Shaking Earth.* Chicago: Univ. of Chicago Press. An overview of the culture history of Mexico and Guatemala, emphasizing synthesis rather than detail. Very useful bibliographical notes.

Part I

General

BRAIDWOOD, ROBERT J., and GORDON R. WILLEY, eds.
 1962 *Courses Toward Urban Life.* Viking Fund Publications in Anthropology no. 32. New York: Wenner-Gren Foundation for Anthropological Research, Inc. Patterns and processes in food collecting, food production, and the

emergence of urbanism and civilization. Papers by Willey on Mesoamerica, Rouse on the Intermediate Area, and Haury on the Greater Southwest are particularly relevant for Middle America.

BENSON, ELIZABETH P.
1967   *The Maya World.* New York: Thomas Y. Crowell. A concise introduction to the Maya and their culture.

COE, MICHAEL D.
1962   *Mexico.* New York: Praeger. General introduction to the culture history of pre-Hispanic central and southern Mexico.
1966   *The Maya.* New York: Praeger. The prehistory of the highland and lowland Maya, with particular emphasis on the Classic era.

JENNINGS, JESSE D., and EDWARD NORBECK, eds.
1964   *Prehistoric Man in the New World.* Chicago: Univ. of Chicago Press for William Marsh Rice Univ. A series of papers including: arguments for the early arrival of man in the New World; general developments in northern Mesoamerica (Mexico) and southern Mesoamerica (Maya areas); transpacific contacts; North and South American cultural connections; linguistics.

KATZ, FRIEDRICH
1972   *The Ancient American Civilizations.* New York: Praeger. Descriptions and contrasts between the evolution of pre-Hispanic civilization in Mesoamerica and in the central Andes.

MACNEISH, RICHARD S., ed.
1967   *The Prehistory of the Tehuacan Valley.* Austin: Univ. of Texas Press. A six-volume series presenting detailed archaeological and botanical data from the many occupations of the Tehuacan Valley from the earliest phase to the arrival of the Spaniards.

MEGGERS, BETTY J., and CLIFFORD EVANS, eds.
1963   *Aboriginal Cultural Development in Latin America: An Interpretative Review.* Smithsonian Miscellaneous Collections, vol. 146, no. 1. Washington, D.C.: Smithsonian Institution. Useful summary articles on northern Mexico, central Mesoamerica, southeast Mesoamerica, and lower Central America.

SANDERS, WILLIAM T., and BARBARA J. PRICE
1968   *Mesoamerica.* New York: Random House. Discussion of the rise of civilization and urbanism in Mesoamerica as a result of the dynamics of population growth and ecological adaptations.
1972   Population, Agricultural History, and Societal Evolution in Mesoamerica. In *Population Growth: Anthropological Implications,* ed. Brian Spooner, pp. 101–53. Cambridge: The MIT Press. Presentation of population profiles from various geographical areas within Mesoamerica with discussion of the ecological factors involved in the variations observed.

WEAVER, MURIEL PORTER
1972   *The Aztecs, Maya, and Their Predecessors.* New York: Seminar Press. A general introduction to the archaeology of Mesoamerica.

WILLEY, GORDON R.
1966   *An Introduction to American Archaeology. Vol. 1. North and Middle America.* Englewood Cliffs, N.J.: Prentice-Hall. A detailed, richly illustrated presentation of New World archaeological findings arranged by culture area and cultural tradition. Chapters 1–4 are relevant for studies of Middle America.

WILLEY, GORDON R., ed.
   1956   *Prehistoric Settlement Patterns in the New World.* Viking Fund Publications in Anthropology no. 23. New York: Wenner-Gren Foundation for Anthropological Research, Inc. Includes useful papers on the Guatemalan highlands, the Maya lowlands, the central Mexican symbiotic region, north-central Mexico, and the northeastern periphery of Mesoamerica.

Chapter 1

BUTLAND, GILBERT J.
   1966   *Latin America, A Regional Geography.* 2nd ed. London: Longmans, Green. Part I provides a useful introduction to the geography of Mexico and Central America in terms of major physiographical provinces.

PALERM, ANGEL, and ERIC R. WOLF
   1960   Ecological Potential and Cultural Development in Mesoamerica. In *Studies in Human Ecology,* pp. 1–37. Washington, D.C.: Pan American Union, Social Science Monographs no. 3. Ecological characteristics of physiographic regions within Mesoamerica and of the northern and southern frontiers.

Chapter 2

FLANNERY, KENT V.
   1968   Archeological Systems Theory and Early Mesoamerica. In *Anthropological Archeology in the Americas,* pp. 67–87. Washington: The Anthropological Society of Washington. Stability and change in systems of food procurement from 8000 to 200 B.C.

HAYNES, C. VANCE, JR.
   1969   The Earliest Americans. *Science* 166:709–15. Succinct discussion of the archaeological and geological evidence relating to the problem of the antiquity of man in the New World.

Chapter 3

HAWKES, J. G.
   1969   The Ecological Background of Plant Domestication. In *The Domestication and Exploitation of Plants and Animals,* ed. Peter J. Ucko and G. W. Dimbleby, pp. 17–29. Chicago: Aldine. An excellent consideration of some of the preconditions and processes that underlay the domestication of plants.

MACNEISH, RICHARD S.
   1958   Preliminary Archaeological Investigations in the Sierra de Tamaulipas, Mexico. *Transactions,* American Philosophical Society, vol. 48, pt. 6. Part 4, Conclusions, provides a summary of the way of life of the early food-collectors and food-producers of Tamaulipas.
   1964   Ancient Mesoamerican Civilization. *Science* 143:531–37. A basic summary of changing subsistence and settlement patterns in the Tehuacán Valley from the late Pleistocene to the Spanish conquest.

MANGELSDORF, PAUL C.; RICHARD S. MACNEISH; and WALTON C. GALINAT
   1964   Domestication of Corn. *Science* 143:538–45. Review of archaeological finds of primitive maize with particular emphasis on the development of cultivated forms as seen in the Tehuacán Valley sequence.

WILKES, H. GARRISON
    1972   Maize and Its Wild Relatives. *Science* 177:1071–77. Consideration of
    the importance of teosinte and *tripsacum,* wild relatives of maize, in the
    evolution of hybrid forms of maize.

Chapter 4

BENSON, ELIZABETH P., ed.
    1968   *Dumbarton Oaks Conference on the Olmec.* Washington, D.C.: Dumbarton
    Oaks Research Library and Collection. A series of scholarly papers concern-
    ing the Olmec.
BERNAL, IGNACIO
    1969   *The Olmec World.* Berkeley: Univ. of California Press. Discussion of the
    geography and archaeology of the Olmec heartland, the nature of Olmec
    society, and Olmec influence in Mesoamerica.
COE, MICHAEL D.
    1968   *America's First Civilization.* New York: American Heritage. A good
    introduction to the Olmec.
COE, MICHAEL D., and KENT V. FLANNERY
    1964 Microenvironments and Mesoamerican Prehistory. *Science* 143:
    650–54. Contrasting patterns of adaptation to local resources by inhabi-
    tants of Salinas La Blanca and the Tehuacán Valley.
FLANNERY, KENT V.; ANNE V. T. KIRKBY; MICHAEL J. KIRKBY; and AUBREY W.
    WILLIAMS, JR.
    1967   Farming Systems and Political Growth in Ancient Oaxaca. *Science*
    158:445–54. Discussion of the agricultural potential of the Valley of Oaxaca
    and the factors behind the growth of village-farming communities and elite
    centers during the Formative.
FORD, JAMES A.
    1969   *A Comparison of Formative Cultures in the Americas.* Smithsonian Con-
    tributions to Anthropology, vol. 11. Washington, D.C.: Smithsonian Institu-
    tion. A major contribution to a school of thought that considers trans-
    Pacific contact to have been a major stimulus to the developments of the
    Formative period in the New World.
PADDOCK, JOHN, ed.
    1966   *Ancient Oaxaca.* Stanford: Stanford Univ. Press. Part I, a summary of
    the culture history of Mesoamerica before the rise of the Toltecs; Part II, the
    culture history of Oaxaca; Part III, papers on select aspects of Oaxacan
    prehistory.

Chapter 5

BRONSON, BENNET
    1966   Roots and the Subsistence of the Ancient Maya. *Southwestern J. of
    Anthro.* 22:251–79. Arguments in favor of intensive utilization of root crops
    by Formative and Classic era Maya.
BULLARD, WILLIAM R., JR.
    1960   Maya Settlement Patterns in Northeastern Petén, Guatemala.
    American Antiquity 25:355–72. Discussion of conditions underlying settlement
    pattern and delineation of zonal relationships between rural house ruins,
    minor elite centers, and major centers.

COE, WILLIAM R.
1965 Tikal, Guatemala, and Emergent Maya Civilization. *Science* 147:1401–19. Evidence of Formative developments in the Maya lowlands with particular emphasis on Formative levels at Tikal.

DUMOND, D. E.
1961 Swidden Agriculture and the Rise of Maya Civilization. *Southwestern J. of Anthro.* 17:301–16. Consideration of the potentialities of swidden agriculture for supporting the rise of centralized society in the Maya highlands.

ERASMUS, CHARLES J.
1968 Thoughts on Upward Collapse: an Essay on Explanation in Anthropology. *Southwestern J. of Anthro.* 24:170–94. A stimulating essay that queries whether the collapse of Classic Maya civilization and the seeming degeneration of the succeeding Postclassic cultures represent social catastrophe or social organizational change and advance.

HAVILAND, WILLIAM A.
1970 Tikal, Guatemala and Mesoamerican Urbanism. *World Archaeology* 2:186–99. The nature of the settlement pattern at Tikal, demographic estimates, and the case for Tikal as an urban center.

KIDDER, ALFRED V.; JESSE D. JENNINGS; and EDWIN M. SHOOK
1946 *Excavations at Kaminaljuyu, Guatemala.* Washington, D.C.: Carnegie Institution of Washington, Publication 561. Part I, Introduction, and Part IX, General Discussion, are particularly useful for general reading.

MILLON, RENÉ
1967 Teotihuacán. *Scientific American* 216:38–48. General discussion of the valley and the city, and their significance in Classic Mesoamerica.

PALERM, ANGEL
1955 The Agricultural Basis of Urban Civilization in Mesoamerica. In *Irrigation Civilizations: A Comparative Study,* ed. Julian H. Steward, pp. 28–42. Washington, D.C.: Pan American Union. Classification of Mesoamerican agricultural systems in relation to population density and settlement pattern with particular emphasis on irrigation.

PULESTON, DENNIS E., and OLGA S. PULESTON
1971 An Ecological Approach to the Origins of Maya Civilization. *Archaeology* 24:330–37. Examination of the hypothesis that the first settlers of the Maya lowlands were riverine fishermen and agriculturalists.

RATHJE, WILLIAM L.
1970 Socio-political Implications of Lowland Maya Burials: Methodology and Tentative Hypotheses. *World Archaeology* 1:359–75. Contrasting burial patterns at Uaxactun and Barton Ramie during the Early and Late Classic are considered as possible evidence for increasing social stratification.
1971 The Origins and Development of Lowland Classic Maya Civilization. *American Antiquity* 36:275–85. A model emphasizing the importance of long-distance trade as a critical factor underwriting the rise of centralized sociopolitical organization in the Maya lowlands.

SANDERS, WILLIAM T.
1965 *The Cultural Ecology of the Teotihuacán Valley.* The Pennsylvania State University, Dept. of Sociology and Anthropology. Traces the growth of pre-Hispanic agriculture, settlement pattern, and demography in the Teotihuacán Valley with consideration of the functional relationships be-

tween them. Particular emphasis on the conditions underlying the rise of urbanism.

THOMPSON, J. ERIC S.
1966   *The Rise and Fall of Maya Civilization.* 2d ed. Norman: Univ. of Oklahoma Press. A basic work dealing with the culture history of the ancient Maya and the content of their civilization.

WILLEY, GORDON
1964   An Archaeological Frame of Reference for Maya Culture History. In *Desarrollo Cultural de los Mayas,* ed. Evon Z. Vogt and Alberto Ruz, pp. 137–78. Mexico: Universidad Nacional Autonoma de Mexico. General survey of the rise, florescence, and decline of pre-Columbian Maya culture.

WILLEY, GORDON R., and DEMITRI B. SHIMKIN
1971   The Collapse of Classic Maya Civilization in the Southern Lowlands: a Symposium Summary Statement. *Southwestern J. of Anthro.* 27:1–18. A recent review of evidence and consideration of theories dealing with the lowland Maya collapse.

Chapter 6

ANDREWS, E. WYLLYS, 4th
1968   Dzibilchaltun, a Northern Maya Metropolis. *Archaeology* 21:36–47. Introduction to the culture history of the site.

BARLOW, R. H.
1949   *The Extent of the Empire of the Culhua Mexica.* Ibero-Americana no. 28. Berkeley: Univ. of California Press. Detailed identification of the towns and provinces composing the Mexica empire and the tribute demanded from them.

CHAPMAN, ANNE C.
1957   Port of Trade Enclaves in Aztec and Maya Civilizations. In *Trade and Market in the Early Empires,* ed. Karl Polanyi, Conrad A. Arensberg, and Harry W. Pearson, pp. 114–51. Glencoe: The Free Press. Analysis of long-distance trade between Aztec and Maya, the pochteca and their Maya counterparts, and activities at the ports of trade.

COE, MICHAEL D.
1964   The Chinampas of Mexico. *Scientific American* 211:90–98. Methods of land reclamation, particularly chinampa construction, in the Basin of Mexico during the Postclassic.

DUTTON, BERTHA P.
1955   Tula of the Toltecs. *El Palacio* 62:195–251. Site description and general discussion.

KIRCHHOFF, PAUL
1948   Civilizing the Chichimecs: A Chapter in the Culture History of Ancient Mexico. In *Some Educational and Anthropological Aspects of Latin America,* Latin-American Studies, V, pp. 80–85. University of Texas, Institute of Latin-American Studies. Identification of the Chichimecs and discussion of the dynamics of their relationships with agrarian Mesoamerica, particularly the Toltecs.

MEIGHAN, CLEMENT W.
1974   Prehistory of West Mexico. *Science* 184:1254–61. Summary of knowledge to date of the indigenous cultural traditions and external contacts of west Mexico from 2000 B.C. to A.D. 1500.

SPORES, RONALD
1967   *The Mixtec Kings and their People*. Norman: Univ. of Oklahoma Press. The culture history of the Mixtec with emphasis on the sixteenth century. 1969   Settlement, Farming Technology, and Environment in the Nochixtlan Valley. *Science* 166:557–69. An examination of population growth, local adaptation, and cultural development from 700 B.C. to A.D. 1600 in a Mixtec valley in the Mixteca Alta region of western Oaxaca.

SOUSTELLE, JACQUES
1961   *Daily Life of the Aztecs on the Eve of the Spanish Conquest*. Stanford: Stanford Univ. Press. An excellent general summary of Aztec culture.

STANISLAWSKY, DAN
1947   Tarascan Political Geography. *Amer. Anthropologist* 49:46–55. Growth and expansion of the Tarascans.

Chapter 7

COE, MICHAEL D.
1962   Costa Rican Archaeology and Mesoamerica. *Southwestern J. of Anthro.* 18:170–83. The archaeological sequence for Greater Nicoya reveals that this was long a Mesoamerican frontier region.

HAURY, EMIL W.
1945   The Problem of Contacts Between the Southwestern United States and Mexico. *Southwestern J. of Anthro.* 1:55–74. A good introduction to the subject.

JOHNSON, FREDERICK
1948   Central American Cultures: An Introduction. In *Handbook of South American Indians*, vol. 4, *The Circum-Caribbean Tribes*, ed. Julian H. Steward, pp. 43–68. Washington, D.C.: U.S. Government Printing Office. A general introduction to the peoples and cultures of lower Central America.

KELLEY, J. CHARLES
1960   North Mexico and the Correlation of Mesoamerican and Southwestern Cultural Sequences. In *Men and Cultures,* ed. Anthony F. C. Wallace, pp. 566–73. Philadelphia: Univ. of Pennsylvania Press. General discussion with particular emphasis on the Chalchihuites culture and its relationships with Hohokam.

SAUER, CARL
1934   *The Distribution of Aboriginal Tribes and Languages in Northwestern Mexico*. Ibero-Americana no. 5:1–94. Berkeley: Univ. of California Press. Detailed reconstruction of the location of the diverse peoples of the northwest prior to Spanish influence.

STONE, DORIS
1972   *Pre-Columbian Man Finds Central America*. Harvard University, Cambridge: Peabody Museum Press. Introduction to the archaeology of Guatemala, El Salvador, Honduras, Nicaragua, Costa Rica, and Panama emphasizing the importance of ties with Mesoamerica and South America.

Part II

General

Gibson, Charles
  1966   *Spain in America.* New York: Harper and Row. Summary and analysis of colonial Spanish-American history. Very useful bibliographical essay.

Chapter 8

Elliott, John Huxtable
  1963   *Imperial Spain, 1469–1716.* London: Edward Arnold. Interpretative synthesis of Spanish history from the marriage of Ferdinand and Isabella to the end of Hapsburg rule.
Johnson, H. B., Jr., ed.
  1970   *From Reconquest to Empire: The Iberian Background to Latin American History.* New York: Knopf. A series of readings explore the Iberian roots of various institutions and orientations that were transplanted to the New World colonies.
Parry, J. H.
  1966   *Europe and a Wider World 1415–1715.* 3rd ed., rev. London: Hutchinson and Co. General introduction to the early centuries of the "expansion of Europe."
Vicens Vives, Jaime
  1970   *Approaches to the History of Spain.* 2d ed. corr. and rev. Trans. and ed. Joan Ullman. Berkeley: Univ. of California Press. A succinct account of interrelationships of land, economy, and society in Iberia.

Chapter 9

Chamberlain, Robert S.
  1966   *The Conquest and Colonization of Honduras, 1502–1550.* New York: Octagon Books. (Also Carnegie Institution of Washington, Pub. no. 598.) Informative study of the conquest and Hispanic settlement of Honduras.
  1966   *The Conquest and Colonization of Yucatan, 1517–1550.* New York: Octagon Books. (Also Carnegie Institution of Washington, Pub. no. 582.) The early colonial history of Yucatán.
Díaz del Castillo, Bernal
  1956   *The Bernal Díaz Chronicles; The True History of the Conquest of New Spain.* Trans. and ed. Albert Idell. Garden City, N.Y.: Doubleday. A first-hand account of Cortes's conquest of Mexico written by a companion-in-arms in his later years.
Leon-Portilla, Miguel, ed.
  1962   *The Broken Spears: The Aztec Account of the Conquest of Mexico.* Boston: Beacon Press. Selections from native accounts which record the conquest of Tenochtitlán from the point of view of the conquered.
Powell, Philip Wayne
  1952   *Soldiers, Indians and Silver: The Northward Advance of New Spain,*

1550–1600. Berkeley: Univ. of California Press. The conquest of the silver-rich territory between Queretaro and Saltillo in the face of bitter Indian resistance.

SAUER, CARL ORTWIN
    1966   *The Early Spanish Main*. Berkeley: Univ. of California Press. Summary and interpretation of the initial Spanish conquest and settlement of the major Caribbean islands and adjacent mainland prior to 1521.

Chapter 10

DIFFIE, BAILEY W.
    1967   *Latin-American Civilization, Colonial Period*. New York: Octagon Books. General introduction with emphasis on economy and society.

GREENLEAF, RICHARD E., ed.
    1971   *The Roman Catholic Church in Colonial Latin America*. New York: Knopf. A series of papers on the church as a political-economic institution and an intellectual catalyst of conquest and colonization between 1492 and 1810.

HANKE, LEWIS
    1949   *The Spanish Struggle for Justice in the Conquest of America*. Philadelphia: Univ. of Pennsylvania Press. Reprint ed., 1965. Boston: Little, Brown. Examination of Spanish efforts to find a satisfactory Indian policy.

HARING, CLARENCE H.
    1947   *The Spanish Empire in America*. New York: Oxford Univ. Press. Reprint ed., 1966, New York: Harcourt, Brace & World. A basic descriptive history of colonial institutions.

RICARD, ROBERT
    1966   *The Spiritual Conquest of Mexico*. Trans. L. B. Simpson. Berkeley: Univ. of California Press. Discussion of the role and work of the Mendicant Orders in New Spain during the sixteenth century.

STEIN, STANLEY J., and BARBARA H. STEIN
    1970   *The Colonial Heritage of Latin America: Essays on Economic Dependence in Perspective*. New York: Oxford Univ. Press. Penetrating examination of factors underlying the socioeconomic patterns of Latin American colonialism and the continuation of these patterns into the nineteenth century.

Chapter 11

BORAH, WOODROW
    1951   *New Spain's Century of Depression*. Ibero-Americana no. 35. Berkeley: Univ. of California Press. Demographic changes and economic conditions in Mexico from 1576 until about 1700.

CHEVALIER, FRANÇOIS
    1963   *Land and Society in Colonial Mexico: The Great Hacienda*. Trans. Alvin Eustis. Berkeley: Univ. of California Press. The evolution of the great estate and the rise of a landed aristocracy during the seventeenth century.

DAVIDSON, DAVID H.
    1966   Negro Slave Control and Resistance in Colonial Mexico, 1519–1650. *Hisp. Amer. Hist. Rev.* 46:235–53. General discussion of the position of the Negro in colonial society.

GIBSON, CHARLES
  1955   The Transformation of the Indian Community in New Spain. *J. of World Hist. (Cahiers d'Histoire Mondiale)* 2:581–607. Indian community history from the sixteenth to the nineteenth centuries emphasizing the place of native communities within the larger colonial sphere and the effect of these relationships on community life.
  1964   *The Aztecs under Spanish Rule: A History of the Indians of the Valley of Mexico, 1519–1810.* Stanford: Stanford Univ. Press. Detailed study of the reactions and adaptations of the native populace of the Valley of Mexico to the institutions and demands of colonial rule.

LEONARD, IRVING A.
  1959   *Baroque Times in Old Mexico.* Ann Arbor: Univ. of Michigan Press. Cultural, literary, and intellectual aspects of seventeenth-century New Spain.

LOCKHART, JAMES
  1969   Encomienda and Hacienda: The Evolution of the Great Estate in the Spanish Indies. *Hisp. Amer. Hist. Rev.* 49:411–29. Encomienda and hacienda are shown to be separate manifestations of a continuous process of estate building. The discussion is continued by Robert G. Keith, "Encomienda, Hacienda and Corregimiento in Spanish America: A Structural Analysis," *Hisp. Amer. Hist. Rev.* 51(1971):431–46.

MCALISTER, LYLE N.
  1963   Social Structure and Social Change in New Spain. *Hisp. Amer. Hist. Rev.* 43:349–70. Analysis of the groups and associations composing the colonial society of New Spain.

MÖRNER, MAGNUS
  1967   *Race Mixture in the History of Latin America.* Boston: Little, Brown. Summary of research to date on the dynamics of race relations during the colonial and postcolonial periods.

WEST, ROBERT C.
  1949   *The Mining Community in Northern New Spain: The Parral Mining District.* Ibero-Americana no. 30. Berkeley: Univ. of California Press. Description of the economic life of a seventeenth-century mining community in northern New Spain.

Chapter 12

BRADING, DAVID A.
  1971   *Miners and Merchants in Bourbon Mexico, 1763–1810.* Cambridge: Cambridge Univ. Press. Mining, commerce, and society in the late colonial period.

FOSTER, GEORGE
  1953   Cofradía and Compadrazgo in Spain and Spanish America. *Southwestern J. of Anthro.* 9:1–28. Comparative analysis of the European background and general characteristics of these institutions and their applicability to Latin American cultures.

MCALISTER, LYLE
  1957   *The fuero militar in New Spain 1764–1800.* Gainesville: Univ. of Florida

Press. Factors underlying the emergence of the military as a privileged institution.

WHITAKER, ARTHUR P.
1970   Changing and Unchanging Interpretations of the Enlightenment in Spanish America. *Proc. Amer. Phil. Soc.* 114:256–71. Survey of works on this theme since 1942.

WOLF, ERIC
1957   Closed Corporate Peasant Communities in Mesoamerica and Central Java. *Southwestern J. of Anthro.* 13:1–18. A comparative study of the colonial pressures underlying the formation of defensive rural communities and a delineation of the characteristics of these communities.

Chapter 13

BANNON, JOHN FRANCIS, ed.
1964   *Bolton and the Spanish Borderlands.* Norman: Univ. of Oklahoma Press. Selections from the works of Herbert E. Bolton including his classic paper, "The Mission as a Frontier Institution in the Spanish American Colonies."

FLOYD, TROY S.
1967   *The Anglo-Spanish Struggle for Mosquitia.* Albuquerque: The Univ. of New Mexico Press. The impact of British occupation of the Caribbean coast of Central America from the Spanish point of view.

GRIFFEN, WILLIAM B.
1969   *Culture Change and Shifting Populations in Central Northern Mexico.* Anthropological Papers, no. 13. Tucson: The Univ. of Arizona Press. History of the indigenous inhabitants of north-central Mexico and the processes of colonial culture contact that led to their extinction.

HELMS, MARY W.
1969   The Cultural Ecology of a Colonial Tribe. *Ethnology* 8:76–84. Adaptations of the Miskito Indians to Anglo-Spanish conflicts on the Caribbean coast of Central America.

MACLEOD, MURDO J.
1973   *Spanish Central America: A Socioeconomic History, 1520–1720.* Berkeley: Univ. of California Press. Description and explanation of the cycle of prosperity, depression, and recovery that characterized colonial Central America, with associated social and demographic features.

SOLNICK, BRUCE B.
1970   *The West Indies and Central America to 1898.* New York: Knopf. A summary of Caribbean history from Columbus to the end of the nineteenth century.

SPICER, EDWARD H.
1962   *Cycles of Conquest: The Impact of Spain, Mexico, and the United States on the Indians of the Southwest, 1533–1960.* Tucson: Univ. of Arizona Press. Detailed analysis of patterns and processes of culture contact among tribes of Sonora, Chihuahua, Arizona, and New Mexico.

STRICKON, ARNOLD
1965   Hacienda and Plantation in Yucatan. *América Indígena* 25:35–63. Interpretative summary of the changing social and economic patterns of Yucatán from the conquest to the twentieth century and their effect on rural Maya life-styles.

Part III

General

ADAMS, RICHARD N.
   1967   *The Second Sowing. Power and Secondary Development in Latin America.*
   San Francisco: Chandler. Observations and analyses of the nature of contemporary Latin America emphasizing the special social, economic, and
   political adaptations necessary to adapt to demands of rapid population
   expansion and industrial technologies.

BLACK, C. E.
   1966   *The Dynamics of Modernization.* New York: Harper & Row. Introduction to the concepts, problems, and processes of "modernization" or
   "nation-building" and its effects on world affairs today and in past centuries.

CUMBERLAND, CHARLES C.
   1968   *Mexico: The Struggle for Modernity.* London: Oxford Univ. Press. Informative discussion of the social and economic issues of the colonial period
   and the nineteenth century that finally gave rise to the Mexican Revolution,
   and the direction of change in twentieth-century Mexico. Excellent bibliographical essay and useful statistical tables.

HEATH, DWIGHT B., and RICHARD N. ADAMS, eds.
   1965   *Contemporary Cultures and Societies of Latin America.* New York: Random
   House. A series of papers and essays on delineation of cultural entities, land,
   agriculture and economy, social organization, and world view with strong
   emphasis on Middle America.

KARNES, THOMAS L.
   1961   *The Failure of Union; Central America, 1824–1960.* Chapel Hill: Univ. of
   North Carolina Press. Discussion of the numerous attempts at political federation by the Central American republics and analysis of the reasons for their
   failure to achieve this goal.

MÖRNER, MAGNUS, ed.
   1970   *Race and Class in Latin America.* New York: Columbia Univ. Press.
   Survey of the present state of knowledge of a complex subject with new
   interpretations and reassessments. Included are papers on "The Integration
   of the Negro into the National Society of Mexico," "Mestizaje in Mexico
   during the National Period," and "The Impact of Mid-Nineteenth Century
   Economic Change upon the Indians of Middle America."

NEEDLER, MARTIN C., ed.
   1970   *Political Systems of Latin America.* 2d ed. New York: Van Nostrand
   Reinhold. Informative papers concerning economic and political development in each of the Middle American countries emphasizing the variety
   rather than the commonality of experiences among them.

PARKER, FRANKLIN D.
   1964   *The Central American Republics.* London: Oxford Univ. Press. Detailed
   historical accounts of Guatemala, El Salvador, Honduras, Nicaragua, and
   Costa Rica with emphasis on twentieth-century political organization and
   development and economic conditions; education, art, and religion are also
   considered.

RODRÍGUEZ, MARIO
    1965 *Central America.* Englewood Cliffs, N.J.: Prentice-Hall. Political and
    economic conditions and trends within Central America as a whole during
    the nineteenth and twentieth centuries. Useful bibliographical essay.

TAX, SOL, et al.
    1952 *Heritage of Conquest.* Glencoe, Illinois: Free Press. A series of papers
    considering social, political, religious, and economic aspects of rural, gener-
    ally "Indian," cultures of contemporary Middle America with emphasis on
    Mexico-Guatemala (Mesoamerica). A good starting point for further study.

WOLF, ERIC R.
    1955 Types of Latin American Peasantry: A Preliminary Discussion. *Amer.
    Anthropologist* 57:452–70. Characteristics of the corporate "Indian" commu-
    nity compared with those of the "open" rural community.
    1956 Aspects of Group Relations in a Complex Society: Mexico. *Amer.
    Anthropologist* 58:1065–78. The nature of the interpersonal and intergroup
    ties and relationships that have linked local communities with the wider
    national whole during the colonial and republican periods.

WOLF, ERIC R., and EDWARD C. HANSEN
    1972 *The Human Condition in Latin America.* London: Oxford Univ. Press.
    Economic, political, and ideological characteristics of Latin American culture
    emphasizing the nature of the social relationships through which these vari-
    ous aspects are expressed.

Chapter 14

HUMPHREYS, R. A., and JOHN LYNCH, eds.
    1965 *The Origins of the Latin American Revolutions, 1808–1826.* New York:
    Knopf. A series of papers considers the role of the Enlightenment, the
    Jesuits, foreign powers, social and economic discontent within the colonies,
    and a rising sense of nationalism in paving the way for independence from
    Spain.

STANGER, FRANCIS M.
    1932 National Origins in Central America. *Hisp. Amer. Hist. Rev.* 12:18–45.
    Analysis of those characteristics of colonial Central American society and
    economy that underlay its political fragmentation after independence from
    Spain.

WOLF, ERIC R., and EDWARD C. HANSEN
    1967 *Caudillo* Politics: A Structural Analysis. *Comp. Studies in Soc. and Hist.*
    9:168–79. The preconditions leading to the emergence of caudillo rule, the
    definitive characteristics of this form of political organization, and the factors
    behind its decline.

Chapter 15

WILKIE, JAMES W., and ALBERT L. MICHAELS, eds.
    1969 *Revolution in Mexico: Years of Upheaval, 1910–1940.* New York: Knopf.
    Firsthand accounts and scholarly descriptions of the background and events
    of the revolution from the outbreak of hostilities through the Cárdenas
    administration.

WOLF, ERIC R.
1969   *Peasant Wars of the Twentieth Century.* New York: Harper & Row. Chapter 1 interprets the major preconditions underlying the Mexican Revolution and considers the various movements of which the revolution was composed. A concluding chapter compares the Mexican experience with five other revolutions of our times (Russia, China, Viet Nam, Algeria, and Cuba).

ZEA, LEOPOLDO
1949   Positivism and Porfirism in Latin America. In *Ideological Differences and World Order, Studies in the Philosophy and Science of the World's Cultures,* ed. F. S. C. Northrop, pp. 166–91. New Haven: Yale Univ. Press. Examination of the social, political, and economic doctrines propounded by the thinkers and theorists of the Porfirian generation.

Chapter 16

BAYLEN, JOSEPH O.
1954   American Intervention in Nicaragua, 1909–33: An Appraisal of Objectives and Results. *Southwestern Soc. Sci. Quart.* 35:128–54. An extended analysis of the pros and cons of United States intervention in Nicaragua.

HOUK, RICHARD J.
1953   The Development of Foreign Trade and Communication in Costa Rica to the Construction of the First Railway. *The Americas* 10:197–209. Economic conditions in Costa Rica during the colonial period and in the nineteenth century with emphasis on the development of coffee as an export crop.

JONES, CHESTER LLOYD
1940   *Guatemala, Past and Present.* Minneapolis: Univ. of Minnesota Press. Reprint ed., 1966, New York: Russell & Russell. A basic sourcebook emphasizing social, economic, and political conditions in Guatemala particularly during the nineteenth century and the early twentieth century.

KEPNER, CHARLES D., JR., and JAY HENRY SOOTHILL
1935   *The Banana Empire.* New York: Vanguard Press. Growth and activities of United Fruit Co. and its competitors. See also Kepner, *Social Aspects of the Banana Industry* (New York: Columbia Univ. Press, 1936), and Charles H. Wilson, *Empire in Green and Gold* (New York: Henry Holt, 1947).

MACAULAY, NEILL
1967   *The Sandino Affair.* Chicago: Quadrangle Books. Detailed account of the struggle between Augusto Sandino's guerrilla forces and United States Marines in Nicaragua between 1927 and 1933.

MUNRO, DANA G.
1918   *The Five Republics of Central America.* Carnegie Endowment for International Peace. Reprint ed., 1967, New York: Russell & Russell. Observations and analyses of the economic and sociopolitical conditions of the Central American republics during the nineteenth and early twentieth centuries.

REED, NELSON
1964   *The Caste War of Yucatán.* Stanford, California: Stanford Univ. Press. Part I, general survey of Yucatán at midnineteenth century; Part II, detailed description of military aspects of the war; Part III, the fate of the *Cruzob* or refugee Maya of Quintana Roo.

WOLF, ERIC R., and SIDNEY W. MINTZ
1957   Haciendas and Plantations in Middle America and the Antilles. *Soc. and Econ. Studies* 6:380–411. Comparative analysis of the hacienda and the plantation as two "types" of social systems.

Chapter 17

ADAMS, RICHARD N.
1970   Brokers and Career Mobility Systems in the Structure of Complex Societies. *Southwestern J. of Anthro.* 26:315–27. Cultural brokers and power brokers and processes of individual and group mobility as means to achieve access to power and as links between levels of society. Case materials based on a study of the national social structure of Guatemala.

AVILA, MANUEL
1969   *Tradition and Growth. A Study of Four Mexican Villages.* Chicago: Univ. of Chicago Press. Change and development in Chan Kom, Soteapan, Mitla, and Tepotzlán from the 1930s until early 1960s.

BRANDENBERG, FRANK
1964   *The Making of Modern Mexico.* Englewood Cliffs, N.J.: Prentice-Hall. A general discussion with information on many topics.

CANCIAN, FRANK
1965   *Economics and Prestige in a Maya Community.* Stanford, Calif.: Stanford Univ. Press. A study of the structure and function of the civil-religious hierarchy of Zinacantán, a Maya township in the highlands of Chiapas. References to additional sources on this topic.

CORNELIUS, WAYNE A., JR.
1969   Urbanization as an Agent in Latin American Political Instability: The Case of Mexico. *Amer. Pol. Sci. Rev.* 63:833–57. Discussion of the reasons for rural-urban migration in Mexico, conditions migrants encounter in the city, and their reactions to urban life. See also David J. Fox, "Urbanization and Economic Development in Mexico," in *Cities in a Changing Latin America,* ed. D. J. Fox and D. J. Robinson (London: Latin American Publications Fund), pp. 1–21.

FRIEDRICH, PAUL
1968   The Legitimacy of a Cacique. In *Local-level Politics,* ed. Marc J. Swartz, pp. 243–69. Chicago: Aldine. Analysis of the multifaceted role of the political boss or power broker in rural Mexico as exemplified by the activities of the cacique of a contemporary Tarascan community.

STAVENHAGEN, RODOLFO
1970   Classes, Colonialism, and Acculturation. In *Masses in Latin America,* ed. Irving Horowitz, pp. 235–83. New York: Oxford Univ. Press. Various types of interethnic relationships that structure the interactions between mestizos and rural "Indian" populations in the southern highlands of Mexico (Chiapas) and adjacent Guatemala.

VERNON, RAYMOND
1963   *The Dilemma of Mexico's Development.* Cambridge: Harvard Univ. Press. An analysis of the roles and relationships between government and private enterprise in the growth of the national economy of Mexico from 1860 to 1960.

WATERBURY, RONALD
    1970   Urbanization and a Traditional Market System. In *The Social An-thropology of Latin America,* ed. Walter Goldschmidt and Harry Hoijer, pp. 126–53. Los Angeles: Univ. of California. Detailed discussion of the traditional Oaxacan market system.

WHETTEN, NATHAN L.
    1948   *Rural Mexico.* Chicago: Univ. of Chicago Press. Basic sourcebook detailing the conditions of life in the Mexican countryside from before the revolution to about 1945. Emphasis on the effect of revolutionary reforms, particularly land redistribution, on rural life-styles.

WILKIE, JAMES W.
    1970   *The Mexican Revolution: Federal Expenditure and Social Change since 1910.* 2d ed. rev. Berkeley: Univ. of California Press. Social and economic development discussed in terms of national budgets and federal expenditures. Attempts to measure "poverty" and link changes in poverty level with politics of modernization.

Chapter 18

ADAMS, RICHARD N.
    1956   Cultural Components of Central America. *Amer. Anthropologist* 58:881–907. Systematic classification and identification of the diverse cultures and peoples that compose Central America today.
    1957   *Cultural Surveys of Panama-Nicaragua-Guatemala-El Salvador-Honduras.* Washington, D.C.: Pan American Sanitary Bureau, Scientific Publication no. 33. A general description of basic aspects of the rural culture characteristic of the small towns and countryside of Hispanic Central America.
    1970   *Crucifixion by Power.* Austin: Univ. of Texas Press. Analysis of the national social structure of Guatemala, with particular emphasis on the period from 1944 to 1966, relating national structure to regional and local levels on the one hand and to international events on the other.

ANDERSON, CHARLES W.
    1961   Politics and Development Policy in Central America. *Midwest J. of Pol. Sci.* 5:332–50. Discussion of the varied approaches to social and economic development advocated by political movements in Costa Rica, El Salvador, and Guatemala which views them as political instruments designed to mobilize and consolidate political support.

BEHRENDT, RICHARD F.
    1949   The Uprooted: A Guatemala Sketch. *New Mexico Quart. Rev.* 19:25–31. Brief account of Esteban Pazuj, an Indian carpenter in Guatemala, and his experiences and dissatisfactions as a laborer on a United Fruit plantation.

BIESANZ, JOHN, and MAVIS BIESANZ
    1944   *Costa Rican Life.* New York: Columbia Univ. Press. A basic introduction to Costa Rica emphasizing everyday life.
    1955   *The People of Panama.* New York: Columbia Univ. Press. A basic introduction to the peoples and cultures of Panama.

BROWNING, DAVID
    1971   *El Salvador, Landscape and Society.* Oxford: Clarendon Press. A cultural geography of El Salvador exploring the interrelationships between man and land from prehistoric to contemporary times.

EBEL, ROLAND H.
   1964   Political Change in Guatemalan Indian Communities. *J. of Inter-Amer. Studies* 6:91–104. Description of traditional political structure of Indian communities and detailed analysis of the changes that occurred after 1944 in two communities.

GOLDKIND, VICTOR
   1961   Sociocultural Contrasts in Rural and Urban Settlement Types in Costa Rica. *Rural Sociology* 26:365–80. Comparison of settlement patterns, general life-styles, and degree of national integration characteristic of rural districts, villages, towns, and city.

LANGLEY, LESTER D.
   1970   U.S.-Panamanian Relations since 1941. *J. of Inter-Amer. Studies and World Affairs* 12:339–66. Traces and analyzes the course of relations between these two countries as a case study of the conflicting fluctuations between cordiality and hostility that have marked the United States' reception in Latin America since World War II.

MARTZ, JOHN D.
   1959   *Central America, The Crisis and the Challenge.* Chapel Hill: Univ. of North Carolina Press. Detailed analysis of Central American political affairs from World War II until about 1960.

MOSK, SANFORD A.
   1954   Indigenous Economy in Latin America. *Inter Amer. Econ. Affairs* 8:3–25. Analysis of the nature and functioning of regional economies of highland Guatemala and their interrelationships with the national economy.

NUNLEY, ROBERT E.
   1960   *The Distribution of Population in Costa Rica.* Washington, D.C.: National Academy of Science, National Research Council, Pub. no. 743. History of population growth and expansion of settlement from the colonial period to 1950.

TAX, SOL
   1937   The Municipios of the Midwestern Highlands of Guatemala. *Amer. Anthropologist* 39:423–44. A good introduction to the distinctive characteristics of the highland municipios of Guatemala.

WHETTEN, NATHAN L.
   1961   *Guatemala, The Land and the People.* New Haven: Yale Univ. Press. A basic sourcebook on the people and culture of Guatemala.

Chapter 19

ASHCRAFT, NORMAN
   1973   *Colonialism and Underdevelopment: Processes of Political Economic Change in British Honduras.* New York: Teachers College Press. The economic history of British Honduras and its effects on social and political life.

AUGELLI, JOHN P.
   1962   The Rimland-Mainland Concept of Culture Areas in Middle America. *Annals, Assoc. of Amer. Geographers* 52:119–29. A classification of the cultural and racial diversity of Middle America (including the West Indies) based on a division of the area between a "Euro-African Caribbean Rimland" and a "Euro-Indian Mainland."

HANSEN, ROGER D.

    1967   *Central America: Regional Integration and Economic Development.* Washington, D.C.: National Planning Association, Studies in Development Progress, no. 1. Problems of economic development in Central America with emphasis on the Central American Common Market. See also Carlos M. Castillo, *Growth and Integration in Central America* (New York: Praeger, 1966).

OLIEN, MICHAEL D.

    1970   *The Negro in Costa Rica: The Role of an Ethnic Minority in a Developing Society.* Wake Forest University Developing Nations Monograph Series no. III. Winston-Salem: Overseas Research Center, Wake Forest University. A series of four papers explores the culture history of the Caribbean lowlands of Costa Rica with particular emphasis on the role of Negro populations in Costa Rican economy and society during the colonial and republican periods.

REINA, RUBEN E., and NORMAN B. SCHWARTZ

    1974   The Structural Context of Religious Conversion in Peten, Guatemala: Status, Community, and Multicommunity. *Amer. Ethnologist* 1:157–91. A general description of the central Petén with emphasis on factors relating to religious conversion.

WADDELL, D. A. G.

    1961   *British Honduras: A Historical and Contemporary Survey.* London: Oxford Univ. Press. Introduction to the political, economic, and social conditions of British Honduras. See also A. H. Anderson, *Brief Sketch of British Honduras,* rev. ed. (Belize, 1958).

WYNIA, GARY W.

    1972   *Politics and Planners: Economic Development Policy in Central America.* Madison: Univ. of Wisconsin Press. Discussion of the political and economic difficulties faced by development planners in Central America since World War II.

Community Studies and Related Accounts

Community studies provide an excellent source for detailed, intimate views of village and town life in various areas of Middle America. A selection of recent works is listed here. For additional accounts published prior to 1952 see Howard Cline, "Mexican Community Studies," *Hisp. Amer. Hist. Rev.* 32(1952):212–42, and the bibliography in Sol Tax et al., *Heritage of Conquest* (Glencoe: Free Press, 1952).

BELSHAW, MICHAEL

    1967   *A Village Economy.* New York: Columbia Univ. Press. Study of a small agricultural community in the highlands of central Mexico.

COLBY, BENJAMIN, and PIERRE L. VAN DEN BERGHE

    1969   *Ixil Country: A Plural Society in Highland Guatemala.* Berkeley: Univ. of California Press. Conflict and cooperation between Ixil and Ladinos in a rural area of Guatemala.

DIAZ, MAY N.

    1970   *Tonalá: Conservatism, Responsibility and Authority in a Mexican Town.* Berkeley: Univ. of California Press. Reaction of a traditional rural town to the industrial world emanating from the nearby city of Guadalajara.

FOSTER, GEORGE M.
  1967   *Tzintzuntzan: Mexican Peasants in a Changing World.* Boston: Little, Brown. The history and traditions of this ancient Tarascan community, current customs, and its position within modern Mexico.

FRIEDRICH, PAUL
  1970   *Agrarian Revolt in a Mexican Village.* Englewood Cliffs, N.J.: Prentice-Hall. An account of the preconditions leading to agrarian revolt and of the uprising that finally erupted in the Tarascan village of Naranjan during the 1920s.

GONZALEZ, NANCIE L. SOLIEN
  1969   *Black Carib Household Structure.* Seattle: Univ. of Washington Press. Effects of migratory wage labor on the social and economic organization of Black Carib families.

GUITERAS-HOLMES, CALIXTA
  1961   *Perils of the Soul: The World View of a Tzotzil Indian.* Glencoe, Illinois: Free Press. Manuel, a native of the community of San Pedro Chenalhó, Chiapas, describes and interprets the meaning of life as he knows it.

GWALTNEY, JOHN L.
  1970   *The Thrice Shy: Cultural Accommodation to Blindness and Other Disasters in a Mexican Community.* New York: Columbia Univ. Press. The burden of life in San Pedro Yolox, a Chinautec community in highland Oaxaca.

HELMS, MARY W.
  1971   *Asang: Adaptations to Culture Contact in a Miskito Community.* Gainesville: Univ. of Florida Press. Life in a contemporary community of Miskito-speaking Indians in eastern Nicaragua viewed within the context of past and present contact experiences.

KEARNEY, MICHAEL
  1972   *The Winds of Ixtepeji: World View and Society in a Zapotec Town.* New York: Holt, Rinehart & Winston. The defensive strategies of Oaxacan villagers to guard against a hostile world.

LESLIE, CHARLES
  1960   *Now We Are Civilized.* Detroit: Wayne State Univ. Press. How the Zapotec of the Oaxacan town of Mitla view themselves and the changing world around them.

LEWIS, OSCAR
  1959   *Five Families.* New York: Basic Books. An intimate account of daily life in five Mexican families, one living in a rural Nahuatl village, three of various backgrounds living in Mexico City slum tenements, and one well-to-do family established in a prestigeful residential sector of the city.
  1960   *Tepoztlan: Village in Mexico.* New York: Holt, Rinehart & Winston. Life in an ancient highland community in the state of Morelos.
  1961   *The Children of Sanchez.* New York: Random House. Inside view of the daily lives of five members of a lower sector family living in a slum tenement in the heart of Mexico City.
  1964   *Pedro Martínez: A Mexican Peasant and His Family.* New York: Random House. An autobiographical narrative of a Nahuatl-speaking rural Mexican who discusses his life as a Zapatista, a village leader, a poor campesino, and a husband and father.

LOOMIS, CHARLES P., JULIO O. MORALES, ROY A. CLIFFORD, OLEN E. LEONARD
1953 *Turrialba: Social Systems and the Introduction of Change.* Glencoe, Illinois: Free Press. Conditions of life in the town of Turrialba, Costa Rica, and on the large estates and small farms of the surrounding hinterland.

MADSEN, WILLIAM
1960 *The Virgin's Children: Life in an Aztec Village Today.* Austin: Univ. of Texas Press. Tecospa, a village of Nahuatl-speakers close to Mexico City, retains many traditional customs.

NASH, JUNE
1970 *In the Eyes of the Ancestors: Belief and Behavior in a Mayan Community.* New Haven: Yale Univ. Press. Account of the Tzeltal community of Amatenango, Chiapas, documenting the stress and conflict that result when traditional behaviors meet new sociocultural changes.

NASH, MANNING
1958 *Machine Age Maya: The Industrialization of a Guatemalan Community.* Chicago: Univ. of Chicago Press. Reaction of the Quiché Maya of the highland community of Cantel to the introduction of a large textile factory to their town.

NELSON, CYNTHIA
1971 *The Waiting Village: Social Change in Rural Mexico.* Boston: Little, Brown. General ethnography with emphasis on the reception of community development programs in the Tarascan community of Erongarícuaro on the shore of Lake Pátzcuaro in Michoacan.

REDFIELD, ROBERT, and ALFONSO VILLA ROJAS
1962 *Chan Kom: A Maya Village.* Rev. ed. Chicago: Univ. of Chicago Press. First edition, 1934. Classic study of the mode of life of a Maya community in north-central Yucatán.

REINA, RUBEN E.
1966 *The Law of the Saints: A Pokomam Pueblo and Its Community Culture.* Indianapolis: Bobbs-Merrill. Life in the Maya community of Chinautla, near Guatemala City, emphasizing the structure and functioning of the powerful *cofradías* or religious organizations that influence much community life.

ROMNEY, A. KIMBALL, and ROMAINE ROMNEY
1966 *The Mixtecans of Juxtlahuaca, Mexico.* New York: Wiley. General ethnography with emphasis on child-rearing practices in a Mixtec *barrio* (neighborhood) of a community in Oaxaca.

SPICER, E. H.
1954 *Potam, A Yaqui Village in Sonora.* American Anthropological Association Memoir 77. Economic and political organization, social structure, and ceremonial life emphasizing those features of Yaqui culture that may be related to its persistence and continued integration.

STONE, DORIS
1962 *The Talamancan Tribes of Costa Rica.* Papers of the Peabody Museum of Archaeology and Ethnology, vol. 43, no. 2. Cambridge: Peabody Museum, Harvard University. Aspects of contemporary culture of the Cabécares and the Bribri, two Talamancan tribes of eastern Costa Rica.

STOUT, DAVID B.
1947 · *San Blas Cuna Acculturation: An Introduction.* New York: Viking Fund Publications in Anthropology no. 9. Historical background, directions of culture change, and description of San Blas Cuna culture in 1940.

TAX, SOL
1953 *Penny Capitalism: A Guatemalan Indian Economy.* Smithsonian Institution, Institute of Social Anthropology no. 16. The economic system of Panajachel, a Quiché community on the shores of Lake Atitlán.

TAYLOR, DOUGLAS MACRAE
1951 *The Black Carib of British Honduras.* New York: Viking Fund Publications in Anthropology no. 17. Black Carib culture in 1947–48 and in historical perspective.

TURNER, PAUL R.
1972 *The Highland Chontal.* New York: Holt, Rinehart & Winston. Discussion of the sociocultural and personality systems of the isolated highland Chontal of Oaxaca and their place within the wider Mexican nation-state.

VOGT, EVON Z.
1970 *The Zinacantecos of Mexico.* New York: Holt, Rinehart & Winston. An introduction to the world—social, ceremonial, economic—of the Tzotzil Indians of the municipio of Zinacantan in the highlands of Chiapas. More detail is available in Evon Z. Vogt, *Zinacantan: A Maya Community in the Highlands of Chiapas* (Cambridge: Harvard Univ. Press, 1969).

WHITEFORD, ANDREW H.
1964 *Two Cities of Latin America*, Garden City, N.Y.: Doubleday. Description of the social sectors ("classes") of the city of Querétaro, Mexico, and comparison with Popayán, Colombia.

WILKIE, RAYMOND
1970 *San Miguel: A Mexican Collective Ejido.* Stanford, Calif.: Stanford Univ. Press. Study of life in a highly capitalized collective ejido in the Laguna cotton region of north central Mexico emphasizing the effects of demographic and economic changes.

YOUNG, PHILIP D.
1971 *Ngawbe: Tradition and Change among the Western Guaymí of Panama.* Illinois Studies in Anthropology no. 7. Urbana: Univ. of Illinois Press. Historical perspectives and contemporary culture of the Chibchan-speaking western Guaymí inhabiting the mountains of western Panama.

ZANTWIJK, RUDOLF A. M. VAN
1968 *Servants of the Saints: The Social and Cultural Identity of a Tarascan Community in Mexico.* New York: Humanities Press. Community life in contemporary Ihuatzio placed within broader historical and national contexts.

Index